VORTICISM
AND ABSTRACT ART IN THE FIRST MACHINE AGE

Volume 2
Synthesis and Decline

William Roberts
*The Vorticists at the Restaurant de la Tour
Eiffel: Spring 1915*, 1961–2. Left to right, seated:
Hamilton, Pound, Roberts, Lewis, Etchells and
Wadsworth. Standing: Dismorr, Saunders, Joe
the waiter and Rudolph Stulik, the proprietor of
the restaurant.

Richard Cork

VORTICISM

AND ABSTRACT ART IN THE FIRST MACHINE AGE

Volume 2
Synthesis and Decline

UNIVERSITY OF CALIFORNIA PRESS
Berkeley · Los Angeles

UNIVERSITY OF CALIFORNIA PRESS
Berkeley and Los Angeles
Copyright © Richard Cork 1976
ISBN 0-520-3269-1
Library of Congress Catalog Card Number: 75-37227

Set in Monotype Imprint and printed in Great Britain by
Lund Humphries, Bradford and London
Designed by Peter Guy

Contents

List of Illustrations in Volume Two

To aid conciseness, the word 'lost' is used whenever the whereabouts of an original work is unknown.
Height is stated before width in the measurements listed and they are all given to the nearest half-centimetre.
Where relevant, the number under which a work was listed in the catalogue of *Vorticism and its Allies*, the exhibition held at the Hayward Gallery, London, March–June 1974, has been added in italics at the end of an entry. The number which precedes each entry refers to the page on which the illustration appears.
All the illustrations are reproduced by courtesy of the various museums and other bodies cited in this list to whom the publishers extend grateful thanks.

Publisher's Acknowledgements

For permission to use copyright material acknowledgement is made to the authors cited below and to the following:

From *Poet and Painter, being the Correspondence between Gordon Bottomley and Paul Nash 1910–1946* edited by Claude C. Abbott and Anthony Bertram to Oxford University Press; from *Life for Life's Sake. A Book of Reminiscences* by Richard Aldington to Cassell & Co. Ltd; from *Painter's Pilgrimage* by A. Allinson to Miss M. Mitchell-Smith; from *Random Recollections* by Malcolm Arbuthnot to Miss A. E. Wisdom; from *Theory and Design in the First Machine Age* by Reyner Banham to the Architectural Press Ltd; from *Since Cézanne* by Clive Bell to Chatto and Windus Ltd and Quentin Bell; from *Art* by Clive Bell to Quentin Bell, Chatto and Windus Ltd and G. P. Putnam's Sons; from *The Journals of Arnold Bennett* to Mrs Dorothy Chesterton Bennett; from *Flight of the Dragon* by Laurence Binyon to John Murray (Publishers) Ltd; from *The Bomberg Papers* by David Bomberg to Mrs Lilian Bomberg; from *Henri Gaudier-Brzeska 1891–1915* by Horace Brodzky to Faber and Faber Ltd; from *Exhibition. The Memoirs of Oliver Brown* to Evelyn, Adams and Mackay; from *Fernand Léger et Le Nouvelle Espace* by Douglas Cooper to Lund Humphries Ltd; from *Café Royal. Ninety Years of Bohemia* by Deghy and Waterhouse to Hutchinson Publishing Group Ltd; from *Cubists and Post-Impressionists* by A. Jerome Eddy to A. C. McClurg, Chicago; from *A Life of Gaudier-Brzeska* by H. S. Ede to H. S. Ede and Cambridge University; from *The Sculptor Speaks* by Jacob Epstein and Arnold Haskell to the Estate of Jacob Epstein; from *Let There Be Sculpture* by Jacob Epstein to Curtis Brown Ltd, on behalf of the Estate of Jacob Epstein; from *Return to Yesterday. Reminiscences 1894–1914* by Madox Ford to Victor Gollancz Ltd; from *Cubism* by Roger Fry to Thames and Hudson Ltd; from *The Flowers of the Forest* by David Garnett to Chatto and Windus Ltd; from *The Golden Echo* by David Garnett to Chatto and Windus Ltd; from *Alvin Langdon Coburn: Photographer* edited by Helmut and Alison Gernsheim to Faber and Faber Ltd; from *Mark Gertler: Selected Letters* to Rupert Hart-Davis; from *Cubism* by John Golding to Faber and Faber Ltd and Harper & Row Inc; from *South Lodge* by Douglas Goldring to Constable & Co. Ltd; from *Odd Man Out* by Douglas Goldring to Curtis Brown Ltd; from *Laughing Torso* by Nina Hamnett to Constable & Co Ltd; from *Edward Marsh: Patron of the Arts* by Christopher Hassall to Longmans and Harcourt Brace Jovanovich, Inc.; from *Frightfulness in Modern Art* by W. H. Higginbottom to Cecil Palmer; from *Lytton Strachey: A Critical Biography* by Michael Holroyd to William Heinemann and Holt, Rinehart & Winston Inc; from *The Life of Henry Tonks* by Joseph Hone to William Heinemann Ltd; from *Gaudier Brzeska Drawings and Sculpture* by Mervyn Levy to Cory, Adams and Mackay; from *Blast No.1, Blast No.2, The Caliph's Design. Architects! Where is your Vortex?* and *Wyndham Lewis the Artist, from Blast to Burlington House* by Wyndham Lewis to Mrs G. A. Wyndham Lewis; from *Time and Western Man* by Wyndham Lewis to Methuen & Co Ltd (originally published by Chatto and Windus) and Mrs G. A. Wyndham Lewis; from *Blasting and Bombardiering* by Wyndham Lewis to John Calder (Publishers) Ltd and University of California; from *Tarr* by Wyndham Lewis to John Calder (Publishers) Ltd; from *Rude Assignment. A Narrative of My Career* by Wyndham Lewis to Hutchinson Publishing Group Ltd; from *Dear Miss Weaver* by Jane Lidderdale and Mary Nicholson to Faber and Faber Ltd and Viking Press; from *David Bomberg. A Critical Study of his Life and Work* by William Lipke to Evelyn, Adams & Mackay; from *The Young Bomberg 1914–1925* by Alice Mayes, an unpublished memoir © Denis Richardson to Denis Richardson; from *This Difficult Individual Ezra Pound* by Eustace Mullins to Fleet Publishing, New York; from *Paint and Prejudice* by C. R. W.

Nevinson to Methuen & Co. Ltd and Harcourt Brace Jovanovich Inc; from *Gaudier: A Memoir* by Ezra Pound to the Estate of Ezra Pound and the Marvell Press; from *Ripostes* by Ezra Pound to the Estate of Ezra Pound; from Ezra Pound's prefatory note to *The Complete Poetical Works of T. E. Hulme* to the Estate of Ezra Pound and Faber & Faber Ltd; from 'Cavalcanti' from *Literary Essays of Ezra Pound* to Faber & Faber Ltd and New Directions Publishing Corporation; from *The Art of Wyndham Lewis* by Charles Handley-Read to Faber & Faber Ltd; from *Contemporary British Art* by Herbert Read to Penguin Books Ltd; from *Pound/Joyce: Letters and Essays* edited by Forrest Read to Faber & Faber Ltd and New Directions Publishing Corporation; from *The Man From New York* by B. L. Reid to Oxford University Press; from *Cometism and Vorticism. A Tate Gallery Catalogue Revised, Abstract and Cubist Paintings and Drawings, A Reply to my Biographer, Sir John Rothenstein, Memories of the War to End War* and *A Press View at the Tate Gallery* by William Roberts to William Roberts and the Favil Press Ltd; from *Collected Poems of John Rodker* to The Hours Press, Paris; from *The Future of Futurism* by John Rodker to Routledge & Kegan Paul Ltd; from *The Letters of Wyndham Lewis* edited by W. K. Rose to Methuen & Co. Ltd and Mrs G. A. Wyndham Lewis; from *Modern English Painters* Vol.I and Vol.II by Sir John Rothenstein © Sir John Rothenstein 1952 to MacDonald & Jane's new edition 1976; from *Evolution in Modern Art* by Frank Rutter to George G. Harrap & Co Ltd; from *Since I Was Twenty-Five* by Frank Rutter to Constable & Co. Ltd; from *Art in My Time* by Frank Rutter to Rich and Cowan Ltd; from *Modern Masterpieces* by Frank Rutter to The Hamlyn Publishing Group Ltd; from *Letters of Eric Gill* edited by Walter Shewring to Jonathan Cape Ltd and Devin-Adair Co; from *The New Art. A Study of the Principles of Non-Representational Art and their Application in the Work of Lawrence Atkinson* by Horace Shipp to Cecil Palmer; from *Great Morning* by Osbert Sitwell to Macmillan; from *The Life of Eric Gill* by Robert Speaight to Methuen and P. J. Kennedy & Sons; from *The Life of Ezra Pound* by Noel Stock to Routledge & Kegan Paul Ltd and Pantheon Books Inc.; from *T. S. Eliot: Symposium* edited by Tambimuttu and Richard March to Frank Cass Ltd; from *A Portrait of the Artist as the Enemy* to G. Wagner; from *Vile Bodies* by Evelyn Waugh reprinted by permission of A. D. Peters & Co Ltd; from *The Modern Movement in Art* by R. H. Wilenski to Faber and Gwyer; from *Beginning Again* by Leonard Woolf to the Author's Literary Estate, The Hogarth Press and Harcourt Brace Jovanovich, Inc; from *Roger Fry: A Biography* by Virginia Woolf to the Author's Literary Estate, The Hogarth Press and Harcourt Brace Jovanovich.

Biographical Outlines of the Artists Associated with Vorticism

MALCOLM ARBUTHNOT
1874–1967
Born 1874 in London, and brought up in East Anglia. Studied painting under C. A. Brindley. Became well-known as an innovatory photographer, 1900–10, exhibiting regularly at the London Photographic Salon, writing articles and reproducing his work in *The Amateur Photographer*. Befriended Coburn and elected to the 'Linked Ring' 1907. Held a one-man show of *Impressions* at *The Amateur Photographer*'s Little Gallery, London, March 1909. One-man show of *Camera Portraits* at the Goupil Gallery, London, June–July 1912. Appointed manager of Kodak's Liverpool branch, 1912. Organized a Post-Impressionist exhibition at the Sandon Studios, Liverpool, February – March 1913 and met Lewis early 1914. Signed *Blast No.1*'s manifesto, summer 1914, and from then until 1926 ran a successful portrait studio at 43 and 44 New Bond Street. Also pursued painting and sculpture. Elected Fellow of RSA 1939 and a member of RI 1944. Died December 1967 in Jersey.

LAWRENCE ATKINSON
1873–1931
Born 17 January 1873 in Chorlton upon Medlock, near Manchester. Educated at Bowden College, Chester, and then studied singing and music in Berlin and Paris. Taught singing in Liverpool and London, and gave concert performances. Self-taught as an artist, he exhibited in the July 1913 Allied Artists' Association Salon, and moved from Fauvism to Vorticism when he joined the Rebel Art Centre early 1914. Signed *Blast No.1*'s manifesto, summer 1914, appeared in the 'Invited to Show' section of the June 1915 Vorticist Exhibition and published a book of poems called *Aura*, 1915. Exhibited with the London Group, June 1916, and designed the cover of Edith Sitwell's *Wheels* magazine 1918. Held a one-man show of *Abstract Sculpture and Painting* at the Eldar Gallery, London, May 1921. Concentrated on sculpture in later life and awarded Grand Prix for his carving *L'Oiseau* at the 1921 Milan Exhibition. Died 21 September 1931 in Paris.

DAVID BOMBERG
1890–1957
Born 5 December 1890 in Birmingham, the fifth child of a Polish immigrant leather-worker. Family moved to Whitechapel 1895, and c.1906–07 Bomberg apprenticed to lithographer Paul Fischer, while studying with Walter Bayes at the City and Guilds evening classes. Broke his indentures to become an artist 1908, and attended Sickert's Westminster School evening classes. Studied at the Slade School 1911–13 and met Lewis, December 1912. Visited Paris May–June 1913 and included in the 'Cubist Room' section of the *Camden Town Group and Others* exhibition at Brighton, December 1913–January 1914. Included in the January–February 1913 and the February–March 1914 Friday Club exhibitions at the Alpine Club Gallery. Founder-member of the London Group, in whose first exhibition he participated, March 1914. Contributed to the Whitechapel Art Gallery's *Twentieth Century Art* exhibition, which he helped to organize, May–June 1914. One-man show at the Chenil Gallery, Chelsea, July 1914. Included in 'Invited to Show' section of the June 1915 Vorticist Exhibition, and enlisted in the Royal Engineers, November 1915. Married Alice Mayes March 1916, transferred to Canadian Regiment December 1917 to paint war picture and returned to England November 1918. One-man show at the Adelphi Gallery, London, September 1919. In later life changed his style completely, travelled widely and married again to Lilian Holt. Died 19 August 1957 in London.

ALVIN LANGDON COBURN
1882–1966

Born 11 June 1882 in Boston, Massachusetts, the son of a shirt manufacturer. Introduced to photography by his cousin, F. Holland Day, 1890. First exhibition in Boston 1898. First one-man show in London Photographic Salon, 1900. Founder-member of Photo-Secession, 1902. Elected to the 'Linked Ring', 1903. Portfolio appeared in *Camera Work*, 1904, when he moved to London and met George Bernard Shaw. One-man show at the Royal Photographic Society, 1906, and befriended Arbuthnot around the same time: the two men took photographs of each other. Included in the International Exhibition of Pictorial Photography at the Albright Gallery, Buffalo, 1910. Contributed photographic illustrations to H. G. Wells' *The Door in the Wall*, 1911. Visited New York 1912, when he married Edith Clement. Returned to London 1912 and met Ezra Pound 1913. Took Pound's photograph. One-man show of *Camera Pictures* at the Goupil Gallery, London, October 1913, and published portrait collection called *Men of Mark* the same year. Photographed Epstein 1914 and Lewis and Wadsworth 1916. Invented Vortoscope late 1916. Exhibited *Vortographs and Paintings* in one-man show at the Camera Club, London, February 1917. Elected Honorary Fellow of the Royal Photographic Society 1931, and became naturalized British subject 1932. Died 23 November 1966 in Rhos-on-Sea, North Wales.

JESSICA DISMORR
1885–1939

Born 1885 in Gravesend. Educated at Kingsley School, Hampstead *c*.1897–1901, and studied at the Slade School 1902–03. Studied under Max Bohm at Etaples *c*.1905–08. From 1910–13 studied painting in Paris at the Atelier La Palette, under Metzinger, Fergusson, Segonzac and Blanche. Contributed illustrations to several issues of *Rhythm* magazine 1911, and exhibited in the Allied Artists' Association Salons of July 1912 and July 1913. Exhibited with Peploe, Fergusson and Rice at the Stafford Gallery, 1912. Frequently lived in Paris 1913–14. Included in the Salon d'Automne, 1913, and met Lewis the same year. Joined the Rebel Art Centre, Spring 1914, and signed the manifesto in *Blast No.1*, summer 1914. Exhibited at July 1914 Allied Artists' Association Salon, and spent much of the war in France doing voluntary war-work. Participated as a member of the movement in the June 1915 Vorticist Exhibition, contributed illustrations and writings to *Blast No.2*, July 1915, and included in the January 1917 New York Vorticist Exhibition. Contributed poems and 'Critical Suggestions' to the *Little Review*, 1919. Exhibited with other ex-Vorticists in Group X at the Mansard Gallery, March–April 1920, elected to the London Group 1926 and became completely abstract by the 1930s, contributing to *Axis*, No.8, 1937. Died 29 August 1939 in London.

SIR JACOB EPSTEIN
1880–1959

Born 10 November 1880 in New York. Studied at the Arts Student League in New York and then at the Académie Julian in Paris. Moved to London 1905 and became a British subject 1907. Between 1907–08 executed his earliest important commission, eighteen figures for the façade of the British Medical Association's building in the Strand, which prompted the first of many public scandals in Epstein's lifetime. Close friendship with Eric Gill. Produced two decorated relief pillars for Madame Strindberg's Cabaret Theatre Club 1912, and installed his monumental *Tomb of Oscar Wilde* at Père La Chaise Cemetery, Paris, autumn 1912. Met Modigliani, Picasso, Brancusi and other radical artists in Paris, then returned to England 1913. Settled in Pett Level, Sussex to carve in isolation.

Exhibited at the July 1913 Allied Artists' Association Salon, the *Post-Impressionist and Futurist Exhibition*, October 1913, and the 'Cubist Room' section of the *Camden Town Group and Others* exhibition in Brighton, December 1913–January 1914. One-man show at the Twenty-One Gallery, December 1913–January 1914. Became close friend of T. E. Hulme, who defended his work in *The New Age*. Exhibited as founder-member in March 1914 London Group show, participated in the Whitechapel Art Gallery's *Twentieth Century Art* exhibition, May–June 1914, and contributed two illustrations to *Blast No.1*, summer 1914. Displayed original version of *Rock Drill* at March 1915 London Group exhibition, and exhibited in March 1916 Allied Artists' Association Salon. Displayed second version of *Rock Drill* at the London Group, June 1916. Held one-man show at the Leicester Galleries, February–March 1917. Called up 1917 and demobilized 1918. In later life renounced radical ideas, concentrating on portrait busts. Knighted 1954. Died 19 August 1959 in London.

FREDERICK ETCHELLS
1886–1973
Born 14 September 1886 in Newcastle upon Tyne, the son of an engineer, and educated at Macclesfield Grammar School. Studied at the Royal College of Art *c.*1908–11 and afterwards rented a studio in Paris, where he met Picasso, Braque and Modigliani. Participated in Fry's mural scheme for the Borough Polytechnic 1911, while teaching part-time at the Central School, London. Exhibited in Friday Club, February 1912, and collaborated with Duncan Grant on mural in Brunswick Square for Adrian Stephen and his sister Virginia (Woolf). Contributed to the *Second Post-Impressionist Exhibition* at the Grafton Galleries, October 1912–January 1913. Joined Omega Workshops 1913, visited Dieppe with Lewis the same summer and in October walked out of Omega with Lewis and the other rebels. Contributed to the *Post-Impressionist and Futurist Exhibition*, October 1913, and the 'Cubist Room' section of the *Camden Town Group and Others* exhibition in Brighton, December 1913–January 1914. Founder-member and exhibitor at the London Group exhibition, March 1914, and joined the Rebel Art Centre spring 1914. Contributed illustrations to *Blast No.1*, summer 1914, and participated as a member in the June 1915 Vorticist Exhibition. Contributed illustrations to *Blast No.2*, July 1915, and then included in the January 1917 New York Vorticist Exhibition. Did not fight in War on medical grounds, but painted large picture for Canadian War Memorials Fund. Included in the Group X exhibition at the Mansard Gallery, March–April 1920. Soon after gave up painting, took his ARIBA and became an architect. Designed pioneering Crawford building in Holborn 1930, and translated Le Corbusier's *Towards a New Architecture*. Married Hester Sainsbury in 1932. Died 16 August 1973 in Folkestone.

HENRI GAUDIER-BRZESKA
1891–1915
Born Henri Gaudier, 4 October 1891, in St-Jean de Braye, near Orleans, the son of a carpenter. Visited England on a scholarship 1906 and again 1908. Started work as a sculptor in Paris, 1910, and met Sophie Brzeska, with whom he lived from this time, adding her surname to his own. Settled in London January 1911, where he soon met John Middleton Murry, Alfred Wolmark, Horace Brodzky and Epstein. Aroused controversy by exhibiting in the July 1913 Allied Artists' Association Salon, befriended T. E. Hulme and Ezra Pound and affiliated himself briefly with the Omega Workshops, 1913–14. Exhibited with the Grafton Group at the Alpine Gallery, January 1914, and contributed as a founder-member to the March 1914 London Group exhibition. Joined the

Rebel Art Centre, spring 1914. Participated in the Whitechapel Art Gallery's *Twentieth Century Art* exhibition, May–June 1914, contributed an illustration and essay to *Blast No.1* and signed its manifesto, summer 1914. Chairman of artists' committee for July 1914 Allied Artists' Association Salon, of which he wrote a preview in *The Egoist*. Included as a member in the June 1915 Vorticist Exhibition and contributed an essay and illustration to *Blast No.2*, July 1915. Killed serving with the French army, 5 June 1915, at Neuville-Saint-Vaast. *Memoir* published by Pound 1916. Memorial Exhibition held at the Leicester Galleries, May–June 1918.

CUTHBERT HAMILTON
1884–1959

Born 15 February 1884 in India, the son of a judge. Studied at the Slade School on a Slade scholarship 1899–1903, contemporary with Lewis. Taught art at Clifton College 1907–10. Collaborated with Lewis on decorations for Madame Strindberg's Cabaret Theatre Club, 1912–13, and included in the last month of the *Second Post-Impressionist Exhibition* at the Grafton Galleries, January 1913. Joined the Omega Workshops, summer 1913, accompanying Lewis, Etchells and Wadsworth when they left the Omega in October the same year. Contributed to the *Post-Impressionist and Futurist Exhibition*, October 1913, and to the 'Cubist Room' section of the *Camden Town Group and Others* exhibition at Brighton, December 1913–January 1914. Participated in the March 1914 London Group exhibition and joined the Rebel Art Centre, spring 1914. Contributed an illustration to *Blast No.1*, summer 1914, and signed its manifesto. Served as a special constable in the First World War and was the most abstract of the artists who exhibited in Group X at the Mansard Gallery, March–April 1920. Also displayed pottery at Group X, made at the Yeoman Potteries which he had founded, and around this time began to experiment with sculpture. Died 13 March 1959 in Cookham.

WYNDHAM LEWIS
1882–1957

Born 18 November 1882 on board his American father's yacht off Amherst, Nova Scotia. His mother was British. Educated at Rugby School, 1897–8, and studied at the Slade School 1898–1901. Between 1902 and 1908 travelled widely, visiting Madrid with his friend Spencer Gore, Holland, Munich, and Paris, spending summer holidays in Brittany. Settled in England 1908, while continuing to visit Paris every year, and published short stories in *The English Review*. Met Pound 1909, and contributed as a founder-member to the first Camden Town Group exhibition, June 1911. Showed again in second Camden Town Group exhibition, December 1911, and at the July 1912 Allied Artists' Association Salon. Included in the *Second Post-Impressionist Exhibition*, October 1912–January 1913, and the third Camden Town Group show, December 1912. Contributed to the July 1913 Allied Artists' Association Salon, joined the Omega Workshops around the same time, and walked out of the Omega, October 1913. Contributed to the *Post-Impressionist and Futurist Exhibition*, October 1913, and wrote a catalogue preface for the 'Cubist Room' section of the *Camden Town Group and Others* exhibition at Brighton, December 1913–January 1914. Decorated a dining-room for Lady Drogheda, 1913–14. Exhibited as a founder-member in the March 1914 London Group show, and at the same time founded the Rebel Art Centre. Contributed to the Whitechapel Art Gallery's *Twentieth Century Art* exhibition, May–June 1914, edited and contributed to *Blast No.1*, summer 1914 and exhibited in the July 1914 Allied Artists' Association Salon. Decorated Ford's study at South Lodge, November 1914. Included in the March 1915 London

Group show and wrote catalogue preface for the June 1915 Vorticist Exhibition, to which he contributed. Edited and contributed to *Blast No.2*, July 1915. Decorated a 'Vorticist Room' in the Restaurant de la Tour Eiffel, 1915. Joined army as a gunner 1916 and participated in the January 1917 New York Vorticist Exhibition. Seconded as a war artist, December 1917, to paint a picture for the Canadian War Memorials Fund, and published first novel, *Tarr*, 1918. Held one-man show at the Goupil Gallery, February 1919, and wrote catalogue preface for Group X exhibition at the Mansard Gallery, March–April 1920. Married Gladys Anne Hoskins 1930, and continued to write and paint prolifically. Lost his sight 1951. Died 7 March 1957 in London.

CHRISTOPHER NEVINSON
1889–1946
Born 13 August 1889, the son of the war correspondent and author H. W. Nevinson. Studied painting at St John's Wood 1908, and the Slade School, 1909–12. Exhibited at the July 1911 Allied Artists' Association Salon, and the Friday Club exhibitions of February 1912 and January–February 1913 at the Alpine Club Gallery. Studied in Paris at Académie Julian and *Cercle Russe* summer 1912 – spring 1913, and became friendly with Severini, Modigliani and other radical French artists. Exhibited at the July 1913 Allied Artists' Association Salon, the October 1913 *Post-Impressionist and Futurist Exhibition* and the 'Cubist Room' section of the *Camden Town Group and Others* exhibition at Brighton, December 1913–January 1914. Welcomed Marinetti with a dinner at the Florence Restaurant, November 1913, and exhibited in the February–March 1914 Friday Club show. Joined preliminary discussion with Lewis about *Blast* and thought of its name. Contributed as a founder-member to the March 1914 London Group exhibition, and joined the Rebel Art Centre soon afterwards. Included in the Whitechapel Art Gallery's *Twentieth Century Art* exhibition, May–June 1914, and published with Marinetti in June 1914 the 'Vital English Art: Futurist Manifesto' which the other members of the Rebel Art Centre repudiated. Exhibited in the July 1914 Allied Artists' Association Salon and served with the Red Cross in Europe. Showed his first war pictures in the March 1915 London Group exhibition. Married 1915. Included in the 'Invited to Show' section of the June 1915 Vorticist Exhibition as a 'Futurist', and contributed an illustration to *Blast No.2*, July 1915. Served in the Royal Army Medical Corps until 1917, and held two very successful one-man shows at the Leicester Galleries, September–October 1916 and March 1918. Painted war picture for the Canadian War Memorials Fund 1918 and renounced Futurism. In later life his work became far more traditional. Died 7 October 1946 in London.

WILLIAM ROBERTS
b.1895
Born 5 June 1895 in London. Apprenticed 1909 to the poster-designing and advertising firm of Sir Joseph Causton Ltd., to learn commercial art. At the same time attended evening classes at St Martin's School of Art. Won a precocious LCC scholarship in drawing to the Slade School 1910, where he studied for three years. Executed a tempera wall painting for Fulham Girls' Club 1911, and won a Slade Scholarship 1912. Left the Slade summer 1913, and travelled in France and Italy. Joined the Omega Workshops after Lewis and the other rebels had left, and exhibited with the New English Art Club December 1913. Included in the Grafton Group show at the Alpine Club Gallery, January 1914, and contacted spring 1914 by Lewis, who borrowed two of his pictures to hang in the Rebel Art Centre. Contributed to the Whitechapel Art Gallery's *Twentieth Century Art* exhibition, May–June 1914. Work illustrated in *Blast No.1*,

summer 1914, and signed its manifesto. Exhibited in the March 1915 London Group show and as a member in the June 1915 Vorticist Exhibition. Contributed illustrations to *Blast No. 2*, July 1915. Joined the Royal Field Artillery 1916, participated in the January 1917 New York Vorticist Exhibition and returned to England 1918 to paint a large picture for the Canadian War Memorials Fund. Demobilized 1919, and executed three paintings for the Restaurant de la Tour Eiffel. Contributed to Group X at the Mansard Gallery, March–April 1920, and held first one-man show at the Chenil Gallery in November 1923. Issued a series of pamphlets and books on his early work from 1956 to 1976. Elected a Royal Academician 1966. Lives in London.

HELEN SAUNDERS
1885–1963

Born 4 April 1885 in London, the daughter of a director of the Great Western Railway. Educated at home in Bedford Park. Studied at the Slade School, 1906–07, and at the Central School. Exhibited in the February 1912 Friday Club exhibition at the Alpine Club Gallery, and in the Allied Artists' Association Salons of July 1912 and July 1913. Joined the Rebel Art Centre, spring 1914 and contributed to the Whitechapel Art Gallery's *Twentieth Century Art* exhibition, May–June 1914. Signed the manifesto in *Blast No. 1*, summer 1914, as 'H. Sanders'. Participated as a member in the June 1915 Vorticist Exhibition, and contributed a poem and illustrations to *Blast No.2*, July 1915. Assisted Lewis with the decoration of the 'Vorticist Room' at the Restaurant de la Tour Eiffel, summer 1915, and exhibited at the July 1916 Allied Artists' Association Salon. Worked for the Records Office in London during the War. Included as a non-member in the November–December 1916 London Group exhibition, and then participated in the January 1917 New York Vorticist Exhibition. Continued to paint in a more representational style in later life, sometimes close to the work of her friend Jessica Dismorr. Died 3 January 1963 in London.

DOROTHY SHAKESPEAR
1886–1973

Born 14 September 1886 in London, the daughter of a solicitor who worked in India and the minor Edwardian novelist Olivia Shakespear. Educated at Crowborough School, Sussex, and St James's School, Malvern. Self-taught as an artist, and specialized from an early age in landscape watercolours. Met Ezra Pound 1908. Both Dorothy and her mother attended the lectures Pound gave on Medieval Literature at the Regent Street Polytechnic 1909–10, and he later introduced her to Lewis and Gaudier. Impressed by the Rebel Art Centre when taken there by Pound for Saturday afternoons, spring 1914. Married Pound April 1914, but always kept her maiden name of Shakespear when painting, because she wanted to keep her work separate from her husband's. Lewis encouraged her during the Vorticist period, and she contributed a decoration and an illustration to *Blast No.2*, July 1915. Always remained an amateur artist, never holding or seeking an exhibition. In later life acknowledged a debt to Vorticism, which can be seen informing the many landscape studies she executed after 1920. Died 8 December 1973 near Cambridge.

EDWARD WADSWORTH
1889–1949

Born 29 October 1889 in Cleckheaton, Yorkshire, the son of a wealthy worsted spinning magnate, and educated at Fettes College, Edinburgh *c*.1902–6. Studied engineering at Munich 1906–7 but became more interested in painting, attending the Knirr School in his spare time. On returning to England went to Bradford

School of Art, where he gained a scholarship to the Slade School. Studied at the Slade 1908–12. Married Fanny Eveleigh and spent honeymoon in the Canary Islands, April–May 1912, afterwards travelling in France and Spain. Exhibited in the Friday Club at the Alpine Club Gallery, February 1912 and January–February 1913. Included in the last month (January 1913) of the *Second Post-Impressionist Exhibition*. Joined the Omega Workshops summer 1913 and exhibited in the July 1913 Allied Artists' Association Salon. Left the Omega with Lewis and the other rebels October 1913, and contributed to the *Post-Impressionist and Futurist Exhibition* the same month. Included in the 'Cubist Room' section of the *Camden Town Group and Others* exhibition at Brighton, December 1913–January 1914, and exhibited as a founder-member in the March 1914 London Group show. Joined the Rebel Art Centre, spring 1914, and participated in the Whitechapel Art Gallery's *Twentieth Century Art* exhibition, May–June 1914. Contributed illustrations, and translations from Kandinsky's *Uber das Geistige in Der Kunst*, to *Blast No.1*, summer 1914, and signed its manifesto. Included in the July 1914 Allied Artists' Association Salon, visited Rotterdam July 1914, and contributed to the March 1915 London Group exhibition. Contributed as a member to the June 1915 Vorticist Exhibition, and reproduced his work in *Blast No.2*, July 1915. Served in the Royal Naval Volunteer Reserve on the island of Mudros until invalided out 1917. Included in the January 1917 New York Vorticist Exhibition, and then employed supervising dazzle camouflage for ships in Bristol and Liverpool. Painted large picture for the Canadian War Memorials Fund, and held a one-man show at the Adelphi Gallery, March 1919. Exhibited in Group X at the Mansard Gallery, March–April 1920, and in later life pursued a more representational style, apart from a period in the 1930s when associated with Unit One. Elected Associate of the Royal Academy 1944. Died 21 June 1949 in London.

Chapter 12: Vorticism in Practice: Lewis and Wadsworth

The Great War had granted the rebels little more than a year in which to submit *Blast No. 1*'s heady assertions to the acid test of paintings, drawings and sculpture. It was a pitifully brief lifespan for any innovatory movement to be allotted; and since Vorticism's very right to existence was constantly being challenged by several of the artists so grudgingly coerced into its ranks, the odds were weighed heavily against the emergence of a coherent corpus of work. But before the trenches finally put an end to their activities, the Vorticists, alongside those who hovered on the edge of the group, did manage to create a style that can now be recognized as both original and homogeneous; and that, in view of the large number of vital pictures which have since been tragically mislaid or destroyed, stands as a considerable achievement. There were, of course, internal variations and inconsistencies within the overall framework of this style. The danger was even foreseen by Pound, who warned in his 1914 'Vorticism' article that 'no artist can possibly get a vortex into every poem or picture he does. One would like to do so, but it is beyond one'. Arguing quite naturally from a literary vantage-point, he explained that 'certain things seem to demand metrical expression, or expression in a rhythm more agitated than the rhythms acceptable to prose, and these subjects, though they do not contain a vortex, may have some interest, an interest as "criticism of life" or of art. It is natural to express these things, and a vorticist or imagiste writer may be justified in presenting a certain amount of work which is not vorticism or imagisme, just as he might be justified in printing a purely didactic prose article. Unfinished sketches and drawings have a similar interest; they are trials and attempts toward a vortex'.[1]

And yet such lapses were endemic in the very nature of a group situation. It always seems a somewhat arbitrary act to lump together a collection of diverse artistic temperaments under one heading, especially when that label has been propagated by someone as domineering and self-centred as Lewis. But is the term 'Vorticism' any less meaningful than its counterparts – Impressionism, Fauvism, Cubism, Futurism or Expressionism? Several of these movements did not even have the chance to coin a title of their own: it was thrust upon them, as a term of abuse, by insensitive critics who wished to denigrate a phenomenon they could not understand. The English rebels at least had the comfort of knowing that their name had been thought up by one of their number; and although it is easy to sympathize with their unwillingness to subsume private identities in Lewis's overpowering egotism, the benefits deriving from the birth of the movement were by no means exclusively channelled towards their self-styled leader's interests. In the context of pre-war London, where any new movement had to shout out its new ideas as loudly as possible to be heard above the babble of opposing forces, it was absolutely vital to form a pressure-group. The rebels were committed to overthrowing all existing aesthetic adversaries, from Marinetti down to the bedrock of the Royal Academy, and the most efficient way to effect a revolution was to form themselves into a battalion of fighters. Left on their own, the gospel they all wanted to preach – albeit in individual ways – would be broken up in a myriad small pockets of dissent. Better by far to come together and allow Lewis his streak of megalomania if it meant that a soporific nation would be aroused from its complacency by the force of an editorial pen. There is reluctant admiration, as well as understandable annoyance, in Roberts' memory of 'Lewis's tall form in heavy overcoat and grey sombrero, with scarf flung flamboyantly over one shoulder, striding along, the broad shoulders tilted slightly, like a boxer advancing to meet an opponent. In a sense, acquaintanceship with Wyndham Lewis was like a contest, in which you came out of your corner fighting – and the best man won'.[2] It was immensely bracing to know such a man, and the relationship did not need to be a permanent one. The rebels were only at the beginning of their careers, after all, and could retain the option to repudiate the strait jacket of the movement at a later date when the singularities of their own visions had matured. But for the moment, despite the inherent disadvantages of a corporate ideology, it was advisable to remain united and accept Vorticism as a necessary evil.

Besides, it simply was not possible for Lewis or anyone else to stand beside his political allies in their studios and dictate the form that their creative work ought to assume. 'At no time was it intended that either Mr Lewis, or Gaudier or myself or Mr Wadsworth or Mr Etchells should crawl into each other's skins or that we should in any way surrender our various identities,' wrote Pound, surveying the progress of the movement in 1916, 'or that the workings of certain fundamental principles of *the arts* should force any one of us to turn his own particular *art* into a flat imitation of the external features of the particular art of any other member of our group'.[3] It depended entirely on the individual concerned, and 'flat imitation' is always a danger even when there is no official movement to encourage its growth. In any one generation, some artists are bound to be more gifted, ambitious or assured than their contemporaries: if all the avant-garde groups that sprang into being at the beginning of this century had never existed, it would still be easy in retrospect to detect which artist fell under the spell of another, who forged ahead and who felt content to follow from a distance.

The reality of the situation was defined with fairness by Pound, who stressed that 'it cannot be made too clear that the work of the vorticists and the "feeling of inner need" existed before the general noise about vorticism. We worked separately, we found an underlying agreement, we decided to stand together'.[4] Only the last clause of this explanation can be justifiably disputed. For plenty of the work executed by the rebels before Vorticism arrived displays nascent characteristics which the movement itself was to develop into a more coherent style, even if the preliminary springboard lay in the inspiration of Cubism or Futurism. The strident energy, the classical detachment, the urge to define forms in rigid entities, the explosive iconoclasm and the obsession with mechanical imagery can all be detected in many of the paintings and sculptures they executed prior to the summer of 1914. And so Lewis can never be accused of claiming for the movement he outlined in *Blast No. 1* attributes which he knew did not then exist. Rather did his manifestos seek to gather together the strands of original experiment that could be seen in the work of the artists he had met at the Omega, the Cabaret Club or Hulme's Salon, and whose friendship he had consolidated for a while in the ill-fated Rebel Art Centre. The method by which he chose to weave those strands into a web of aesthetic doctrine was overbearing, certainly – Pound was being euphemistic when he wrote that 'we decided to stand together' – but the impulse which instigated the founding of Vorticism was never spurious. It was the manner of Lewis's actions, not the matter behind them, which can be called to account.

The works are there to prove the truth of this interpretation, and one of the best ways to pinpoint the singularity of Vorticist pictures is to compare their attitude towards the machine with those of their European rivals. For many radical artists of the day were preoccupied, to a greater or lesser degree, with the challenge of mechanical imagery. It was the element that symbolized more than anything else the spirit of the new century they were attempting to express, and it is all too easy to dismiss the Vorticists' use of machines as a superficial fad borrowed wholesale from their immediate forebears on the continent. Pound was right when he declared in an 'Affirmations' article of February 1915 that 'a feeling for . . . machines' was 'one of the age-tendencies, springing up naturally in many places and coming into the arts quite naturally and spontaneously in

England, in America, and in Italy'. He effectively extracted the mystique from this obsession by describing it as an instinctive process, a manifestation of simple enjoyment and pleasure rather than a rarefied pursuit conducted by artists who dabbled in abstraction. 'We all know the small boy's delight in machines', he wrote sensibly. 'It is a natural delight in a beauty that had not been pointed out by professional aesthetes. I remember young men with no care for aesthetics who certainly would not know what the devil this article was about, I remember them examining machinery catalogues, to my intense bewilderment, commenting on machines that certainly they would never own and that could never by any flight of fancy be of the least use to them. This enjoyment of machinery is just as natural and just as significant a phase of this age as was the Renaissance "enjoyment of nature for its own sake", and not merely as an illustration of dogmatic ideas.'[5]

Pound's dissertation is a useful corrective for the tendency to seek profound

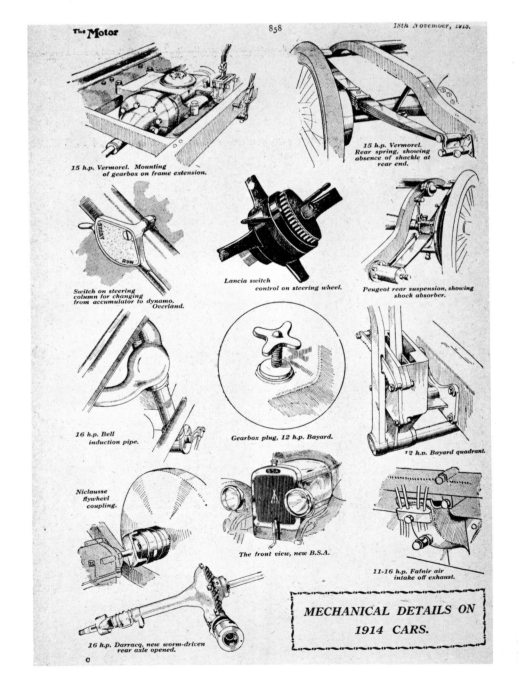

'Mechanical details on 1914 cars'
Illustration from *The Motor*, 1913

motives behind the employment of mechanistic motifs in avant-garde art of this period. It is difficult, now, to appreciate just how stimulating the proliferation of mechanical objects must have been to anyone prepared to view them as laudable inventions rather than a threat to the quality of human life. Machines constituted a rich seam of new forms, and they were waiting to be tapped – just as the Quattrocento to which Pound had alluded seized on the pictorial tool of perspective with a similar enthusiasm. 'Machinery is the greatest Earth-medium', cried Lewis in *Blast No. 1*, partially accounting for his statement by adding that 'it sweeps away the doctrines of a narrow and pedantic Realism at one stroke'.[6] Mechanical imagery possessed for the Vorticists the inestimable advantage of providing a ready-made stock of abstracted forms, thereby ensuring that the man who expressed his own time by incorporating such a vocabulary in his art automatically freed himself from the duty to retain many external references to nature. The machine provided, in fact, a stylistic as well as thematic inspiration for the artist courageous enough to tackle it head-on. And the Vorticists considered that they, more than anyone, did so with the necessary amount of verve. 'We are proud, handsome and predatory', Lewis announced in 'Our Vortex', and as if to demonstrate the truth of his claim went on to declare that 'we hunt machines, they are our favourite game. We invent them and then hunt them down'.[7] Not for them the hysterics of the Futurists, who succeeded only in reducing the fine lines of an automobile to a mess of chaotic speed. 'To represent a machine in violent movement is to arrive at a blur', Lewis wrote later. 'And a blur was as abhorrent to the Vorticist as a vacuum is to nature. A machine in violent motion ceases to look like a machine. It looks, perhaps, like a rose or a sponge. For in violent enough displacement the hardest thing takes on the appearance of the softest. A statue cut out of basalt would become more fluid than flesh, if whirled round sufficiently swiftly. So the very spirit of the machine is lost – the hard, cold, the mechanical and the static. And it was these attributes for which Vorticism had a particular partiality.'[8]

The English rebels would never, for instance, have warmed to the way Boccioni uses the motif of a railway engine in his study for *States of Mind: The Farewells*, a painting they would all have seen at the first Futurist London exhibition in 1912. The engine itself is included no less than four times in the painting, and such simultaneous views of the machine were anathema to the Vorticist: when Etchells drew *Hyde Park* as part of his 'impressions of a car journey through London',[9] he concentrated on one impression only, that of a bridge over the Serpentine. But his stance would never have been entertained by Boccioni, who sets up an endless rhythmic flow which dominates the angular shapes and welds the whole design into one emotional unity. The embracing couples on the left of *The Farewells* look like a series of repetitions of the same group, while those on the right have been condensed into a wedge of writhing movement. In Etchells' drawing, by contrast, the figures traversing the bridge are all single, stationary configurations, hieratic and crisply defined.

Both artists are playing off mechanical objects against groups of people; and yet there the resemblance ends. For Boccioni uses the train as one more means of conveying an agitated, subjective, almost expressionist mood. He and his fellow Futurists aimed not at abstraction but empathy, an identification of object with emotion. 'We do not want to observe, dissect and translate into images', wrote Boccioni, rejecting objective analysis as the basis for painting; 'we identify ourselves with the thing, which is profoundly different'.[10] If Futurist manifestos exalted mechanics and the triumphs of scientific invention, their actual paintings were rarely concerned with mechanical forms. They wanted to humanize the machine rather than mechanize man.

But this humanism was not tough enough for the Vorticists. As Lewis said,

Umberto Boccioni
Study for States of Mind: The Farewells, 1911

Frederick Etchells
Hyde Park, 1914–15

Pablo Picasso
The Aficionado, or *Torero*, 1912

they 'accepted the machine-world...the inner world of the imagination was not an asylum from the brutality of mechanical life. On the contrary, it identified itself with that brutality, in a stoical embrace...The artist observed the machine from the outside'.[11] In *Hyde Park*, therefore, which was shown in the 1915 Doré Galleries Exhibition, Etchells takes a potentially picturesque scene as the pretext for a display of Vorticist detachment. The figures are levelled with their environment in a bleak geometric scaffolding of urban forms. The lower right half of the design spins off into a complex of other impressions drawn from his car journey, but they do not interfere with the measured calm of the design. So determined is he to distil all the constituents of his picture into an 'hallucination or dream ... with a mathematic of its own', that it is hard at first to decipher his precise meaning. Any passion the drawing possesses is a by-product of the tight, formal discipline Etchells applies to its subject-matter. Boccioni's emotion, however, could not possibly be evaded or pushed aside: the fragments of train, telegraph poles, lovers and clouds of smoke are all subservient to the melodramatic depiction of a 'State of Mind'. Where Vorticism used the machine as a basis for the construction of a brutal world – 'the Vorticist made rather a point of being tough', explained Lewis, 'so that he might be in harmony with his material' – Futurism simply regarded it as one more means of celebrating its own exalted feelings.

The Cubism evolved by Picasso, Braque and Gris, on the other hand, never showed any outward interest in the machine: when Lewis wrote 'BLAST Bouillon Kub (for being a bad pun)'[12] in his Vorticist manifesto he was poking fun at the way in which the title of a Picasso painting shown at Fry's 1912 Post-Impressionist Exhibition summed up the Cubist obsession with domesticity. But Lewis did not just object to Picasso's lack of interest in mechanical themes; he also loathed the Spaniard's method of depicting the human image as an edifice of semi-abstract planes. In a painting like *The Aficionado*, it was the architectural quality of the figure that Lewis hated most of all. 'In Picasso's portrait the forms are those of masonry, and, properly, should only be used for such', he complained. 'They are inappropriate in the construction of a man, where, however rigid the form may be, there should be at least the suggestions of life and displacement that you get in a machine.' As far as Lewis was concerned, the best way to inject the maximum amount of vitality into the portrayal of a human being was to equate him with a mechanism. 'Picasso's structures are not ENERGETIC ones, in the sense that they are very static dwelling houses', he wrote. 'A machine is in a greater or less degree, a living thing. Its lines and masses imply force and action, whereas those of a dwelling do not.'[13]

Lewis put these beliefs into practice with a work like *Vorticist Design*, which uses the same basic vocabulary as *The Aficionado* and yet produces a totally different result. Not only have Picasso's calm rectilinear planes become edgy, jostling diagonals, each one fighting against its neighbours: the whole structure of the design is changed from a passive edifice to a resolutely active machine. Lewis refuses to align his image with a mechanism in any literal way, although suggestions of saw-tooth edges, levers, pistons and even gun-barrels can be detected among the nervously delineated components of the picture. Rather does he imply the analogy, through every creaking twist and swerve of contour, leaving us to decide whether the end-product is closer to a robot than a blast-furnace.

One element which needs no debating in *Vorticist Design*, however, is its aggression. This is a machine equipped and hungry for battle; and it provides a graphic illustration of the theories Lewis outlined in *Blast No. 1* to reject the typical warlike subject-matter of 'the old style', in which 'two distinct,

Wyndham Lewis
Vorticist Design, c. 1914

heroic figures were confronted, and one ninepin tried to knock the other ninepin over'. Now, Lewis argued, 'we all today (possibly with a coldness reminiscent of the insect-world) are in each other's vitals – overlap, intersect, and are Siamese to any extent'. Hence the sinister feeling in *Vorticist Design* that a struggle is taking place within this single structure, that it contains at least two figures locked in mortal combat. And Lewis explained how his dogmatic ideas about the modern world dictated the degree of abstraction in his art when he declared in the same *Blast No. 1* essay that 'just as the old form of egotism is no longer fit for such conditions as now prevail, so the isolated human figure of most ancient Art is an anachronism'. He admitted that 'the human form still runs, like a wave, through the texture or body of existence, and therefore of art', but simultaneously insisted that 'THE ACTUAL HUMAN BODY BECOMES OF LESS IMPORTANCE EVERY DAY. It now, literally, EXISTS much less'.[14]

No such literary considerations engaged Picasso's attention when he painted *The Aficionado*, which is built up solemnly out of a series of sober facets until it stands on the canvas as a more or less self-sufficient formal entity. The written words, the humour of the moustache and the diagrammatic representation of facial features are all kept in their place as subsidiary factors, and their wit appears insignificant beside the dour monumentality of the whole construction. Lewis seized on this in his writings, claiming that 'the word, even, CUBISM, is a heavy, lugubrious word. The Cubists' paintings have a large tincture of the deadness (as well as the weightiness) of Cézanne'. They were worlds apart from *Vorticist Design*, which was – in accordance with Lewis's theories – 'electric with a more mastered, vivid vitality'.[15] And one obvious means of attaining that vitality was to break away from *The Aficionado*'s emphasis on planar integration, allowing the main image in *Vorticist Design* to rear up in isolation against a backdrop of pencil shading, and supporting it equally firmly on a floor of horizontal pen-strokes. Despite the advanced degree of abstraction employed in the picture, therefore, these strategies give it strong figurative overtones. They are the stage-props in Lewis's theatrical tableau; and even if he has left the narrative uncertainties of his 1909 *Theatre Manager* watercolour far behind, the gulf between his literary inspiration and Picasso's formal preoccupations is still as wide as it was then.

Lewis's impatience with Cubism's refusal to invest its art with any specific meaning other than a purely stylistic one knew no bounds. The mechanistic overtones which he persisted in thinking their canvases contained infuriated him, simply because they were not followed through and developed into a potent force. 'Picasso's latest work . . . is a sort of machinery', he declared in *Blast No. 1*. 'Yet these machines neither propel nor make any known thing: they are machines without a purpose. If you conceive them as carried out on a grand scale, as some elaborate work of engineering, the paradox becomes more striking. These machines would, in that case, before the perplexed and enraged questions of men, have only one answer and justification. If they could suggest or convince that they were MACHINES OF LIFE, a sort of LIVING plastic geometry, then their existence would be justified.'[16] The Cubists would never have understood this viewpoint: even Léger, who placed himself firmly outside Picasso's interpretation of Cubism and employed overtly mechanistic imagery in his work of this period, did not regard an evocation of the machine as his main purpose. By 1913, when he painted his pioneering *Contrast of Forms* series, the tubular figures he previously depicted had given way to a reliance on those tubular shapes for their own sake. They are let loose in an abandoned chain of movement, each one described with the utmost simplicity and yet adding up to a complex whole as they jostle with the equally elementary square

Fernand Léger
Contrast of Forms, 1913

Edward Wadsworth
War-Engine, c. 1915

blocks. If human bodies are still invoked, their connotations have almost disappeared; and metallic objects have taken their place as completely as they do in Wadsworth's *War-Engine*, which was reproduced in *Blast No. 2*.

The Vorticist's picture uses a conglomeration of abstract shapes to create a meticulously detailed metaphor of aggression. *War-Engine* does not refer to any known weapon: it is a Vorticist substitute, a new creation, just as Lewis would have wanted it to be. Wadsworth describes with a near-scientific precision what modern, mechanized war meant to his imagination, and in that sense his design is as literary as Lewis's *Vorticist Design*. He has 'hunted down' this machine, and then 'invented' it on paper, thereby beginning to fulfil *Blast No. 1*'s prediction that 'engineer or artist might conceivably become transposable terms, or one, at least, imply the other'. And the bleak objectivity of the picture faithfully obeys Lewis's order that 'in a Vorticist Universe we don't get excited at what we have invented'.[17] Wadsworth does not seek to impress with bluster or sensationalism: he prefers to state unassailable pictorial facts with as much cold authority as he can muster.

Léger, however, does not feel he has to invent a machine at all. He conveys his feelings about the dynamism of contemporary life through the formal motion of his shapes and nothing else. For him, it was the abstract language – stated with all the simplicity of a basic primer – rather than the subject-matter of machinery that reflected the essential vitality of his age. As he himself explained, 'modern mechanical achievements, such as colour photography, the cinematograph, the profusion of more or less popular novels and the popularisation of the theatres have made completely superfluous the development of visual, sentimental, representational and popular subjects in painting'.[18] And he would, on the evidence of his 1913 work no less than this statement, have included *War-Engine* among this outmoded 'representative' art, despite its ostensibly abstract format. For Léger considered that his *Contrast of Forms* dealt with form alone, whereas Wadsworth agreed with Lewis's belief that a total, exclusive use of abstraction would always be an impossibility. 'The general character of the organizing lines and masses of the picture inevitably betray it into some category or other of an organized terrestrial scene or human grouping', Lewis declared in *Blast No. 2*; 'especially as the logic and mathematics at the bottom of both are the same.'[19] And Wadsworth tacitly admits the truth of this statement by calling his so-called 'abstract' design a *War-Engine*.

The difference between Vorticism's use of the machine and its role in the work of other radical movements is therefore very plain; but there was another branch of Cubism that employed mechanical imagery with as much avidity as the English rebels, and its arch-exponent was Duchamp. Indeed, it was he who came closer than any other continental painter to the Vorticists' detached view of machinery. If his painting of *The Bride* is compared with Lewis's *Portrait of an Englishwoman*, illustrated in *Blast No. 1*, the relative attitudes of the two artists become clear. For both these pictures transform the theme of femininity into a series of frankly mechanistic shapes. Lewis, true to his iconoclastic temperament, destroys all traces of his woman and replaces her with an arrangement of thick black bars, most of which ascend in a diagonal succession towards the top of the design. They suggest industrial girders, even gun-barrels, and their repetitive oblongs consciously refute the curves that are normally associated with the visual depiction of a female. In fact, the phallic thrust of these dark bands constitutes a perverse denial of a woman's ideal contours, despite the fact that Pound thought the design 'presented cool beauty'.[20] Duchamp likewise banishes all representational traces of his bride in favour of an elaborate cluster of organic and scientific forms. He has performed a surgical operation on her, plucking out a whimsical compound of genitalia and intestines and mixing them

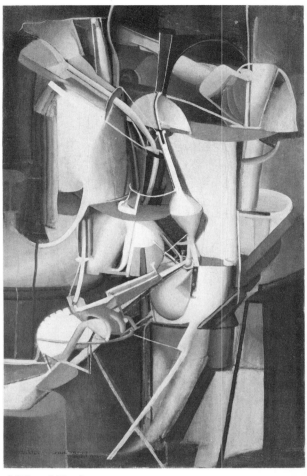

△ Marcel Duchamp
The Bride, 1912

◁ Wyndham Lewis
Portrait of an Englishwoman, 1914

in with pistons, tubes and levers borrowed from an automaton. His composition circulates around the picture-surface like the course of an alimentary canal, whereas Lewis's bristles with tensile force. The two men are united in their removed attitude towards the machine, but however mutually aloof Duchamp and Lewis may appear, they are nevertheless opposed in other, more subtle ways. Despite the subversive intentions lying behind both pictures, *Portrait of an Englishwoman* does not share the cynical, negative outlook expressed in *The Bride*. When Lewis reproduced his picture in the Vorticists' magazine, he saw it as one more method of 'blasting' the English into a discussion of the movement outlined in writing elsewhere in the journal. He was, at heart, positive in his ambitions, aiming to establish an art that would reflect the precise pulse of modern experience. Duchamp, by contrast, painted *The Bride* in a spirit of witty, sophisticated nihilism, and afterwards devoted his life's work to undermining the foundations of all existing aesthetics, including those Lewis was trying so hard to formulate.

For all the similarities between Vorticism and its rivals, then, the movement had managed to dip into the pool of avant-garde ideas and come up with an independent catch of its own. The artists who first exhibited together as a group in the 'Cubist Room' at Brighton had come of age, and assumed a national identity. Pound was not merely blustering when he advised H. L. Mencken in March 1915 that 'in any case you might keep in mind the fact that Vorticism is not Futurism, most emphatically NOT. We like Cubism and some Expressionism, but the schools are not our school'.[21] The Great English Vortex may not have succeeded in making its countrymen realize that it had, as Lewis wrote afterwards, 'hustled the cultural Britannia, stepping up that cautious pace with which she prefers to advance',[22] but it certainly left an unmistakable mark on the works of the many considerable artists associated with its fundamental cause. Even those who, like Bomberg and Epstein, could never actually bring themselves to be branded as Vorticists can now be seen to have participated in the general style that was evolved. And if Lewis predominates as the tripartite originator, organizer and oracle of the movement, he was not necessarily its most outstanding practitioner.

All the same, Lewis would not have been unduly pompous if he had stood back and claimed, before he left for the war in the spring of 1916, that he had managed to bully a recalcitrant circle of compatriots into acknowledging the need for a concerted assault on the accepted beliefs of their age. At this stage he was, as he later wrote, 'a man of the *tabula rasa*', who 'thought everything could be wiped out in a day, and rebuilt nearer to the heart's desire'.[23] For Lewis had genuinely convinced himself that 'the time had come to shatter the visible world to bits', and he 'really was persuaded that this absolute transformation was imminent'. Only a man capable of considering himself to be 'a little like the Christians of the First Century who believed firmly that the end of the world was at hand'[24] could have been foolhardy or tenacious enough to embark on such an adventure, and the wonder is that he managed to achieve anything at all. He could reasonably be proud of his progress from the time of the June 1911 Camden Town Group exhibition, when the *Sunday Times* had prophetically complained that 'visitors may be shocked at the elongated noses in the squarely-drawn heads by Mr Wyndham Lewis',[25] up to the moment in July 1914 when the uncertainty of those 'shocks' blossomed into the confidence of *Blast No. 1*.

A measure of just how many hopes he had then entertained for Vorticism can be gauged from a speech Lewis gave at the opening of a Leeds Arts Club exhibition in May 1914, just before he decided to bring his movement out into the open. 'In the course of a short address', reported the *Yorkshire Post* on 18 May, 'Mr Wyndham Lewis said that, roughly speaking, there were three movements in modern painting, namely, futurist, cubist, and expressionist, the two latter being the first in date. He was of the opinion, however, that eventually we should find these three sub-divisions no longer existing, but that we should get one art, which, it was to be hoped, would be modern art.' A few weeks after these prophetic and revealing words were uttered, Vorticism was launched in the firm belief that it would indeed be able to synthesize the most positive modernist impulses in this all-embracing 'one art'. Lewis's ambitions at that stage refused to satisfy themselves with anything less.

'I am always regretting that I was not born in a volcanic land; in the matter of art anyhow', he had written to John soon after the movement was launched; 'the sort of place where the aesthetic structures have a slight shake-up every day and are periodically swallowed up altogether. What's the good of being an island, if you are not a *volcanic* island?'[26] And if, by 1916, Vorticist politics had failed to uproot those 'aesthetic structures' from their firmly embedded position in the subsoil of English culture, he could rest happy in the knowledge that Vorticist art had managed to portray the country as the weapon *Blast No. 1* envisaged:

an 'industrial island machine, pyramidal workshop, its apex at Shetland, discharging itself on the sea'.[27] Creative stamina, at least, had forced the volcano to erupt and solidify into a new imaginative order.

Nowhere is this order given more specific expression than in the pictures that survive from the Vorticist period by Lewis himself. Most of them are outwardly non-representational, in spite of his prediction in *Blast No. 2* that 'a great deal of effort will automatically flow back into more natural forms from the barriers of the Abstract',[28] and a small group of mixed-media designs keep these barriers raised as high as possible. They are all dated 1915, and form a series of almost musical variations on the theme of an ideal Vorticist structure. In one, the *Composition in Red and Purple*, Lewis lays down a collection of thick wedges in black ink which surge up in a characteristic diagonal direction towards the upper edge of the paper; and he then proceeds to inject venom with areas of flaming crayon and gouache, pitching extreme colours together so that they

Wyndham Lewis
Composition in Red and Purple, 1915

Wyndham Lewis
Vorticist Composition, 1915

clash and swear at each other. But however violent the tonal oppositions may be, they are still controlled by the vigorous black scaffolding of the architectural complex they enliven: the Vorticist, after all, would never allow iconoclastic emotions to get the better of geometrical discipline.

This bias towards classical order is even more evident in another of his 1915 designs, *Vorticist Composition*, where a similar conglomeration of interlocking shapes thrust in a taut diagonal. Juxtapose this composition with the last and it is easy to see Lewis ringing the changes, moving from one related idea to the next, pushing his forms around and playing off a multiplicity of angles against the occasional semicircle. They show him meditating aloud, trying to get nearer to the hard, essentially haughty world he carried as a vision in his mind. In *Vorticist Composition* a deep lilac wash slices down in a zigzag through the centre of the shapes, and the entire design was once framed by Lewis himself with dazzling silver foil; but neither element would ultimately be permitted to interfere with the proud lines of the superstructure Lewis had erected to substantiate his dream.

Are these pictures totally abstract, or do they embody those figurative references which Lewis's contemporaneous writings insisted were always present in a work of art? The best answer is to be found in his 'Review of Contemporary Art' essay, where he explains that if 'you live amongst houses, a "town-dweller"', your 'familiarity with objects gives you a psychological mastery akin to the practised mastery of the workman's hand'. Lewis obviously believed in the value of incorporating an instinctive knowledge of his surroundings in these *Compositions*, albeit in a very indirect manner which removed his work from any suspicion of imitation. If, as he stated, 'Nature itself is of no importance', and 'it is always the POSSIBILITIES in the object, the IMAGINATION, as we say, in the spectator, that matters', then he could see 'no reason why you should not use this neighbouring material, that of endless masonry and mechanical shapes, if you enjoy it'. Lewis manifestly did delight in his urban context, and suggestions of it can even be seen influencing the most free and ostensibly abstract of all his mixed media designs, the remarkable *Composition in Blue*.

Here, although the main brunt of the arrangement is borne by the sharp ink lines that enclose the middle with their protective angles, the black oblongs hovering at the top and the area of sheer ultramarine washing the corner of the paper, the picture telescopes in towards a distant centre where crayon describes the outlines of a mysterious architectural cavity. It looks almost like the entrance to a city of Lewis's own imagining, and imparts a meaning to the composition which its abstract elements would not otherwise have held. It bears out, too, the warning Lewis stressed in his 'Review' article when he wrote that 'if you do not use shapes and colours characteristic of your environment' and 'wish to escape from this, or from any environment at all, you soar into the clouds, merely. That will only, in its turn, result in your painting what the dicky-birds would if they painted. Perhaps airmen might even conceivably share this tendency with the lark'.[29] *Composition in Blue* avoids this danger by ensuring that the floating ensemble of lines and colours dominating the design are firmly attached to the tiny urban metaphor lodged at its heart.

But Lewis did not want his picture to be limited simply to city references. Putting into visual terms Pound's insistence in the 'Vorticism' essay that 'the imagiste's images have a variable significance', he made sure that the central form in *Composition in Blue* could be seen as an armoured head as well as an architectural cavity. Once this new reference has been grasped, it is possible to read the entire complex of lines extending from the 'head' to the bottom edge of the design as the torso and legs of a figure. Such an interpretation immediately transforms the meaning of the surrounding elements, turning them into the directional

Wyndham Lewis
Composition in Blue, 1915

Wyndham Lewis
Design for Red Duet, 1915

arms of opposing forces reminiscent of Lewis's earlier *Plan of War* painting. But this alternative reading does not render the other, urban meaning redundant: the two coexist, refusing to be mutually exclusive and adding richness to a work which manages to be both precise and ambivalent, specific and multi-referential.

The more closely Lewis's pictures of this period are scrutinized, the clearer it becomes that tissues of literary meaning are enfolded in their outwardly abstract structure. *Design for Red Duet*, for instance, a drawing for which Lewis expressed a special regard by reproducing it both in *Blast No. 2* and as the frontispiece of the Vorticist Exhibition catalogue, appears as deeply committed to the viability of a non-figurative language as any of the *Compositions*. It would seem hard to pin down any intention in the drawing other than the emotions conveyed by its tense, haughty formal disposition. But the clue to its deeper purpose is contained in an article called 'Wyndham Lewis Vortex No. 1', which appeared in *Blast No. 2* about thirty pages away from the *Red Duet* drawing. Subtitled 'Be Thyself', the clipped sentences of the essay advised its readers to 'be a duet in everything', for 'the Individual, the single object, and the isolated, is, you will admit, an absurdity'. Lewis was arguing that the Vorticist should never fall into the trap of thinking that his creative persona was compatible with his animal persona. 'There is Yourself: and there is the Exterior World, that fat mass you browse on', he wrote, clearly distinguishing between the spiritual and the social sides of man. 'Do not confuse yourself with it, or weaken the esoteric lines of fine original being' he warned, determined to tell everyone not to 'settle down and snooze on an acquired, easily possessed and mastered, satisfying shape'.

The reason why Lewis was so anxious to establish this duality lay in his belief that it was impossible to realize a full personal potential without it. Just as he stressed the opposition between 'Art' and 'Life', so he thought that the man who failed to dissociate his intellectual from his physical nature ended up by aping reality in his work rather than reforming it into a genuine artefact. And the artist who bowed down to the influence of external appearances was committing creative suicide. Lewis had dramatized this problem before, when he wrote 'Enemy of the Stars' and published it in *Blast No. 1*. There the dilemma was expressed as an allegory in which the two characters, Arghol and Hanp, symbolized pure intelligence and sensual animal respectively. They are tragically inseparable, the two halves of a human who realizes the disparity in his own personality but cannot do anything about it. As Arghol bitterly explained in the explosive, compressed prose that served as a literary equivalent for Lewis's own art: 'Men have a loathsome deformity called Self; affliction got through indiscriminate rubbing against their fellows: Social excrescence. Their being is regulated by exigencies of this affliction. Only one operation can cure it: the suicide's knife.'[30] The problem is resolved at the end of the 'play' by death: Hanp stabs the sleeping Arghol and then throws himself into a canal. The message of the parable was dramatically apparent, and Lewis defined it in his 'Be Thyself' article by insisting that 'you can establish yourself . . . as a Machine of two similar fraternal surfaces overlapping . . . Any machine then you like: but become mechanical by fundamental dual repetition . . . Hurry up and get into this harmonious and sane duality'.[31]

The twin mechanisms in *Design for Red Duet* served, therefore, as a pictorial parallel for the way in which Lewis reconciled these conflicting personae in his own working life. 'No clear outlines, except on condition of being dual and prolonged', Lewis ordered, realizing that the harsh contours of the drawing could only be arrived at by appreciating the difference between creative and mimetic urges. 'You must catch the clearness and logic in the midst of contradictions' he urged, thereby inferring that his mechanical imagery was the direct

Wyndham Lewis
Red Duet, 1914

outcome of an ability to synthesize his personality, allowing its receptive side to exist but knowing all the time that the conceptual was the side that made Vorticist art. And out of this self-knowledge came the further realization that the most abstract picture necessarily contained a representational strain within itself.

Even the large gouache version of *Red Duet*, probably displayed at the Vorticist Exhibition and eventually acquired by Pound, referred back to the literary problems discussed in these theoretical writings, for all its unprecedentedly schematic appearance.[32] Lewis, massing his black segments into martial ranks, intersperses them with a scalding combination of scarlet, mauve and crimson gouache. And as the various particles stand upright, march diagonally across the picture-surface or arrange themselves into heraldic emblems, so they inexorably assume the character of a challenge. The colours gell with these bullet-like forms into an unshakable pattern of defiance, as if their creator was declaring war on every artist weak enough to admit the irrelevant contours of the visible world into his work. For the Vorticist had to make sure that he sifted all these accidental superfluities through the filter of his imagination until the abstracted essence remained: only then could he feel free to arrange them in an inevitable sequence on his picture surface. 'In a painting certain forms M U S T be so', Lewis had commanded in *Blast No. 1*; 'in the same meticulous, profound manner that your pen or a book must lie on the table at a certain angle, your clothes at night be arranged in a set personal symmetry, certain birds be avoided, a set of railings tapped with your hand as you pass, without missing one'.[33] This crucial sense of order was for Lewis tantamount to a physical need; and *Red Duet*'s overwhelmingly clear-cut organization is a positive exemplar of Lewis's resolution of duality in his own personality. Dorothy Shakespear, who knew the picture intimately while it hung in Pound's home, thought that Lewis had here taken as his starting-point the Changing of the Guard at Buckingham Palace.[34] And if that was indeed so, *Red Duet*'s transformation of the scene demonstrates how resolutely Lewis sacrificed the incidental pleasures of representation for the sake of his refined, metaphorical ideal. It blares out his victory with as much discordant noise as he felt could be infused into the design without endangering its overall organization. *Red Duet* may appear to be the most extreme abstraction Lewis ever executed, but its implacable emotional impact sums up his underlying aesthetic philosophy as well.

It was, nevertheless, the theme of the city that engaged most of Lewis's attention at this period. He returned to it incessantly, and the twenty pages of his so-called 'Vorticist Sketch-Book' bear witness to an obsession with the kind of quintessential industrial structures recommended as the artist's true subject-matter in *Blast No. 1*'s manifestos. Once again, the interest coincides with Futurism, but this time it is the ideas and designs of Sant'Elia that provide

◁ Wyndham Lewis
Composition V, 1914–15

▽Antonio Sant'Elia
Architectural Dynamism, c. 1913–14

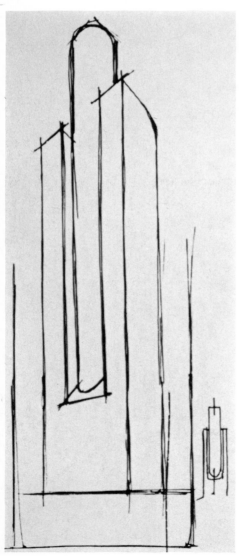

the best point of comparison. This young Italian visionary was an architect and Lewis was a painter; but the resemblance between a Sant'Elia drawing like *Architectural Dynamism* and a page called *Composition V* from Lewis's 'Vorticist Sketch-Book' is too compelling to be ignored. Both sketches outline the bare bones of a projected city-scape, dominated by skyscraper towers as simplified in their cubic volumes as Europe's most advanced painting and sculpture. Sant'Elia was envisaging structures which he would ideally have designed and built in the main urban centres of Italy, and only his premature death in the Great War prevented him from attempting to do so. 'We must invent and re-build *ex novo* our Modern city like an immense and tumultuous shipyard, active, mobile and everywhere dynamic', he wrote in his *Messaggio* of 1914, 'and the modern building like a gigantic machine.'[35] Lewis would have heartily concurred with such sentiments – he confessed later that 'I greatly relished, and still do, a really hideous city like Birmingham or Pittsburgh' – but his job was to present an abstracted metaphor of this city rather than draw up plans for the architecture itself. Sant'Elia's most astonishing drawings are detailed representations of the actual electric generating stations, hangars and blocks of flats he would dearly have loved to construct as a professional practising architect, whereas the notations in Lewis's 'Sketch-Book' are the germs of ideas for paintings where all his complex feelings about the urban situation could be expressed.

The series of repeated rectangles ascending the upper half of his lively *Composition III* can, for example, easily be read as the windows of a modern office block; and yet they are so intermingled with less identifiable fragments of

Wyndham Lewis
Composition III, 1914–15

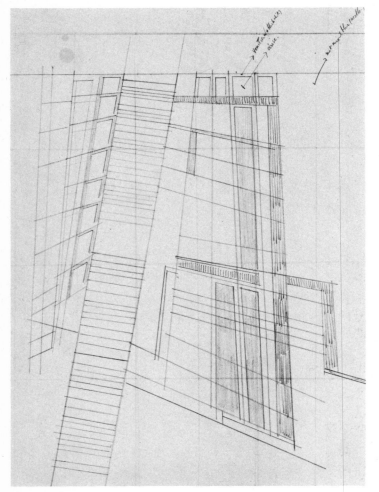

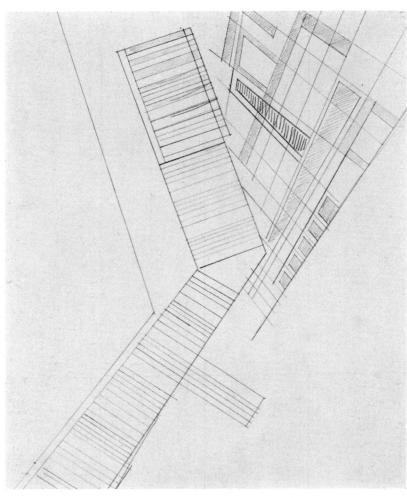

△ Wyndham Lewis
Composition VI, 1914–15

▽ Wyndham Lewis
Composition VIII, 1914–15

geometry that it would be inadvisable to pin them down to such a specific descriptive function. In any case, Lewis had himself warned against a literal interpretation of his work in *Blast No. 2*, where he wrote that 'a Vorticist, lately, painted a picture in which a crowd of squarish shapes, at once suggesting windows, occurred. A sympathizer with the movement asked him, horror-struck, "are not those windows?" "Why not?" the Vorticist replied. "A window is for you actually A WINDOW: for me it is a space, bounded by a square or oblong frame, by four bands or four lines, merely." '[36] The moral was clear. Lewis did not want to rule out the possibility of his ideograms containing references to the outside world, but neither did he relish the prospect of being limited by the spectator's instinctive desire to search for recognizable objects in his pictures. He aimed for a flexible compromise that left the question open: then there could be a supple flow of understanding between the work of art and its viewer, whereby the latter would be free to let his imagination roam although he was subject all the while to the precise intentions of the artist. 'The sense of objects, even, is a sense of the SIGNIFICANCE of the object, and not its avoirdupois and scientifically ascertainable shapes and perspectives.' Lewis wrote in *Blast No. 2*; and it was this kind of meaning, half overt and half intangible, with which he was concerned when he jotted down his first inspirational thoughts in the 'Vorticist Sketch-Book'.

Succeeding pages from the 'Sketch-Book' show him actively striving for a more freewheeling vision of the city than Sant'Elia could ever have attained with his diagrams of a new environmental reality. Lewis's *Composition VI*

Wyndham Lewis
New York, 1914

incorporates a ladder motif climbing up from the bottom of the paper until it joins the familiar window-rectangles to impart a dizzy sensation of height. And this same motif becomes the instigator of an unnerving vertigo in *Composition VIII*, where it sweeps in from the left towards a vortex-like centre. Then, in order to give more substance to the image, Lewis brought ink and gouache into play and executed a startling design in his 'Sketch-Book' which has since been given the evocative title *New York*.[37] It was obviously created in a great hurry, and the feverish, often erratic scratchings of the pen add an extra urgency to the picture, as Lewis rapidly delineates the surging forms of twentieth-century urban civilization. True to his classical bias, the areas blocked in with light and midnight blues assume solid, firm proportions; but they are set at an extreme diagonal emphasis on the page, and cut through by anarchic lines of fluorescent scarlet which add tension as they pierce the larger elements and dart around them like so many flashes of abstract lightning.

Lewis was ready now to transpose this vision into a full-scale oil painting, and a canvas called *Workshop* – exhibited both at the second London Group show and the Vorticist Exhibition – is one of the results of his attempts to do so. Although the only surviving contemporary description of the picture refers to it as 'a Vorticist impression of a studio', there is no reason to suppose that Lewis had suddenly switched his attention from the exciting theme of a city to the altogether more domestic one of an atelier.[38] Why on earth should he have decided to abandon the central obsession of his work and revert to the Cubist subject-matter he so vehemently despised? The title *Workshop* may possibly suggest such a volte-face, but it could equally well stand as Lewis's wry nickname for the city as a machine given over to the processes of labour. He almost admitted as much in his novel, *Tarr*, when he made Tarr himself refute Anastasya's insistence that 'all the world's a stage' by declaring that 'it was an actor that said that. I say it's all an atelier – "all the world's a workshop", I should say'.[39] And the *Blast* manifestos' image of England as an 'industrial island machine, pyramidal workshop' explains Lewis's motives when he painted this picture still more fully. The whole nation would become an urban structure, and when he expressed his thoughts about the city most clearly in prose, he described a place that coincides only too well with the structure created in this painting. 'Men must be penned and herded into "Their Time", and prevented from dreaming, the prerogative of the Lord of the Earth', he explained in *Blast No. 2*. 'They must also be prevented from drifting back in the direction of their Jungle. And the best way to do this is to allow them to have a little contemporary Jungle of their own. Such a little up-to-date and iron Jungle is the great modern city. Its vulgarity is the sort of torture and flagellation that becomes the austere creator.'[40]

The harsh network of lines stamped across the surface of *Workshop* can, therefore, be seen as the boundaries of a prison erected to keep the city's inhabitants satisfied with their environment. They imply a sense of restriction, of inflexible laws imposed with a force that would make it virtually impossible for the average man to break out and start an alternative existence in more emancipated surroundings. Lines plunge forward, swerve abruptly to link up with other lines, double back on each other, brusquely contradict their neighbours' directional emphases, and gather into convoluted knots in their efforts to ensure that no-one is immune to their all-pervasive influence. The ladder shapes already employed in the 'Vorticist Sketch-Book' come into their own at the top of the picture, arranging themselves into regularized series as if to reflect the immovable nature of the world they inhabit. And over on the left, the window shapes take on the cruel power of a grid, their flat, unbroken anonymously applied layers of paint ruling out the possibility of any penetration through to a freedom beyond.

It is a tough, unpleasant, even repellent picture, which strives to parallel in its formal organization the dissonance and daunting stress which Lewis diagnosed as the essential twentieth century zeitgeist. No one single section of this maddeningly awkward composition glides smoothly into another: expectations are aroused concerning one kind of linear movement only to be rudely denied or rebuffed by a neighbouring area, and each regular sequence of geometrical patterning is flouted before it has a chance to take control of the whole design. Nothing is consistent, everything is wilfully contradictory; and Lewis seems determined to starve *Workshop* of every ploy to which a painting can usually resort in order to flatter the viewer's eye. All the manifold attractions of the oil medium have been sacrificed at the altar of the Vorticist's need to evolve an art capable of expressing the raw tension of modern life. *Workshop* appears half-finished, straining outwards to burst through the boundaries of its design and thereby find complete repose and fulfilment. It is held back, however, by a controlled energy which insists upon order and rigid confinement, tempering Vorticism's unruly explosive impulses with the sinews of classical discipline.

But is *Workshop* as claustrophobic a work as this interpretation makes out? Although the linear basis of the picture is self-evident, colour plays an important role as well, and its outspoken blend of bright pinks, maroons, blues, ochres

▷Wyndham Lewis
Workshop, 1914–15

and sepias argues that Lewis wanted to celebrate the city even while he stressed its ability to compartmentalize human beings. Generous bands of white provide an outlet and a space to breathe in several areas, notably at the bottom where one of them is connected to a giant stretch of brown and dark red which moves up the right-hand side and turns to leave the outer edge of the design unconfined by any lines at all. These relatively liberated areas of the picture seem to bear out Lewis's declaration in *Blast No. 2* that 'really – as I have often insisted – this modern Jungle is not without its beauty (what do you think of 21st Street, or the town of Elberfeld?) and has very little that is civilised about it. It is at present, too, replete with a quaint and very scientific ferocity'.[41]

He had a classic love-hate relationship with the city, and the extraordinary tonal contrasts of *Workshop* – laid down in a completely impersonal, prosaic paint-surface that could have been put on with a trowel as easily as a brush – reflect his fascination with this 'ferocity'. For just as he announced in *Blast No.1* that 'the surfaces of cheap manufactured goods, woods, steel, glass, etc., already appreciated for themselves, and their possibilities realised, have finished the days of fine paint', so he wanted to carry out his prediction in the same periodical that 'even if painting remains intact, it will be much more supple and extended, containing all the elements of discord and "ugliness" consequent on the attack against traditional harmony'.[42] This passage, written around the beginning of 1914, was obviously intended as an indication of the work he himself proposed to do. And *Workshop* carries out his programme to the letter,

Wyndham Lewis
Composition IV, 1914–15

serving at the same time as an expression of Lewis's most considered thoughts about the 'iron Jungle' which the Vorticist had a duty to incorporate in his art. Discord becomes a new harmony, ugliness grows into a beauty of its own, and if this metamorphosis posited a world with extremely ambivalent qualities, Lewis was able to present them all in the paradoxical construction of *Workshop*. Even while it alienates the spectator with its unrelieved starkness and jarring formal non-sequiturs, the painting seduces through the originality with which it prophesies a new condition of man.

But what of this man, encapsulated within the taut confines of the city Lewis had presented with such perception? *Workshop* avoided the problem by refusing to include any trace of figurative imagery, and yet that did not mean the creator of the 'Vorticist Sketch-Book' was altogether set against placing humans in the environment he had evolved for them. Other leaves from the 'Sketch-Book', like the complex *Composition IV*, include tentative figurative references among the stern horizontals and verticals which seem to have been drawn up with a ruler to emphasize their authority. Indeed, the only shapes that disturb the rectilinear nature of the drawing suggest the energy of human limbs; and in a strong *Composition II*, which reinforces the formal arrangement of the previous drawing by simplification and the use of a simple orange wash, Lewis disrupts the equilibrium of the large forms with the pencilled shapes of those same limbs in the right centre of his design. But although the jerking motion of the limbs is directly at variance with the calm, monolithic bar of orange nearby, they do

Wyndham Lewis
Composition II, 1914–15

not for one moment threaten to break out of their surroundings. The bar simply shifts slightly, as if condescending to accommodate the demands of this puppet and satisfy his outburst of high spirits. Lewis was obviously working towards another major statement on canvas, this time drawing on the format of these two studies to execute a painting in which humans would be allotted their appropriate place within the hierarchy of urban existence. And instead of concentrating on the motif of one single figure, he finally decided to portray an entire mass of humanity swarming through the interstices of his city.

The resultant picture was entitled *The Crowd*, shown at the second London Group exhibition and then lost from sight until it appeared in a private collection under the name of *Revolution*.[43] But Frank Rutter's enthusiastic description of the painting in his *Sunday Times* review of the London Group show removes all reasonable doubt that the surviving oil, well over six feet in height, is *The Crowd* itself. 'First and foremost there is Mr Wyndham Lewis's huge decoration *The Crowd*', he wrote appreciatively in March 1915, 'a wondrous pattern of imaginative parquetry, formed apparently of brick forms of dull red, which combine very happily in juxtaposition to the old gold bands that form the principal lines of the composition.'[44]

It is the remarkable austerity of these 'old gold bands' that impress most in front of the original picture: they prove that Lewis has had the courage to restrict himself to a bareness worthy of Mondrian in 1915. Not that a Cubist painter like Braque had by this time balked at a greater degree of simplicity – in 1913 he managed, with *The Clarinet*, to let the burden of his composition rest on one broad strip of brown paper traversing most of the width of the picture-surface. It possesses a severe authority comparable to Lewis's 'bands'; but Braque's work was a collage, and still clung to the tradition of the domestic still-life. *The Crowd*'s theme was at once far wider and more literary than that, and it is pertinent to compare it not so much with Mondrian's comparably recti-linear *Pier and Ocean* series of the same date as with Russolo's enormous painting of *The Revolt*, which Lewis would have seen in the Futurists' first London exhibition at the Sackville Gallery.

Both pictures employ large strips of colour that dominate references to urban architecture and groups of diminutive, toy-like figures. Both, too, say a lot about the impersonality and uniformity of industrial society, and use a vast scale to help impose this feeling on the spectator. Here, however, the irreconcilable differences between Futurism and Vorticism disrupt further similarities. Russolo's gaggle of humanity symbolizes, according to the Sackville Gallery catalogue, 'the revolutionary element made up of enthusiasm and red lyricism', and is shown in 'collision' with 'the force of inertia and reactionary resistance of tradition'. His 'bands' are, therefore, the 'vibratory waves' of this revolution: the familiar 'lines of force' propagated by the Futurist Manifestos, and directly opposed in their continuously expanding, accelerating movement to their static, four-square counterparts in *The Crowd*. The mood of *The Revolt* is one of triumph, as in Boccioni's *The City Rises*; and the Sackville catalogue explained, in its uncertain English, that 'the perspective of the houses is destroyed just as a boxer is bent double by receiving a blow in the wind'. *The Crowd*, on the other hand, labours under no such idealistic delusions about modern life's capacity for glorious self-renewal. Lewis's standpoint is dispassionate, coldly appraising and removed from the callow note of subjective involvement that Russolo displays. The editor of *Blast No. 1* had, after all, loathed the enthusiasm of Boccioni's *The City Rises* so much that he had dismissed it as 'sheer unadul-terated Belgian romance: blue clouds of smoke, pawing horses, heroic grimy workers, sententious skyscrapers, factory chimneys, etc'.[45] And the figures he portrayed in *The Crowd* are far indeed from being masters of their surroundings.

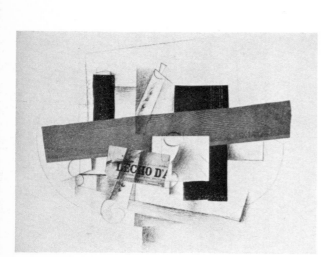

Georges Braque
The Clarinet, 1913

Luigi Russolo
The Revolt, 1911

▷Wyndham Lewis
The Crowd, 1914–15

Apart from three faceless robots who stand motionless at the bottom of the canvas near a downtrodden neighbour, who slinks away from them towards the left corner with his mouth opened in a cry of helpless protest, the human element has been frozen into minute particles of scarlet geometry. They crop up at sporadic intervals all over the vast expanse of the composition, framed at one moment by the oppressive rectangularity of the grid on the right, half hidden by a giant 'band' over on the left and everywhere dwarfed by the immutable abstraction that Lewis has laid down on his picture-surface with all the loftiness of a dictatorial town-planner. The vertiginous liveliness of *Workshop* has now given way to complete prosaism as the massive girders of colour assert a bullying function, pushing the inconsequential lattice of figures into tiny spatial pockets which they have decreed should be left unaffected by the brutality of their weight. And the predominant dull brown casts its gloomy pall over the entire composition, making even the occasional introduction of red, yellow and white seem downcast and anaemic. In the middle of the picture, a matchstick figure leaps out suddenly from the schematic pattern which traps his companions and brandishes a miniature flag in the air. But the gesture is scarcely noticeable, the act of a child showing off his new plaything rather than a signal that will ignite potent revolution among his fellows. Directly above, other groups sway feebly into action and a second flag is held aloft, only to be confronted by the enclosing bar of brown on its right. Every attempt at spirited action is dampened by the brooding force of uniformity; and as if mirroring this trough of depression, Lewis's paint is applied thinly, scarcely managing to block in the dry, listless outlines of his design. The brushwork repels close examination, implying that the artist's own natural vitality was dissipated as he elaborated on his cheerless theme.

'Dehumanization', he had written in *Blast No. 1*, 'is the chief diagnostic of the Modern World', and *The Crowd* gives this pronouncement its most depressing embodiment. But for all the relentlessness of his painting, Lewis did not view this situation pessimistically, as a Kafkaesque nightmare. Although he wrote in the same article that 'impersonality becomes a disease with . . . the modern town-dweller', he remained characteristically cool and analytical about the malaise. If he thought that 'promiscuity is normal', and 'such separating things as love, hatred, friendship are superseded by a more realistic and logical passion', then the Vorticist must measure up to this harsh reality and not evade it by running back to the cloud-cuckoo land of the New English Art Club. Lewis's personal solution was to elevate his awareness of this new spiritual condition into a rationale for his own stylistic move towards abstraction. 'This superseding of specific passions and easily determinable emotions by such uniform, more animal, instinctively logical Passion of Life . . . is, then, the phenomenon to which we would relate the most fundamental tendencies in present art, and by which we would gauge its temper', his *Blast No. 1* essay concluded.[46] And it is not hard to see him taking these theories to their logical conclusion in *The Crowd*, where the 'dehumanized' geometric 'town-dwellers' are inextricably caged up inside the crushing 'uniformity' of the immense rectilinear slabs which exert their control over every inch of the design. Even the letters spelling out 'E N C L O' are prevented from finishing off the word to which they belong: the emotional connotations of the fragment that has been allowed to remain, no less than its abrupt decapitation, add their own special bite to the overall message of confinement.

There was, too, one further level of meaning that Lewis wanted to inject into *The Crowd*. In *Blast No. 2*, he published the 'first part' of 'The Crowd Master', a projected story headed '1914. London, July'. Most of it was taken up with the activities of Thomas Blenner, a retired lieutenant from the Indian army;

but Lewis introduced the story with a chorus-like prelude on the behaviour of the London crowd in those tense days before the final declaration of world war. For him, 'THE CROWD is the first mobilisation of a country', and having established itself 'with all its vague profound organs au grand complet', it 'serpentines every night, in thick well-nourished coils, all over the town, in tropic degustation of news and "stimmung"'. The undulating motion described here may not accord with the strict angularity of the human forms in Lewis's painting, but it soon becomes apparent that the same mood of foreboding and regularized emotion is being explored. 'THE INDIVIDUAL and THE CROWD: PEACE and WAR', the story continued, frankly equating mass emotion with the madness that makes war possible. And in order to emphasize that no-one is immune to its influence, Lewis pointed out that 'we all shed our small skin periodically or are apt to sometime, and are purged in big being: an empty throb'. It was his familiar distinction between the two personae of man; but this time they were separated up into 'Man's solitude and Peace; Man's Community and Row', and Lewis's ideal creative 'duet' was now threatened by a powerful exhortation to join the suicidal impulse of a whole nation. 'The Crowd is an immense anaesthetic towards death' he wrote, explaining how easy it was, when 'Duty flings the selfish will into this relaxed vortex', to confuse the act of enlistment with artistic militancy. 'A fine dust of extinction, a grain or two for each man, is scattered in any crowd like these black London war-crowds', Lewis warned. 'Their pace is so mournful. Wars begin with this huge indefinite Interment in the cities.'[47] Over and above its other meanings, then, *The Crowd* also distilled the atmosphere of a death-wish; and if its sombre mood seems almost to approach the timbre of an elegy, this was fully commensurate with Lewis's grim realization that war threatened the very survival of the movement he was trying to develop through works as ambitious as this drily cerebral yet monumental painting.

Enough of Lewis's mature Vorticist work has survived to show how the movement's ideals were given pictorial life in his own paintings, drawings and watercolours. But how much more did he achieve in other pictures which have since been lost? *Workshop* and *The Crowd* are, chronologically, the first oil-paintings that now exist in Lewis's œuvre, all the rest having been mislaid or destroyed. And yet both these works were completed some time before March 1915, when they were displayed in the second London Group exhibition. Around January, Lewis had told Pound in a letter that 'I am doing a power of painting. If I get my head blown off when I am pottering about Flanders, I shall have left something'.[48] Little did he know, when he gave his friend this proud progress report, that three of his five vital contributions to the 'Picture' section of the Vorticist Exhibition – *Man and Woman*, *Two Shafts* and *Democratic Composition* – were to disappear and not even be commemorated in photographic form. Only scraps of evidence, such as his later memory of a 'canvas in golden yellows and mustards, looking like the cross-section of a bee-hive, which it is a pity I was not able to preserve', can now be salvaged out of the nine months of creative activity left to him from the end of the Vorticist Exhibition to the start of his army career in the spring of 1916.[49] A diverting invitation card to a 'Vorticist Evening' at the Restaurant de la Tour Eiffel in February 1916 still exists, decorated with an assured little sketch of a sinister robot man offering a drink to an even more formidable woman, her hat emblazoned with a cluster of gun-barrels. It proves that the movement's social activities continued, at least; and a photograph survives, taken by Alvin Langdon Coburn just before Lewis joined the army, which shows him seated in front of a vast abstract canvas with a determination that demonstrates how much the rebel cause meant to him. He looks tired and strained; but his defiant pose, no less than the striking heraldry

YOU ARE INVITED
TO A
VORTICIST EVENING
TO BE HELD AT THE
RESTAURANT DE LA TOUR EIFFEL,
1 PERCY STREET,
TOTTENHAM COURT ROAD, W., ON
WEDNESDAY, FEBRUARY 23, 1916,
9 TO 11 P.M.

THIS TICKET IS TO ADMIT
ONE PERSON.

Wyndham Lewis
Invitation to a Vorticist Evening, 1916

△Edward Wadsworth
Photograph of Lewis and Frank Newbold (?)
at High Greenwood House, Hebden Bridge, 1915

▷Alvin Langdon Coburn
Wyndham Lewis in his Studio, 1916

of the lost painting propped up behind him, testifies that he continued his investigations into the possibilities of a non-representational language right up until the last precious moments of his life as a civilian. This tantalizing glimpse of a Vorticist picture that has no name, and was presumably never given the chance to outlast the duration of the Great War, can stand as evidence of Lewis's resolve to keep the movement alive for as long as was practicably feasible. Viewed in this light, it almost becomes a tragic symbol of aspirations that were doomed to remain unfulfilled.

But however many of Lewis's Vorticist productions have gone astray, a considerable corpus of his colleagues' contemporaneous work still survives to fortify and enrich the principles expounded in his pictures and theoretical writings. Wadsworth, for instance, whose contributions to the rebel aesthetic approximate most nearly to those of Lewis, created a marvellously consistent series of woodcuts throughout the Vorticist period, and they show how the collective style managed to mature during 1914 and the following year. According to Roberts, Wadsworth's 'relations with Lewis were closer than any other member of the Group',[50] a statement backed up by Lewis himself when he wrote that 'Wadsworth was the painter most closely associated with my Vorticist activities'.[51] Photographs exist of a walking holiday the two men undertook together at Hebden Bridge in August 1915; and although none of Wadsworth's Vorticist paintings has been traced to prove whether this kinship meant that his large-scale works were too heavily indebted to Lewis, the woodcuts help to discredit this supposition by providing many admirably independent variations on the themes favoured by Vorticism. It is far too easy to imagine that Wadsworth's self-effacing character is symptomatic of a deficiency in his art, and Aldington pointed out in *The Egoist* that 'Mr Wadsworth is personally so retiring and generous to his fellow painters that his own work is sometimes a little under-estimated'. But Aldington went on to affirm that Wadsworth 'has a very energetic conception of design',[52] and nowhere is this more apparent than in the Vorticist woodcuts.

When exactly Wadsworth first discovered the advantages of this particular medium is not known for certain. Only a handful of the woodcuts are dated, hardly any more can confidently be given titles and the chronology of the series is often a matter of speculation rather than certainty. Pound, after telling Harriet Monroe in a letter of November 1914 that 'Wadsworth, a young painter, not nearly so important as Lewis, but good, might interest you as he has a bee for industrial centres and harbours', does mention that 'he is doing woodcuts at the moment'.[53] But this was at least a year after Wadsworth had executed his *Newcastle* woodcut – one impression of which, formerly in Jessie Dismorr's collection, is signed and dated 1913 – and this print already exhibits a precocious degree of abstraction.[54] It is therefore tempting to conclude that he started experimenting with the medium as soon as he broke away from the Omega and Post-Impressionism in the autumn of 1913.

Edward Wadsworth
Cleckheaton, 1914

His print of *Cleckheaton*, stylistically comparable with the *L'Omnibus* painting shown at Rutter's exhibition the previous October, could well represent the next chronological step in Wadsworth's prolonged love affair with the act of engraving on wood. Its inscribed date of 1914 is at first surprising, in view of its decisive return to representation after the abstraction of *Newcastle*. But in the end, *Newcastle*'s crudeness of execution shows what an unpractised adventure it is, and explains why Wadsworth should then have felt the need to backpedal a little on his stylistic development. He turned to his roots for the purpose: Cleckheaton was Wadsworth's birthplace, and he knew its industrialized profile well. No sentimentality accompanied his choice of subject, however. His vision of Cleckheaton is as turbulent as Etchells' similar view of Dieppe, and as infected by a Cubo-Futurist sense of unease.

It permits the geometrical frames of windows to continue on into space beyond the walls in which they are supposed to be situated, and flouts a consistent perspective in the interests of a dynamic pattern. For this miscellaneous jumble of tall stacks and roofs tilt and sway in whatever direction he chooses, sliding into each other and almost collapsing under the force of their creator's fierce attack. Black saw-tooth edges suddenly erupt from nowhere, expressing nothing other than Wadsworth's subjective interpretation of the machine-world; and towards the bottom of the print a small zigzag of white streaks into the surrounding darkness, entirely emancipated from the representational shapes all around and defiantly asserting the artist's right to escape from the limitations of external reality. Its presence obtrudes uneasily in a design which also incorporates elements as solid and tangible as the carefully delineated column of bricks on the right, and Wadsworth must have resolved to allow himself a greater degree of pictorial freedom in the woodcuts he executed after *Cleckheaton*.

Edward Wadsworth
Mytholmroyd, c. 1914

A remarkable start is made with the undated print of *Mytholmroyd*, a small Yorkshire manufacturing town. In the catalogue of Wadsworth's first one-man show at the Adelphi Gallery in 1919, it was listed as the first item and described by Etchells as a work 'produced before the war'.[55] And compared with *Cleckheaton*'s robust gaucherie, it announces a sophistication and poise quite new in Wadsworth's work. Taken together, indeed, they provide an object lesson in the difference between an artist under the influence of foreign movements and one beginning to break through to an independent alternative of his own. For both prints are concerned with the same kind of theme: one towards which Wadsworth was drawn with a more instinctive fascination than Lewis. The editor of *Blast* remembered his friend's willingness to tackle such subjects when he wrote, many years later, that 'I found colleagues from the industrial North, like Wadsworth, more ready to accept . . . that machine forms had an equal right to exist in our canvases'.[56] And he also recalled 'Wadsworth taking me in his car on a tour of some of Yorkshire's cities. In due course we arrived on the hill above Halifax. He stopped the car and we gazed down into its blackened labyrinth. I could see he was proud of it. "It's like Hell, isn't it?" he said enthusiastically'.[57] Only someone as privileged as Wadsworth, whose wealthy father had ensured that his childhood was spent at a safe distance from this harsh environment, could have savoured its savagery without wondering about the plight of the workers who had to live there.

The incident actually occurred 'about 1920'; but it can equally well be seen as indicative of Wadsworth's attitude during the Vorticist period, for Lewis considered that his ally 'had machinery in his blood, and . . . depicted a machine with as much loving care as another man would lavish on a bunch of grapes'.[58] In *Mytholmroyd* this 'machinery' is hidden inside the façades of the buildings that house them, and yet its imagery infects every inch of the design. Wadsworth set himself the task of abstracting away from identifiable objects far more than in *Cleckheaton*, turning an aerial view of a northern town into a minimal statement of angular shapes. Roofs, bricks and chimneystacks are all passed through the refinery of his vision until they become cool, precise segments of Vorticist geometry. Wadsworth's freshly acquired sense of economy allows him to restrict the composition to a few bare elements, and the generous expanse of empty paper surrounding the print gives it room to isolate the projecting diagonal emphases with telling effect.

If *Mytholmroyd* still adheres to the underlying framework of the reality it depicts, another beautiful two-colour woodcut called *Yorkshire Village* uses the example of Cubism to approach a more autonomous structure of the artist's own ordering.[59] Plucking a theme straight out of the mainstream of recent French painting – one that stretched from the pioneering geometry of Cézanne's celebrated views of Gardanne through to the Horta de San Juan landscapes by Picasso that had already inspired Wadsworth in his 1913 farmyard pictures – this woodcut succeeds in infusing it with fresh life by refashioning it according to the principles of Vorticism. *Yorkshire Village* is as classical as its closest French prototype, Derain's 1910 painting of *Cadaquès*, and a comparison between the two works reveals just how far Wadsworth refined this time-honoured motif of houses climbing up a hillside into a tight pyramidal cluster. In Derain's version the empty expanse of foreground, with its wavering lines and random brushmarks, ensures that the conventions of a pictorial view are still retained. The structure of the buildings themselves is emphasized with severity, it is true, but the schematic effect of their bare planes is softened by the traditional apparatus of landscape painting: the distant sea, patches of foliage and a clearly defined stretch of sky.

Four years later, however, Wadsworth succeeded in transforming the same basic constituents into a self-sufficient conglomeration of brittle forms, so simplified that they can be read either as a splintered grid or as a representation of the way light falls on the roofs and walls of northern buildings. The two levels of meaning coexist in perfectly attuned harmony, for the design has cut away all the secondary contours lingering on in Derain's *Cadaquès* and zoomed into a close-up of essential shapes. Like the dancing kaleidoscope of Bomberg's *In the Hold*, the fragments set up a syncopated rhythm as Wadsworth alternates between triangles of black, oblongs of dark grey-green and slices of brilliant white. The interplay between representation and abstraction injects a certain tension into the placid monumentality of the whole composition, providing an admirable exemplar of the way a Vorticist sought to reconcile the dynamics of Futurism with the detached stasis of Cubism. *Yorkshire Village* strikes a subtle balance between rigidity and vitality, purifying its subject-matter into a precise diagram whilst retaining a knife-edge connection with the shifting dynamics of visible reality. Read the shapes as an actual town, and they resolve themselves into a calm, stationary mass; but read them as a non-representational pattern and they shift, glide and dissolve into an ambiguous flux. Their duality constitutes an ideal demonstration of the extent to which Vorticism was able to

△Edward Wadsworth
Yorkshire Village, 1914

▽André Derain
Cadaqués, 1910

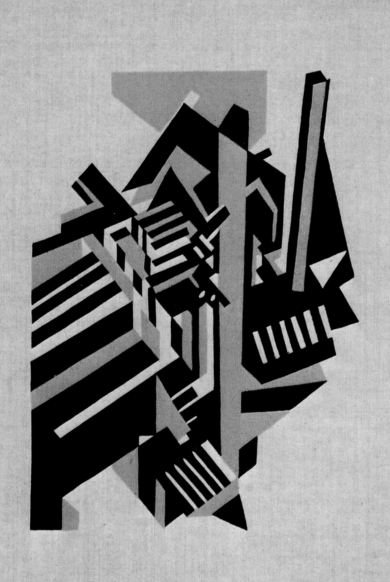

take another movement's theme and transform it into a new entity, as provocative as it was individual. Deprived of all the props and associations conveyed by a conventional landscape, *Yorkshire Village* changes from a picturesque rural prospect into a clean-cut, jagged structure that has more in common with Lewis's urban abstractions than with the ambience of Derain's lazy Mediterranean afternoon.

And sure enough, Wadsworth soon turned back to the direct industrial inspiration of *Mytholmroyd* in order to execute *Bradford: View of a Town*, bristling this time with frankly mechanical shapes and even more severely abstracted than its predecessor.[60] Nothing can be tied down to a descriptive role any more. Wadsworth forces the flat, impersonal finish of his chosen medium to accentuate the one-dimensional character of the design, translating every hint of windows, roofs and real machines into a series of tough geometrical notations. The colours are stamped onto the paper with a precision that utterly precludes the participation of a human hand in their creation. They are as mechanical in execution as the shapes they assume: style and subject-matter meet in a perfect union. Only the minutely calculated order of the composition betrays the workings of an artist's mind, playing off each area of colour against its neighbours in black or white, and carefully ensuring that the convoluted twists and counterthrusts gathered up at the heart of the design slot together with the clarity of a jigsaw puzzle.

Wadsworth's use of the woodcut serves to emphasize the neat, exact, fundamentally tidy nature of his art. He rarely allowed himself to admit any personal handwriting into the vocabulary of his prints, and always limited them to a narrow yet select range of diagrammatic constituents. If he could never be counted among the most violent of the Vorticists, and felt completely at home on a markedly small scale, his woodcuts nevertheless acted as the testing ground for an imagination that was prepared to court extremism with no qualms whatsoever. In order to prove just how uncompromising Wadsworth managed to be, it is revealing to examine his woodcut of *The Open Window* and watch him see next page interpreting another motif derived from a French source, eradicating all inessentials and ending up with a spare, muscular variation of his very own.[61] The debt that this print owes to Delaunay's prolonged devotion to the idea of a cityscape viewed through the artist's studio window is apparent both stylistically and thematically. Delaunay had, of course, shown with the rebels in Rutter's October 1913 exhibition; but the painting of *The Cardiff Football Team* which he displayed there, with its giant advertisement lettering and dynamic references to aeroplanes and Ferris wheels, had more influence on Nevinson than the Vorticists. It seems certain, however, that Wadsworth came across examples of Delaunay's city views – probably in photographic form – and decided to explore an identical subject himself. For *The Open Window* borrows not only its primary conception but also the technique of rendering whole areas of its design in a chequer-board schema of rectangles and squares from a Delaunay painting like *Window on the City No. 4.*

Both pictures shatter the subject, pick up the pieces and reassemble them in a fragmented pattern that does its best to deny representation and perspective alike. But while Delaunay clings to recognizable elements – the Parisian apartment blocks, the distant Eiffel Tower and the billowing curtains framing the composition – Wadsworth escapes almost entirely from such descriptive considerations. The 'chequer-board' is used by Delaunay as a Divisionist tool, sensitive to the variable play of tone and light, whereas *The Open Window* enlarges its individual rectangles and brings them flush with the surface of the paper. For all Delaunay's use of abstracted Cubist planes, his picture is still half in love with the poetic mysteries of spatial recession: it is significant that

Robert Delaunay
Window on the City No. 4, 1910–11

◁ Edward Wadsworth
Bradford: View of a Town, c. 1914

△Edward Wadsworth
The Open Window (dark and light grey and
black), *c.* 1914

▷Edward Wadsworth
The Open Window (red, green and black), *c.* 1914

the original inspiration for his window paintings came from Mallarmé. Wadsworth, on the other hand, banishes depth from his design and concerns himself with a puzzling arrangement of window frames, chequered stripes and an assorted complex of other geometric forms which rebuff any attempt to comprehend logical reality. Indeed, the insistent repetition of shapes suggests a meditation on the idea of reflected images: the window may be open, but Wadsworth is more interested in evoking the magic of shapes mirrored in the glass than the vista of the city beyond. The deep nocturnal grey colours of one version reinforce this interpretation, for these complex refracted segments would stand out at night far more than in the daylight. But Wadsworth piled more vibrant colours on top of each other in alternative versions, so that they flare up, bleed together and interweave in an allusive, tantalizing manner. No less than six different colour versions of *The Open Window* survive, testifying at once to Wadsworth's partiality for this print and to his fascination with the sea-change a single image could undergo when fed through various permutations. It was a process to which the woodcut medium readily lent itself, and Wadsworth exploited it to the full, transforming *The Open Window* from a muted, passive

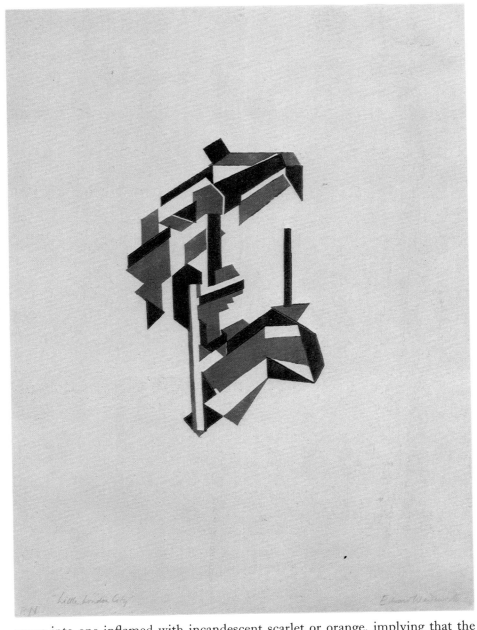

Edward Wadsworth
Little London City, c. 1914

scene into one inflamed with incandescent scarlet or orange, implying that the room had suddenly been invaded by the fieriness of city illuminations and advertisement displays. The most dense version piles blue, brown, umber and black on top of each other into an embossed, relief-like surface, almost as if Wadsworth was loading layer after layer of his memories on to the image he had originally depicted in grey and black alone. In all its brilliant variations, the poetry of an urban interior is presented with as much eloquence as in Delaunay's painting, but the means used to achieve it are more tautly deployed.

This sense of tautness soon dictated that Wadsworth pare down the language of his woodcuts, and move further towards total abstraction. The example set by Lewis, no less than the theoretical precedents laid out in the passages from Kandinsky's theoretical writings which he had translated for *Blast No. 1,* encouraged him to execute a print like *Little London City,* where the ostensible subject is translated into an austere equation of minimal forms.[62] Only the hints of a vertical chimney on the right and a warehouse roof above are permitted to act as a guide to the economical vocabulary Wadsworth employs here. The ochre tint of the paper plays an important role now that the shapes are

Edward Wadsworth
Semaphore, c. 1914

separated more decisively from each other, isolated and given space to register as self-sufficient entities no longer reliant on an attachment to outward reality.

Little London City never quite lets go of the urban reference suggested in its title; but Wadsworth finally pushed his art into an extreme of non-representation in another, closely related woodcut which celebrated its freedom from description by calling itself *Semaphore*.[63] And just as real semaphore depends on an alphabet of terse, clear-cut signals to communicate its messages, so this remarkable print consists entirely of autonomous shapes which stand or fall on their abstract significance alone. Wadsworth restricts its colours to a discreet combination of grey and black, as if to emphasize the purist finality of his intentions. The forms are all linked together in one mechanistic structure, and yet the result does not suggest a solid object: its various components jerk, tilt, slope, slide, touch and balance of their own accord, as independent members of a democratic whole. Complete abstraction, Wadsworth seems to be saying, does not need to attach itself to a dominant image any more.

This dialogue is taken to a still more defiant conclusion in the large two-colour print entitled *New Delight*, which schematizes *The Open Window*'s chequered stripes into regulated blocks of symmetrical dimensions and abandons *Semaphore*'s tight organization in favour of a more scattered alternative.[64] The print marks a climax in his experiments with abstraction, witnessing as it does a determination to let the disposition of shapes and colours speak for themselves, refusing to rely on external connotations to convey their emotional impact. Although Lewis's theoretical writings constantly returned to the impossibility of creating a picture that implied nothing outside its own terms of reference, Wadsworth here seems to confound his friend's thesis with disarming confidence. His woodcuts might be classified as minor works of the rebel movement because of their size, but within their diminutive proportions they often commit the most outrageous acts of revolutionary excess. For *New Delight* lives up to the feeling of liberation implied in its title by breaking all the rules, refusing to placate the viewer with a single clue about its subject-matter and assembling a clangorous, discordant design to add to the cognitive discomfort. It is a notably decentralized arrangement, forcing the eye to travel disconsolately over its splintered parts in search of a focus that does not exist. The various particles fly out in a multitude of conflicting directions, echoing neighbouring shapes without ever actually repeating them: the two pale triangles on the right remain obstinately dissimilar, just as the stripes never quite run in parallel lines with their related counterparts.

And yet, despite the explosive overtones contained in this woodcut, its ultimate effect is reflective rather than destructive. These shapes do not attack or aggravate; they hover in space, calmly asserting their right to exist without in any way threatening to disrupt with the kind of furious energy that Lewis usually infused into his work. *New Delight* succeeds in disguising its extremism in an atmosphere of harmony, unruffled and serene. Its smooth, even finish makes Lewis's contemporaneous designs look fidgety and irritable, full of pen hatchings and unresolved details that have been overlooked in the heat of the moment. No wonder the Vorticist leader never attempted woodcuts himself: a glance at Wadsworth's would have been enough to convince him that it suited a deliberate, painstaking imagination far more than his own hasty and impulsive working methods. There is passion in *New Delight*, but it is a passion borne of exactitude and thoroughness. Not a fragment more than its creator intended has been included in the tight orchestration of this remarkable print, and such self-control could never have been commensurate with the congenital impatience and improvised energy of Lewis.

The profound difference between the two men was acutely analysed by Pound

▷Edward Wadsworth
New Delight, c. 1914–15

"New Delight"

Edward Wadsworth

F.P.N.

Edward Wadsworth
Fustian Town/Hebden Bridge, c. 1914

Edward Wadsworth
*Untitled: Abstract Woodcut (Brown Drama?), c.*1914–16

in his article on 'Edward Wadsworth, Vorticist', published by *The Egoist* in August 1914. 'I cannot recall any painting of Mr Wadsworth's where he seems to be angry', the poet wrote perceptively. For while it was 'natural that Mr Lewis should give us pictures of intelligence gnashing teeth with stupidity . . . and that he should stop design and burst into seething criticism', Pound found it 'as hard to conceive Mr Wadsworth expressing himself in any other medium save paint as it is to conceive Mr Lewis remaining unexpressed'. A straightforward enjoyment of picture-making seemed to characterize Wadsworth's art in Pound's eyes, and he declared that 'there is a delight in mechanical beauty, a delight in the beauty of ships, or of crocuses, or a delight in pure form. He liked this, that or the other, and so he sat down to paint it'. This at once set him apart from Lewis's infatuation with 'crashing and opposing and breaking', and the poet saw the two men's work 'almost as a series of antitheses. Turbulent energy: repose. Anger: placidity'.

The differentiation was extraordinarily well expressed, and Pound proved how far he had succeeded in understanding Wadsworth's outlook when he asserted in the same essay that 'the vorticist can represent or not, as he likes. He *depends* – depends for his artistic effect – upon the arrangement of spaces and line, on the primary media of his art. A resemblance to natural forms is of no consequence one way or the other.' A similar philosophy must have guided Wadsworth when he executed the woodcuts, with their constantly shifting attitude towards the value of representational references. *New Delight* may look like a final, dogmatic step towards the viability of abstraction as a satisfying pictorial language, but its roots are still in the northern industrial world, and it belongs to a series of woodcuts which often proclaim a closer relationship with descriptive appearances. Wadsworth wanted above all to remain flexible in his approach to the problem, so that he was free at any given time to move from one convention through to the other without creating any sense of broken boundaries or personal inconsistency. And Pound showed an instinctive sympathy with this outlook by describing an 'amazingly fine line block of "Vlissingen"', which he himself owned, in purely formal terms. Although he admitted that 'the "motif" is ships in a harbour', he insisted that the picture was basically 'a very fine organisation of forms. That is to say, there are a whole lot of forms, all in keeping, and all contributing to the effect . . . There is a definite, one might say a musical or a music-like pleasure for the eye in noting the arrangement of the very acute triangles combined like "notes in a fugue" in this drawing of Mr Wadsworth's. One is much more at ease in comparing this new work to music'. The analogy enabled Pound to write about an unnamed 'black and white' design in a particularly sensitive passage, enthusing over 'a thing like a signal arm or some other graceful unexplained bit of machinery, reaching out, and alone, across the picture, like a Mozart theme skipping an octave, or leaving the base for the treble'. Pound's ear for the rhythms of prose here expresses Wadsworth's use of pictorial interval in an unusually accurate manner: the pauses in the sentence, no less than the meaning they convey, mirror the action of the visual elements in these woodcuts with uncanny precision.

On another level, moreover, Pound took Wadsworth's woodcuts as an example of the influence which he considered Eastern art had exerted on the evolution of Vorticism. Taking a lost 'arrangement in pure form' called *Khaki*, which he explained bore that title 'simply because it is necessary to call pictures something or other for ease of reference in conversation', the poet declared that it 'does not "look like" anything, save perhaps a Chinese or Japanese painting with the representative patches removed. The feeling I get from this picture is very much the feeling I get from certain eastern paintings, and I think the feeling that went into it is probably very much the same as that which moved certain Chinese painters'.[65] Pound tended to attach more importance to the stimulus of Eastern art than did the Vorticist artists themselves: he was, after all, very involved both in the haiku tradition and in translations of Chinese poetry, and it was surely his decision to bless Koyetzu, Rotatzu and Korin in *Blast No. 2*. But Lewis did pay tribute to the importance of Geomancy in his essay on 'Fêng Shui and Contemporary Form' in *Blast No. 1*, and towards the end of his 'Review of Contemporary Art' in *Blast No. 2* he categorically asserted that 'the least and most vulgar Japanese print . . . is a masterpiece compared to a Brangwyn, a Nicholson, or a Poynter'.[66] Elsewhere in the magazine, he pointed out how ludicrous it was to worry too much about the illustrational subject-matter of art, declaring that 'the Japanese did not discriminate very much between a Warrior and a Buttercup. The flowering and distending of an angry face and the beauty of the soldier's arms and clothes, was a similar spur to creation to the grimace of a flower'. And Etchells, for one, did actually praise the 'Korinesque treatment'[67] of a post-war Wadsworth woodcut called *Dock Scene*, as if to imply that Vorticism owed some at least of its taut linear energy, startling viewpoints and innate sense of abstract pattern to Eastern precedents.

Edward Wadsworth
Façade, c. 1914

Edward Wadsworth
Street Singers, c. 1914

The smaller Wadsworth's prints became, the more hermetic he allowed himself to be in his use of non-representational forms. A tiny untitled *Abstract Woodcut*[68] offers an especially tantalizing example of his talent for constructing a solid, tangible machine which still manages to elude descriptive classification. Wadsworth's professional knowledge of machinery – he had, after all, studied engineering at Munich in 1906 and was the son of a worsted spinning magnate – enabled him to invest his imaginative structures with an impressive functional authority. The whole ensemble is built up with such weight and inevitability that it comes as a shock to realize that this modern megalith has been bodied forth on a flimsy sheet of paper no more than a few inches in size. Wadsworth fully understood the advantages to be gained from the drastic compression of an image, and delighted in the woodcut's ability to encompass most of the properties of a painting on such a minute scale. The monumentality of the forms, combined with the additional solidity of colour, helps to make this image burst out of its tiny dimensions and assume the proportions of a major statement. As Etchells wrote in his introduction to Wadsworth's 1919 exhibition, the woodcut 'does not demand wall space but yet can have the seriousness and dignity of a large painting in an accessible form'.

The more Wadsworth's prints of this productive pre-war period are examined, the more versatile his newly-found abstract vocabulary appears. At one moment, in a woodcut called *Façade*, he takes as his starting-point the gleaming fabric of an industrial environment and turns it into a crisp study in contrasts between black and white.[69] No additional colours help him to enliven the image this time: it stands or falls in monochrome alone, and passes the test with resilience. Although the title of the work suggests an architectonic structure of some kind, it cannot be pinned down. The ascending shafts cluster together like rank growths in a jungle of metal, neither building nor machine but an unclassifiable amalgam of both. They bristle with a tensile force which derives from Wadsworth's direct opposition of light and dark, exchanging the real world of northern factories for a Vorticist recreation that attempts to crystallize the essence of twentieth-century automation.

How could such a style possibly incorporate the presence of human figures as well? In general, Wadsworth avoided the problem by eliminating them from his work; and yet one print, showing a trio of standing forms who could easily be suspected of harbouring some unmechanical traits, does survive to reveal how he tackled the challenge. *Street Singers* is the only one of his pre-war woodcuts to possess a figurative title,[70] but the buskers' bodies have been meta-morphosed so completely into angular fragments of geometry that they could equally well be seen as enormous cranes ranged in a row at the dockside. Either interpretation is possible, and Wadsworth makes sure that the ambiguity is real by allowing these jagged shapes to hover half-way between humanity and machinery, singers and robots. Vorticism enjoyed this multiplicity of meaning, regarding it as one manifestation of the increased freedom which abstraction offered the artist. And Wadsworth undoubtedly shared Lewis's determination to exploit a subtle and ambivalent impulse that delighted in evading outright proclamations of intent in favour of a wider reference.

Not that Wadsworth's virtuoso command of the woodcut medium failed to extend itself in the direction of bold, forthright designs now and again. If *Street Singers* is devious about its content, another untitled *Vorticist Composition* shouts its message out with an exclamatory vigour that threatens to invalidate Pound's praise of Wadsworth's innate 'placidity' and 'repose'. This explosive print, on one level utterly abstract but also suggesting an aerial view of oblong

Edward Wadsworth
Untitled: Vorticist Composition (The Port?),
c. 1914–15

boats moored by a dockside – presumably like an unidentified woodcut of *The Port* – is possibly the most aggressive of all the woodcuts.[71] The steady progression of an army is invoked too, linking up on a third level with the battle diagrams Lewis used in *Plan of War*. But it is impossible to disentangle the associations of war from the iconoclastic intentions of Vorticist aesthetics: the two aims merge into one double-edged attack, as committed to the destruction of the English art establishment as to a realistic assessment of the meaning of mechanized strife. The rebels did not shrink away from the inhumanity of this combat, like so many of their fellow countrymen; and neither did they glorify the advent of an international upheaval. Their aim was always to provide an unsentimental, clear-eyed assessment of the true conditions pertaining to twentieth-century life, and if this meant that the critics would be tempted to equate their work with the evil impulses of war, then it was a risk well worth taking. How else could the programme outlined so tenaciously in both issues of *Blast* be put into action?

All the same, *Vorticist Composition* is markedly more combative than Wadsworth usually permitted himself to be in his woodcuts. One of the largest and most imposing of these prints, *Illustration*, reverts once again to a tightly controlled format that holds back naked aggression in the interests of classical detachment.[72] Unlike the majority of the series to which it belongs, this design is signed and dated 1915, suggesting that Wadsworth conceived his woodcuts on a grander scale as Vorticism entered into its second and final year of active

Edward Wadsworth
Illustration (Typhoon), 1915

life. It is, too, an unprecedentedly inflexible composition, with the long strands of white extending their strength around its borders like steel bands. They effectively seal off the left side of the picture and ensure that the blank area in the middle does not enlarge its boundaries any further. Everywhere there is a feeling of restriction, as if Wadsworth had decided to stand back from the image and assert his dominance over every facet of its construction: even the motif of ascending oblongs that had been used with such conspicuous brashness in *Vorticist Composition* is here securely contained inside its black surround.

The unrelieved starkness of monochrome reinforces this feeling of oppression, as palpable in its own way as the brooding menace of Lewis's *The Crowd*. *Illustration*, however, does not admit the existence of human figures at all: its heartless organization sets out to celebrate a world overshadowed by the power of machinery alone. And this interpretation is confirmed by Wadsworth himself, who quoted the passage from Conrad's *Typhoon* which this print illustrates in his 1919 exhibition catalogue: '. . . the iron walls of the engine room. Painted white, they rose high into the dusk of the skylight, sloping like a roof: and the whole resembled the interior of a monument, divided by floors of iron grating, with lights flickering in the middle, within the columnar stir of machinery'. The quotation is somewhat inaccurate – in particular it misses out a phrase about 'a mass of gloom' – but it is nevertheless clear that Wadsworth's woodcut was directly inspired by Conrad's sombre evocation of a ship's power-house. *Typhoon* was written during the period when Conrad and Ford collaborated most closely together as a writing team on *Romance*, and so it is likely that Ford first awakened Wadsworth to the possibilities of illustrating the book in a thoroughly unconventional sense, creating a self-sufficient equivalent to Conrad's prose while admitting that Vorticism still retained strong links with the reality *Typhoon* describes.

The idea would have appealed at once, for Conrad's work deals with a world which Wadsworth always found especially congenial. While Lewis chose to concentrate his interests most of all on the theme of the modern city, he was instinctively attracted to the excitement of harbours and shipping. Throughout his life he showed a predilection for maritime subjects, and gave vent to this fascination in an outstandingly successful 1914 woodcut of *Rotterdam*, a large print which was reproduced in *Blast No. 2* and shown in the Vorticist Exhibition. A whole page of photographs in Wadsworth's family album is inscribed 'Rotterdam: July 1914', to prove that his interest in the motif was awakened by a visit to the port. And he was so devoted to the subject that he also executed a lost painting of the same title in 1914 and displayed it at the second London Group exhibition: the only extant record of the picture describes it as 'a Vorticist conception of the harbour of Rotterdam, with brilliantly coloured funnels of moored ships, depicted in the abstract, in strong blues, red and black and white'.[73] If the painting was as exuberant and celebratory as it sounds, Lewis would have approved, for he declared in *Blast No. 2* that 'I cannot see how the Port of Rotterdam can be bettered'.

Juxtapose the surviving woodcut of *Rotterdam* with the earlier *Mytholmroyd* composition, and it is immediately apparent how far he progressed in less than a year towards a closer understanding both of abstraction's possibilities and the unique character of his own artistic personality. Nobody but Wadsworth could have created *Rotterdam*: the peculiarly sturdy forms, the immaculate precision of execution and the balanced equilibrium that prevails over a potentially anarchic design, all these attributes belong supremely to his work of this period rather than anyone else. *Mytholmroyd*'s reliance on the visible facts of a scene is here dispensed with, and in its place a hard-hitting overall consistency based on his favourite motif of castellated oblongs has been established. Wadsworth

Edward Wadsworth
Rotterdam, 1914

turns them to good account by restricting the design to a brilliant black and white, as dazzling in its intense contrasts as the Op Art aesthetic it so vividly adumbrates. And the strange diagonal columns help to restore a necessary sense of balance, literally propping up the surging elements below with their rigid strength. They lean sideways as well, subject to the same pressures as the ships and buildings; yet there is never any suspicion that these linear hawsers will snap. They are the guy-ropes for the whole wind-blown design, and Vorticism's bias towards order ensures their continuing tautness.

'I have some preference for "Rotterdam"', Gaudier told Wadsworth in a letter from the trenches, acknowledging the gift of several woodcuts. 'I do not know why, as the same qualities persist through them all, at the same degree. When you send me some more, as I am greedy to see much vorticism just now, print them on the thin. The reason is this, I have room for them in my knapsack and the less weighty the individuals are, the more I shall be able to stuff in'.[74] And Lewis, even though he never tried his hand at the medium himself, shared Gaudier's admiration for its unique properties in a 'Note' on an exhibition of Expressionist woodcuts by Kandinsky, Marc, Pechstein and others written specially for the catalogue of a Spring 1914 show called *Modern German Art* at the Twenty-One Gallery. He was far more appreciative of this form of Expressionism than its paintings, and explained that 'where the Germans are best – disciplined, blunt, thick and brutal, with a black simple skeleton of organic emotion – they best qualify for this form of art'. In other words, the closer they approximated to the ideals of Vorticism the better artists they became in Lewis's eyes. 'The quality of the woodcut is rough and brutal, surgery of the senses, cutting and not scratching: extraordinarily limited and exasperating' he wrote, insisting that 'it is one of the greatest tests of fineness.' And while he criticized the exhibition by declaring that 'all the things gathered here do not come within these definitions', he openly connected its best qualities with Vorticist principles in his conclusion to the 'Note'. 'Some woodcuts by Mr H. [*sic*] Wadsworth, though not part of the German show, are to be seen in the Gallery', he added; and proceeded to praise an unnamed print in words that could easily be applied to *Rotterdam*. 'One, of a port, is particularly fine', he enthused, 'with its white excitement, and compression of clean metallic shapes in the well of the Harbour, as though in a broken cannon-mouth.'[75] Such an appreciation of his friend's grasp of the medium's powerful potential can stand as a fitting tribute to Wadsworth's prowess in his woodcuts. They are the chamber music of Vorticism: modest in scale, impeccably organized and yet full of a driving originality that puts them among the most resolved products of the movement as a whole.

It is all the more a matter for regret, then, that none of Wadsworth's paintings still exists to show how he translated his ideas into sizeable canvases. Photographs of the markedly abstract *Caprice* and another closely related picture, taken at the Rebel Art Centre in March 1914, prove that he was among the first of the rebels to approach non-representational painting. But only an illustration of a work called *Cape of Good Hope* in *Blast No. 1* gives any indication of how Wadsworth developed this new language in succeeding canvases. The reproduction is poorly printed, which makes it hard to tell whether the painting of that name exhibited at the 1914 AAA Salon is the one shown in *Blast No. 1*: clear traces of brushwork are discernible, and yet its pronounced linearity could mean that it is a

Edward Wadsworth
Cape of Good Hope, 1914

gouache study for the final painting. Either way, however, the decisive nature of the composition suggests that it was fully worked out in Wadsworth's imagination by the time he executed this version; and it seems reasonable to take the *Blast No. 1* photograph as a guide to the *Cape of Good Hope* painting which Gaudier approved of in his *Egoist* review of the AAA salon. The young sculptor asserted that Wadsworth's 'bigger picture, No. 113, gives more pleasure on account of the warmer pigments used and the construction: growing in a corner and balanced at the other by a short mass'.[76]

The description implies that Gaudier saw the picture as a wholly abstract design; but if *Cape of Good Hope* is compared with *Rotterdam* or *Illustration* it is obvious that Wadsworth has here allowed himself – in this relatively early Vorticist work – a degree of representation that he later relinquished. For the composition could easily be seen as an aerial view of moored ships in a harbour; and this interpretation becomes even more convincing in a limpid watercolour, which looks like a study for the main section of the painting.[77] However much this interpretation threatens to limit the picture to an unnecessarily literal degree, it does remain true that the design parallels the verbal hymn to a port published in *Blast No. 1*. For in the 'bless' part of the introductory manifestos,

Edward Wadsworth
Study for Cape of Good Hope, 1914

Gino Severini
Flying over Rheims, c. 1915

other unidentifiable spare parts, all set down with an engineer's exactitude that would have gratified Hulme. Although the painting is less closely attached to representational elements than *Cape of Good Hope*, it is still possible to appreciate the subtlety with which Wadsworth merges views of the ground below with details from the machine itself. Where the Futurists would have drawn on a number of disparate memories and arranged them in a picture that did nothing to disguise their heterogeneous origins, the Vorticists preferred an abstracted amalgam which wedded all the diversity into one stylistically consistent image. *A Short Flight* dispenses with easy clues as to its contents in favour of a solid metaphor, an imaginative equivalent with terms of reference far wider than those provided for by overt description.

When Severini drew his charcoal impression of *Flying over Rheims* a year later, for instance, he leaned far more heavily on the outward reality of his subject. However much he slices up his aeroplane and the distant glimpses of the ground, shakes them around and sprinkles them onto the hectic surface of his composition, the wings of the machine are as instantly recognizable as the rose window of the cathedral beneath. Despite the faceted planes that collide with each other all over the picture – heralding his imminent espousal of Cubist doctrines – Severini does not aim for the compact unity of Wadsworth's interpretation. *Flying over Rheims* is at once less dogmatic and more attached to its source than *A Short Flight*, and is not afraid to court the blurred, chaotic sensations of a journey through the air. Its hazy definition mirrors the Futurists' romantic enjoyment of the new machine age; and if Severini's emotions seem more immediately understandable than Wadsworth's tough detachment, they nevertheless lack the mystery of *A Short Flight*, and its concomitant reverberations.

Part of Wadsworth's analytical attitude towards aeroplane flight in this picture may derive from his keen professional interest in the pictorial possibilities opened up by such voyages. As early as 1912, when he exhibited his lost 'bird's-eye-view' of *Long Acre* at the Friday Club, it had been apparent that he was fired by the new approach to reality which airborne passengers were offered: one critic presumed *Long Acre* was painted 'from an aeroplane'.[83] Wadsworth did not record whether he actually flew at this period, although he very probably did. But for the purposes of his art he hardly needed to: the technique of aerial photography had recently been developed, and its products would have been enough to suggest stimulating avenues for the artist to explore. Just as Lewis seems to have employed battle diagrams and games in the evolution of highly abstract paintings like *Plan of War* or *Slow Attack*, so Wadsworth found that aerial views helped him to divest his art of descriptive props. If machinery supplied the Vorticist with a ready-made abstract language, so did the geometry of ground plans; and it is possible to watch Wadsworth progressively raising his angle of vision, through *L'Omnibus*, *The Sandpit*, *Mytholmroyd* and *Bradford*, until it reaches the stage of a full aerial blueprint in *Caprice* and *Cape of Good Hope*. No wonder *Blast No. 1*, possibly at his suggestion, blessed no less than four celebrated pilots of the day. Even the extreme fragmentation of *New Delight* may derive from Wadsworth's glimpse of a northern town as he flew straight over its roofs and railway lines, realising that the organisation of forms he saw below him pointed towards the emancipated language he sought in his art.

When Wadsworth's daughter was asked about the likelihood of such flying activities, she told the author that 'possibly he *might* have had a trial flight during the '14–'18 War – I don't know – certainly neither of us can recall his ever referring to such an event . . . And since he was so interested in machines, also in the then "great" flights of the pioneers, I *feel* he *would* have mentioned the fact sometime or other'. But if this testimony throws doubt on the idea of Wadsworth

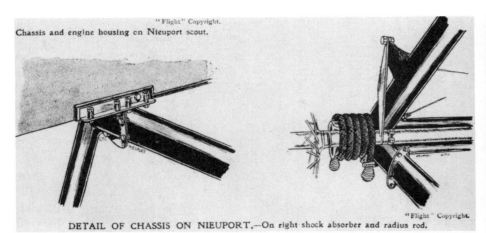

"Flight" Copyright.

Chassis and engine housing on Nieuport scout.

"Flight" Copyright.

DETAIL OF CHASSIS ON NIEUPORT.—On right shock absorber and radius rod.

△Aerial photographs of (above) Belmore and (below) Eastleigh Junction, 1914

▽ Diagrams of a Nieuport aeroplane, 1914

climbing into a cockpit and gaining his source material from first-hand experience, it is still easy to imagine him eagerly feeding off the verbal and visual information provided in generous quantities by *Flight* magazine. For the pages of this lavishly illustrated journal, which described itself with justifiable pride as the 'First Aero Weekly in the World', were permeated with the spirit of flying adventure throughout the 1914 period. New models and technological advances were reported week by week, the praises of the latest pilot heroes sung with wide-eyed consistency, and details of aeroplane machinery illustrated in diagrams that often look like abstract designs from *Blast*. Wadsworth could well have been inspired by the contents of *Flight*, and agreed in particular with a long and comprehensive article exploring 'Further Developments of Military Aviation' which it published on 14 February 1914. Although the author, Lieutenant-Colonel F. H. Sykes, admitted that 'photography is difficult from an aeroplane owing to the fact that the observer is often rather cramped, and the camera has to be fixed in the bottom of the machine', he went on to declare that 'in my opinion there are considerable possibilities in the science of aerial photography, and it is well worth developing'.

So indeed it was, and *Flight* echoed Sykes's sentiments by carrying pictures like an aerial view of St. Peter's, or even of Harrogate from a balloon, with a regularity which itself reveals how much of a marvel these strangely schematic patterns must then have seemed. According to the magazine's own captions, aerial photography was to be valued for the relatively factual knowledge it supplied about the appearance of interesting landmarks. But from Wadsworth's standpoint the full-page group of four views taken from a plane at over 4,000 feet, which appeared in *Flight* on 11 December 1914, would have been the inspiration for Vorticist art rather than a straightforward geographical aid. The view of Belmore's cultivated fields reproduced in the upper right corner of this group is similar to his most abstract designs: works like *Composition* or *Enclosure*, both of them executed in 1915, which will be discussed shortly. And the photograph of Eastleigh Junction illustrated in the bottom right corner, its aerial view partially obscured by the geometrical structure of the plane, combines machine and ground-plan in the same way as the two-in-one organisation of *A Short Flight*. Malevich was, of course, the artist who actually disclosed in his 1927 book *The Non-Objective World* how aerial photographs stimulated the Suprematist in his search for an abstract interpretation of the contemporary environment. But Wadsworth's Vorticist pictures had already openly announced their close relationship with the terrestrial structuring which perpendicular views suggested to radical painters aiming at a symbiosis between their form-language and the images produced by the modern world.

Just how much the Vorticists' insistence on this degree of abstraction allowed the onlooker full reign for his own interpretative responses is shown by Lewis's

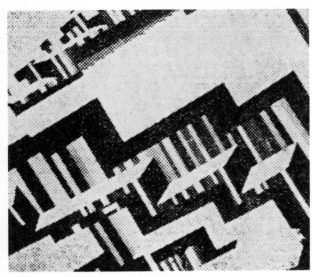

Edward Wadsworth
Blackpool, c. 1915

Edward Wadsworth
Composition, 1915

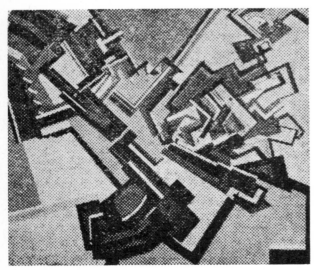

Edward Wadsworth
Combat, c. 1915

reaction to Wadsworth's painting of *Blackpool.* Quite possibly inspired by the view to be seen from the top of Blackpool Tower, the picture is now lost; but a very poor photograph of *Blackpool* which appeared in the *Daily Mirror* – showing a series of coloured stripes, enclosed within dark zigzag bands, rising up diagonally in majestic ranks from the lower right corner – does survive to supplement Lewis's description of the painting in *Blast No. 2.* After praising it unreservedly as 'one of the finest paintings he has done', Lewis went on to state that 'its striped ascending blocks' signified 'the elements of a seaside scene, condensed into the simplest form possible for the retaining of its vivacity'. Attuned as he was to the wider meanings of Vorticism's non-representational language, Lewis was able to assert with remarkable confidence that 'its theme is that of five variegated cliffs', and describe how 'the striped awnings of Cafés and shops, the stripes of bathing tents, the stripes of bathing-machines, of toy trumpets, of dresses, are marshalled into a dense essence of the scene'. A more descriptive treatment of the theme, he implied, could not possibly contain such a comprehensive survey of its fundamental characteristics; and the colours – 'the harsh jarring and sunny yellows, yellow-greens and reds are especially well used, with the series of commercial blues' – helped in their own special way to give substance to this brash locale. Precisely because the painting was so firmly rooted in a particular experience of reality, Lewis saw it as an admirable exemplar of the ideal balance between representation and abstraction that his theoretical expositions of Vorticism always emphasized. 'Much more than any work exhibited in the last year or so by any English painter of Cubist or Futurist tendencies it has the quality of LIFE' he wrote, determined to stress the importance of retaining a positive link with human experience. 'In most of the best and most contemporary work, even, in England, there is a great deal of the deadness and heaviness of wooden or of stone objects, rather than of flashing and eager flesh, or shining metal, and heavy traces everywhere of the too-thorough grounding in "Old Master" art, which has characterized the last decade in this country', he continued. 'Several of the Italian Futurists have this quality of LIFE eminently: though their merit, very often, consists in this and nothing else. Hardly any of the Paris Cubists have, although it is true they don't desire to have it. To synthesize this quality of LIFE with the significance or spiritual weight that is the mark of all the greatest art, should be, from one angle, the work of the Vorticists.'[84]

It was a vaguely stated ambition, the definition of a painter who was trying to be his own critic and succeeding only as far as it was feasible for a man to stand outside his art and analyse its motives. But if this proposed combination of 'life' and 'significant, spiritual weight' is applied to *Composition,* a work which bears more than a little resemblance to *Blackpool,* Lewis's meaning becomes clearer.[85] For Wadsworth has here attained a synthesis of the two impulses, counteracting the onrushing crescendo mounted by the stripes with the stabilizing force of the elongated diagonals, which scythe a path through the oblong ranks and check their course. In other words, the vitality of surging motion has been regulated by these dramatic linear interruptions. And yet nothing is at a standstill: just as the blocks themselves possess considerable substance along with their movement, so the opposing diagonals add their own tension to the picture even as they seek to control it. The requisite balance has been reached, based on the kind of knife-edge calculation that Lewis respected most. Both 'weight' and 'life' are upheld in full measure, reconciled in a union which could easily be broken and subside in favour of one quality alone. *Composition* might only exist as a photograph, but the complexity of its formal attributes are striking enough to make convincing sense out of Lewis's theoretical contentions. And if Wadsworth's large painting of *Combat* could be appraised in anything other than the

Edward Wadsworth
Study for a Vorticist Painting (?), *c.* 1914

murky photograph which appeared at the time of its inclusion in the Vorticist Exhibition, it too might be found to fulfil the same precepts.[86] For the composition, which is obviously related to Wadsworth's drawing of a *War-Engine* in *Blast No. 2*, is only allowed to explode outwards in fragments of machine imagery because it is controlled at the same time by a firm overall structure.

In the lamentable absence of a surviving Vorticist oil by Wadsworth, his contribution to the movement has to be assessed from the series of woodcuts, a number of poor reproductions and the small group of gouaches that still exist in their original form. One of them, an untitled study, is little more than a swift sketch for a projected painting like *Cape of Good Hope*, but its value lies in the spectacle it affords of Wadsworth thinking instinctively in abstract terms as he roughs out the broad outlines of an idea.[87] The picture must have been executed at the height of the Vorticist period, for the movement's distinctive vocabulary is here deployed with a confidence that argues prolonged familiarity. The whole mechanistic ensemble seems, paradoxically, to grow in an organic manner: a rhomboid gives birth to a rectangle, which in turn sprouts a semicircle or an oval. Wadsworth doubtless came to regard these industrial shapes as living entities, and in this rapid study they spread themselves over the rough sketching paper with a spontaneity which fully endorses Lewis's later claim that 'I considered the world of machinery as real to us, or more so, as nature's forms, such as trees, leaves and so forth'.[88]

Edward Wadsworth
Abstract Composition, 1915

These words apply even more forcibly to another of Wadsworth's few gouaches, *Abstract Composition*, an elaborately finished exposition of the mature Vorticist style.[89] Here the entire knot of shapes springs from a tiny complex in the lower half of the picture, progressively unfolding and enlarging itself into grander proportions as it stretches out in a multitude of varying directions. The colours echo this movement and articulate its development, beginning with small areas of intense blue that sing out from the kernel of the design, and then relaxing in broad stretches of restrained ochre, light brown, pale grey and a discreet green. Viewed in their entirety, the forms take on the solidity of a sculptural group, moving out in clumps and imposing their authority like giant bars of metal clamped down over the squared-up lines of the page beneath. They should be violent, explosive, self-assertive; but the muted colours, no less than the deliberated gravity of the whole ponderous structure, prevents *Abstract Composition* from proclaiming its rebellious intentions with the acerbity of a Lewis. Gaudier was right when he wrote to Wadsworth from the trenches, thanking him for 'your letter with the woodcuts; it's a great relief to touch civilization in its tender moods now and then'.[90] Wadsworth was, in the main, too gentle an artist to produce wholeheartedly aggressive images for the movement he supported with such distinction.

Even the largest and most substantial of his Vorticist gouaches, a marvellous

Edward Wadsworth
Enclosure, 1915

composition called *Enclosure* which he included in the Vorticist Exhibition, could hardly be described as a militant work. Its fundamental colour combination of boisterous reds and blues is certainly as brash as the orchestration of *The Mud Bath*, *Red Duet* and *New York*. But it is softened with a cooler and more rational blend of cream, umber and coffee, which prevents the design from becoming rasping; and Wadsworth's essentially neat, orderly method of organising his component parts likewise fosters pictorial decorum. It would, nevertheless, be foolish to deny that *Enclosure* possesses a profoundly unsettling and discordant structure. Sequences of form are interrupted, pushed off course and contradicted with the wilful bloody-mindedness of Lewis's *Workshop*, while Wadsworth takes an impudent delight in subjecting the striped blocks slung across the surface of his picture to the most uncomfortable juxtapositions and densely packed crowding. There is a frozen jazz quality about the composition which is characteristic of many Vorticist works, and helps to explain why a lot of Art Deco designs look like popularised, decorative spin-offs from the Vorticist vocabulary. Indeed, the ascending, descending, swaying, converging, receding and advancing anarchy of movement set up by Wadsworth's serried ranks can be said vividly to evoke the freewheeling improvisation of a jazz performance.

At the same time, however, this tensile virtuosity of pattern is allied to a richness of potential meaning which shows how the Vorticists managed to invest an increasing degree of abstraction with an equally increasing referential range during 1915. *Enclosure* may be the most non-representational of Wadsworth's extant works, but it also encourages a wealth of valid interpretations, all of which rise directly out of its formal organisation: aerial views of cultivated fields, the colliding directional forces of opposing armies, the brittle vigour of the Vorticist's urban environment. However mutually exclusive these possible areas might sound, they flow together into a convincing synthesis. Fields can be affected by mechanisation, after all, and modern city life is in many respects similar to a bitter military battle. Wadsworth willingly embraces these amalgamations of meaning, and sets a firm limit to any suspicion of unqualified dynamic optimism by quite literally 'enclosing' his picture with plane after overlapping plane of collaged strips, which stamp lean authoritarian boundaries across the frantic activity beneath. In this sense, they recall Lewis's analysis in 'The Crowd Master' of how 'T H E P O L I C E with distant icy contempt herd London. They shift it in lumps here and there, touching and shaping with heavy delicate professional fingers'.[91] But if *Enclosure* is compared with Lewis's painting of *The Crowd*, which uses the fragment 'E N C L O' within its design, Wadsworth is at once seen to be more sunny and balanced in his outlook. When one of his friends watched him finish *Enclosure* and voiced his disapproval and incomprehension, Wadsworth turned to him without a trace of defensiveness or reproach and replied, quite simply: 'But this is the future.'[92] Such an attitude, which tempered the visionary urgency of a prophet with the clear-eyed realism of a stoic, and refused to accept that a vital appreciation of the modern condition should necessarily entail romantic sentimentality, lies at the very core of the Vorticist aesthetic.

Chapter 13: Vorticism in Practice: Roberts and Bomberg the Outsider

None of the other allies could be summarized as gentle in his attempts to revolutionize English art. Roberts, for example, was a precocious, prickly teenager whom Etchells remembered as 'terribly young, but a real rebel';[1] and he was almost as much of a temperamental outsider as his friend Bomberg. It is difficult to believe that he had only just celebrated his nineteenth birthday when his signature appeared in the *Blast No. 1* manifesto: for although he was the baby of the whole group in terms of age – even Gaudier was almost four years older – his sturdy self-confidence ensured that he bowed to no-one in the development of his style. Helen Saunders described in a letter to Jessie Dismorr his 'resentful old-gentleman-sulky urchin manner', combined with a 'peculiar honesty and simplicity',[2] and this awkward disposition caused him to abstain from participating in any kind of partisan activity long after his allies had committed themselves to a communal cause.

While most of the nascent Vorticists were forming ranks in 'The Cubist Room' exhibition, he stayed away and contributed instead to the far more traditional and catholic New English Art Club show of December 1913. And when they went on to create a stir in the first London Group exhibition of March 1914 he was again absent, having appeared two months before with Fry's Grafton Group at the Alpine Gallery. Lewis had to go to his studio and ask for permission to hang *Dancers* and *Religion* in the Rebel Art Centre, an institution with which Roberts refused to become affiliated through official membership. And it is significant that the first public show where he actually appeared alongside the other Vorticists was the Whitechapel Gallery's *Twentieth Century Art* exhibition of May 1914, a survey that set out to be a comprehensive *Review of Modern Movements* rather than a shop window for English abstraction. Roberts' persistent desire to remain outside Lewisian dogma would have been well satisfied by his inclusion in a section described by the catalogue's resolutely non-political introduction as 'the fourth group', a collection of artists who had 'abandoned representation almost entirely'. A guarded proviso added that only 'some members of the group have recently established a "Rebel Art Centre" ' and he must have been happy with such an exemplary display of tact.[3] So much so, that he contributed no less than eight pictures to the show, ranging from the relative archaism of his Slade *Resurrection* drawing through to the lost painting of *The Parting*, which he later described as an 'abstract' work.[4]

Very far from non-representational, however, is a 1914 drawing inscribed *At the Fox-Trot Ball*, where Roberts seems momentarily to forsake the ruthless carpentry of his earlier *Dancers* painting.[5] Broad, undulating curves replace the mechanistic angularity of the *Dancers* with a more fluid, naturalistic idiom. Roberts is not afraid to particularize facial features or details of clothing in among his sweeping rhythms, and the irregular motion of the wash shows his willingness to admit realistic observation into his work. There is little attempt here to confuse the spectator by playing off figuration against abstraction: everything is easily identifiable, nothing admitted for its own sake as a formal prop. And yet, for all its seeming directness, *At the Fox-Trot Ball* is in many ways a disturbing drawing. Roberts pitches the perspectival angle as steeply as he had previously done in *The Return of Ulysses*, establishing an aerial viewpoint that accentuates the dramatic positions taken up by the dancers' arms. Seen from above, they resolve themselves into sinister pincer shapes, like the tentacles of so many crabs extending their full length into space and then stopping to wave. Caught in this weird pose, the figures appear to be engaged in an activity half-way between dancing and struggling, and this feeling is reinforced by their forbidding surroundings: the crazily tilted floor leads up at a giddy inclination to the claustrophobic bare walls hemming the figures in at the top of the design. A bleak setting indeed for a supposedly festive party.

William Roberts
At the Fox-Trot Ball, c. 1914

The creation of this threatening, highly theatrical atmosphere was fully in accordance with the tenor of Roberts' previous work. Whether it was a Slade drawing like *David Choosing the Three Days' Pestilence* or a later, more esoteric allegory like *Religion*, he was never afraid to indulge a preference for grotesque form and a stylistic artifice that amounted almost to Mannerism. Lewis, from the time of *The Theatre Manager* onwards, often indulged in a similar strain of self-conscious exaggeration, and it would be tempting to speculate about his possible influence over the younger artist. But Roberts' own personality asserts itself so forcibly even in his student drawings that it would be facile to suggest he ever plundered wholesale from the pictures Lewis had already exhibited in London. The two men did not really come into fruitful contact with each other before the spring of 1914, and Roberts was always sufficiently independent of his fellow artists to evolve a distinctive style. Even Bomberg, who may have originally encouraged him to embrace the uncompromising abstraction of *Dancers*, could never be said to have contributed towards the formation of Roberts' markedly idiosyncratic outlook.

Nobody else could conceivably have produced the large gouache drawing of *The Toe Dancer*, which was executed towards the end of 1914 and shown at the second London Group exhibition in March 1915.[6] It is an extraordinary work, the most elaborate of Roberts' pictures to have survived from this period now that all his Vorticist paintings are lost, and its theme is as bizarre as the style of the drawing itself. For the artist later testified that he was here letting the full force of his imagination loose on 'the dances performed by the wife of Stewart Gray the Hunger-Marcher at their home in old Ormonde Terrace in the autumn of 1914'.[7] Around that time, Roberts had moved into this house to live in an artists' commune run by Gray, whom Epstein remembered as 'a strange character'. He had, apparently, been 'a respectable lawyer in Edinburgh, and "kicked over the traces", and had led a contingent of "hunger marchers" to London. He finally got hold of some sort of derelict house where the lease had not expired [and] turned it into a caravanserai for artists and models'. It was, according to Roberts, a 'bohemian paradise' and Epstein described its ramshackle idealism when he recalled that 'this refuge was without gas or electric light, so that candles were used, and it seldom had water. No room had a lock, as most of the metal work had been carried away. Here the artists lived, and there was a life class at which I sometimes drew, and sometimes the artists, among others Roberts and Bomberg, a mysterious Indian artist, and some models, would have parties. Whether Stuart [*sic*] Gray ever received any rent was a question, but the old man who resembled a Tolstoy gone wrong would prowl about at night in a godfatherly fashion and look over his young charges'.[8]

This, then, is the macabre setting for *The Toe Dancer*. And Roberts emphasizes its other-worldliness by freezing the entire scene in the angry glare of a light that catches room, limbs and features alike in a brittle clarity. The eerie black shadow of the dancer is flung out across the foreground of the composition, as if Roberts wanted to make sure that the most abstract element in his drawing was displayed to full effect. But it does not ultimately detract from the dancer herself, petrified into a motionless statue as she performs a robot-like arabesque for the audience. Her hair has been beaten into a curving metallic cylinder, her buttocks are like a pair of steel helmets and her left leg is a bewildering amalgam of cartilage and piston. Yet the shading on her arms and torso painstakingly describes the play of light on human skin, and the fingers of her left hand are treated with full representational accuracy. Roberts is toying with different stylistic conventions once again, delineating faces everywhere with such compelling naturalism that Gray himself can be detected in a portrait-head on both the left and the right sides, and at the same time forcing his figures to

◁William Roberts
The Toe Dancer, 1914

adopt supremely artificial attitudes.[9] Everywhere, the most penetrating kind of mimetic observation is married to fantastic abnormality as Roberts tries to achieve his own private resolution of the balance between representation and abstraction that Lewis had recommended as the Vorticist ideal in *Blast No. 1*. *The Toe Dancer* ought to be merely whimsical, a misconceived jumble of conflicting idioms; but Roberts fills in each concentrated millimetre of the picture with such intensity that its blend of geometry and description, surrealism and verisimilitude coheres into a hard-won unity.

The Toe Dancer remains as an ideal testament to Gray and his madcap adventures, as well as marking an impressive step forward in Roberts' own progress towards creative maturity. Many of the formal elements of *At the Fox-Trot Ball* – the steeply inclined viewpoint, arbitrary exaggeration and ominous overtones – are carried over into this more ambitious work, where the introduction of mechanistic imagery heralds the major Vorticist canvases that Roberts executed the following year. Lewis obviously hoped he would move away from representation towards a more extreme form of abstraction, for after praising *The Toe Dancer* as 'a very brilliant drawing . . . infinitely laboured like a 15th Century engraving in appearance, worked out with astonishing dexterity and scholarship', and declaring that 'it displays a power that only the few best people possess in any decade', he criticized its lingering traces of a Slade-inculcated academicism. 'Michael Angelo is unfortunately the guest of honour at this Lord's Supper' he complained, implying that Roberts had composed his design like a grandiose religious pageant of the Renaissance. 'But Buonarotti', he added, in order to reassert his admiration for the picture, 'is my Bete-Noir.'[10]

Nothing else by Roberts has survived to bridge the considerable stylistic gap between *The Toe Dancer* and his contributions to the 1915 Vorticist Exhibition. The artist himself sadly recorded that '*The Bombardment of Scarborough*, a painting rejected by the New English Art Club in 1915 – it was perhaps asking too much of the New English that they should be interested in abstract art at that date – has disappeared without trace'.[11] And another, equally important work entitled *Boatmen*, which Roberts remembered as 'a large abstract composition',[12] has likewise never been seen since it was shown alongside *The Toe Dancer* in the second London Group exhibition. The sarcastic description of this painting in the *Observer*, whose critic asserted that 'there is not even a suggestion of recognisable form in the jumble of rectangular colour stripes which Mr Roberts exhibits as "Boatmen"',[13] hints at a picture that abandoned the hybrid style of *The Toe Dancer* and went back for inspiration to the extremism of the earlier *Dancers* painting. And this hypothesis is fully confirmed by Lewis's detailed appreciation of *Boatmen* in *Blast No. 2*, where he wrote that it 'is very different from the drawing' of *The Toe Dancer*. 'It is a very powerful, definitely centralised structure, based on a single human group', Lewis explained, pointing out that the picture was in fact rooted in a figurative inspiration. 'All the limbs and heads, as well, have become, however, a conglomeration of cold and vivid springs bent together into one organised bunch', he continued, outlining the mechanical vocabulary that Roberts was now employing. 'The line of colour exploited is the cold, effective, between-colours of modern Advertising art. The beauty of many of the Tube-posters – at least when seen together, and when organised by a curious mind – is a late discovery. The wide scale of colour and certain juxtapositions, in "Boatmen", however, suggests flowers, as well. It is the most successful painting Mr Roberts has so far produced, I think.'[14] This passage, which was quoted by Konody in his review of *Blast No. 2* as an example of Lewis's 'brilliant attempt to disguise [his] purpose in language as obscure as the drawings in criticizing the work of his fellow Vorticists',[15] can now be seen rather as a vivid demonstration of the way Lewis reacted to his colleagues' work, delighting in the multifarious images that *Boatmen* conjured up in his imagination. Springs, flowers and tube posters would not normally be compatible with a painting of naval workmen, but Vorticist abstraction brought them all to mind in the same complex artefact.

Many years later, Roberts admitted that 'Vorticism for me is the work I did for the Doré Gallery exhibition, together with the drawings in the second Blast (War number) whilst a member of the Group';[16] and although none of the four large paintings he displayed at the Vorticist exhibition is extant, a handful of assorted studies have survived to give some indication of their appearance. One of these drawings, an unnamed preliminary sketch which was called *Street Games* after it came to light a few years ago, could perhaps be identified as a working drawing for *Overbacks*, the first of Roberts' paintings to be listed in the Doré Galleries catalogue.[17] The only record of *Overbacks* describes it as 'a vorticist impression, portrayed with great vitality in an ultra-modern composition of colours, against a millet-yellow background',[18] and this generalized description does not help to prove whether the picture had any connection with the theme of *Street Games*. But the people who can so clearly be seen crouching down in the foreground of this drawing could possibly be engaged in a game like leap-frog that would justify the title *Overbacks*. A figure outlined hastily in pencil at the top of the page is relatively naturalistic, which suggests that Roberts started his Vorticist works in a methodical manner by progressively simplifying and abstracting notations jotted down in a straightforward, realistic style. In *Street Games*, the figures who have been drawn most fully in ink are the most removed from external appearances: the head of the woman on the extreme left is rendered as a stark circle, and her skirt is in the process of becoming as solid as the buttress shape filling up the lower right corner. By the time Roberts tackled the final canvas, she would probably have become a mechanical configuration, with the skirt acting more as a volume that counterbalances the weight of the 'buttress' than as a recognizable article of clothing. All the figures visible in this study must eventually have been levelled with their abstract surroundings, retaining the vivacity and essential movement of their poses but subordinated nonetheless to the formal requirements of the finished Vorticist canvas.

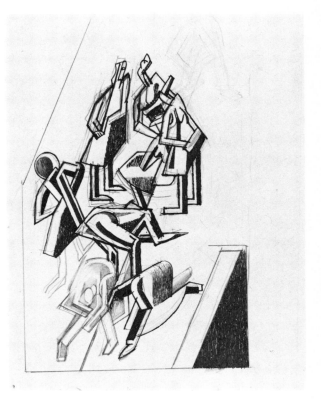

William Roberts
Street Games: Study for Overbacks (?), *c.* 1915

The same could equally well be said of the surviving study for another Doré exhibit entitled *Jeu*, a small scribble inscribed *Dominoes* that gives no more than a rough summary of the painting's final contents.[19] This time, Roberts has himself linked the drawing with his lost picture, and its chessboard theme accords well with the only recorded description of *Jeu* as 'a simple composition of lines and planes, in fresh brilliant colours: an abstract suggestion of gaming'.[20] The subject immediately recalls Pound's poem, the 'Dogmatic Statement on the Game and Play of Chess' published in *Blast No. 2*, and it is tempting to wonder if Roberts was directly inspired by Pound, or even vice versa. For the geometrical format of a chequered board was in itself a tailor-made symbol for the new art, and Roberts ensured that its heraldic pattern could be seen to the full in his painting by tipping up the table-top outlined in *Dominoes* at a notably steep angle. So eager was he to brandish the board's coloured squares that the inclination of the table-top no longer agrees with the shadow it casts on the ground below, and the figures seated on either side of the table seem to be experiencing some difficulty with the problem of resting their arms on such a preternaturally raised surface. But the construction of the left-hand player's body shows how Roberts would have so thoroughly transformed this scene for the painting itself that such descriptive inconsistencies would no longer be relevant: his legs are turning into regularized struts, practically indistinguishable from the machine-made legs of the chair beneath him, and his upper half can no longer be disentangled from the chair back as the two shapes already start to merge into one

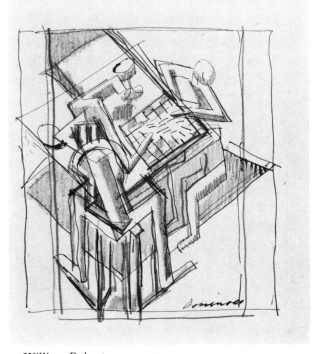

William Roberts
Dominoes: Study for Jeu, c. 1915

ambiguous configuration. *Dominoes* is unfortunately no real substitute for the loss of *Jeu*, but it does offer valuable insights into the creative processes behind Roberts' Vorticist pictures.

These processes are given fuller exposition still in the trio of studies for *Theatre*, the third painting he contributed to the Doré exhibition. For all three drawings show a more advanced stage in the evolution of the final image: even the first, a confused affair riddled with contradictions, unresolved details and scrawled second thoughts, presents a comprehensive idea of the whole design. Like *Street Games*, it all hinges on a strong diagonal line – the edge of the stage – which courses through the centre of the composition and almost divides it up into two equilateral triangles. The figures have been subjected to a certain degree of abstraction, and several areas of the picture have already moved beyond the bounds of logical analysis; but Roberts still shows himself to be under the influence of his motif in the rendering of light. This indebtedness to reality, a specific locale, was precisely the kind of element that the Vorticist

△ William Roberts
Study for Theatre I (recto), *c.* 1915

▷ William Roberts
Study for Theatre II (verso), *c.* 1915

had to purge from his design at a formative stage in its development, and it comes as no surprise to find the action of light far less important in the second of the studies for *Theatre*, executed on the back of the first sketch. Now the whole image has been reversed, and it is no longer possible to decipher its constituents with so much confidence. Roberts allows ambiguity to exert its puzzling control by dispensing with the houselights that contributed so greatly towards articulating the actors from their public in the first sketch, and making the limbs of the audience sprawl into shapes which can no longer be easily associated with the attitudes of humans seated in the front row of the stalls.

It is difficult, however, to gauge how much of this ambiguity is intentional: Roberts' pencil and pen remain tentative and uneasy as they clash with his water-colour wash over a messy, indecisive portion of the design. Only in the third *Study for Theatre* does he iron out all hesitancies, rationalize every lingering descriptive passage into a geometrical component and square the drawing up for transfer to the definitive canvas. Crisp pencilled outlines enclose his previous difficulties in a network of unshakeable pictorial facts, as if the alternatives that had been swimming around freely in his fluid fantasy had suddenly gelled into a tangible substance. Roberts' contours are now firm and exact, and they need

William Roberts
Study for Theatre III, c. 1915

to be; for the composition they describe now treads a thin tightrope between subtle allusion and total disintegration. The intimate scene that was still clearly visible in the first study has become nothing more than a pretext for a full-blown display of Vorticist pyrotechnics, as the fabric of the theatre itself hardens into bullets of angular form which discharge themselves among the figures. And the actors become nothing more than sculptural extensions of the stage, their four faces staring out impassive and unseeing above the heads of the immediate audience, which seems paradoxically to be more active than the performers on the stage. They remain content with their monumental calm, a symbol of the detachment with which the Vorticist was able to change the theme of a theatre, with its atmosphere, life and richly human associations, into a bleak world where aggressive abstract forms take on the potency of the figures they envelop.

The passage from the first study for *Theatre* to the last provides an object lesson in the application of the Vorticist aesthetic to a subject steeped in picturesque associations: compare these drawings with the loving recreations of a music-hall *ambience* which Gore and Sickert produced, and Roberts' ruthless formal logic becomes startlingly apparent. But if the *Theatre* series seems by contrast altogether too cerebral, it must be remembered that these studies are an incomplete record of the lost painting. The extra dimension which colour would lend to the composition is lacking, and only the two surviving studies for Roberts' fourth Doré Galleries exhibit, *Twostep*,[21] afford any idea of the vitality that oil-paint could have injected into his sober working sketches. Colour must have been a very positive force in all his contributions to the show, for *The Athenaeum*'s critic took violent objection to them and declared that 'Mr Roberts has woefully come to grief in a series of sickly cloying colour-schemes'.[22] But the true quality of these controversial 'schemes' is at least suggested in the *Twostep* studies, which begin at the stage where the *Theatre* sketches left off: a detailed pencil drawing of the complete design, squared and numbered according to time-honoured Slade precepts.

Roberts has returned yet again to the dance theme that occupied his energies so much in the past, but he has taken his cue more from the *Dancers* than the later *Toe Dancer*. It is virtually impossible to ascertain with any confidence where the figures are, or how many of them are portrayed. Apart from one legible area, the figurative references are equated so effectively with a classic Vorticist vocabulary of girders and clumps of jutting metal that they enter the realm of guesswork. For Roberts did not want them to be read in the accepted way, even if he always set great store by the retention of a starting-point in outward reality. Rather did he aim at a new type of reading, whereby the effect produced by the figure alone was inseparable from the impact of the non-representational complex surrounding it. It is, therefore, unwise to hunt around in the usual manner for the dancers themselves. By comparing *Twostep* with *Dancers* Roberts can be seen to have gained more confidence in the autonomous power of abstraction; and he lets it engulf the human element in *Twostep* to such a degree that he has obviously decided to stake everything on the ability of shapes and colours to convey his emotions with the minimum amount of help from descriptive connotations.

This ambition receives resonant confirmation in the watercolour version of *Twostep*, the finest of Roberts' surviving Vorticist works and surely a reliable guide to the appearance of the lost painting. The tonal orchestration in this little picture is a revelation of the freedom with which the English rebels employed colour. Its scalding oppositions of orange against scarlet would be as savage as the most headlong Fauve painting were it not for the skill with which Roberts blends them in with more seductive pinks, lilacs, purples, pale blues and a relieving use of white. Instead of merely clashing and swearing at each other,

△William Roberts
Study for Twostep I, c. 1915

▷William Roberts
Study for Twostep II, c. 1915

Bernard Meninsky
St. George and the Dragon, 1915

these two seemingly irreconcilable colours end up by charging the design with an access of urgency: the dancers may not be fully apparent, but the dance itself is evoked with a vengeance as a resolutely modern ragtime orgy, far removed from the civilized elegance that the name *Twostep* implies.

Despite the title Roberts gave to this picture, he probably based its extraordinary panache on memories of a more uninhibited form of dancing. Recalling his early days in the 'spacious cobbled-stoned' Old Cumberland Market, where 'there was a small colony of artists . . . sufficient to have formed a Market Group', he mentioned the wild parties thrown by his friend John Flanagan. 'In Flanagan's balconied rooms were held many an all-nightly revel to the Jazz-music of a gramophone', he remembered affectionately; 'our full-throated singing of "Way down on the Levee" and "Hold your hand out, you naughty boy", if too long sustained in the still small hours, brought visits from constables disturbed on their beats'.[23] And it is exactly this kind of jazz experience that Roberts reflects so vigorously in the *Twostep* watercolour, with its pounding rhythms and exacerbating tonal contrasts.

Indeed, Roberts' decision to spell this normally hyphenated word in such an unorthodox, compressed way is a measure of his impatience with the conventional idea of all ballroom dancing, even a relatively appropriate military two-step. The twentieth century no longer had any time for that kind of polite, stately measure; and Roberts' picture sets out to provide an inflammatory Vorticist substitute, not only subsuming its figures in the greater dissonance of fluorescent colour but also suggesting that humanity now plays second fiddle to the mechanistic fragments which dominate the design and themselves participate in the new, impersonal urban dance demanded by *Blast No. 1*'s 'enormous, jangling, journalistic, fairy desert of modern life'. Roberts' surviving Vorticist works refuse to tackle that industrial subject-matter directly, just as they stop short of the extreme abstraction employed in pictures like *Workshop* or *Enclosure* and always base their compositions on the human figure rather than a maritime or architectural blueprint. *Blast*, however, nowhere insisted that the Vorticist artist grasp the nettle of the machine world to the exclusion of all else: it was enough if he succeeded in impregnating his chosen themes with a formal organisation, a secondary imagery and a vitality inspired by that world. On this level, *Theatre* and *Twostep* are thoroughly Vorticist in their metamorphoses, and Roberts' recent attempts to describe himself simply as an 'English Cubist'[24] do no justice to the originality with which he and his allies evolved from both Cubism and Futurism an art remarkably independent of either paternal movement. It is regrettable that Roberts' retrospective determination to escape from any suspicion of Lewis's overbearing hegemony means that he now has to repudiate his membership of the one movement that coincides with the character of his 1914–15 work.

He was as iconoclastic as Lewis, for all his unwillingness to associate freely with the editor of *Blast*; and when his painter friend Bernard Meninsky asked him to execute a line drawing for the St George's Day celebration number of the *Evening News* in April 1915, he produced a complex abstract composition without caring one jot about the incomprehension of the newspaper-reading public. So did Meninsky, whose uncharacteristically radical design was also reproduced in the St George's Day issue and described there by the artist as a work 'in which the most modern tendencies in pictorial art are shown'.[25] This accomplished exercise is the sole surviving example of Meninsky's brief flirtation with the English rebel movement – Roberts later stated that it was 'the only occasion that he tried his hand at this form of art'[26] – but the *Evening News* insisted on calling it *A Futurist St George*.

The same title was given to Roberts' drawing as well, even though it was a

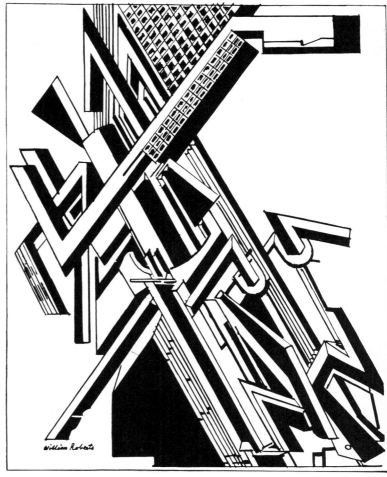

classic demonstration of the Vorticist style.[27] And the *Evening News*, which had politely explained underneath Meninsky's contribution how 'with care and patience this drawing may be understood of the Philistine', claimed in the caption for Roberts' design that 'to the unitiated in the mysteries of Futurism, this drawing will appear rather like a distracted jig-saw puzzle'.[28] But then, the press was hardly likely to sympathize with a work that permitted only the upper half of St George's body to be displayed with any clarity. Roberts has constructed a resolutely streamlined saint, an impersonal robot whose figure merges with the paraphernalia of twentieth-century civilization. No horse is visible in this mechanical jungle, nor is there a romantic landscape; and as for the dragon, whatever traces once existed of its scales and snarling teeth have long since been submerged in the plethora of jagged particles piled up at the foot of the giant diagonal. Only the cheeky circle of an eye incised at the very bottom of the drawing prompts the suspicion that its head lurks there, attached to a pair of angular wings, but they are so embedded in the abstract elements that nothing is certain. Once again, Roberts is sufficiently confident of his non-representational contents to permit them to carry the burden of the picture, expressing the battle between saint and mythological beast in terms of a thrusting formal arrangement. Just as Lewis had taken an openly defiant stand against the public taste by mocking his *Portrait of an Englishwoman* in a scaffolding of phallic shapes, so his young ally revelled in the chance Meninsky's commission gave him to reduce a hallowed national legend to an exercise in forbidding geometry. St George is, quite literally, blasted by a Vorticist who sees no reason why such an outdated symbol should be allowed a definite existence outside the harsh reality of the modern world.

△William Roberts
St. George and the Dragon, 1915

▽ William Roberts
Study for St. George and the Dragon, 1915

William Roberts
Machine Gunners, c. 1915

But if *St George and the Dragon* shows Roberts at his closest to Lewis, both stylistically and spiritually, his affiliations with Bomberg were still as marked as they had ever been. Both these twin loyalties become strikingly evident in his contributions to *Blast No. 2*, a pair of lost monochrome compositions which probably represent his latest surviving Vorticist work: Roberts afterwards declared that his 'connection with Vorticism ended with the publication of my two line-drawings ... in the second Blast'.[29] One of them, simply entitled *Drawing* in the magazine but actually named *Machine Gunners* by the artist, is close to *Before Antwerp*, Lewis's cover design for the War Number.[30] For both drawings evince a similar desire to combine abstraction with an instantly understandable subject, one which would mirror the international conflict in the most direct fashion permissible within the overall context of the Vorticist aesthetic. Lewis achieves it by forming his comparatively realistic soldiers out of the same vocabulary as his non-figurative background, but he barely avoids an uncomfortable clash between two incompatible ways of seeing. Roberts conquers the problem with more ease by simplifying his gunners' bodies into schematic puppet shapes that fit in well with the broad, unfussy areas of abstraction around them. If his drawing lacks the sombreness of *Before Antwerp* – the gunners look almost like toy soldiers enacting a scene out of a comic-strip

William Roberts
Combat, c. 1915

battle – its neat facility nevertheless makes Lewis's composition appear laboured. Roberts rings the changes between abstraction and description with admirable flair, weaving in limbs with their geometrical counterparts so deftly that the transition is never even seen to be happening.

The other Roberts illustration for *Blast No. 2*, a much larger design entitled *Combat*, abandons this straightforward vein and courts ambiguity again. The soldiers have now become inextricably entangled with each other, their weapons and a network of Vorticist geometry. Certain small representational clues are retained, but on the whole there is no fixed boundary between figures and objects. Follow the composition around and it will soon be evident that arms grow into girders, heads into zigzags without the slightest hesitation. Roberts has emancipated himself from the need to distinguish between the idioms he uses, just as Bomberg had previously achieved a freewheeling amalgamation of styles in his masterly works of 1914. In *The Mud Bath*, it is no longer possible to state whether the configurations dominating the painting are men or machines: they exist as independent creations and are all the more affecting for their ability to do so. The same is true of *Combat*, too, where a Bombergian marriage of the human and mechanical is enacted with such bewildering success that it helps to explain why Roberts and Bomberg seemed 'inseparable' at that period.[31]

Bomberg, however, succeeded in moving even further away from the need to describe natural forms. He must have executed at least one sizeable painting after the completion of *The Mud Bath* in the summer of 1914 – he joined the army only in November 1915 – but nothing has survived except an assorted series of daring watercolours and drawings which are very rarely dated. The titles of the six works he displayed in the 'Invited to Show' section of the Vorticist exhibition have a blunt simplicity that has made them impossible to trace, but they do suggest a more extreme degree of abstraction than *The Mud Bath* employed. Two of the paintings are called *Decorative Experiment* and the third *Small Painting*, while the drawings are merely referred to as *Design in White* or *Design in Colour*. Rebecca West confirmed the non-representational nature of these works when she remembered Lewis taking her, around the time of the Vorticist show, 'to see Bomberg's white paintings, basically I think because he wanted to look at them himself. One of them was oblong, but they were all large and abstract'.[32] Bomberg obviously wanted to avoid giving these pictures titles which would attach them to any specific subject-matter, and it certainly makes sense to imagine them as being close in style to his remarkably refined watercolour of an *Abstract Composition*. Its medium does not necessarily rule it out as a possible candidate for one of two *Designs in Colour* exhibits at the Doré Galleries. One critic of the show stated that 'Mr Bomberg has a very pretty watercolour design of pseudo-calligraphic character';[33] and its dogged refusal to elaborate on a few skeletal pencil outlines washed in with primary areas of red, yellow, blue and brown could easily represent the summation of Bomberg's experiments with abstraction. The form jerking its way out of the central mass towards the upper left edge can no longer be connected with a human limb at all, and its light blue tone prevents its identification as the lever or handle of a machine. Bomberg has made sure that it eludes both these classifications, standing instead on its own merits as a manifestation of the 'Pure Form' ideal he had proposed in his Chenil Gallery manifesto. And a similar conclusion must be reached about another astonishing *Drawing* in black chalk, which does not even allow colour to give volume to the sinewy lines traced so sparingly on its surface. A slight layer of white heightener has been applied to the large vertical shape in the middle of the picture, but it hardly succeeds in differentiating this focal image from the other lines. They are all set free to twist, turn, double back and

David Bomberg
Abstract Composition, c. 1914

frolic with each other in a spirit of carefree abandon that mirrors Bomberg's own relief at escaping almost entirely from the need to represent.

Could a work as extreme as *Drawing* belong only to the 1915 period? The question implies that Bomberg progressed in a steady, logical manner towards total abstraction before active service called a halt to his production, and yet this is demonstrably not so. For one thing, Hulme had enthused over a 're-markable drawing' called *Zin* in his review of the 1914 Chenil Gallery one-man show which could easily be identified as the selfsame *Drawing* that has just been tentatively placed in the Vorticist Exhibition period. After noting that *Zin* 'contains hardly any representative element', Hulme went on to show how 'in the upper part, which strikes me as best, there are no recognisable forms at all, but only an arrangement of abstract lines outlining no object . . . Perhaps the best way of describing it would be to say that it looks like a peculiarly interesting kind of scaffolding'. His description fits in well with the character of *Drawing*,

David Bomberg
Drawing: Zin (?), *c.* 1914

and suggests that the two pictures may in reality be identical; but Hulme's enquiring mind did not rest content with a superficial survey of *Zin*'s appearance. He plunged immediately into an honest discussion of the problems confronting the writer who wishes to expatiate on the merits of an abstract work of art.

'It is very difficult to state why one considers a drawing of this kind good when one hasn't it before one', he confessed, revealing the candour that made him a penetrating and constructive critic rather than a superficially destructive one. 'I should probably find it difficult to say what I found interesting in it if I had the drawing here before me and could show it you', he persisted. 'Its interest depends on qualities peculiarly indescribable in words. Indescribable not for any mysterious reason, but because forms are of their nature rather indescribable, and even difficult, to point out. They depend, for example, very often on a three dimensional relation between planes which is very difficult to get at.' Unlike the vast majority of English reviewers, who would never for one moment have acknowledged that the rebel art posed a challenge to their own powers as writers, Hulme was fascinated by the idea that abstraction might eventually discredit the whole concept of verbal art criticism. 'The artist in front of a picture endeavouring to explain it, by inexpressive motions of his hands, has often been laughed at; but laughed at, I think, for a wrong reason', he continued. 'It is supposed that he waves his hands, makes strange gestures with his thumbs, peculiar twists with his wrists, because he lacks the power of expressing himself in words; because he is a painter, in fact, and not a literary man. This I believe to be a mistaken view of the phenomenon. He is not using his hands through poverty of words, through lack of ability to express himself in the proper manner. He is trying to describe the qualities of the picture in the only way they can be described.'[34] It was a startling conclusion for a man actually engaged in criticizing an exhibition to reach, and only Hulme had the requisite frankness to set down his doubts in print. But he would never have done so had he not realized that the advent of abstract art would ultimately overthrow every received notion about aesthetics. In that sense, it was a measure of his respect for Bomberg's courage and independence.

Nowhere are these dual qualities more apparent than in the marvellous series of watercolours he executed around the idea of *The Dancer*. It was this theme, more than any other, that fired rebel artists in their search for the perfect equation between form and content. From Lewis's *Kermesse*, through Gaudier's *Red Stone Dancer* to Roberts' several treatments of the subject, it ran like a connecting thread through the convoluted imagery of Vorticist art; and Bomberg, the man who insisted on staying outside the official movement, proved his underlying kinship by returning to this motif with obsessive consistency. Helen Rowe, who knew Bomberg very well during the Ormonde Terrace period, told his widow that the *Dancer* watercolours were inspired by a Russian ballet dancer called Maria Wajda, who frequented Stewart Gray's colony. But they seem also to owe something to a girl called Sophie Cohen – later Sonia Joslen – who was a member of the tightly-knit East End group Bomberg grew up with. 'I always enjoyed dancing at this period', Mrs Joslen recalled. 'And in 1913, when I went down to Southborne to join a summer school dancing out-of-doors on the cliffs with Margaret Morris, Bomberg followed me down there with a few friends. He was in love with me at the time, and thought it a great lark to watch us all cavorting around at this open-air camp. The *Dancer* watercolours came out of his interest in all this, and I think you can see the bodies' movements clearly in the designs.'[35]

Bomberg's obsession with the dance theme links up, too, with the general awakening of interest in dancing's potential which Diaghilev's triumphant London seasons aroused. 'The arrival of the Russian Ballet in London had a marked effect on the taste of Londoners', Oliver Brown recalled. 'It was in 1911 that Diaghilev brought the Imperial Russian Ballet in full force to Covent Garden with Karsavina and Nijinski, arousing immediate attention. The younger generation in London was infatuated . . . There is no doubt that these constant visits of the Russian Ballet made a lasting impression and exerted a considerable influence on visual taste.'[36] Douglas Goldring, who still enthused many years later about the time when 'the Russian Ballet first electrified the town', fondly recorded his visit to '*Le Pavillon d'Armide*, in which Cechetti gave a marvellous performance as the premier danseur de caractere in a costume like a Christmas cracker'. And can it be doubted that it was the exotic costumes, as much as the ballet's innate ability to concentrate on the formal properties of the human body, which fired artists like Bomberg in their desire to celebrate the dance in their work? Jessie Dismorr had shown her regard for its inspiration as early as 1911, in her *Rhythm* illustration of Isadora Duncan, while Gaudier paid an equally specific tribute to the Diaghilev troupe in his early group of Bolm and Tamara Karsavina performing a duet in *L'Oiseau de Feu*. And Goldring helped to account for Gaudier's devotion when he remembered that '*Petrouchka* and *L'Oiseau de Feu* were my favourites among Diagileff's earliest productions, with *Le Spectre de la Rose* – shall I ever forget Nijinsky's leap through the young virgin's window? – as a close third'.[37] Gaudier, working at an earlier stage of his life as a sculptor, modelled his homage to the ballet in a Rodinesque vein, reproducing the movements of the performers with tender accuracy. But when Bomberg started his watercolour series of *The Dancer* not long afterwards, he perhaps took his cue from abstract treatments of the theme like Picabia's 1913 watercolour of *Star Dancer and Her School of Dancing* and went to the other extreme, creating a totally non-representational equivalent of the movement which had excited him.

Francis Picabia
Star Dancer and Her School of Dancing, 1913

See next page

Firmly dated 1913, this design must be one of Bomberg's first works to break away completely from representational intent, and thereby helps to discredit the theory that he was at his most uncompromising only in 1915. Indeed, the picture's stern structure is positively puritanical in its determination to banish every trace of a figurative reference. There is an air of heavy deliberation about the composition, as if the exclusion of irrelevant associations cost Bomberg the price of his normal spontaneity. The crayon defines *The Dancer*'s contours without any sense of the life-enhancing arabesque movement which gives some of the succeeding *Dancer* pictures their wonderful lightness and sprung tension, and the picture's real merit resides in its dogmatic statement of formal priorities.

The Vorticists would have understood such an aim, however: Pound quoted with approval in *Blast No. 2* a passage from Laurence Binyon's *The Flight of the Dragon*, where the fundamental ingredients of a work of art are actually equated with the physical movements Bomberg was attempting to express in these watercolours. 'Every statue, every picture, is a series of ordered relations, controlled, as the body is controlled in the dance, by the will to express a single idea', he declared, usefully summarizing Bomberg's ambitions in a succinct metaphor. To succeed, the *Dancer* watercolours had to be co-ordinated with the same blend of discipline and inspiration that a good dancer possesses, and they must be informed by absolutely single-minded motives. Not that this meant Bomberg ought to approximate more closely to his source-material and reintroduce descriptive elements into his art: in a third sentence reproduced in large capitals by Pound in *Blast No. 2*, Binyon emphasized that 'IT IS NOT ESSENTIAL THAT THE SUBJECT-MATTER SHOULD REPRESENT OR BE LIKE ANYTHING IN NATURE; ONLY IT MUST BE ALIVE WITH A RHYTHMIC VITALITY OF ITS OWN'.[38]

△ David Bomberg
The Dancer, 1913

▷ David Bomberg
The Dancer, 1913–14

▷ David Bomberg
The Dancer, 1913–14

Bomberg probably never came across these sentiments until they were printed in the Vorticists' journal in 1915, but he did not need to. The rest of the *Dancer* series carry out Binyon's precepts to the letter, celebrating the infinite variety of balletic movement in designs that seem to trace the ceaseless flow of limbs in motion. Sometimes the effect is lyrical and delicate, the lines darting restlessly all over the picture-surface as they struggle to reflect the mercurial quality of a dancer's actions. And then the mood changes slightly, the pattern shifts and tries to assume a more permanent character, rising up out of a firmly built base with the solidity of a sculpture on a plinth. Bomberg seems to have been more satisfied with this approach, for the most majestic designs fill out and expand into extravagant structures that float on the paper like galleons in full sail. As his imagination roams further away from the ostensible theme, so Bomberg's handling of colour becomes more emboldened. Rich crimsons and ceruleans predominate, lending these elaborate designs a splendour entirely in keeping with the lavish spectacles that Diaghilev's audiences would have witnessed. The mixture of watercolour and gouache is applied liberally, with a loaded brush laying down broken patches of wash and then leaving them to coagulate, stain or dribble at will. No single colour area is evenly painted, for Bomberg enjoys exploiting a controlled form of accident as he splashes his colours onto the paper and watches them run their own course. If Lewis's pronounced linearity marks him out as the most Florentine of the rebels, Bomberg is the most Venetian, and he saturates these *Dancer* pictures with a painterly freedom that is only just brought under control by the principal contours of the composition. It is all the more to be regretted, therefore, that when his close friend

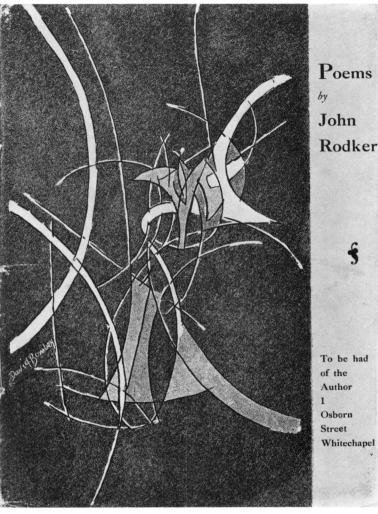

△David Bomberg
The Dancer, 1913–14

▷David Bomberg
The Dancer: Cover of *Poems by John Rodker*, 1914

△Alexander Rodchenko
Compass and Ruler Drawing, 1915–16

John Rodker decided to illustrate one of them on the cover of his *Poems* – privately printed in 1914 – Bomberg castrated its delicate tonality by re-executing it in a slightly altered monochrome version.[39] Deprived of their sustaining colours, these thin crescents of form seem starved and ineffectual, even though the design itself moves closer to the idea of a dancing figure than its more high-flown counterparts. Indeed, it is remarkable how insistently this cover design recalls Rodchenko's slightly later *Compass and Ruler Drawing*, where Bomberg's geometrical leanings have been taken to their logical conclusion (could Rodchenko have seen a copy of Rodker's *Poems*?) and given a vitality lacking in the *Dancer* cover.

The original watercolour is, however, the subtlest and most disciplined example of the entire *Dancer* series. Its minimal, surprisingly curvilinear spiral of shapes represents the nearest Bomberg ever came to the vortex symbol he did so much to avoid in political terms, and relies to an astonishing extent on the vibrancy of the pink, blue and orange washes which give it life. It does also possess the closest connections both with the dancing activities of its present owner, Sonia Joslen, and with the work of John Rodker, who dedicated his *Poems* to Mrs Joslen and was married to her at the time when Bomberg executed these water-colours.[40] For one of Rodker's poems, written in 1915, was actually called *Dancer*, and it provides a striking verbal parallel to Bomberg's treatment of the same theme:

This is Niobe
whirling in anguish

David Bomberg

David Bomberg
The Dancer, c. 1914

over her dead ones!
gathering the poor strayed limbs

Whirling she sucks them into her,
they fade through and into her;
Her swiftness whirls the air into one large round sob.

Now a bitter ellipse – wickedly whirling:
so tight   so crushed by air:
so shaped by the thumb of air
and levered on humming heels;
her pointed head
drills the skiey vault:
makes heaven's floor tremble![41]

The staccato quality of Rodker's vers libre, alleviated only in places by the occasional archaism, has the same bareness that Bomberg achieved in his water-colour. And the poem's insistent whirlpool imagery, no less than its Vorticist-like references to 'drills' and a 'bitter ellipse', comes near to simulating the concerns of English rebel art as a whole.

Perhaps it was the inspiration of this link between Rodker's poetry and Bomberg's own work that prompted the latter to supplement his *Dancer* pictures with words. For he afterwards printed six lithographs based on the theme, wrote a short poem to supplement their meaning and published them together as a booklet entitled *Russian Ballet*. It did not appear until 1919, and Bomberg probably executed the prints at that time as well; but the designs obviously belong to the pre-war period on stylistic grounds, and Bomberg's first wife Alice Mayes recorded that, in order to make the lithographs, 'David took six of the little drawings he had coloured before he went away to the War'.[42] Her statement makes absolute sense, for the booklet contains at least three compositions that can be regarded as the culmination of Bomberg's prolonged pre-war obsession with the dance. And just as the watercolours had swung wildly in their con-struction from opulence over to severity, so the lithographs proved to be enormously varied in style. Executed with an assurance that proves Bomberg had remembered the lessons of his early apprenticeship with the lithographer Paul Fischer around 1906, they stand as a grand summary of his various formal experiments with the dance motif. One of the best, based around a group of stick-like forms gesticulating in a shallow space reminiscent of *The Mud Bath*, sends shafts of vivid purple running in Vorticist diagonals behind its orange participants. This frieze of limbs cranking its way across the composition bears a much closer relationship with the human figure than any of the watercolours, and marks a conscious return to the schematic methods of the *Acrobat* drawings. A strong tension is built up between the solid, unrelieved purple bands, raking the picture with the intensity of stage spotlights, and the more uneven nature of the limbs, glancing in the light as they pick their way through the formal obstacles Bomberg has laid in their path. But he denies this clarity in another of the most important lithographs, where the poised movement outlined so well in the previous print is broken up and dissipated in a shower of almost pointillist strokes. Whether or not the intention was to capture the effect of a certain kind of trick lighting employed by Diaghilev, it remains true that Bomberg hardly ever employed this device anywhere else in his work. For an artist fascinated above all by volume and mass, this relatively weightless composition comes as a surprise: the occasional insertions of uninterrupted ochre, blue and umber hardly counteract the evanescent impression created by these small stabs of black scattered all over the surface of the design.

David Bomberg
The Russian Ballet lithographs, 1914–19

The abrupt stylistic transitions employed in these lithographs – two of the smaller prints depend for their effect on sudden areas of illumination blazing out of otherwise penumbral surroundings – are reflected in the text of the accompanying poem. Bomberg carefully arranged the order of the booklet so that each of the six pictures faced a portion of text on the opposite page, in the following sequence:

Methodic discord startles . . .
Insistent snatchings drag fancy from space,
Fluttering white hands beat – compel. Reason concedes.
Impressions crowding collide with movement round us –
the curtain falls – the created illusion escapes.
The mind clamped fast captures only a fragment, for new illusion.

Although the clipped, compressed verse could not possibly be intended as a literal translation of the pictorial images, it does remain true that the lithograph facing the fourth section of the poem, 'impressions crowding collide with movement round us', directly expresses Bomberg's verbal sentiments. Huge, unwieldy boulders of form brood over the scene, scarely giving the areas of orange-yellow a chance to assert themselves at all. The boulders seem almost to crush each other with their overwhelming brutality, acting as a reminder that the 'new illusion' Bomberg created in these abstracted metaphors was not wholly concerned with the beauty of balletic motion. This design seems more concerned with the sensations of shock and surprise, as if the artist's retina found the 'methodic discord' of the ballet an unbearably powerful experience. Small wonder that, when he tried to sell the prints as souvenirs of Diaghilev's 1919 London season, the response was hostile. 'We started a mad escapade, David and I and another artist, which was to go into the stalls of the Alhambra and to offer these booklets for sale (as programmes)' recalled Alice Mayes. 'We had sold five or six of them when Diaghilev spotted us and chased us back into the ninepenny gallery, where we belonged, and the money was refunded to those who had bought the booklet. An attendant explained that it was a mistake, but it was great fun while it lasted.'[43] And even when more conventional selling methods were attempted, the result was equally pitiful: nobody wanted to waste half-a-crown on these puzzling prints. 'David took his hundred unsold copies to Henderson's Bomb Shop in Charing Cross Road,' Alice Mayes continued, 'where they were put out for sale and about ten were sold and then Henderson withdrew them as unsaleable.'[44]

How far can Bomberg's work be regarded as compatible in intention and achievement with the Vorticist movement? He always made such a point of disengaging himself from the group's political activities, and insisting later on that 'I was never a Vorticist',[45] that it would be simple to regard him as the lone individualist he always wanted to be; and yet his connections with the Vorticist aesthetic are too striking to be ignored. Points of contact with Roberts have already been discussed, and *The Mud Bath* contains nothing to contradict the energetic synthesis of abstraction, observation and mechanistic imagery promulgated by Lewis in both issues of *Blast*. Indeed, Alice Mayes recalled that 'one of our first visitors' to the studio in Robert Street which they occupied early in 1915 was Lewis, 'who spent many evenings trying to persuade David to allow him to have one of his drawings published in the new issue of "Blast". David was adamant that he should be "adequately represented" and demanded that five drawings be included in the publication – or none'. The conditions Bomberg laid down about his inclusion in the magazine had therefore been modified somewhat since the spring of 1914, when he threatened to sue Lewis if *Blast No. 1* reproduced any of his works. Alice Mayes even went on to claim that 'later David gave in and allowed two drawings to be published in a later issue of "Blast" ';[46] so it seems as if Bomberg would have actually appeared in the rebels' company had *Blast No. 3* been printed.

It never got beyond the planning stage, but an important drawing exhibited by Bomberg at the Spring 1915 NEAC show does survive to reveal unprecedentedly strong stylistic connections with Lewis's work. And Alice Mayes made clear just how much of a turning-point Bomberg considered this composition to be. 'Soon the easel was occupied by a large piece of paper on which David was planning a picture, which was to meet war time conditions', she wrote, remembering the early days at Robert Street. 'First of all, it was to be entirely naturalistic, for he had done with Cubism "for the duration". This picture was to be truly up-to-date – it was to be called "Billet", and was to depict the new volunteers as they had first arrived at their new billet, to find themselves with one bedstead between them, showing their attempts to find places for themselves . . . I myself took all the postures, as David would have every posture verified by my ability to take and hold it. Hold the posture I did, until often I had to be lifted out of it and vigorously massaged to life again.'[47]

The drawing itself, for which there exist two sizeable and markedly more abstract black chalk studies, bears out Bomberg's desire to back-pedal on his former radicalism and his surprising insistence on using a life model again. The

David Bomberg
Billet, 1915

design is based on the rectangular platform Bomberg had favoured so many times before, and he once more uses it as a foil for the gesticulating activity of monumental limbs. Throughout a large portion of the picture, a densely shaded equivalent of khaki uniforms is deployed to prevent any positive identification of the bodies' poses: when a projecting leg is about to be linked with a torso or an arm, the ink lines intervene and weave an obscuring net over the area involved. But Bomberg now knows precisely how to counteract this maddening allusiveness with plain statement, making sure that the bed-heads framing the composition are rendered with uncluttered directness. And this new descriptive direction is given unequivocal confirmation in the solitary soldier who sits on the farthest side of the bed, his head and trunk transformed into the type of implacable robot that Lewis had so often favoured before entering his most abstract phase. The figure possesses a typically Bombergian solidity, of course, and a massive calm which Lewis's frenetic automatons never displayed: even *Billet*, with its clear narrative implications, shows how much less literary Bomberg was than most of the Vorticists, how his concerns centred more on a purist abstraction of the human figure than on the quintessentially 'modern' themes favoured by *Blast*, and how the mechanistic element in his work was a by-product of formal simplification, not an integral part of a deliberate, programmatic involvement with the twentieth century metropolitan zeitgeist. In all these respects, no less than in his refusal to compromise the fundamentally monumental character of his art with too much Vorticist explosiveness, Bomberg stands apart from Lewis's movement; but in *Billet* the similarities between the two men's work are at the same time self-evident.

And they help to justify, in their turn, any discussion of Bomberg with the other English rebels, for the artist capable of executing *Billet* could not have been so very divorced from the concerns of Vorticism. His continuing personal involvement with the movement is evinced both by Alice Mayes, who recalled that 'Bobby Roberts came in every day'[48] while Bomberg was at Robert Street, and by Lewis's aside in a 1915 letter to Pound that 'we had Bomberg to entertain us, on Saturday'.[49] While Nevinson even told Lewis, around the time of the 1915 Doré exhibition, how pleased he was to hear that Bomberg 'had become a Vorticist'.[50] It was more a matter of personal antipathy that kept him out of the movement: Kate Lechmere thought there was a 'class war' between 'Lewis the Rugby School product and Bomberg the East End Jew',[51] while Sonia Joslen explained this tension more fully by asserting that 'Lewis was a bit anti-semitic, whereas Bomberg was very bombastic and pugnacious'.[52] Bomberg himself drew particular attention to his racial origins years afterwards, when he stated that 'some of Lewis's colleagues who were with him partisan in a very remarkable struggle for supremacy against Royal Academy Art – which before 1911 was still the public conception of What Art Should Be in England – were Jews, some British born as it was my fate to be'.[53]

This memoir, written shortly before his death, happily implies that both he and Epstein – the two most recalcitrant personalities within the English rebel circle – were closely caught up with the cause Lewis tried so hard to propagate in *Blast*. Indeed, there is a distinct note of pride in Bomberg's claim that he was 'partisan', a 'colleague' of Lewis's: something he would never have dreamed of admitting at the time. In 1914, Bomberg's instinctive belligerence forbade him to associate with an openly political alliance like Vorticism. He even positively enjoyed the thrust and parry of conflict with the rebels, revealing later that 'it was Lewis who was naughty and told the critic, how my paintings looked like poached eggs. He was somewhat dry in "polemic" in those early days of 1913 and I liked him more on that account'.[54] Etchells recalled that 'Bomberg was just as aggressive as Lewis: he used to taunt Lewis the whole time, and whenever the two of them met Bomberg would say "Well, Percy, how's old Perce, then?" deliberately using the name Lewis hated'.[55] And Lewis, according to Sonia Joslen, aggravated the situation still further by striking back, making 'pointed jokes about Bobby Roberts going round the whole time with "*Bum*berg" '.[56] Nor was the editor of *Blast* the only Vorticist whom Bomberg succeeded in alienating. Lewis himself remembered that at one stage 'Gaudier was spoiling for a fight. He threatened at Ford's to sock Bomberg on the jaw, and when I asked him why, he explained that he had an imperfect control over his temper, and that he must not be found with Bomberg, for the manner adopted by that gentleman was of a sort that put him beside himself. I had therefore to keep them apart'.[57]

It is a cause for astonishment, in fact, that any of these inflammatory indivi-dualists ever managed to sublimate their own swollen egos within a communal enterprise at all. Only in later life could Bomberg view the period more dis-passionately and bring himself to confess that 'the truth is, the three of us, Lewis, Roberts and Bomberg took equal parts with "Other Vorticists" in helping recover ground lost to art in England. No endeavour for cultural better-ment is ever brought about single-handed'.[58]

Chapter 14: Vorticism in Practice: Etchells, Hamilton, Atkinson, Dismorr and Saunders

Even Etchells, who seems to have been one of the quietest and least assertive of the rebels, never wholly made up his mind about the movement until he finally agreed to exhibit as a Vorticist at the Doré Galleries show. His ambivalent attitude to the idea of official membership is worth stressing, if only to counteract the prevailing tendency – pompously nurtured by Lewis in his autobiographical writings – to categorize the lesser-known artists in the group as obedient disciples following meekly in the path of their self-proclaimed leader. 'The leader legend originates in Lewis's Vorticist Manifesto', Roberts declared angrily; 'and that belongs to journalism, not painting.'[1] Reacting fiercely against the suggestion that he and his erstwhile companions were mere ciphers, Roberts actually went so far as to assert that 'with Etchells we might even find that Lewis was the recipient of a slight "Impact" '.[2] On the evidence of surviving work, it is doubtful whether this claim is justified: Etchells was too wayward as an artist to exert a stylistic influence on anyone else. The paintings and drawings which he executed in 1913 were caught indecisively between the Bloomsbury sensibility and a desire to put the lessons of Cubism to good use; and his contributions to *Blast No. 1* were notable for their indebtedness to Continental precedents.

Other 1914 paintings which have since been lost may, however, have countered the present-day impression that Etchells lagged behind his contemporaries in the search for an independent alternative to the European avant-garde. The untraced pictures called *On Board Ship*, *Still Life* and *Houses at Dieppe* which were included in his contributions to the first London Group show in March 1914 may, for instance, have been more radical. For Rutter recorded in his review of the exhibition that Etchells' work was as advanced as Bomberg's, and he described how both men 'obviously make use of their own arbitrary conventions of form as an exercise to build up patterns which please them', adding rather grumpily that 'it would be better if all who aimed at non-representational art at once dropped descriptive nomenclature'.[3]

These London Group pictures might well have bridged the yawning stylistic gulf which separates Etchells' *Blast No. 1* illustrations from his fully Vorticist drawings like *English Comedian*, where the ineloquent anarchy of *Patchopolis* has given way to a precise essay in abstract geometry. The transition is dramatic and total. At first glance, it looks as if Etchells has exchanged the mannered, eccentric personality so evident in an earlier painting like *The Dead Mole* for deliberate anonymity: it seems impossible to detect any significant difference between this composition and a similar abstraction by one of his allies. The vocabulary is identical, with Lewisian window shapes, diagrammatic structures formed out of angular lines and the emphatic diagonal inclination of the principal mass. But then, just as the drawing is about to be enlisted as proof of Etchells' willingness to bury his former identity in the interests of a collective endeavour, odd quirky details come to the fore. The comedian's face appears, drawn in a profile as elegant and witty as a Cocteau head, on the top of the block pointing towards the upper right corner. Its presence subtly alters the whole design, prompting the suspicion that this rigid network of ink contains references to a mechanistic figure, and that Etchells enjoyed the freedom Vorticist abstraction gave him to indulge his taste for whimsy and caprice in a more sober, veiled form. While Lewis transformed his *Englishwoman* and Roberts his *St George*, Etchells typically chose to subject a more comic national archetype to the same forbidding treatment, turning him from a cheerful entertainer into a computerized automaton.

There may even be a figurative intent lurking somewhere in the lively organization of a gouache called *Stilts*, but this time abstraction triumphs altogether and Etchells restricts himself to an impersonal group of mechanical components.[4] Indeed, if it were not for the signature inscribed so clearly on the picture, it

Frederick Etchells
English Comedian, 1914–15

Frederick Etchells
Gouache: Stilts (?), 1914–15

would be difficult to distinguish this design from related works by other English rebels. The repetition of ascending L shapes lends *Stilts* a definite character, and there is a certain wayward passivity about the formal disposition that marks it out from the forcible, compact arrangements created by Roberts, Lewis or Wadsworth. There is also, alongside this element of compositional wandering so especially noticeable in the straggling forms extending across from the upper right corner, a similar diffidence in the use of colour. While the scarlet of the L shapes is just as fiery as its equivalent in *Red Duet*, the discretion of the background's muted green and brown suggests that Etchells felt uneasy about employing all the aggressive colours which his fellow-rebels favoured. Although *Stilts* is in many ways an admirable design, its ambivalent qualities suggest that Etchells excluded some of his essential self from such non-representational experiments.

If the extreme paucity of his Vorticist works did not preclude definitive judgements about his achievements, it would be tempting to decide that Etchells never really found himself as a creative personality. There is a disconnected quality in the limited number of pre-war paintings and drawings that have survived from his hand: they do not add up to a convincing whole in the way that Lewis's Vorticist œuvre does. No individual vision informs the progress of his work from the Borough Polytechnic murals onwards, and even an admirer like Pound was forced to admit in September 1914 that 'Mr Etchells still remains more or less of a mystery'. All that the American poet could find to say about him was the cryptic comment that 'he is on his travels, whence he has sent back a few excellent drawings'.[5] The implication was that Etchells, potentially a fine Vorticist, was searching rather than finding, and simply not producing enough to form a coherent corpus of work. The artist himself later testified to his irregular, dilettante way of life when he recounted how 'I would paint a picture, sell it and then rush off to Paris and have a roaring time for three or four months on the proceeds'.[6] Such a carefree approach to art is not calculated to yield sustained results – it is surely symptomatic that Etchells displayed only two items in the Vorticist Exhibition 'Picture' section, whereas all the other members sent in four each – and it must remain questionable whether the recovery of his lost contributions to the Doré show would greatly enhance his reputation.

The only description which survives to hint at the likely appearance of one of these paintings, *The Pigeon-Juggler*, simply mentions that it possessed 'great vitality' and 'charming gradations of tone'.[7] But a poorly exposed photograph of the picture does afford more evidence, and shows that Etchells filled his modestly proportioned canvas with the jerking limbs of a Vorticist marionette.[8] The figure, his mechanistic legs bent slightly as he strains to perform his trick, throws his arms out at contrasting right-angles to either side. He is flattened into a schematic, frontal pose which increases the robot-like character of his movements, and the pigeons fluttering above his head have become equally geometric segments of angular form. The only real manifestation of Etchells' quirky personality lies in the choice of subject-matter: its whimsical bias almost contradicts the severity of the style, and could never have been chosen by any other member of the rebel group. It is, moreover, a markedly figurative work, despite all the formal simplifications; whereas nothing now exists concerning his other Doré Galleries exhibit – *Painting* – to indicate whether it too avoided total abstraction.

The very anonymity of its title does, however, suggest that *Painting* might have been closer in style to a drawing called *Progression*, which was illustrated in *Blast No. 2* along with *Hyde Park*. It is his most pleasing and restrained design, based on the unifying motif of repeated triangles. There is activity in

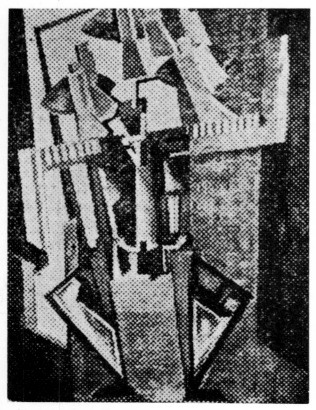

Frederick Etchells
The Pigeon-Juggler, c. 1915

Frederick Etchells
Drawing of *Progression*, 1914–15

Frederick Etchells
Watercolour of *Progression*, 1914–16

Progression, and considerable change; but no positive attack. And even when the artist afterwards decided to wash in his drawing with watercolour, creating tonal combinations as unconventional as Roberts' *Twostep*, the result is notable for its mellow restraint.[9] Indeed, both versions of *Progression* represent the sturdiest bridgehead Vorticism can throw forward to the second phase of abstract art in England. Neither picture is so very far removed from the measured equilibrium of a characteristic thirties abstraction like Cecil Stephenson's 1937 *Painting*, which displays a similar confidence in the self-sufficiency of a few controlled formal elements organised in a calm horizontal configuration across the picture-surface. It is most unlikely that Stephenson was aware of Etchells' native precedent for his own efforts, and *Progression* does contain pockets of dynamic energy and an overall sculptural solidity which the *Painting* consciously excludes. But the fact remains that Stephenson inherited the Vorticists' involvement with machine imagery and even gave two of his own paintings – executed in 1939 and the following year respectively – the specific title *Vortex*. So Etchells' avoidance here of Vorticism's normal combative stance makes *Progression* an ideal pointer towards the interconnections between the rebels of 1914 and their successors in England twenty years later.

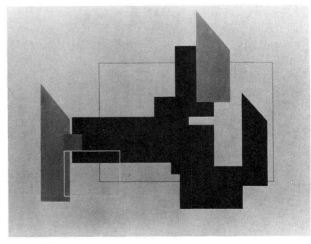

Cecil Stephenson
Painting, 1937

Cuthbert Hamilton
Group, 1913–14

Pablo Picasso
The Accordionist (Pierrot), 1911

The same conclusion could hardly be reached about the lost picture that Cuthbert Hamilton contributed to *Blast No. 1*. It was entitled *Group*, and appears from the photograph reproduced in the Vorticist journal to be a brutally simplified treatment of the human figure.[10] Hamilton cares not a jot for traditional sensibilities, scoring his jagged contours onto the canvas without any regard for felicities of draughtsmanship and smearing his colours as a calculated snub to painterly values. He had not improved his manners since the days of Rutter's show in the autumn of 1913, when Clive Bell classified him as a 'painter who goes out of his way to be ugly'.[11] And if *Group* is compared with a Cubist painting like Picasso's *The Accordionist (Pierrot)* of 1911 – which strips the figure down to a similar series of angular outlines – it is at once apparent that Hamilton is fulfilling Vorticist ideals by substituting the calm stability of Cubism for explosive violence. While Picasso maintains an austere, meditative equipoise, Hamilton declares his appetite for destruction by giving his forms an extrovert flamboyance with which Cubism's analytic desire to render full three-dimensional reality on a flat surface was never concerned.

The slap-happy extremism of *Group* whets an appetite for Hamilton's work that is doomed to remain unsatisfied: none of his paintings has been traced, and he did not contribute anything else to either issue of *Blast*. Moreover, the lamentable dearth of his pictures is echoed by the strange way in which he gradually ceased to involve himself in official exhibitions. After he had shown no less than five pictures at the 'Cubist Room' in December 1913 – two *Heads*, a *Bust*, a *Nude Figure* and *Interior, Soho* – and then sent in *Two Figures* and *Waterloo Bridge* to the first London Group exhibition, Hamilton mysteriously disappeared from public view. His signature was printed at the end of the Vorticist Manifestos, but he was not represented at the Whitechapel's comprehensive survey of rebel art in May; nor, the following March, did he display his work at the second London Group show. And when the Vorticist Exhibition was finally mounted, he disengaged himself so successfully from any form of collective participation that he did not even appear in the 'Invited to Show' section. If, therefore, the loss of Hamilton's work makes him into a shadowy figure hovering on the fringes of the group, he seems to have encouraged this image by deliberately opting out of rebel circles after the publication of *Blast No. 1*. The man whom Bomberg was moved to describe as 'a natural born painter'[12] will doubtless always remain the enigma of the movement.

So will Lawrence Atkinson, whose support for the Great English Vortex likewise evaporated after his first flush of enthusiasm had manifested itself at the Rebel Art Centre. By the time he reluctantly agreed to hang three pictures, each simply listed as *Painting*, in the 'Invited to Show' section of the Vorticist Exhibition, the memory of that signature printed in *Blast No. 1* must have begun to rankle. In the same year, after all, he published a volume of poetry called *Aura*, thereby reiterating a Faustian desire to extend his creative interests in as many directions as possible. And such a man – writer, singer, musician as well as artist – could never have been more than momentarily content to associate himself with a movement dominated so forcefully by the personalities of others. Although his untraced early paintings bore the imprint of many different influences, he appears to have consistently distanced himself from the example of his friends, as if determined all the while to appraise their achievement and only extract what he considered to be worthwhile in terms of his personal development. So much is made clear in Horace Shipp's monograph on the artist, published in 1922 when Atkinson had finally established himself as a non-representational painter and sculptor. 'He has passed through phases of discipleship to many other schools', wrote Shipp, 'and one can find among his works, pieces inspired by the practice of Impressionists, Fauvistes, Cubists, Simultanists.' But at the same time, Shipp was at pains to stress his subject's 'personal method of art education', explaining that 'to Atkinson these movements existed only inasmuch as their results came to him and convinced him of their value. His art study was conducted in the great galleries all over Europe, and by passing contact with the minds of contemporary artists. All the time he was thus travelling, bringing the art of the past and the present to the test of his own individual vision, he was practising expression in every medium and within the theories of every school which presented itself to his notice and seemed to offer what he sought'.[13]

The complete loss of Atkinson's pre-1914 work makes it impossible either to confirm or refute this eulogy to his independent spirit, and it is equally difficult to tell when it was that he decided to let art take precedence over his other multifarious interests. Did his involvement with the activities of Great Ormond Street coincide with a decision to reject the attractions of literature and music? Shipp's rambling and woolly essay does not provide an answer, contenting itself with the strange statement that 'Atkinson has deliberately chosen to express himself in the graphic and plastic arts because he realises the danger of the sensuous appeal of music as a power which holds the mind as he would say "to earth". He has always aimed at a medium and a method which would prove transparent, revealing clearly the non-materiality'.[14] The passage would have made strange reading to Pound, who constantly emphasized that music was the medium towards which all art should ideally aspire, and began his 'Vorticism' article in *The Fortnightly Review* by quoting Whistler's 'self-evident' assertion that 'it is no more ridiculous that a person should receive or convey an emotion by means of an arrangement of shapes, or planes, or colours, than that they should receive or convey such emotion by an arrangement of musical notes'.[15] In common with most avant-garde theorists of the time, Pound considered that music should be envied for its purely abstract nature, and emulated precisely because it existed untrammelled by any descriptive considerations. But to Atkinson, a man described by Shipp as 'in the greatest sense of the word . . . a mystic', painting contained the potential to surpass music. Accordingly, he abandoned the wilful eclecticism of his early period and, possibly galvanized by the experiments of his temporary allies at the Rebel Art Centre, formulated a style which Shipp considered to be 'a phase of directed Cubism'.[16]

At some stage during the course of 1914, Atkinson finally shook off the teachings he had imbibed in Paris at Fergusson's *La Palette* and, as Shipp recorded, 'found that the structural values in an object interested him more than the merely decorative ones'. As a result, he concerned himself exclusively 'with structure and the relationship of the planes and masses, but always with a view to what they revealed rather than merely what they were. He saw, for instance, in an object certain directions of growth, certain potentialities of movement; he saw forces which thwarted that growth or influenced it; dynamics which curbed or accentuated the lines of movement; he saw masses which affected the balance, and he saw too the reactions between an object and its environment'.[17] All these considerations are plainly evident in the strongest of Atkinson's two surviving paintings, the so-called *Painting*, which might conceivably have been one of his contributions to the Vorticist Exhibition.[18] For despite its minimalism, there are clear indications in this richly coloured picture of a standing figure, leaning forwards in a familiar diagonal towards the top left corner as it strides across the surface, even if most of the body has disappeared into the fabric of lines and colours which Atkinson has evolved as a means of reducing his theme to its lowest common denominator. The method derives ultimately from the most 'hermetic' period of Cubism: Picasso's most abstract

Lawrence Atkinson
Painting, c. 1914–18

△ Lawrence Atkinson
Painting, c. 1914–18

▷ Lawrence Atkinson
Abstract Composition, c. 1914–15

period in 1910 produced works which obscure their figuration far more than Atkinson. But Picasso was unhappy with such an extreme divorce from the reality of a model, whereas Atkinson prefers to start with an idea rather than a motif in his studio. For all its abstraction, Cubist work still relates to a specific experience witnessed by the artist, while *Painting* is a far more generalized account of intellectual ideas about the interaction between a figure and its surroundings. 'Atkinson realizes that an object does not exist to itself alone, but that it is affected by its environment and in turn reacts towards it', wrote Shipp. 'Environment is thus given emotional as well as a structural value. This element of what he has called "spatial accordancy" is one which is of profound importance in his work.'[19]

When, therefore, the identifiable sections of the figure in *Painting* merge with planes that seem to represent no particular image, Atkinson can be seen translating his awareness of environmental forces into pictorial terms. But another element, derived this time from Futurism, is put into action in the upper half of the picture, where a series of slender forms are virtually repeated as they glide up towards the top. Their motion proves the accuracy of Shipp's declaration that Atkinson utilized 'the Futurist tenet that the single point of time was an arbitrary restriction, having been accepted by the necessities of representational art but possessing of itself no fundamental aesthetic value'. The forms in the top section of *Painting*, however, contain no suggestion of the Futurists' blurred subjectivity. They are bounded by thin, dry contours that clearly separate one shape from the next, just as Vorticism demanded. And Shipp testified to this when he pointed out that Atkinson's use of simultaneity concentrated exclusively 'upon one object, and the time element was allowed to intrude only because movement was so much an essential to the object in question that presentation of it demanded the suggestion of its progress'.[20] Lewis and the other rebels would have agreed with such an approach, and its presence in *Painting* helps to explain why Atkinson consented to ally himself with them during his Rebel Art Centre days.

Whether the Vorticists would have approved of the other Atkinson painting surviving from this period is open to doubt, however.[21] For despite the systematic and coolly deliberate way in which every element in the composition has been reduced to a minimal plane of restrained grey, brown or pink, its origins as a still life remain clear. In other words, it embraces precisely the kind of domestic theme which *Blast* was at pains to blame Cubism for prolonging, even if the objects concerned have here been transformed into an almost sculptural presence, elongated, sharp-pointed and faintly menacing. Not until the 1930s, when Ben Nicholson took the genre even further towards abstraction, would English painting dare treat a still life as summarily as Atkinson does in this gentle but at the same time skeletal work. The hesitancy of its brushwork and construction is part of its attraction, preventing it from becoming too schematic or drily resolved. But such delicate virtues placed him apart from the other rebels, and Atkinson's decision to employ this sacrilegious motif is a measure of the divide separating him from the group he chose to leave when it came to participating in the Vorticist Exhibition.

Atkinson's temporary underlying kinship with his fellow rebels is, however, firmly revealed in the large crayon *Abstract Composition*, which builds up its assemblage of mechanistic forms into a monumental pyramid.[22] Of all his extant works, this picture is the most related to the vocabulary employed by the other rebels: the elongated shapes stretching across the lower right corner are topped by sharply beaked heads that recall Lewis's *Enemy of the Stars* drawing, even if figurative connotations play only a minor part in the overall conception of the design. Atkinson piles girder upon girder until a structure as implacable as

Lewis's Vorticist cityscapes has been evolved; but his use of abstraction conveys neither the violence nor the industrial connotations implicit in Lewis's contemporaneous work. For *Abstract Composition* employs soothing, almost pastoral colours: a pale lime in the background acts as a foil to a discreet blend of bleached ochres, greys, whites and umbers. They harmonize the picture, and make it ingratiating rather than openly aggressive – a far cry from the startling tonal contrasts which the Vorticists liked to exploit. This is the distinctive quality in Atkinson's temperament which marks him out from his allies, a refined delicacy that prompted Shipp to summarize his work as 'fundamentally beautiful and appealing, dealing only occasionally with unlovely facts, expressing

Lawrence Atkinson
Abstract Composition, c. 1914–16

almost invariably the deeply pleasing things and emotions'.[23] Such a man was
bound to be only momentarily involved with a movement dedicated to upheaval
and destruction. While the Vorticists vented their spleen on a hostile and reactionary public by charging their work with pictorial acid, Atkinson retired into
an ethereal world where earthly passions were negated and a puritanical desire
to meditate on aesthetic fundamentals asserted itself.

This fanatical degree of self-abnegation was hardly calculated to endear him
to a cause associated above all with exclamatory displays of defiance. Atkinson
possessed an unworldly reserve that automatically placed him outside the main
impulses of the movement; and it resulted in personal designs like *Abstract
Composition*, which transforms all the outward characteristics of the Vorticist
style into a shy, retiring, even poetic affair.[24] Where the explosive diagonals and
jagged fragments of an urban architecture suggest an *active* portrayal of the
dynamism inherent in modern life, Atkinson's quiet colours produce a *reflective*
interpretation. It would be an irredeemably schizophrenic picture if the strain
of dreaminess did not seep through into the very character of the enclosing lines:
they are as unassertive as the tonal orchestration, drawn with a cautious whisper
which completely contradicts the scabrous vigour of mainstream Vorticist art.
Lewis could hardly have been in sympathy with such a temperament for very
long; and Atkinson, for his part, can be seen in the process of moving away from
the group's spirit in a watercolour of *The Lake* that must terminate his links
with the rebel aesthetic.

Presented by the artist to Shipp himself in 1921, but possibly executed some
years earlier, the composition can be read – like certain Vorticist works – as an
aerial view. Atkinson has departed so radically from his subject that a literal
interpretation is inadvisable: the title is a positive obstruction, in fact, and
hinders any enjoyment of the work on the purely abstract, subconscious level
that Atkinson cherished. 'He holds that the artist also is most likely to fulfil his
function by releasing his mind from the obsession of the conscious and working
at the dictates of these forces deep down within us all', Shipp wrote, affirming
Atkinson's belief that 'generations of race knowledge have led us to give a
certain definite value and meaning to various forms'. And yet in *The Lake*
this reliance on the subconscious, which Atkinson derived not from Kandinsky
but 'the teachings and theories of Goethe and of his disciple Rudolf Steiner',
clashes uncomfortably with the desire to cling fast to a descriptive theme. The

Lawrence Atkinson
The Lake, c. 1914–18

picture is in no sense a straightforward landscape, and neither is it a liberated metaphor like the best Vorticist designs. It is a halting compromise, both cerebral and bloodless, and serves as a reminder that Atkinson could sometimes dissipate his talents in a wan form of refinement. Even Shipp admitted as much, when he wrote of 'this second period' that 'his work suffered occasionally from . . . over-sophistication and too great a reliance upon its intellectual quality. In the most experimental stage in the work of almost any artist there will usually be a period when his own concentration upon art will lead him to assume that his fellows and those who see his pictures are thinking with his mind. It was the recognition of this error, and of its limiting effect upon his language as a painter, alongside of his growing conception of the bases of art, which led Lawrence Atkinson to the third period – that of Pure Abstraction'.[25] By that time, Pound had dismissed him as a 'bad imitator'[26] of Lewis, the war was over, and Atkinson had severed whatever links remained to connect him with Vorticist principles. He deserves a place in the history of English rebel art because he shared, for an instant, the group's independent stand against the challenge of Cubism and Futurism. But his signature was little more than a passing token: like Bomberg and Epstein, he was at once too isolated an individual and too proud to commit himself to a communal endeavour.

The female members of the movement, by contrast, were only too delighted to place themselves at the disposal of Lewis's most egotistical interests. Goldring could not contain his amusement when he recalled that, during the *Blast No. 1* inaugural tea party, 'Jessie Dismorr, an advanced painter and poetess whom I had met a year or two earlier in Provence . . . was ordered by the Master, after a counting of heads, to get tea for us. She obeyed, with as much promptitude as I used to obey my guru'.[27] Her loyalty to Lewis was afterwards defined by her close friend R. H. M. Ody as based on a respect for his standing 'as leader of this radical new movement'; and Mr Ody was convinced that, 'from what I know of her character, the relationship was purely platonic, and on his side partly commercial'.[28] But Lewis undoubtedly gave encouragement to Dismorr as well, going out of his way to tell her in a 1915 letter that 'you are unconvincingly modest about your work'.[29] And he had good reason for his praise, for Mr Ody explained that Dismorr personified 'the Edwardian phenomenon of the New Woman', to whom 'the Declaration of the Rights of Woman proclaimed in *Howards End* . . . would have appealed'. She apparently 'possessed all [Forster's] novels',[30] and took their liberated sentiments to dramatic extremes: Kate Lechmere remembered the sensation that was caused 'when Dismorr decided one day to take off all her clothes in the middle of Oxford Street'.[31] Indeed, so unpredictable was her behaviour that Etchells later described her as being 'always a bit dotty – she used to go on the whole time about what she called "the hole of birth"'.[32] Mental illness did, unfortunately, dog her at various times throughout her life.

In view of this controversial reputation, it comes as something of a surprise – not to say an anticlimax – to find her executing work as disciplined as the tiny *Design* illustrated in *Blast No. 2*. If Dismorr was under the spell of Lewis's personal charisma, the language employed in this drawing shows her to have been stylistically indebted to him as well. The hatched shading, the cage structure and the vertiginous pattern of thrusting diagonals all relate clearly to Lewis's 'Sketch-Book' designs, although the nervous subtlety of Lewis's handling has given way to a schematized clarity that borders on the banal. Dismorr deliberates so ponderously over each stroke of the pen, and explains each section of her picture with such heavy-handed care that the effect is finally one of naïvety. It would be easy to dismiss *Design* as a second-rate pastiche of other artists' ideas,

were it not for the presence in *Blast No. 2* of some poetry and prose by Dismorr which demonstrate a personal feeling for the geometrical power of her urban environment. 'Gigantic cubes of iron rock are set in a parallelogram of orange sand', she wrote of the British Museum in 'London Notes'. 'Ranks of black columns of immense weight and immobility are threaded by a stream of angular volatile shapes. Their trunks shrink quickly in retreat towards the cavernous roof.' The short sentences, as curt and abrupt as the organization of *Design* itself, prove that Dismorr did genuinely apprehend the character of her surroundings in terms of Vorticist abstraction. 'Towers of scaffolding draw their criss-cross pattern of bars upon the sky, a monstrous tartan', she wrote in her 'Notes' on Piccadilly. 'Delicate fingers of cranes describe beneficent motions in space.' And in a description of Fleet Street, she helped to account for the rebels' obsession with the meaning contained in their diagrammatic drawings when she pointed out how 'curiously exciting are so many perspective lines, withdrawing, converging; they indicate evidently something of importance beyond the limits of sight'.[33]

It comes as a disappointment, after the sensitivity of these written observations, to find Dismorr executing a design as wilfully crude as *The Engine*, which was also illustrated in *Blast No. 2*.[34] Once again, she juxtaposes a few broadly defined, simple forms, avoiding the often bewildering complexity of her fellow-

△ Wyndham Lewis
Composition I, 1915

◁ Jessica Dismorr
Design, c. 1915

Jessica Dismorr
The Engine, c. 1915

Jessica Dismorr
Abstract Composition, c. 1914–15

members' work. And for the second time, the final product seems oddly feeble-minded. Despite the undeniably dramatic presence of the huge arrow-shape rising up from the left, all the potential tension oozes out of a composition that is too slack to have any concerted impact. There is no structural unity to bind the various segments together into a whole: instead, they dwindle and fall apart, partially dissipating the instantaneous shock administered to the senses by the black arrow.

Could it be that a feminine temperament was congenitally incapable of sustaining the amount of aggression needed to create a convincing Vorticist work of art? This male chauvinist hypothesis might seem tenable when Dismorr's *Abstract Composition* is examined, a picture which may have been one of her four contributions to the Vorticist Exhibition. They were listed in the catalogue as *Shapes, Interior, Movement* and *Design*, titles which suggest that she had by this stage abandoned all representational intentions. A translation of Kandinsky's treatise *On the Spiritual in Art* came into her possession in 1914,[35] which may have helped her to embrace the full implications of abstraction; but the painting itself is also strangely reminiscent of Bomberg's *The Mud Bath*. For both pictures set sculptural configurations into motion around a vertical column, even if Dismorr injects none of the knife-edge vitality of Bomberg's masterpiece into her sluggish mechanisms. They have the largeness of form which characterized *The Engine* and *Design*, relying to a similar extent on a few broad masses and dispensing with intricate detail altogether. No more than half-a-dozen shapes circulate in this undefined spatial area, and the black background sets them off with far greater intensity than the *Blast No. 2* drawings achieved. But the arrangement still appears dangerously rudimentary, and the colours Dismorr has chosen to enliven her cumbersome forms – muted pinks, greens, and purples – make the painting tasteful, almost chic in feeling.

And yet, when she tried to put the mechanical imagery of *Abstract Composition* into words by equating her own body with a machine, the result was as brutal as the most uncompromising of Lewis's designs. In a poem called 'Monologue', published in *Blast No. 2*, she puts the obsession with the 'hole of birth' that Etchells remembered into stern practice:

My niche in nonentity still grins –
I lay knees, elbows pinioned, my sleep mutterings blunted against a wall.
Pushing my hard head through the hole of birth
I squeezed out with intact body.
I ache all over, but acrobatic, I undertake the feat of existence.
Details of equipment delight me.
I admire my arrogant spiked tresses, the disposition of my perpetually
      foreshortened limbs,
Also the new machinery that wields the chains of muscles fitted beneath
      my close coat of skin.
On a pivot of contentment my balanced body moves slowly.[36]

The poem seems to enact the creation of a new human species, the kind of robot that Lewis had imagined so often in his drawings. And the 'pivot of contentment' could almost be a verbal equivalent for the movement portrayed in *Abstract Composition*, where fragments of 'the new machinery' float in a collected equilibrium around the erect pillar, implying that Dismorr could only achieve personal and creative satisfaction at this period by taking on the attributes of the machine world outlined in *Blast*.

If, therefore, Dismorr never succeeded in matching the finest pictorial achievements of the other Vorticists, she did manage to express her own individual vision through verse and prose; and in one picture, called *Landscape*, she showed her true mettle by constructing an impregnable fortress out of the picturesque motif of a mountain. This pen and wash study for a now destroyed painting outlines a monumental mass of geometry, as if the dwelling-place of the mechanistic race described in 'Monologue' had been cut in half to reveal a cross-section of its insides. The structure stands rigid, defined with immense plasticity by the pen-nib Dismorr has used to etch out its contours. It rises up from the ground like some immense theatrical flat, a fitting backdrop for an implacable play enacted by Vorticist automatons. And its emphatic sense of order links up yet again with another of Dismorr's written contributions to *Blast No. 2*, a brief story entitled 'June Night'. A parable of the artist's own conversion from Fauvism to Vorticism, it describes how the heroine suddenly decides to refuse

Jessica Dismorr
Landscape: Edinburgh Castle (?), *c*. 1914–15

the 'romantic' overtures of her lover Rodengo, realizing that 'cool normality and classicalism tempt me'. She escapes from him and takes a nocturnal walk through London, a 'wander in the precincts of stately urban houses'. Before long, these buildings come to symbolize her change of heart. 'Moonlight carves them in purity. The presence of these great and rectangular personalities is a medicine. They are the children of colossal restraint, they are the last word of prose. (Poetics, your day is over!) In admiring them I have put myself on the side of all the severities. I seek the profoundest teachings of the inanimate. I feel the emotion of related shapes. Oh, discipline of ordered pilasters and porticoes! My volatility rests upon you as a swimmer hangs upon a rock.'[37] It is surely not too fanciful to view *Landscape* as Dismorr's most successful attempt to create her own visual embodiment of the 'colossal restraint' she so passionately admired; and if it is identical with the drawing Dismorr executed around then of *Edinburgh Castle*, she here succeeded in reducing a picturesque, romantic motif to a classical structure which bears out the resolve dramatised in 'June Night'.[38]

Helen Saunders, however, seems to have reserved her most unqualified admiration not so much for Vorticism as for the personal charms of its official spokesman. 'Both Dismorr and Saunders were very delightful girls', Etchells recalled, 'but Saunders was completely potty about Lewis. If Lewis had painted Kate Greenaway pictures, Saunders would have done them too: she had a schoolgirl "pash" on him.'[39] Saunders herself afterwards testified to her quietness and passivity in Lewis's company when the Vorticist circle met for Monday suppers in Soho. She confessed that her friend Harriet Weaver 'was as silent in "company" as I was myself, and I can't remember anything that either of us said!'[40] But perhaps her awed devotion to Lewis led to a clash with Dismorr, for Saunders told her fellow-paintress in November 1915 that 'I am very sorry for the detestable spirit that has been behind some of my conduct to you – I have done the right thing but with (sometimes) an evil spirit – it would have been better if I had done the wrong thing under those circumstances'.[41]

There may, possibly, have been friction between the two women over Saunders' collaboration with Lewis on the murals for the dining-room at the Restaurant de la Tour Eiffel in the summer of 1915. Indeed, for an artist as egotistical as Lewis to have allowed another hand to work with him on such a project argues that Saunders was willing to lose some of her own creative identity and obey the dictates of her hero: Lewis would never have agreed to the intrusion of a separate personality in a commission which he knew would be appraised as his achievement. But this supposed subservience cannot be proved for certain. Nothing survives of the Tour Eiffel's 'three abstract panels'; and the trio of designs presented to the Tate Gallery many years later by Saunders' sister are by no means rehashed copies of Lewis's style, even though their former owner considered that they probably all dated from the period when the Restaurant scheme was being executed.[42]

One of them, an *Abstract Multicoloured Design*, actually appears to bear the imprint of Orphism over and above its primary debt to Lewis. The burgeoning repetition of semi-circles around the central area of the picture recalls the disc motif which had become the hallmark of Robert Delaunay's art two years before.[43] And Saunders' rather uncontrolled use of a variety of watercolour washes – an extraordinary mixture which throws together ice blue, green, ochre, crimson, cosmetic pink and peach with little sense of pictorial cohesion – echoes Robert Delaunay's belief that he could create movement in space solely through colour variations. 'In purely coloured painting it is colour itself which by its interplay, interruptions and contrasts forms the framework, the rhythmic development, and not the use of older devices like geometry', he insisted. 'Colour is form and subject.'[44] To Delaunay, Saunders' picture could still have appeared to be an essentially linear work that depended for its effect upon 'older devices like geometry', in spite of its indebtedness to his formal vocabulary. For Saunders has aimed at an odd compromise between two influences, transforming the effulgent orbs of Orphism into the vicious sickles of Vorticism and allowing curvilinear elements to jostle uncomfortably with the more angular shapes of Lewisian derivation. She has attempted a private variation of her own, and ended up with a stylistic mélange that does not entirely cohere. But it does, even so, display an infectious audacity which conveys much of the delight in dissonant colour Lewis recommended in *Blast No. 1*.

Her partiality for a contrast between curves and straight lines receives more convincing expression in the second of these 1915 designs, the *Monochrome Composition with Ascending Figures*. Its swell of semicircles, twisting themselves first to the right and then in a partially fulfilled figure of eight round to the left, are integrated with the abrupt angles of the robot men who dominate the design with their erect diagonal column. Although these blank, expressionless figures use each other's shoulders as a catapult to shoot themselves further into the distance they are still conceived as part of a surface pattern. Smaller

Helen Saunders
Abstract Multicoloured Design, c. 1915

semicircles emblazoned like military uniforms on their torsos emphasize this flatness by linking up with larger counterparts, and the altogether more abstract shapes playing around the column of men likewise ensure that this thrusting pillar does not establish any real spatial recession. A brittle tension is thereby set up between the singleminded directional impetus of the figurative elements, and the one-dimensional play conducted by the abstract elements. It is a forbidding design, sufficiently devoid of feminine sensibility to explain why Lewis found it possible to collaborate with Saunders on the Tour Eiffel decorations, and its vitality comes as a relief after Dismorr's work.

Indeed, both the harshness and the vigour expressed by the picture are given verbal reinforcement in Saunders' poem, 'A Vision of Mud', which was published in *Blast No. 2* and proved that a grim sense of foreboding permeated her view of life. Inspired no doubt by the mounting horror of war, the poem imagines a death caused by slow suffocation in a universal sea of mud, and the only sensations that register on the victim's mind are as startling as the imagery of *Monochrome Composition with Ascending Figures*:

Helen Saunders
Monochrome Composition with Ascending Figures, c. 1915

The drums thud and the fifes pipe on tip-toe.
They are trying to pierce and dart through the thick envelope of the drum's beating.
They want to tear jagged holes in the cloud.
I try to open my eyes a little.
A crowd of india-rubber-like shapes swarm through the narrow chinks.
They swell and shrink, merge into one another like an ashen kaleidoscope![45]

As this extract from the poem implies, Saunders thought in terms of an abstract vocabulary in most of her Vorticist work. For the sounds and forms which threaten to overwhelm her in 'A Vision of Mud' possess the same aggressiveness as the splintered fragments assembled in the third 1915 picture, *Vorticist Composition with Figure in Blue and Yellow*. And this time, the description of human bodies has given way to a work which successfully obscures figurative content in a mass of restless particles. Saunders seems determined to eradicate any kind of repose from her picture, and insists on setting off each separate shape at such a dizzy angle to its neighbour that all approximations to a stable horizontal or vertical are avoided. A fierce animation results, enlivened both by a clear lemon wash singing out from the left side and by the forms at the bottom of the picture which isolate themselves into the movement of dancing legs. But dionysian abandon is never fully achieved: Saunders' execution is a little too gauche and awkward to achieve the requisite amount of panache. In other words, it honourably fails to measure up to the ideals Lewis expounded when he proposed an art that would be 'electric with a more mastered, vivid vitality, which is the conception of their mission held by most of the Vorticists'.[46] *Vorticist Composition with Figure in Blue and Yellow* reaches out for this kind of pictorial energy, yet its hastiness precludes complete success.

The same faults detract from the vitality of *Vorticist Composition with Figure*, another work from this period executed in pencil, indian ink, and watercolour. Saunders has here given the automaton who dominates the picture-surface a greater figurative prominence, allowing his strong diagonal form to merge with the abstract elements surrounding it. There is plenty of energy in the thrusting axes of this design, no less than in the virulent combination of pink, blue, green and yellow washes which Saunders – never afraid of risky tonal oppositions – uses to envenom her linear structure. But if it is examined closely, the fabric of the composition begins to look hurried and ill-considered: shape follows shape almost haphazardly, without any real sense of overall organization, and the

Helen Saunders
Vorticist Composition with Figure, c. 1915

Helen Saunders
Vorticist Composition with Figure in Blue and Yellow, c. 1915

Helen Saunders
Design for a Book Jacket (?), *c.* 1915

careless handling of line only compounds Saunders' failure to do full justice to her original conception.

Perhaps she could only manage to ally intention and execution with complete success when she dispensed with figuration altogether. For although there are hints of a tree form in a *Design for a Book Jacket* carried out around this time, its outstanding impact depends almost entirely on an arrangement of non-representational elements.[47] Saunders uses pink, green, yellow, and black to articulate and reinforce a spare, muscular work which traps its main vertical motif in a mesh of taut forces. Some dive down from the right as if to crush the 'tree' itself, while others lock around its base like a protective cage. The two strain against each other, held in a tense balance by Saunders' ability to overcome her

Helen Saunders
Dance (?), *c.* 1915

weaknesses and compose a picture that now pays as much attention to the whole as it does to the parts. *Design for a Book Jacket* uses this new confidence to transform a shape taken from nature into a mechanistic Vorticist alternative, just as Dorothy Shakespear managed to do in her *Plane Tree* watercolour.

The fact that clear references to gesticulating figures are included in another elaborate watercolour, here titled *Dance*, ought therefore to rule out the possibility of Saunders achieving this hard-won balance once more.[48] But against all the odds, in a design which moves from totally abstract schematic segments to the most frank indication of jumping, waving bodies, the synthesis still holds. This is perhaps the most purely joyful of all surviving Vorticist pictures: despite the menacing implications of the uppermost forms, which extend pincer-like heads in attitudes of aggression towards the figures, the blaring yellow ground provides an ecstatic keynote for the entire design. Floating freely through a spatial area unconfined by any hint of conventional gravity, the dancers perform with an abandon which recalls Roberts' *Twostep* and suggests that Vorticism – so far as Saunders was concerned, at least – reserved a place for human spontaneity within its otherwise depersonalized world.

This world is reasserted in *Vorticist Composition in Green and Yellow*, where

Helen Saunders
*Vorticist Composition in Green and
Yellow, c.* 1915

she uses the classic Vorticist vocabulary of lancing diagonals in a tightly constructed picture which would be unequivocally sombre and bleak without her
singing blend of gouache washes.[49] The various elements do not quite lock together with the finely judged inevitability of the best Vorticist designs, but they
still provide an excellent demonstration of the movement's ability to fuse two
ostensibly opposed qualities in one work. The lines and colours are at once
pressed firmly against each other, so that they mesh into a solid stasis, and
dynamically shooting away from each other with the force of an explosion.
Architectural repose is thereby matched equally against iconoclastic vigour,
amounting together to the ideal union which Lewis defined when he paradoxically asserted that 'the Vorticist is at his maximum point of energy when
stillest'.[50]

The maxim was likewise upheld in the two full-page illustrations Saunders
contributed to *Blast No. 2*, and a tiny preparatory scribble for one of them, the
Island of Laputa, suggests that she needed to take a design through several
painstaking stages before it took on the authority of a definitive Vorticist statement. Squared up in accordance with the method practised by both Bomberg
and Roberts, this little study shows Saunders in private, tempering the harsh
contours of her abstraction with female waywardness. The pen-strokes on the
left are delicately applied, and the main structure is outlined with a diffidence
which implies that Saunders shrank back from absolute rigidity even when her
imagination decreed it to be necessary. This clash of opposing impulses within
herself may help to account for the uncertainties of the 1915 watercolours, but
she resolved them in the *Island of Laputa* by eliminating the sketch's hesitation
by the time she completed the final version.[51]

The fundamental disposition of masses remains identical, and yet every single
line has been straightened out, toughened and redefined in the interests of
maximum clarity. The mess of ink splattered like pointillist dots over the lower
right corner of the preliminary study now becomes a crowd of precise triangles,
graded so carefully that they seem to be falling towards a sedentary heap at the
bottom of the composition. And the hatched area on the left has asserted itself
as a far more positive force than it was in the sketch: instead of being no more
than a quiet foil for the main structure, the strokes now take on a life of their
own as Saunders carves them into the paper and insists that they dazzle the
optical nerves with their jarring movements. Freedom of handling and adventi-
tious charm has everywhere been replaced by a diagrammatic logic fully commensurate with the character of the kingdom described in *Gulliver's Travels*.
Lewis's satirical intelligence would, of course, have found much to admire in
Swift – in one of *Blast No. 1*'s opening manifestos he made sure that the thick
capitals spelt out 'BLESS SWIFT for his solemn bleak wisdom of laughter' –
and he probably passed on this enthusiasm to his female ally.[52] But *Gulliver*
must have been widely appreciated within the rebel circle, for Etchells recalled
that 'Saunders did the drawing and then wanted a title for it, so I suggested the
Island of Laputa from Swift. The names of most Vorticist drawings were added
after they had been finished'.[53] His proposal was singularly apt: all the English
abstractionists would have been delighted with the idea of an island where
geometry, music and mathematics dictate every principle of life. Whereas
Swift wanted to attack the dangers of an uncritical belief in the power of science,
taking the abstracted mentality of the islanders to a horrifying conclusion and
showing how the most inhuman atrocities could be committed in the sacred name
of progressive research, the rebels would have seen Laputa as an amusing parallel
to their own beliefs.

Gulliver might almost be describing the ideal menu for a Vorticist dinner
when he noted how, at a meal on the island, 'in the first Course, there was a

△Helen Saunders
Study for Island of Laputa, c. 1915

◁Helen Saunders
Island of Laputa, c. 1915

Shoulder of Mutton, cut into an Æquilateral Triangle; a Piece of Beef into a Rhomboides; and a Pudding into a Cycloid'. Saunders divides up the geometrical sections of her design with a similarly dogmatic passion, and she must have warmed to a civilization where tailors measure Gulliver's 'Altitude by a Quadrant, and then with Rule and Compasses, described the Dimensions and Out-Lines of my whole Body'. None of the rebels could have failed to feel at home with the conceptual habits of a people whose 'Ideas are perpetually conversant in Lines and Figures. If they would, for Example, praise the Beauty of a Woman, or any other Animal, they describe it by Rhombs, Circles, Parallelograms, Ellipses, and other Geometrical Terms; or else by Words of Art drawn from Musick'. Lewis, frustrated in his desire for an aesthetic revolution, would surely have envied the power of a flying island that could, if its subjects below 'still continue obstinate, or offer to raise Insurrections', resort to literal iconoclasm 'by letting the Island drop directly upon their Heads, which makes a universal Destruction both of Houses and Men'. Obviously, Saunders' design does not depend in any mimetic way on Swift's airborne fortress, which was 'exactly circular' in dimensions; but the cold, metallic character of her Vorticist 'island' accords surprisingly well with Gulliver's description of 'a vast Opake Body . . . the Bottom flat, smooth, and shining very bright from the Reflexion of the Sea below'.

Helen Saunders
*Atlantic City, c.*1915

Vorticism was never concerned with illustration of any kind, and it is significant that the title of Saunders' drawing was only applied after its completion. All the same, it manages to exemplify the literary bias in rebel art, and can now be seen as a ready-made pictorial parallel to Swift's Laputa, an invention that goes a long way to answering Lewis's prayer in the 'Cubist Room' foreword for 'a machine . . . built to fly or kill with'. Now, only eighteen months after Lewis wrote those words, a style had been evolved to embody this ideal, and it was entirely fitting that *Island of Laputa* should have been shown as one of Saunders' contributions to the 'Drawings' section of the Vorticist Exhibition. She displayed no less than four items in the 'Picture' section as well, but of the names listed in the catalogue – *Atlantic City*, *English Scene*, *Swiss Scene*, and *Cliffs* – only a study for the first of these has survived. Like *Laputa*, it was reproduced in *Blast No. 2* where, sandwiched in between Roberts' *Combat* and Wadsworth's *Rotterdam*, it more than held its own as a vigorous example of the mature Vorticist style. The theme is identical with the subject-matter of Lewis's 'Sketch-Book' designs, and Saunders shares not only the vocabulary employed by her mentor but also his iconoclastic attitude towards the city. Huge splinters of form cut through the architectural complex at the centre, but they do not dislodge the static window-shapes arranged in steady horizontals and verticals. Rather do they illuminate the motif, accentuating its dynamism and charging it with an energy that would not otherwise be evident. Jagged cryptograms of lightning flash across the lower right corner, bent not so much on destroying as adding to this generalized summary of industrial power. 'BLESS THE ARABS OF THE ATLANTIC', Lewis had cried in *Blast No. 1*, and *Atlantic City* celebrates the dynamic fervour of those 'BLEAK WAVES' even while it incorporates them in an urban context. Lewis may have dominated Saunders' work, but such a composition proved her eminently capable of fulfilling the tough programme expounded by the Vorticist Manifestos. It ably counterbalances hectic movement with the classical restraint advocated in the theories of Hulme, Pound and Lewis, and shows that she was as fully alive to the frenetic quality of modern city life as she was determined to express it in her art.

Chapter 15: Vorticism in Practice: Gaudier-Brzeska

Despite his instinctive love of wild life in all its manifestations, Gaudier was capable of responding to the stress and pressure of his urban environment as well. Towards the end of his 'Vortex' essay in *Blast No. 1* he compared his own generation of sculptors with the African and Oceanic races and concluded that, just as these primitives had found 'the soil was hard, material difficult to win from nature, storms frequent, as also fevers and other epidemics', so 'WE the moderns: Epstein, Brancusi, Archipenko, Dunikowski, Modigliani, and myself, through the incessant struggle in the complex city, have likewise to spend much energy'.[1]

Apart from providing a useful check-list of Gaudier's sculptural heroes, the passage shows how closely he identified with the other rebels' response to the experience of existing in twentieth-century London. If Lewis likened the capital to a 'modern Jungle', Gaudier's love of archaic art made him take the image further and equate the tomtoms of tribal dances with the roar of contemporary mechanisms. For all the sophistication of his inventions, Man was still forced to pit his strength against the domineering force of an industrial environment; and where the prehistoric artist had expressed his reaction to the world in terms of the chase, drawing its schematized contours on the surface of his cave walls, the Vorticist turned the machine into a similar kind of fetish and made it the centre of his art. 'Early stone-age man disputed the earth with animals', Gaudier explained in his 'Vortex' article. 'His livelihood depended on the hazards of the hunt – his greatest victory the domestication of a few species. Out of the minds primordially preoccupied with animals Fonts-de-Gaume gained its procession of horses carved in the rock. The driving power was life in the absolute.'[2]

And thousands of years later, this same need for a creative 'absolute' inspired Gaudier himself to produce a pastel like *Abstract Composition*, which gives vent to his condition by enacting the 'incessant struggle in the complex city' in terms of line and colour. With its suggestions of engineering spare parts, and an electric combination of lemon, orange and lime, this design brings Gaudier the sculptor close to the iconography of pictorial Vorticism. The rigid geometry of propellers and crank-shafts is married to the curvilinear rhythms of cables and levers; and the picture plays these two different stylistic elements off against each other, alternating constantly between the organic and the mechanical, dynamism and stability. The presence of some strong horizontal and vertical forms is counter-balanced by the freewheeling anarchy of other, far less ordered shapes, while the fluorescent colours add their own subversive contribution to the energy of the whole. It could almost be a portrayal of the modern interaction between humans and machines, expressed in the non-representational language which Gaudier had decided could best convey the zeitgeist of a new century.

His 'Vortex' essay in *Blast No. 1* proves that he had convinced himself of the need for such a radical abstraction by the summer of 1914. Teeming with deliberately controversial theories and an impressively confident grasp of sculptural history, it roams freely through the achievements of the past and judges the style of each successive culture from a purely formal standpoint. Like Clive Bell before him, who had lauded primitive art at the expense of Hellenism and the Renaissance, Gaudier brusquely declared that 'the fair Greek saw himself only. HE petrified his own semblance. HIS SCULPTURE WAS DERIVATIVE his feeling for form secondary. The absence of direct energy lasted for a thousand years'. Better by far to dismiss such an enfeebled imitation of reality and admire 'the HAMITE VORTEX of Egypt', which 'RETAINED AS MUCH OF THE SPHERE AS COULD ROUND THE SHARPNESS OF THE PARALLELOGRAM'.[3]

Every race was submitted to the rigorous scrutiny of a man committed to Vorticism's unyielding principle, and many were found wanting. 'The Indians

Henri Gaudier-Brzeska
Abstract Composition, c. 1914

felt the hamitic influence through Greek spectacles', Gaudier asserted. 'Their extreme temperament inclined towards asceticism, admiration of non-desire as a balance against abuse produced a kind of sculpture without new form perception.'[4] The judgements were incisive, and the English language so trenchantly employed that Pound was forced to 'confess that I read it two or three times with nothing but a gaiety and exhilaration arising from the author's vigour of speech'.[5] The American poet could not fail to respond to the headlong stylistic exuberance of a sentence like 'from Sargon to Amir-nasir-pal men built man-headed bulls in horizontal flight-walk'; and neither can his innate respect for the Renaissance have altogether deterred him from cheering Gaudier's spirited affirmation that the 'VORTEX IS ENERGY! and it gave forth SOLID EXCREMENTS in the quattro e cinquo cento, LIQUID until the seventeenth century, GASES whistle till now. THIS is the history of form value in the West until the FALL OF IMPRESSIONISM'. But now, a fresh generation of rebel artists had returned from this European decadence to abstract fundamentals, selecting and welding the discoveries of the primitive into a supreme synthesis of old and new. 'We have been influenced by what we liked most, each according to his own individuality', Gaudier insisted, 'we have crystallized the sphere into the cube, we have made a combination of all the possible shaped masses – concentrating them to express our abstract thoughts of conscious superiority.'[6]

The claim was as haughty as it was uncompromising, and much of its unflinching determination is reflected in the inflexible structure of *Vorticist Composition*, perhaps the most commanding of all Gaudier's rebel pictures. Strangely enough, his subtle use of pale yellows, orange, dark blue and black here creates a sense of solidity that recalls Bomberg's obsession with palpable volume. The diagrammatic simplicity of the design emphasizes flatness and surface pattern, but the beautifully gradated shading allows depth to coexist at the same time. Forms are suggested as well as described, and even the most dominant tend to fade away into an undefined space where dark shadows take on the significance of the more fully elaborated shapes. Gaudier pulls his crayon across the paper, giving his mechanized components a paradoxically velvet texture that softens these cylinders, tubes and girders into objects of meditative splendour. And the measured tempo of this most classical composition achieves the 'concentrated' quality Gaudier advocated in his 'Vortex' credo: *Vorticist Compositon* has not only 'crystallized the sphere into the cube' – it has also made the compact strength of cubic units inform the framework of a dynamic Vorticist vision. For this drawing steers a marvellously original course between Cubist monumentality and Futurist flux, providing English rebel art with another example of what Lewis described in *Blast No. 2* as 'the reformed and imaginatively co-ordinated impression that is seen in a Vorticist picture'.[7]

Stability and motion are both held together within the confines of one work, just as they are in an emblematic pastel called *Signals*, which replaces the discretion of *Vorticist Composition* with an incandescence of fiery colours. The blades of railway signals, as sharp and aggressive as steel knives, provide the main figurative point of reference; but the experience of a train journey presented here is a comprehensive one that encompasses the circular glare of an engine's headlamps and the undulating contours of its passage through space. Oranges, greens and a deep midnight blue are laid down as hard, undiluted symbols of the lights that would assail the eye during such a journey, and their rawness complies with Pound's insistence on 'the primary pigment'.

Signals takes its place beside all the other Vorticist interpretations of modern industrial life, evincing Gaudier's ability to furnish the movement with paradigms of a world dominated by those 'forms of machinery, Factories, new and

Henri Gaudier-Brzeska
Signals, c. 1914

Henri Gaudier-Brzeska
Vorticist Composition, c. 1914

vaster buildings, bridges and works'[8] which Lewis had recommended as the ideal subject-matter in the *Blast No. 1* manifestos. But when the young sculptor turned away from pictorial activities and addressed himself to his central concern with carving, he eschewed mechanical themes and attempted instead to infuse their formal lessons into the construction of animals and birds. He had been fascinated by wild life ever since he drew a golden eagle's wing on a trip to the Bristol City Museum in 1908; and by 1912 he had begun to pay regular calls on London Zoo to capture the essential outlines of monkeys, wolves, tigers or elephants. The obsession remained with him while his drawing style changed from curvilinear outlines to angular geometry: a swan's serene, galleon-like placidity is evident in every minimal line of one beautiful 1914 study, and the forms of a dog can still be discerned in the ostensibly non-figurative construction of a 1914 *Drawing*, one of his most memorable sketches.

It is difficult, at first glance, to associate this spare arrangement of curves and straight lines with the gentle contours of a domestic pet. There is nothing in the least ingratiating about Gaudier's transformation of his playful motif into a dogmatic summary of skeletal shapes. The distortions are dictated more by the

Henri Gaudier-Brzeska
Swan, 1914

Henri Gaudier-Brzeska
Drawing (of a Dog?), *c.* 1914

internal logic of an imaginative abstraction than any fidelity to the outward appearance of the original subject-matter. Gaudier has moved so far towards an autonomous Vorticist vocabulary that he is interested above all else in producing a formal harmony of notations on the page; and he carefully varies the pressure on his charcoal so that the picture gains as much from the interplay of thick and thin, dark and light lines as it does from its fundamental connection with a dog. 'In Vorticism the direct and hot impressions of life are mated with Abstraction, or the combinations of the Will',[9] Lewis wrote in *Blast No. 2*, and Gaudier's drawing carries out this programme to the letter by forcing its outward theme to conform with the mechanistic imagery of rebel art.

At first, Gaudier was far less willing to accept the full implications of the Vorticist aesthetic when he applied its precepts to the creation of sculpture. His small marble carving of a *Dog*, probably executed at the beginning of 1914 and nicknamed the 'Dachshound' by Sophie Brzeska,[10] retains much of its model's comfortable roundness even as it cuts away the superfluities and arrives at a simplified extract. Gaudier still clings to endearing irregularities: he cannot yet bring himself to regulate every detail of his carving in accordance with the

Henri Gaudier-Brzeska
Dog, c. 1914

geometrical inspiration of the main masses. But he does manage to assert the primacy of his working material, tucking the haunches neatly into the body on one side and wrapping the dog's tail firmly round the other side so that the essential lozenge of the marble is emphasized as an autonomous shape in its own right. The result, for all its austerity, is imbued with much of what Pound described as Gaudier's 'abnormal sympathy with, and intelligence for, all moving animal life, its swiftness and softness'.[11] And yet the debt to Epstein's *Dove* carvings is more explicit here than anywhere else: Pound's assertion that 'Epstein reigned for a time in [Gaudier's] bosom' is borne out in *Dog*, which arrives at the same stylistic compromise between description and abstraction as Esptein's earlier copulating birds had done.

Not that the influence was a permanent one, even in one as young as Gaudier. Fired by the need to strip his subject of all irrelevant associations, he proceeded to cut another – even tinier – block of marble into a stern proclamation of sculptural priorities. The motif this time is a duck, but it has been fashioned with such ruthlessness that the creature it professes to represent has lost all its

Henri Gaudier-Brzeska
Duck, c. 1914

feathery delicacy and become a functional tool. The *Duck*'s head has been transformed into the head of a hammer, whilst its tail has become as hard as a prehistoric flint. And the only markings Gaudier now permits himself to make are strictly geometrical: an eye is summarized in a cursory circle, scratched out roughly in the surface of the marble. It seeks to stress the framework of basic units underlying all things, just as the tiny triangle incised on the tip of the tail echoes the larger triangle formed by the *Duck*'s hind-quarters. The whole body is sliced up into self-sufficient sections of form, with clear divisions separating each one from its immediate neighbours. Gaudier wanted to ensure that his carving was seen as a sum of abstracted parts, over and above its subsidiary role as a mimetic representation of natural life.

Having committed himself to the rebel standpoint in such relatively minor works, the 22-year-old sculptor soon felt confident enough to tackle animal themes on a larger and more ambitious scale. He came into possession of some veined alabaster and decided to carve a complex of *Stags*, completing it in time to exhibit the finished product at the first London Group show in March 1914. The catalogue tacitly acknowledged the strong non-figurative element in the sculpture by listing it simply as an *Alabaster Group*; and Fry, for one, was sufficiently antagonized by its extremism to censure the piece in his review of the exhibition. After praising the much earlier and more naturalistic of Gaudier's contributions – the stone *Maternity* and a marble *Torso* – the Omega leader balked at *Stags* and admitted that he was 'not sure that [Gaudier] is not more inspired by contact with nature than by abstract problems of plastic design'.[12] The complaint was only to be expected, for Gaudier has composed his stags with a freedom that makes them almost impossible to read as identifiable animals. The stern geometry of *Duck* lingers on in the pure almond shape carved into one stag's head to signify an eye, but elsewhere anatomical reality has been dispensed with in favour of an interlocking series of biomorphic shapes. Bellies, legs and antlers are all treated as the swollen parts of an ambiguous whole, and they burgeon mysteriously out of a decentralized composition which avoids any fixed focal point. The eye is forced to travel round the entire mass, searching for a clue with which to interpret the meaning of these huddled, vegetable forms. They appear wilfully to defy analysis, and sprout from their base like natural outcrops of the alabaster itself. Gaudier has obviously decided to follow the

△ Henri Gaudier-Brzeska
Stags, 1914 (photograph from *Blast No. 1*)

◁ Henri Gaudier-Brzeska
Stags, 1914

dictates of the material he uses in his search for an allusive style, part schematic
and part organic, that will resolve his struggle to make form and content more
nearly indivisible. The veins streaking their way across the surface of the
sculpture help him by calling attention to the nature of the medium, and their
pronounced markings transform these recumbent animals into a sensitively
orchestrated conglomeration of flecked pebbles. Indeed, it could be argued that
Gaudier has exploited the abstract potential of this built-in linear camouflage,
which runs like a crazy pink tattoo all over the forms and foils any attempt at a
straightforward representational reading.

It does not do, all the same, to overestimate the bizarre quality of *Stags*. In
his review of the London Group show, Pound contrasted Epstein's 'austere
permanence' with Gaudier's 'abundant and pleasing' personality, concluding
that 'his animals have what one can only call a "snuggly", comfortable feeling,
that might appeal to a child. A very young child would like them to play with,
if they were not stone and too heavy'.[13] For all its proof of stylistic radicalism,
Stags is a gentle work, and its slow-moving somnolence has little in common
with the explosive iconoclasm of most Vorticist art. Small wonder that Lewis
later remembered Gaudier, in the context of the movement, as 'a good man on
the soft side, essentially a man of tradition – not "one of Us" '.[14] And in accordance with his misgivings about the young sculptor, the editor of *Blast* allowed
only a single illustration of Gaudier's work to be reproduced in the first issue of
his magazine: *Stags* itself, carefully photographed from an angle where the
animals' fecund proportions take on the menacing power of boulders.

But Lewis should have reserved his judgement on a man whose ideas developed
with such prolific rapidity in the last year of his life. By the time *Blast No. 1*
appeared in July 1914, Gaudier had gone on to create an image of outright
aggression that went a long way towards satisfying Lewis's impatient demands
for an art of total iconoclasm. He probably took as his cue a small cut brass *Fish*
which he presented to Mrs Kibblewhite 'as a gift to thank her for all that she
had done for him', telling her with a characteristically puckish sense of humour

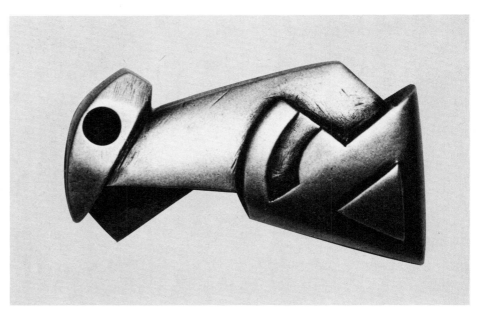

Henri Gaudier-Brzeska
Fish, 1914

that it was 'a little toy to keep in her handbag'.[15] For this diminutive carving, with its sharp, pointed beak and armour-plated flanks, must have encouraged Gaudier to cast around for a combative motif that would justify the warlike appearance of his new breed of mechanical creatures.

Whether Gaudier actually witnessed the dramatic incident he finally chose, perhaps during a walk in one of London's parks, is unknown: he may simply have decided to transpose the viciousness of his *Fish* to a more extended tableau in the privacy of his own studio, relying on memories or a friend's description of the theme. The preliminary wash study for *Bird Swallowing Fish* does not solve the question of the sculpture's origin; for although its swift delineation of the main sculptural idea possesses the spontaneity of a sketch from life, Gaudier has already extracted the essence of the subject and distorted natural forms to suit his own ends. At this stage details like the end of the fish's tail and the bird's beak, which would assume greater importance as the idea developed, are entirely subservient to the summary of an abrupt physical action – in itself a vivid paradigm of Vorticism's insistence on 'the point of maximum energy'. If anything, the balance between the struggling protagonists is tipped too heavily in the fish's favour: it is reduced to a pair of sharp, cutting triangles, whereas the softer, more curvilinear body of the bird seems slightly overwhelmed by the forceful impact of the encounter. Gaudier more than redresses this anomaly in a confident pencil study, which considerably enlarges the bird's bulk and tightens its contours so that the fish assumes rather too passive and contained a role. The structure of all the interlocking components is clarified as well, and purged of any over-reliance on blurred Futurist movement which the wash sketch might easily have encouraged. Not that Gaudier's sharp pencil lines lose sight of the whiplash speed and force with which the bird raises itself up on its legs and dives down to snatch at the victim enclosed in its beak. There is a streamlined efficiency about the manoeuvre that drives home the suddenness of the act, and Gaudier heightens its instantaneous impact by selecting a split second in time. A moment later, the fish will have been swallowed and the bird's back lowered down once more, thereby destroying the heraldic V-shape that dominates the design with the force of an exclamation.

Gaudier attempted to meet the challenge of translating this transitory event into the permanence of sculpture in an elaborate ink drawing, where the precarious poise of the pencil study has given way to a firmly based object, rendered in its full three-dimensional solidity. The thrusting legs have been dispensed

Henri Gaudier-Brzeska
Wash Study for Bird Swallowing Fish, 1914

Henri Gaudier-Brzeska
Pencil Study for Bird Swallowing Fish, 1914

Henri Gaudier-Brzeska
Ink Study for Bird Swallowing Fish, 1914

with, folded neatly back along each side of the bird's body, doubtless because they interfered with the integrity of the main mass; and the two warring halves of the sculpture are freed to rise up into the air, unrestricted by any formal props. Wings have been added as well, to articulate the bareness of the flanks in the earlier drawing, and the bird's cheeks bulge out to accommodate the size of its catch. There is, however, a sluggish element in this drawing: the shapes remain disappointingly earthbound, weighed down by the sheer density of the hatching Gaudier has lavished on their construction. They lack the lightning vitality of the pencil sketch, and dissipate the illusion of merciless swiftness which any portrayal of the subject had to capture. The solution was clear. Somehow, the final carving had to combine the virtues of all the drawings, endowing itself with the sprung tension of the first two while retaining the volumetric significance of the third.

Gaudier set to work on a plaster model, and produced a remarkable synthesis of all the best qualities outlined in the studies. This masterpiece of Vorticist sculpture formalizes the anatomical properties of its two protagonists with such rigidity that most of their recognizable features have completely disappeared. The fish slots into the bird like a key that can only fit one particular lock, and they are wedged together into a single dynamic entity. It is hard, at first, to realize that two separate creatures are depicted rather than a macabre amalgam containing the characteristics of both: they seem indistinguishable from each other, as if the fish was a sinister malignance growing out of the bird's extended beak.

This ambivalence extends through to the very meaning of the act Gaudier has chosen to dramatize. The whole weird operation has been frozen and held up for inspection, so that the most complicated overtones are given full rein. It is no longer a simple matter of one creature consuming another. On the contrary, the fish is not really being devoured at all; it is, rather, ramming itself into the bird's open mouth with all the force at its disposal. The predator's eyes seem to be straining in their sockets, which swell with the effort involved in finding room for this awkward visitor: instead of swallowing, the bird could actually be choking, gorged with the outsize dimensions of a prey he was unwise to chase.

An examination of the sculpture from a lower angle, moreover, shows how equally matched the two combatants are in reality. The fish may be the smaller of the pair, but there is nothing slight about its structure; and its tail sticks up into space like the butt of a weapon, more than balancing the bird's back thrusting itself into an ample triangle at the other end. Both sides shoot down with comparable strength towards the middle, where all the force of the sculpture is concentrated inside the bird's gullet. There the two meet, hidden from view, in a moment of contact that conveys more than a little sexual frisson. Violence and lust are never wholly separable impulses, and Gaudier has exploited this truth in the core of his invention. He has selected the moment of deadlock, when each party is still struggling for survival, and the outcome of this eerie stalemate is still undecided. But despite the tension, there is no hint of a hectic struggle. The dispassionate dictates of Vorticist art ensure that bird and fish have a detached air about them: no emotive expressions, either of fear, greed or hate, are permitted to disturb the unruffled impersonality of the performance. What would normally be a trivial incident, a callous fact of nature, has been metamorphosed through a straitjacket of stiff contours into an intractable ritual. And the belligerence of the formal language found its match in the materials employed: although the original model was carved out of plaster, the catalogue of the 1914 AAA Salon states that *Bird* was first cast in gunmetal.[16] Nothing could have been more appropriate for a sculpture which shows above

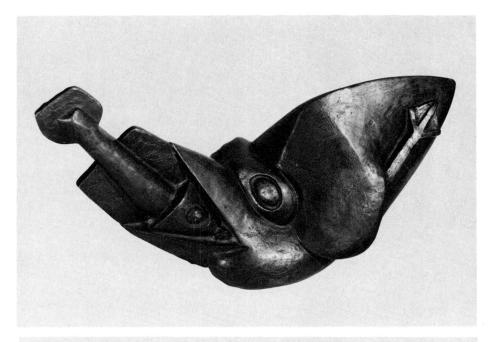

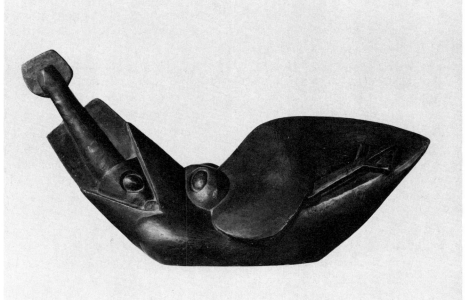

Henri Gaudier-Brzeska
Bird Swallowing Fish, 1914 (two views)

all how Gaudier managed to reconcile his dual involvement with nature and the machine. As Pound explained in 1916, Gaudier's 'long meditation on the relative value of organic and inorganic forms is witnessed by the great number of studies of fishes and birds, in which creatures the division between the two, that is between organic and inorganic forms, is less obvious'.

Even if *Bird Swallowing Fish* now stands as one of Gaudier's supreme achievements, his own imperiously high standards were not wholly satisfied by the finished product. 'Unfortunately', he admitted in his *Egoist* review of the 1914 Salon, 'I now see that had the planes of the wings been convex and the forepart thicker the design would have gained in buoyancy and stateliness.'[17] The last two nouns sum up, with admirable clarity, the two kinds of conflicting ambition embodied in the sculpture, and it is difficult to see how it could have been enhanced by the enlargement of the wings or the fish's half of the composition. An access of bulk might easily have made the work relapse into the kind of bovine sloth represented in the preliminary ink study, and the imbalance between fish and bird could not have been righted without a concomitant loss of tension.

Henri Gaudier-Brzeska
Abstract Figure Drawing, c. 1914

Henri Gaudier-Brzeska
Abstract Design, c. 1914

But Gaudier was restless, always ready to try out new stylistic approaches to the challenge of transforming the wild life that he loved into exactingly original artefacts. Around this time he let himself go completely, and executed a drawing of pure curves and angles so minimal that it is impossible to tell whether animals or humans are caught up in its linear maelstrom. And a wildly executed *Abstract Design* has survived to show this eager appetite for fresh formal solutions in action, smothering the delicate outlines of two gazelles' heads with brusque strokes of watercolour.[18] The gazelles, drawn in the traditional style of Gaudier's earlier period, have been almost completely blotted out by the peremptory contours of an 'animal' constructed according to the rules of rebel art. Crude black washes sweep down the paper, suggesting a snout here and a backside there, while primary colours give the figure a barbaric power which the drawing underneath would never have entertained. The picture symbolizes the drama of Gaudier's conversion from pastoral to radical.

This exhilarating sense of enlarged creative licence found its ultimate expression in the tall limestone carving called *Birds Erect*, the sculpture that marks Gaudier's espousal of near-abstraction.[19] Here, in the summer of 1914, he succeeded in carrying over the full revolutionary daring of studies like *Abstract Design* into a major work, and created a monument to his own extraordinary thirst for experiment. Casting aside the mechanistic rigidity of *Bird Swallowing Fish*, he turned back to the organic vocabulary employed in *Stags*; but this time, he allowed no doubt to exist about the wholly anti-realistic nature of his latest enterprise. When *Stags* was exhibited in the London Group show, Hulme had complained in his *New Age* review that 'the abstractions used do not seem to me to be always thoroughly thought out'.[20] And although the philosopher would never have advocated the use of complete abstraction, it remains true that *Stags* does suffer from a slight confusion of aims. There is no strong demarcation between descriptive and imaginative forms: the presence of a clearly delineated stag's head and body encourages the viewer to seek for the same kind of gentle stylization throughout the sculpture. No such uncertainty is permitted to linger on in the language of *Birds Erect*, however. As if in recognition of his previously divided aims, Gaudier has now rejected all descriptive impulses out of hand and concentrated his attention on the construction of a self-sufficient clump of simplified components. The only clue to the overt representational purpose of the carving lies in its title: these freestanding shapes are indeed 'erect', like a group of birds thrusting out of a nest in readiness for the arrival of food. But there the connection with identifiable reality is cut short; Gaudier wanted to construct an autonomous equivalent to his ostensible theme rather than trying in any way to reproduce an episode from natural life.

At what precise point in the course of 1914 this piece was executed is not known; but it seems likely that Gaudier had it in mind when he prefaced his 'Vortex' essay in *Blast No. 1* with a stern tripartite list of creative precepts:
Sculptural energy is the mountain.
Sculptural feeling is the appreciation of masses in relation.
Sculptural ability is the defining of these masses by planes.[21]
For all three beliefs apply to *Birds Erect* more than any other item in his œuvre, setting out as it does to discover whether enough 'energy', 'feeling' and 'ability' could be expressed in a work that refused to depend for its effect upon a recognizable link with external appearances. The entire burden of the carving rests on Gaudier's personal sensibility: if he could unite the power of a 'mountain' with his feeling for 'masses in relation', and give these qualities eloquent form by 'the defining of these masses by planes', then the result should be able to stand comparison with the best of his figurative sculptures. Accordingly, he started to build a group of upright shapes in the round, determined to produce a primer

Henri Gaudier-Brzeska
Birds Erect, 1914 (two views)

of stone fragments that would vindicate the Vorticist sculptor's right to create, with his fellow-painters, an independent vocabulary which existed outside and apart from the visible world. If Lewis and his other friends could achieve as much on their canvases, he saw no reason why he could not do the same in his chosen medium: as Brodzky later pointed out, possibly remembering Gaudier's own words, ' "Birds Erect" emulates an abstract painting'.[22] But this was not to be a dry, cerebral assertion of theoretical beliefs, a manifesto in limestone. After all, Gaudier had castigated Karl Hagedorn's contributions to the 1914 AAA Salon as 'the worst instance of feelingless abstraction – no emotions; no art', and he would have despised any attempt on his part to produce a lifeless piece of dogma.[23] Moreover, he had to disprove the criticisms of friends like Aldington, who admired his 'beautiful, almost calligraphic line in drawing deer and antelopes', but considered that 'when he worked in stone, all that grace disappeared and he was enslaved by pedantic abstractionist theories'.[24]

No trace of pedantry can be discerned in these crisply articulated segments, grouped together in an ensemble that positively bristles with vitality. Gaudier has set them down on a tall base shaped into four main planes which help to punctuate the continuous movement of the sculpture above and, more importantly, provide an uneven sloping surface for the work to rest on. Another view of the piece shows how the forms have to perch on this severe incline, crowding in on each other as if to save themselves from falling off the edge of a precipice. The instability creates a feeling of tightrope tension: Gaudier is pushing asymmetry as far as he can, in the knowledge that the most exciting composition of 'masses in relation' invariably springs from a willingness to take risks, to shock and surprise. And so he drives his chisel deep into the fabric of the stone, undercutting in layers, carving violent Vorticist diagonals and zigzags into each swaying upright in order to set the whole structure jerking with syncopated motion. The rhythms created by the work as the eye traverses its convoluted, ever-shifting arrangement of surfaces are harsh and jarring. Thick chunks of masonry lean sideways and backwards, sway in to collide with their neighbours or else turn round on themselves and contradict their own directional movement. The abruptness is intimately related to the essential effect of a Vorticist picture, and yet it is not the same: these rough-hewn fragments have an organic warmth which belongs to Gaudier alone, and goes some way towards contradicting the unrest of the sculpture. The stones appear almost to be unfolding and expanding outwards from their base, and the continuously changing surfaces they present when the work is walked around seem to reflect this process of growth. Abstraction gave Gaudier the chance to inject several layers of meaning into one carving, and *Birds Erect* is pregnant with associations of plant life. 'He had several small cacti in his studio', recalled Brodzky, who maintained that the sculpture was directly inspired by their shapes. 'These he liked because they suggested new ideas. All the time, he was going to nature for his forms.'[25] Just as Lewis had always insisted, Gaudier never for one moment lost sight of his response to the outside world, even though *Birds Erect* makes plain his desire to erect in its place an alternative universe of his own ordering.

'This is one of the most important pieces', declared Pound, placing the work in a symbolic position at the very end of his catalogue of Gaudier's *œuvre*. And he made his admiration more than evident by roundly asserting that 'as a composition of masses I do not think I have seen any modern sculpture to match it'.[26] His categorical remark claims more than the carving deserves, but *Birds Erect* is without doubt among the most defiant and extreme sculptures to have been produced anywhere in Europe by 1914. Indeed, one of its most prophetic qualities lies in the frankness with which Gaudier enjoys the intrinsic character of the limestone itself, making its porous texture an integral part of the cool, bleached impact conveyed by the structure as a whole. He adjusted his working methods to suit the specific demands which his innate respect for the sculptor's material imposed on him. It did not matter that poverty forced him to grasp eagerly at any medium he could lay his hands on: the limestone of *Birds Erect* may well have been acquired on one of those nocturnal forays described by Aldington, who recalled that 'he and Epstein (so Gaudier informed me) used to go out late at night and steal pieces of stone from a mason's yard near the Tate Gallery'.[27] What really counted was the use to which the sculptor put the various materials that came his way, enhancing their individual properties rather than hiding them in an attempt to pretend that he only ever employed marble or bronze.

'The sculpture I admire is the work of master craftsmen', Gaudier wrote proudly in *The Egoist*. 'Every inch of the surface is won at the point of the chisel – every stroke of the hammer is a physical and mental effort. No more arbitrary translations of a design in any material. They are fully aware of the different qualities and possibilities of woods, stones, and metals.' And he went on to acknowledge the source of his convictions by explaining how 'Epstein, whom I consider the foremost in the small number of good sculptors in Europe, lays particular stress on this. Brancusi's greatest pride is his consciousness of being an accomplished workman'.[28]

Perhaps Gaudier's most unusual demonstration of the value he attached to particular materials was embodied in the small *Door-Knocker*, a cut-brass abstraction which he made especially for Hulme.[29] In view of its owner's predilections, it is safe to assume that an outright sexual allegory is contained within the genital forms in the lower half of the composition; but the two prominent circles staring out from the top give the carving an animal presence, as wary as an owl. The main interest of the piece, however, lies in its unconventional use of a material that would normally be associated with casting alone. Gaudier could not afford bronze, and so he short-circuited the problem by chiselling into its nearest equivalent: brass. 'The door-knocker is an instance of an abstract design serving to amplify the value of an object as such', he wrote in his preview of the 1914 AAA Salon, implying that the Vorticist style was ideally suited to the task of enhancing the functional properties of everyday appliances. 'No more cupids riding mermaids, garlands, curtains – stuck anywhere! The technique is unusual; the object is not cast but carved direct out of solid brass. The forms gain in sharpness and rigidity.'[30] *Door-Knocker* lives up to Gaudier's words by assuming the appearance of a gleaming monster, half reptile and half geometrical machine, a true product of its own unyielding material.

Moreover, his passion for controlling the entire business of making a sculpture even extended as far as the implements he used for his carvings. 'As if his . . . constant chipping at stone were not enough to occupy his hands . . . he made his own tools at a forge', wrote Pound. 'It might take a full day to temper his chisels. These chisels were made from old steel spindles sent him by Mr Dray, who had . . . a factory somewhere in the indefinite "North". This also may have been an economy, but it was the sort of economy Gaudier liked. He liked to do the "whole thing" from start to finish; to feel as independent as the savage.'[31] The importance of this emphatic belief in the sanctity of materials for the future development of sculpture hardly needs to be emphasized. Pound summarized many of the principles taken up by Henry Moore and a whole later generation when he described the 'new form' in an 'Affirmations' article as 'energy cut into stone, making the stone expressive in its fit and particular manner. It has regard to the stone. It is not something suitable for plaster or bronze, transferred to stone by machines and underlings. It regards the nature of the medium, of both the tools and the matter. These are its conventions and limits'.[32]

Perhaps the most unusual product of Gaudier's sympathy with Pound's

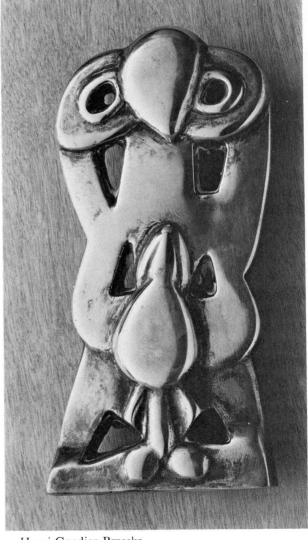

Henri Gaudier-Brzeska
Door-Knocker, 1914

△ Henri Gaudier-Brzeska
Carved Toothbrush Handle, 1914 (front and back)

▽ Henri Gaudier-Brzeska
Ornament/Toy, 1914 (front and back)

prophetic words was the *Carved Toothbrush Handle*, made from an everyday object which most sculptors would never have considered worthy of serious attention.[33] Gaudier thought otherwise, attracted no doubt by the idea of working with bone, by the unusual shape of the handle and by the financial economy of the enterprise. He would also have been amused by the almost Duchampian wit implicit in the act of transforming such a humble appliance into a work of art, and the project certainly paid dividends. From both front and back, the toothbrush has lost all trace of its normal function and become an essay in geometrical abstraction, a totemic cult-object. The familiar triangles have been incised on its surface at both ends, to emphasize the fact that it does not possess a conventional top or bottom; but one tip is rounded into a helmet as if to suggest an image of armoured aggression. The real fascination of the piece lies, however, in the extraordinary variety of forms Gaudier has invested in his tiny, fragile material: now solid and bulky, now cut right through, now narrowed down to a sliver and finally ribbed like the manufactured edges of a real toothbrush.

But it was in another cut brass sculpture, the *Ornament/Toy* which Hulme purchased for £2 and carried around in his pocket, that Gaudier came closest of all to the cold militancy of the Vorticist ideal. According to Pound, it was 'the first experiment and the best of the three' brass carvings, and he described it as a *Toy*.[34] Yet Gaudier himself listed the work more appropriately as an '*ornement torpille!*'[35] – in other words, a type of flat torpedo fish capable of giving an electric shock. It was a metaphor after Lewis's own heart, for this little piece of metal can easily be seen as a standing robot figure, as harsh and combative as the 'Primitive Mercenaries in the Modern World'[36] whose birth was announced in the *Blast No. 1* manifestos. Like Lewis's mechanized automatons, *Ornament/Toy* would be perfectly capable of leading the rebel attack against the forces of reaction: it stands stiff and erect, as if lined up for battle, and its sharp edges seem eminently capable of tearing their way through any struggle. Indeed, it is easy to imagine the pugnacious Hulme using it as a weapon; and its present owner, whose father was given the sculpture by Mrs Kibblewhite as a 'personal memento'[37] after Hulme's death, maintains that although it was essentially 'an abstract object for the philosopher to fidget with while his meditations were maturing, Hulme's character was such that he may well have playfully threatened to brain someone with it'.[38]

Despite its miniature scale, the figure is heroic in implications, both as a warrior and a milestone in the evolution of twentieth-century sculpture. For *Ornament/ Toy* is one of the very first examples of a completely penetrated carving; later, perhaps, than Archipenko's pioneering experiments in the same field, but innovatory nevertheless. Gaudier has pierced through the brass completely, from front to back, in no less than three places. Viewed from behind, these holes register with just as much effect as they do from the opposite side, even if the lowest triangle is no longer stressed by the larger triangle of metal surrounding it at the front. And the back reinforces the image of a human body, possessing as it does a spine motif that runs down from the top into a knot of organic forms towards the bottom. Gaudier often liked to play around with ambiguity – an alabaster *Imp*, carved in the same year, presents an abstract surface on one side and a figurative one on the other – but in this case, high spirits are not allowed to interfere with the essential severity of a hieratic presence. It could almost be a three-dimensional statement of Vorticism's most warlike impulses, and might easily have prompted the enthusiasm of Lewis's comments on Gaudier in *Blast No. 2*, where he praises the 'suave, thick, quite PERSONAL character' of his work and explains how 'it is this, that makes his sculpture what we would principally turn to in England to show the new forces and future of this art'.[39]

One of the most striking manifestations of that new force was Gaudier's attitude towards a base for his sculpture. Not only were *Duck*, *Fish*, *Dog* and *Ornament/Toy* intended to be handled as playthings and slipped into their owners' pockets, thereby deflating any excessive fine art pretensions they might otherwise have possessed: even the substantial *Bird Swallowing Fish* asked to be picked up by its projecting tail and wielded like a weapon rather than automatically rested on a static pedestal. Just as *Toothbrush*'s lowly material reflected Gaudier's delight in making a virtue of economic necessity and transforming the most ordinary substance, so the base upon which *Birds Erect* was placed seems to be used not so much as a plinth as a foil, an integral part of the entire sculpture. Gaudier never wrote about his feelings towards the prospect of a vanishing base, and so it is impossible to tell whether such a programme formed a consistent part of his working philosophy. But he does appear to implement such an aim in many of his carvings, and Pound backed it up by asserting in a *New Age* article on Vorticism published on 14 January 1915 that 'if you clap a strong magnet beneath a plateful of iron filings, the energies of the magnet will proceed to organise form . . . The design in the magnetised iron filings expresses a confluence of energy. It is not "meaningless" or "inexpressive"'. Nor were Gaudier's sculptures, despite the fact that their unorthodox materials and lack of a conventional base lowered them to a level as mundane as that of the iron filings lying in their plate. The 'confluence of energy' involved in their making ensured

Henri Gaudier-Brzeska
Garden Ornament, 1914

that they embodied what Pound described as 'order and vitality and thence beauty', and Gaudier proved that these qualities were not dependent upon the consecration either of expensive marble or an ennobling plinth.

Yet however much Gaudier's latest productions can be seen to concur with the Vorticist aesthetic, it has to be admitted that his individuality was simply too strong – and too unformed – to be restricted within the pigeonhole of the rebel movement. He was still a very young man, barely into his twenties, when he departed for France in the autumn of 1914; and he had not entirely grown out of his earlier zest for eclecticism. He no longer made a habit of jumping around from style to style or brandishing his ability to emulate the masters of the past, certainly: the execution of the *Red Stone Dancer* and his subsequent affiliation with the Rebel Art Centre had inaugurated a new phase of concentrated activity, and his written contribution to *Blast No. 1* finally confirmed that his sympathies lay for the most part with the Great English Vortex.

But he still harboured the occasional wish to be a free agent, as uncommitted to any specific partisan group as his mentor, Epstein. Although Gaudier's signature was affixed to the *Blast No. 1* manifesto and his work reproduced in the same periodical, he was not afraid to be disloyal to the rebel cause if it suited him. After he had returned from his first abortive attempt to join the army in France – the army authorities at Boulogne imprisoned him for having previously evaded his military service, but he escaped back to London within two days – he had no qualms about accepting a commission through the auspices of the Omega. Lady Hamilton wanted him to carve two huge garden vases in stone, and Gaudier went so far as to model the plaster maquettes before he 'got very much bored with it, finding the stone much harder than he had expected'.[40] The kind of sensibilities displayed in one of these preliminary versions might well have endeared him to the Bloomsbury sensibilities at Fitzroy Square, and it is significant that he was willing to accept a commission from them at all. He was erratic to the end, and never ceased to delight in confounding the expectations of his immediate circle by seeming to recant his own most deeply held beliefs about art. Aldington, for example, who was always engaged with Gaudier in 'perpetual, acrimonious, and fundamentally amical [*sic*] dispute as to whether Greek art and civilization were worthy of serious consideration', recorded his astonishment when 'we walked together across Hyde Park and Kensington Gardens on his last days in London, and he told me gravely that being in prison had entirely changed his views on art – he was going to abandon the modern style entirely and follow "the Greeks". He even offered to do a classical statue of me as Hercules. If this had ever happened, I suspect I should have emerged in stone as a prize-fighter afflicted with microcephaly, elephantitis, and superb appendages'.[41]

Right up until the end, Gaudier outraged his friends and flouted all the accepted rules about creative integrity. Most of the controversial squibs were reserved for conversation alone, but when he abandoned Lady Hamilton's stone vases at his Putney studio and turned his attention to a carving of more modest proportions, the result was far indeed from an unequivocal reassertion of his commitment to Vorticism. A vigorous drawing for *Seated Woman*, the sculpture which Pound described as 'his last or almost his last work',[42] shows that his original conception envisaged a radically distorted image, full of the thrusting diagonal movements and abstracted simplifications of his rebel carvings. The sketch flattens the figure out into one plane, almost like a bas-relief: the mask-like face, the arms and legs all seem to be crowding towards the surface of the paper on which they are drawn. Such an intensely compressed study would suggest a brutal sculpture, alive with the violence of feeling that had previously characterized a Vorticist work like *Bird Swallowing Fish*. And yet, when Gaudier

Henri Gaudier-Brzeska
Study for Seated Woman, 1914

finally completed his marble version of the *Seated Woman* in late August or early September, he revealed a calm, fundamentally classical figure that bore only the most indirect resemblance either to his immediately preceding sculptures or to the movement he had championed for so many months.

Instead of hard, mechanistic Vorticist angles, the carving revels in the slow curves of a woman. The only real point of contact with rebel principles occurs in the construction of the ponderous arms: the sudden meeting of forearm and head could have provided a destructive climax to the work, and infected it with the kind of callous iconoclasm that Lewis cherished. But this extraordinary decision to cut straight into the woman's right eye fails to disturb the sensual fulfilment of a carving that takes its mood – as Gaudier's respect for his medium would have wished – from the delicate beauty of the white marble itself. Even the back view, which does resolve itself into a more abstract assertion of planar priorities and stresses the diagonality of the girder-like arms, manages at the

▷   Henri Gaudier-Brzeska
▷▷ *Seated Woman*, 1914 (front and back)

▽   Aristide Maillol
      Seated Nude (*Mediterranean*), *c.* 1901

same time to convey a rounded, voluptuous rhythm through the undulating shoulders and the soft hump of the thigh.

Once again, his thoughts had wandered back to the example of Maillol, who had executed Hellenistic figures like the stone *Seated Nude* (*Mediterranean*) that were inspired by the same feeling of monumental stillness. Gaudier's woman is embroiled in a profound, sleeping calm which matches the mood of Maillol's sculpture exactly. The position of the legs in both works is identical, even if Gaudier has truncated his woman's legs just below her knees so that the thighs make a rock-like base for the upper half and nothing can possibly detract from the dominant motif of the sweeping arms. *Seated Woman* could almost be seen as a restatement of the Maillol prototype, an attempt by a young and ambitious sculptor to reconcile his admiration for a famous French predecessor with his need to break away from the tradition which Maillol upheld. It is a transitional work, for all its considerable authority: Gaudier is seen to be pausing for breath, and wondering how best to continue his radical investigations without leaving the Maillol conventions behind altogether.

His continuing susceptibility to the influence of older men is proved in one further way, too, for *Seated Woman* betrays links with the kind of stone *Caryatid* that Modigliani was carving in Paris at the same time. Gaudier's figure conveys a more aloof impression than the splendidly uncomplicated hedonism of Modigliani's stone goddess, but the same strain of lazy fertility permeates both

Amadeo Modigliani
Caryatid, c. 1914

sculptures. Or rather, *Seated Woman* crosses *Caryatid* with the more schematized hauteur of an elongated *Head* that Modigliani exhibited at the Whitechapel Art Gallery in the summer of 1914. Gaudier was bound to have seen and admired it in the Whitechapel show – around the same time he included Modigliani in his list of sculptural heroes in *Blast No. 1* – and he relies on a similar type of African mask in the construction of his woman's facial features. He arrives at a far bulkier format than Modigliani's extreme attenuation, of course: Pound aptly described its effect when he wrote of Gaudier's characteristic 'soft bluntness'.[43] But it seems likely that the memory of the *Head* remained with him when he deliberated over the shape that his *Seated Woman*'s face should assume.

The sources at work behind this carving's placid façade effectively destroy any hopes that Gaudier's final carvings would in any way crown or confirm his links with the Vorticist movement. Lewis recorded his own feelings of disappointment at such lapses when he wrote later that 'I must confess even Gaudier seemed a little too naturalistic and not starkly XX century enough'.[44] He successfully eludes any attempt to force his work into a predetermined pattern; and the fact that his departure for the war in France meant 'all the art-feuds of young London were at truce for half an hour' shows how he succeeded in attracting the admiration of a wide cross-section of bitterly opposed factions. The one thing everyone agreed about was Gaudier's talent, his immense promise, and the normally unsentimental Lewis melted when he recalled the final farewell on the railway platform. 'I remember him in the carriage window of the boat-train, with his excited eyes', he wrote. 'We left the platform, a depressed, almost a guilty, group. It is easy to laugh at the exaggerated estimate "the artist" puts upon his precious life. But when it is *really* an artist – and there are very few – it is at the death of something terribly alive that you are assisting. And this little figure was so preternaturally *alive*.'[45] Only a few months were left to Gaudier from the time of his final enlistment to his death on 5 June 1915. And it would be idle to search for any significant development in his creative thinking among the miscellaneous assortment of letters, postcards and hasty sketches which he sent back to his friends in London from the Front, were it not that he told Pound in October about his decision to compose 'a short essay on sculpture for the *Blast* Christmas No.'[46] The article arrived at the beginning of December, and it reassured his Vorticist friends by announcing that 'MY VIEWS ON SCULPTURE REMAIN ABSOLUTELY THE SAME. IT IS THE VORTEX OF WILL, OF DECISION, THAT BEGINS'.[47]

Dramatically entitled 'VORTEX GAUDIER-BRZESKA (Written from the Trenches)', the essay set out to prove that his ideas had not changed since he wrote the first three lines of his 'Vortex' credo in *Blast No. 1* stressing the supreme importance of formal values. The horror and bloodshed of war had done nothing to make him retract his previous credo: there was plenty of time for thought and observation in the trenches, and he reported that his new experiences had simply strengthened his earlier convictions. 'Just as this hill where the Germans are solidly entrenched, gives me a nasty feeling, solely because its gentle slopes are broken up by earth-works, which throw long shadows at sunset', he wrote, 'just so shall I get feeling, of whatsoever definition, from a statue ACCORDING TO ITS SLOPES, varied to infinity.' Chance configurations of the landscape affected him far more than the prospect of death, and so he concluded that his future work would be controlled by the same emphasis on abstract design as it had done hitherto. 'I SHALL DERIVE MY EMOTIONS SOLELY FROM THE ARRANGEMENT OF SURFACES' he declared, 'I shall present my emotions by the ARRANGEMENT OF MY SURFACES, THE PLANES AND LINES BY WHICH THEY ARE DEFINED.'[48] The extremism was, if anything, even more absolute than it had ever been before: now his very emotions would be 'derived' from the structure of a surface itself. And as a practical example of his renewed radicalism, a substitute for the sculptures he would have executed had the war not prevented him from doing so, he told his rebel friends that 'I have made an experiment. Two days ago I pinched from an enemy a mauser rifle. Its heavy unwieldy shape swamped me with a powerful IMAGE of brutality'. He had been moved by the shape of the rifle, not by the fact that it was a weapon of destruction. And so, discovering that 'I did not like it', he decided to counteract the 'brutality' with an alternative shape of his own. 'I broke the butt off and with my knife I carved in it a design, through which I tried to express a gentler order of feeling, which I preferred', he wrote. 'BUT I WILL EMPHASIZE that MY DESIGN got its effect (just as the gun had) FROM A VERY SIMPLE COMPOSITION OF LINES AND PLANES.'[49]

Amadeo Modigliani
Head, c. 1913

The carving has since been lost, and along with it any indication of what Gaudier's last sculpture looked like. If he had not 'gone out through a little hole in the high forehead',[50] as Ford lamented in his obituary article, he might of course have followed his colleagues and reverted to a more naturalistic form of expression. Even after the 'Vortex' from the trenches had been finished and sent off for publication in *Blast No. 2*, Pound was still worrying over the effect that prolonged exposure to battle would have on his friend's future work. When the poet wrote to Gaudier in January 1915, he 'threatened him that in reaction from his present life in violence, he would react into Condor [*sic*], the nineties, delicate shades and half lights'; and Gaudier replied firmly that 'if I return am sure I shall not work like Condor. But I believe I shall develop a style of my own which, like the Chinese, will embody both a grotesque and a non-grotesque side. Anyway, much will be changed after we have come through the blood bath of idealism'.[51]

What did he mean? The prediction is vaguely worded, but it comes as a surprise nonetheless to find Gaudier talking of 'change' and 'the Chinese' so soon after asserting in his *Blast No. 2* article that his views on sculpture remained 'absolutely the same'. And more disturbing still are the thoughts contained in a later letter of 11 April to Mrs Shakespear, where he reveals that 'I am getting convinced slowly that it is not much use going farther in the research of planes, forms, etc. If I ever come back I shall do more "Mlles. G . . ." in marble'.[52] *Mlle G . . .* was the nickname he gave to an ample classical torso executed in 1913 as a passing tribute to 'those *damn* Greeks', and Pound insisted that 'he had repeatedly stigmatised it as insincere'.[53] Could Gaudier have really intended to go through with such a startling volte-face, or was it just another instance of his weakness for making unpredictable stylistic gestures? Pound was adamant in his opposition to the former suggestion: 'personally I do not believe that "genius" ever "goes back"', he declared flatly. 'It would be a very sickly sign for any man of twenty-two to regard his actual work as anything save a way and a leading toward some further fullness and rightness.' But then, Pound's sympathies lay with the most Vorticist of Gaudier's sculptures, and he admitted that 'I and various people, who seem to me most alive to the significance of Gaudier's work, are interested in the squarish and bluntish period, Gaudier's latest work, the cut brass and the "Birds Erect"'.[54]

Fry, on the other hand, arguing quite naturally from the Bloomsbury standpoint, maintained in 1916 that it was only 'in a few pieces of sculpture' that Gaudier 'tried to treat organic forms with a system of plasticity derived from mechanical objects so as to give to the schemes of planes and to their surfaces the same kind of relations that appears in the planes of machinery. However useful this attempt may have been as an exercise in the problem of plane relations reduced to their simplest terms, I cannot think that the work was in line with Brzeska's special gifts and artistic temperament. Brzeska himself recognized this in his later conversations with me, and states in one of his letters that he intends to return to organic forms'.[55] Fry was as partisan as Pound, but Gaudier's last letters certainly do bear out Fry's thesis, and even Pound admitted that 'for the second number of *Blast*, Gaudier had planned an essay on "The Need of Organic Forms in Sculpture"'. Indeed, Pound reported the substance of 'almost [my] last long talk' with Gaudier, in which the sculptor said that 'his conclusion, after these months of thought and experiment, was that combinations of abstract or inorganic forms exclusively, were more suitable for painting than for sculpture'.[56] The practical application of these thoughts can already be seen in the pronounced organic leanings of *Birds Erect*, and Gaudier might well have gone on to achieve a more complete synthesis of the natural and the mechanical had he survived.

His incipient change of direction is prophetic if measured against the work which the other Vorticists would execute after their return from the war. But the only neutral answer to the question of Gaudier's future evolution lies in the last works themselves, a brace of hasty, crumpled pencil sketches which he sent back from Craonne for exhibition at the second London Group show. One of

Henri Gaudier-Brzeska
A Mitrailleuse in Action, 1914–15

them, *A Mitrailleuse in Action*, shows how closely allied Gaudier still was to the concerns of the Vorticists: the soldier bending over his firing gun is as mechanical as the weapon he holds. Indeed, his whole body is described with such confident precision that it merges with the harsh lines of the gun in one compact mass of aggressive energy. The drawing, with its swift definition of essential shapes, would not have looked at all out of place in *Blast No. 2*, next to an illustration like Roberts' *Machine Gunners*.

Gaudier set his *Mitrailleuse* down with true Vorticist detachment, just as he calmly traced the exploding arcs of a shell that could easily have destroyed him in the other trenches drawing, *One of our Shells Exploding*. His reckless courage became proverbial at the Front – he was promoted for gallantry twice, becoming a corporal and then a sergeant – and he accounted for the analytical nature of this remarkable sketch by explaining in his *Blast No. 2* essay that 'THE BURSTING SHELLS, the volleys, wire entanglements, projectors, motors, the chaos of battle DO NOT ALTER IN THE LEAST, the outlines of the hill we are besieging'.[57] Those 'outlines' represented the permanent values in Gaudier's imagination: the fuss and noise were as unimportant as the hysterics of the Futurists had been in pre-war London. Hence the *Shells* drawing's spare arrangement of curves, which he had successfully extracted from the blurred confusion of a real explosion without losing sight of its underlying power. 'The direct and hot impressions of life' had indeed been 'mated with Abstraction', exactly as Lewis recommended; and it was only natural that the editor of *Blast No. 2* should have reserved special praise in his magazine for this particular sketch. 'His beautiful drawing from the trenches of a bursting shell is not only a fine design, but a curiosity', Lewis wrote. 'It is surely a pretty satisfactory answer to those who would kill us with Prussian bullets: who say, in short, that Germany, in attacking Europe, has killed spiritually all the Cubists, Vorticists and Futurists in the world. Here is one, a great artist, who makes drawings of those shells as they come towards him, and which, thank God, have not killed him or changed him yet.'[58] Soon after these words were written, Gaudier died during an infantry charge; but although the missiles which he drew finally destroyed him, this battered sketch survives to prove that war had not destroyed his belief in Vorticism as well.

Henri Gaudier-Brzeska
One of Our Shells Exploding, 1914–15

Chapter 16: Vorticism in Practice: Epstein and Rock Drill

Jacob Epstein
Bust of Lady Drogheda, c. 1914–15

Jacob Epstein
Head of T. E. Hulme, 1916

Epstein was now the only sculptor left alive to carry on the rebel cause, and one of Gaudier's last regrets was that fighting prevented him from viewing his friend's new productions. 'Hulme has told me in detail what Epstein had lately been doing', he told Pound in a January 1915 letter, 'and from the description I should be glad to see the works, perhaps I will once.'[1] But if he had managed to return to London he might have been surprised and perplexed by the diversity of Epstein's contemporaneous style. The older man really had no right to castigate Gaudier in his autobiography for having 'a volatile nature' that 'caused him to change his style from week to week'.[2] For Epstein himself was equally culpable, not through 'volatility' so much as a rather more suspect desire to placate the sitters who commissioned his portrait busts.

At the very start of the Vorticist period, for instance, when he was involved in the execution of his revolutionary *Flenite* and *Dove* carvings, Epstein was enough of a chameleon to change his skin and execute a disconcertingly slick and facile head of Lady Drogheda. This superficial exercise cannot even be explained away as a conscious stylistic escapade, a raid on the cultures of the past like Gaudier's early aberrations. It is a fashionable image, totally at odds with the originality of the work he was simultaneously creating in the privacy of his Pett Level studio. The only possible explanation for this flaw in Epstein's otherwise stalwart artistic integrity is that he did not basically care about such works. A commission from Lady Drogheda provided him with the financial means to carry on with his genuinely creative preoccupations, and he could not be bothered to expend on it the kind of pioneering inventiveness that went into Lewis's dining-room decorations for the same patroness.

It is less easy to account for Epstein's willing reversion to a straightforward form of naturalism when he modelled the heads of close friends. Even Hulme, who would have been the first to expect a portrait as experimental as the *Flenite* carvings he had earlier defended with such vigour, found his likeness perpetuated in a bronze that was at once traditional and unadventurous. The degree of realistic observation embodied in this sculpture, which was executed in the spring and summer of 1916 when Hulme was stationed at a Royal Marine Artillery Barracks in Portsmouth, contains nothing to suggest that its sitter had recently been a prime advocate of 'a new constructive geometrical art'. Unlike Gaudier, who had used his bust of Pound as the pretext for a brave leap forward by extending the principles of his imaginative work through to the problems of a carved portrait, Epstein here shied away from innovation and contented himself with an undemanding study from life. Indeed, Kate Lechmere remembered the philosopher telling her that Epstein 'actually measured the finished plaster to make sure that it was exactly the same size as Hulme's own head'[3] – an academic notion alarmingly removed from the daring distortions of the *Flenite* figures.

It seems incredible that only a year before he had exhibited a work as radical as the *Marble Mother and Child* at the second London Group show, for this carving aims above all at purging every shred of descriptive excrescence from the human image. The maternity theme he had explored so many times before is here restated in its most purified form: instead of portraying the mother as an inchoate primitive animal, terrified by the new life surging up inside her swollen belly, Epstein chose to depict the calm acceptance and enjoyment of procreation that the advent of childbirth brings. The baby is now placed beside its mother, an entirely separate egg-like ball of white marble balanced so delicately on its slender neck that it appears to be hovering in space. A fully thought-out contrast is established between the two heads, the one a compact oval and the other an elongated sphere; the one rotund and convex, the other shallow and concave. They sit there, those two wonderfully defined entities, in a chaste

Jacob Epstein
Mother and Child, c. 1913–15 (front and back)

and frontal frieze; and the back view emphasizes the vertical rectitude of the mother as opposed to the horizontal expansion of the baby by contrasting her flat, patterned hair with his bald roundness. Epstein does not even allow the mother to show her ears: they are pared away in the interests of her verticality, whereas the baby's ears seem to enhance his floating equilibrium.

The composition is deliberately kept simple, so that the full geometrical strength of the two participants' faces can be displayed with the maximum clarity and the minimum elaboration. They exist apart, and yet they are conjoined by the material of the carving; and the union is strengthened by the mother's protective hand covering her baby's chest. This gesture is an important one, the sole demonstration of feeling in a sculpture otherwise remarkable for its aloof reserve. The two heads do not turn towards each other in a mood of domestic affection: they both face outwards, lost not so much in contemplation of some distant spectacle as in a deep introspection. For the child's eyes are rendered as a single, unseeing horizontal line, while its parent's are mere sockets, a pair of shadowy valleys incapable of vision.

But there is nothing tragic about their lack of sight. Epstein meant them to be abstract symbols of a state of mind, just as Brancusi had pared away human features in his successive versions of the *Sleeping Muse* to arrive at the essence of repose. The *Muse*, and Modigliani's *Heads*, would be the main influence on *Marble Mother and Child*, were it not for the remarkable resemblance that the mother herself bears to one of the most prized items in Epstein's collection of primitive sculpture, the so-called *Brummer Head*. The great curve of the forehead, the distended nose and tapering chin are all close to the construction of the mother's features, and Epstein clinched the likelihood of this source when

Anon
The 'Brummer Head', formerly in Epstein's collection

Jacob Epstein
Drawing, c. 1913

he recalled seeing the *Brummer Head* 'in Joseph Brummer's shop in Paris . . . in 1913'.[4]

His admiration for this great Fang wood carving, which originally surmounted a bark box containing the skulls and bones of ancestors, must have remained with him when he executed his own marble; and he helped to explain the impulses behind the sculpture when he pointed out how the *Brummer Head* 'has qualities which transcend the most mysterious Egyptian work. It is an evocation of a spirit that penetrates into another world, a world of ghosts and occult forces, and could only be produced where spiritism holds sway'. Epstein likewise wanted to create an image that would haunt the imagination, but he combined primitive magic with the urge to make a thoroughly avant-garde artefact, one of the most advanced European sculptures of its time. And its formal inspiration was provided by the *Brummer Head*, too: he later explained how 'on the plastic side also, the [African] head is very remarkable, with its surrounding prongs of hair off-setting the large roundness of the forehead, a perfect example of free wood-carving'.[5] Epstein's head is a virtuoso performance as well, but it was not severe enough to satisfy Lewis's thirst for austerity. 'Had Mr Epstein in his marble group, Mother and Child, not made a Eugène Carrière in stone of the Mother, but treated that head, too, with the plastic solidity of the baby's head, I should have considered it among his best things', he wrote in *Blast No. 2*. 'As it is, "for the Baby's sake", it is very fine.'[6]

However pleased Epstein may have been with this carving, its relatively modest size was not calculated to assuage his ambitions to produce sculpture on the most monumental scale. The three-year period at Pett Level gave him the necessary solitude and time to tackle superhuman tasks, and he soon set about the creation of two huge marble Venuses that would bring together his twin obsessions with pregnancy and copulating doves in a monolithic résumé. It is not known which of the two statues was executed first: looking back on the Pett Level work, he simply recorded that 'it was here I carved the "Venus" ',[7] and when *Second Marble Venus* was first shown at his Leicester Galleries one-man show in the spring of 1917, the catalogue merely listed it without a date as 'Venus. Marble', although the Galleries' director remembered Epstein working on it as early as 1914. Nor did he ever explain why he bothered to carve two large versions of the same subject, even if it seems likely that he approached the task in the same way as the various *Flenite* and *Dove* carvings, tirelessly attempting different formal solutions to the same problem until he felt the possibilities of the motif were exhausted.

The Venuses may even have been executed concurrently, for all the Pett Level works seem to have grown out of each other, suggesting variations and treatments to the sculptor as he executed them. One of his *Blast No. 1* illustrations, for instance, a lost *Drawing* of a pregnant mother enclosed in a mesh of whirling lines that form a cave-like protection around her, stands as a bridge connecting the preoccupations of the *Flenite* figures with the Venuses. The central figure is no longer a rounded, essentially archaic creature as she was in *Female Figure in Flenite*: the head has now taken on the stiff angularity of a geometrical helmet, and the tensely summarized surroundings refer more to a twentieth-century environment than a primitive jungle. It may well have been one of the drawings exhibited in Epstein's first one-man show at the Twenty-One Gallery, for Hulme seized on them as exemplars of his new theories about art in his Quest Society lecture.[8] 'The tendency to abstraction, the desire to turn the organic into something hard and durable, is here at work, not on something simple, such as you get in the more archaic work, but on something much more complicated', he wrote. 'Abstraction is much greater in the second case, because generation, which is the very essence of all the qualities which we

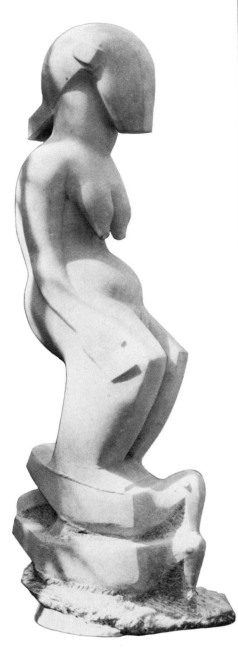

have here called organic, has been turned into something as hard and durable as a geometrical figure itself.'[9]

With his usual perspicacity, Hulme had put his finger on the one extraordinary paradox informing both the marble Venuses. For while they celebrate the wonder of procreation, and become goddesses of fertility, they are at the same time putting into practice Epstein's new-found faith in a rigidly dehumanized stylization. The *First Marble Venus*, only half the size of its partner and therefore perhaps the earlier of the two, does not carry this process as far as the second version. She is the most African of the pair, with enormous pendent breasts and swollen stomach. Her whole body sags under its own titanic weight, thickening so alarmingly around the waist and buttocks that the supporting doves barely seem capable of taking the strain. Their heads drop despondently forward, as if cowed by the weight above, and they thereby remain disconnected from the main mass of the statue. Nor is this the only inconsistency: the vege-

△△ Jacob Epstein
First Marble Venus, c.1913–15 (two views)

△ Anon
The De Miré Figure, formerly in Epstein's collection

Adrian Allinson
*Mr. Epstein doubting the Authenticity of a
South Sea Idol*, 1914

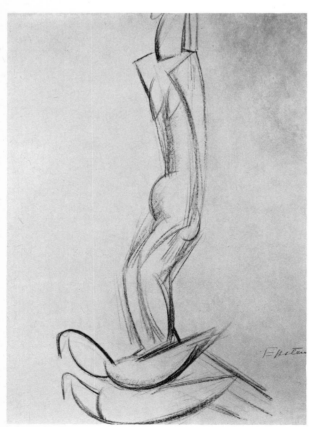

Jacob Epstein
Study for Second Marble Venus, c. 1914–16

table splendour of the figure's mammaries and belly do not quite marry with the stark planar flatness of her head, arms and legs. There is an outright clash, rather than a fully judged contrast, between the abstract severity of the blank, featureless face and the reassuring normality of the breasts below; for Epstein had not yet arrived at a synthesis that would merge his diverse impulses in a convincing unity of idea and form. At one moment, the eye is lulled by the flowering richness of the more naturalistic areas, and then it is disturbed by the life-denying puritanism of the schematic limbs. The dissonance jars, highlighting the incongruity of the fundamental conception: Epstein had failed to learn the lesson embodied in the kind of African prototype that lies behind the *First Marble Venus*.

The *De Miré Figure*, for example, which he acquired for his primitive collection in 1932 and may well have known at this period, manages to combine human curves and godlike stiffness without any sense of conflict. It is a male, of course, and therefore does not have to conquer the same difficulties that beset Epstein's attempt to simplify a female body; but its pose – head erect, arms limp, and legs bending forward at the knees – echoes the *Venus*'s stance in a striking way. Could it have been the specific inspiration behind Epstein's sculpture? It is impossible to know. As a connoisseur of primitive art whose collecting instincts were so well known by 1914 that Allinson was able to caricature them, he must have been aware for many years of the De Miré pieces.[10] He later described them as 'undoubtedly the finest collection of African Art outside a museum', and he considered that this particular Fang figure 'equals anything that has come out of Africa'; so it seems likely that he would have known about it, at least in photographic form, at the time he executed the *Venus*. His comments on this 'great standing figure from Gabun River' likewise illuminate the purpose behind his own carving, for he considered it to have 'the astounding attitude of being held spell-bound by sorcery'.[11]

The *First Marble Venus* appears similarly transfixed, as if under the control of some incantation pronounced at a tribal rite; and the doves would presumably fulfil the function originally performed by 'fetish emblems . . . birds or animals, alligators or insects' which he explained were 'worn by the fetish men moving through the crowds of onlookers, brought to the highest pitch of excitement by drums and chanting'. Moreover, he recaptured the interest with which he must have examined the stylistic characteristics of a sculpture like the *De Miré Figure* when he described how 'we can study at leisure their formal relations and coldly calculate how the parts are correlated, and examine the laws of rhythm and form they embody'. Primitive art provided him with an education as well as a collector's passion, and he helped to elucidate the meaning of his *Venus* when he wrote of African wood carvings that 'as fetishes their importance is religious or, at any rate, magical. They were used to impress, terrify and impart to the beholders a state of mind bordering on, or actually, hallucinatory'.[12]

Epstein's own words go a long way towards explaining the domineering, supernatural quality of his *First Marble Venus*. Standing on the dove 'emblems', which are in the process of performing the intercourse that first caused her stomach to grow, this heavy goddess has a semi-religious authority, half brutal and half beneficent. As a literary symbol, she successfully transmits her meaning; but as a sculptural mass she does not cohere. And so Epstein resorted to his sketch-book, outlining the contours of an altogether more elongated figure with smaller breasts and a far more unified anatomical construction. The drawing shows a sculptor trying to resolve his thoughts, turning the rounded calf of Venus's right leg into a stiff vertical and changing her shoulders into sharp angles. The battle between the demands of a womanly form and Epstein's own desire for schematization is here rehearsed; and to judge from the final carving, the latter impulse finally triumphed. In place of the overblown bulk of the first version, *Second Marble Venus* has grown into an icy column of stone extending eight feet into the air. Her bosom has hardened into a pair of strictly regulated circles and her left arm is now little more than a prefabricated slab. Even the stomach is restricted to one clearly defined section and the neck, following the advice of the drawing, has become a taut pillar to emphasize the proud bearing of a creature no longer rendered inert by her own hefty appendages. The function of the doves has been completely rethought, too: instead of bending down, as they do even in the drawing, to form a separate mass, they now become an integral part of the main figure. Looking up to reflect the new alertness of the sculpture they support, their heads carry on the vertical line of the limbs in one uninterrupted movement. And the cock, his comb inserted like a buttress between the Venus's parted limbs, takes the pressure off her bent knees so that she appears more relaxed than her uncomfortably straining predecessor.

Epstein's fresh ideas pay off to spectacular effect when the carving is seen from the front, an angle that shows how far he has succeeded in retaining the

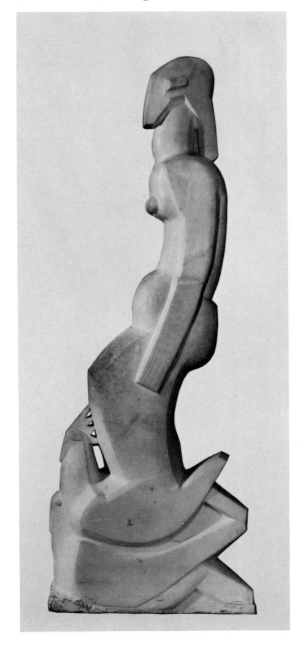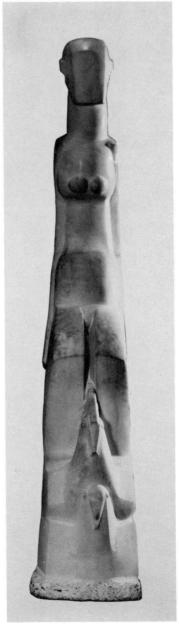

Jacob Epstein
Second Marble Venus, c.1914–16 (two views)

△ Anon
Marble Figure of a Woman (Cycladic),
2,500–2,000 B.C.

▷ Jacob Epstein
Drawing (for Birth), *c.* 1913–14

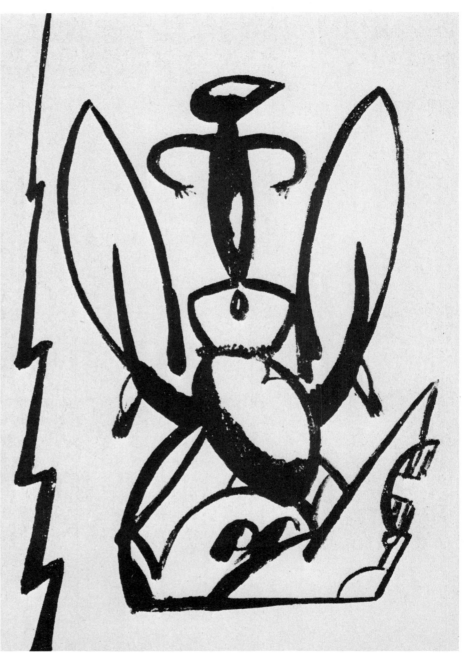

basic shape of the marble block. The Venus here seems literally to be growing out of the stone, and its intrinsic shape hardly appears disturbed by the figure at all. Even the interlocking diagonals of the doves' tails, which from the side extend beyond the goddess and appear to be insufficiently merged with her body, do not now obtrude beyond the bounds of this cubic volume. Epstein has almost created two independent variations on his theme within one sculpture, exploiting the unique possibilities inherent in a three-dimensional medium by making the carving change totally from the rhythmic complexity of the profile to the vertical simplicity of the frontal view. The metamorphosis argues a change of cultures, moving away from the animal involvement of African figures towards the beguiling abstraction of the Cycladic dolls that Epstein would have seen on his regular visits to the British Museum.

The whole attraction of a Cycladic woman lies in the sobriety of her contours: she is pared down to a coolly understated minimal form, a triumph of stylistic consistency. And it was precisely this quality that the *First Marble Venus*

Jacob Epstein
Birth, c. 1913–14

lacked, caught as it was between two violently opposed conventions. A work like the Cycladic doll may have helped point the way out of this dilemma, and Epstein followed its advice to good effect in his final version. The second Venus has appropriated much of the chasteness of her Cycladic prototype, and she rides on the cock's undulating back like a virginal deity newly arisen from the waves. Her pregnancy is symbolic only, a transferred result of the act taking place beneath rather than a proof of her own fertility. She is a ritualistic icon, not a barely disguised object of lust like a Venetian Venus, and her forbidding proportions positively demand worshipful obeisance.

At one stage, Epstein dallied with the idea of creating a masculine equivalent of the *Venus* carvings, and in a lost *Drawing* illustrated in *Blast No. 1* he placed an unequivocally African baby on the belly of a woman screaming with pain. If the drawing is inverted, it can be seen that Epstein actually wanted to represent the agony of a primitive childbirth, with the baby dropping out of the vagina past the mother's parted legs. It was a weird idea, far more controversial than the juxtaposition of a woman with copulating doves, and he was probably wise to take it no further than an unfinished, fragmentary relief carving which repeats the format of the drawing without enhancing it in any way. Realizing perhaps that the project lacked subtlety, Epstein settled as a compromise on the baby's figure alone.

△ Anon
Wooden Bakota Figure, covered with brass
sheet appliqué, formerly in Epstein's collection

▷ Jacob Epstein
Cursed Be The Day Wherein I Was Born,
c. 1913–15

Instead of concentrating on the imagery of jungle voodoo, Epstein forgot about his 'fetish' animals and decided to make this screaming negro into a headlong attack on the plight of the black man in Western society. He himself was a Jew, the son of Polish parents who 'had come to America on one of those great waves of immigration that followed persecution and pogroms in Czarist Russia and Poland',[13] so a personal urgency informs the quotation from Job he gave the sculpture: *Cursed Be The Day Wherein I Was Born*.[14] It is polemical art of the most immediate kind, showing the negro in an attitude of helpless frenzy, his mouth opened out into an accusing cry aimed at the sky. The crouching pose directly recalls the wood and brass bakota ancestral figures which Epstein knew at the British Museum and collected himself, but he gave his sculpture an additional sting by painting the plaster a ferocious scarlet. It is a consciously crude work: Epstein is aping primitive craftsmanship as well as primitive style, and the Press's reaction was hostile when he first displayed the carving at the second London Group show. 'The first thing that frightens one is a large wooden [*sic*] figure by Mr Jacob Epstein of an alleged man', remarked *The Star* drily. 'It is painted bright red, and designed after the Cannibal Islands School. Its title is "Cursed be the Day that I was Born", and one quite agrees.'[15]

The critical sarcasm was predictable, but was this archaizing image really what the twentieth century needed? *Blast No. 1* had championed a programme dedicated to expressing the unique condition of the modern world, and Epstein's own mentor, Hulme, had insisted that 'the new "tendency towards abstraction" will culminate, not so much in the simple geometrical forms found in archaic art, but in the more complicated ones associated in our minds with the idea of machinery'. The philosopher demanded more than exercises compounded out of a fascination for tribal art, and Epstein was the one artist he believed in more than any other. Hulme must have argued with his friend, trying to persuade him to break away completely from the influence of primitivism and produce a sculpture that would fulfil his dreams of a 'new geometric and monumental art making use of mechanical forms'. Even when the philosopher saw the Wilde Tomb for the first time, Epstein remembered that 'Hulme immediately put his own construction on my work – turned it into some theory of projectiles'.[16] And

Jacob Epstein
Winged Figure, c. 1912–13

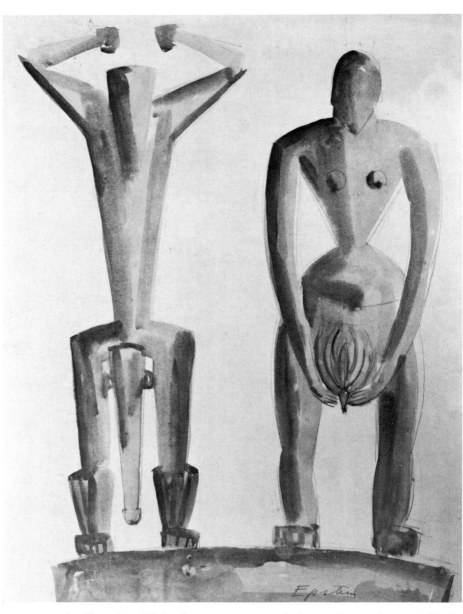

Jacob Epstein
Study for Man Woman (?), 1913–15

sure enough, Epstein did begin to cast around for a theme that would do sufficient justice to Hulme's theoretical recipe.

He drew two streamlined sketches of a robot form in flight, an automated version of the Wilde Tomb; and then deliberated again over the mechanistic potential of a man's form as opposed to a woman's, executing a swift study in fluid wash of a male figure standing next to a female on an ample plinth. He may have been intending to turn the idea into a carving – Epstein's wife listed an untraced 'Man Woman' among the work still unfinished in June 1916[17] – but its importance in the present context consists of the strong connection that exists between the man's body and Epstein's new plans for a mechanical sculpture. For in a drawing that celebrates the sexual properties of both figures in the frankest possible manner, it is the male who shows himself most susceptible to the transformation Hulme desired. The woman, her hands closing proudly underneath the ample vagina she flaunts so openly, remains more or less organic in spirit; but the furiously gesticulating man is in the process of becoming a robot, and his enormous penis has been turned into a metallic piston. This phallic machine was a vitally important invention: it was the germinating motif Epstein had been searching for, and he eventually made it the basis of the

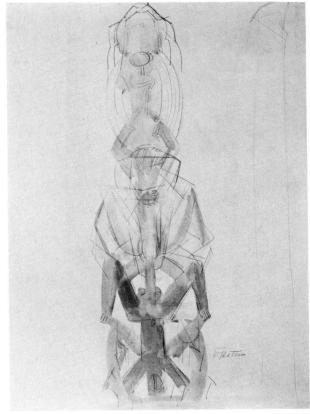

△ Jacob Epstein
Totem, c. 1913

◁ Jacob Epstein
Composition, 1913

projected Hulmean sculpture which was to be known as *Rock Drill.*

First of all, however, he had to rid himself of his obsession with primitive art, and a number of studies survive to show how he gradually eradicated it from his mind. The sculpture was conceived on a monumental scale; and although the chronological sequence of the surviving drawings has to be guessed at, his primary impulse probably led him towards the format of a colossal totem-pole, the kind of monument that a witch-doctor would have erected in the middle of a tribal village. The man stands on his head to form the base of the construction and thrusts his penis into the open vagina of the woman balancing above him on his legs. She, in her turn, raises her arms and holds up a baby, whose stance echoes that of the negro in *Cursed Be The Day Wherein I Was Born.* The whole assemblage, woven together with a multiplication of extra limbs that sprout from the bodies of the copulating pair, is a hymn to procreation, a prehistoric Tree of Life with the new-born generation triumphing at the top. And it is also a celebration of virility, for the totem is in itself a ready-made phallic symbol. Epstein had conceived a powerful image, but he must have realized that it was still imitative of African carvings: the motif was discarded, and in its place he sketched a more abstract crayon drawing of a totem-like penis piercing an aperture.

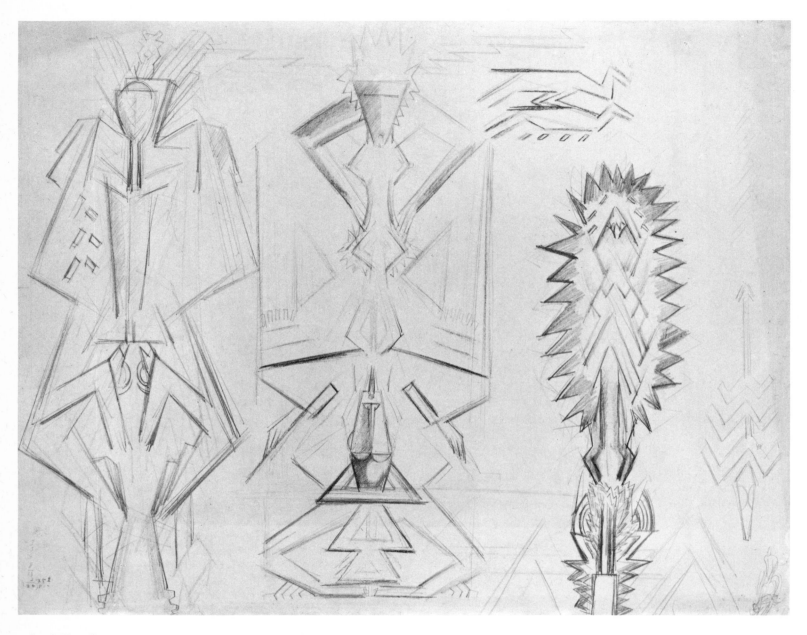

Jacob Epstein
Study for Rock Drill, Venus and Doves, c. 1913

Then, perhaps quite suddenly, a better alternative occurred to him, and he drew three versions of a similar column on one sheet of paper. The project drawn in the centre of the page still shows the man in an inverted position at the bottom, but the Venus-like woman is far less easily distinguishable and the child has disappeared completely. Epstein wanted to focus all his attention on masculinity, and to this end he outlined the figure on the left, who now stands upright and seems to thrust downwards with all his strength on the phallic point of stress between his straining legs. The penis is not so specifically described here, doubtless because Epstein was dissatisfied with such an obvious genital reference; and on the right he considers a possible alternative, sketching an exploding structure that shoots up like a rocket from the bottom of the picture. Mechanical metaphors were evidently beginning to suggest themselves to his imagination and this drawing, which shows how inextricably related all the different Pett Level themes were in Epstein's own mind, reveals the genesis of his eventual solution. He would have seen rock drills at work in the quarries he visited for his materials, and it is quite likely that the form of the sculpture first presented itself while he was watching such a machine cutting into stone, shattering the air all around with its ear-splitting noise. No other modern machine could signify the Vorticists' jarring urban context, and their belief in 'the point of maximum energy', more dramatically.

When precisely did the idea of a rock drill occur to him? The presence of a tiny sketch for the dove carvings on this very same drawing points to a date early in 1913, and Epstein himself recalled that 'it was in the experimental pre-war days of 1913 that I was fired to do the rock drill.'[18] Artists' memories are never automatically accurate, however, and it is reassuring to find that one of Epstein's contributions to the 'Cubist Room' exhibition of December 1913 was actually entitled *The Rock Drill*. It was not, as some historians have assumed, the complete sculpture: Lewis's introduction to the show stated that 'in this room as well are three drawings by Jacob Epstein', and only three contributions by the sculptor are listed in the catalogue.[19] Two more *Rock Drill* drawings were included in his one-man show at the Twenty-One Gallery, which ran concurrently with the 'Cubist Room' exhibition, and Bomberg actually remembered visiting Epstein in the same month in order to see the almost complete first version of the sculpture. 'Did we not call on Jacob Epstein, about December 1913, at a garage in Lamb's Conduit Street, which he was using as a workshop, finishing the large white plaster "Rock Drill" or was it Lewis and I, or the three of us together?' he asked Roberts in 1957, thereby proving that the original *Rock Drill* must have been executed by the end of that year.[20]

If Lewis did indeed accompany Bomberg he would have been an admiring visitor; for he had waxed enthusiastic over the studies for the sculpture in his 'Cubist Room' essay, claiming that Epstein 'finds in the machinery of procreation a dynamo to work the deep atavism of his spirit . . . His latest work opens up a region of great possibilities, and new creation'.[21] And it is not difficult to understand Lewis's excitement when one of these fully-fledged studies for *Rock Drill* is examined, for Epstein's identification of man and machine was the ideal sculptural counterpart to the theories laid down in the Vorticist manifestos. Now, in a vigorous charcoal sketch, the figure is shown mounted on a huge pneumatic drill, the perfect twentieth-century substitute for the penis of Epstein's previous drawings. The shining machine is held, with open symbolism, between the driller's parted legs. It is a confident image: the man's head looks upwards, in an attitude of triumph, and he rests his hands calmly on top of the drill. Only the fierce tautness of Epstein's contours, and the rush of steam issuing from the instrument's side, suggest that there is any strain involved in the act.

See next page

One of the problems thrashed out in these drawings was the precise relationship between the man and his weapon. In another sketch of the front view – dated 1913 – Epstein changes the driller's head into a featureless rectangular block and articulates the streamlined details of his instrument in greater detail. He decided to balance the central pillar with two tripods, branching out from each side of the drill and providing metal slabs upon which the man can rest his feet. The sculpture thereby gains in strength and stability, and an even lower viewpoint is chosen so that it soars upwards in an immensely optimistic movement. Straddling his destructive charge, the driller gains an almost heroic status, and the pyramidal architecture of the surrounding rocks serves to accentuate his power. Mastery of pose has been achieved, then, but the man's actions are strangely ineffective. His hands still lie complacently on the drill, and the machine's forked head hovers indecisively over the ground it should be attacking. Accordingly, Epstein proceeded to tackle his subject from the back, dispensing with the rocky framework altogether and shifting the figure into an open-air setting. This study, which Hulme admiringly reproduced in *The New Age* on Christmas Day 1913 as the first of his 'Contemporary Drawings' series, shows a

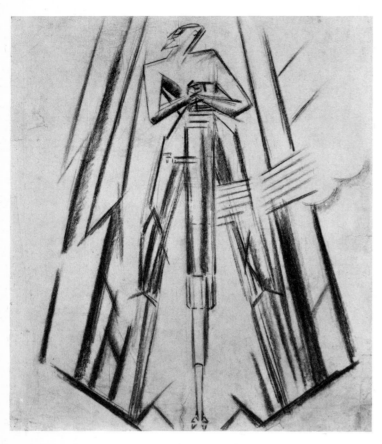

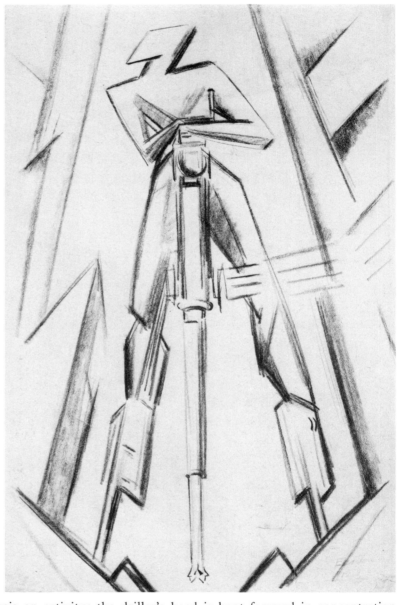

△ Jacob Epstein
Study for Rock Drill (front), *c.* 1913

△△ Jacob Epstein
Study for Rock Drill (front), 1913

▽ Wyndham Lewis
Arghol, 1914

new emphasis on activity: the driller's head is bent forward in concentration rather than turned up to the side, and his right arm is shown in at least three alternative places as Epstein tried to select a more dynamic, proto-Futurist working posture. The man's body has become more mechanical, too, with its inverted triangle of a torso, tight circular buttocks and tubular legs. He is bending slightly at the knees now, to reflect the tension involved in operating the drill, and the ground rises up into a broken mountain as a more positive target for his efforts. But the point of contact between machine and earth remains undescribed: instead of vibrations and steam, a stylized cloud appears behind the man to emphasize his superhuman proportions.

The question is finally settled in another back view, which carries the drill down to the rock and celebrates its energy in a tight complex of expanding arcs. The position of the man's right arm has been sorted out as well, and given a muscular vitality that was previously lacking. Epstein now presents a body strong enough to perform a driller's task, with massively angular shoulder-blades counteracting the extreme slimness of waist and legs. The background has also been elaborated so that man and machine are posed against a panoramic landscape on the horizon. It gives them both an access of liberty, as if to suggest

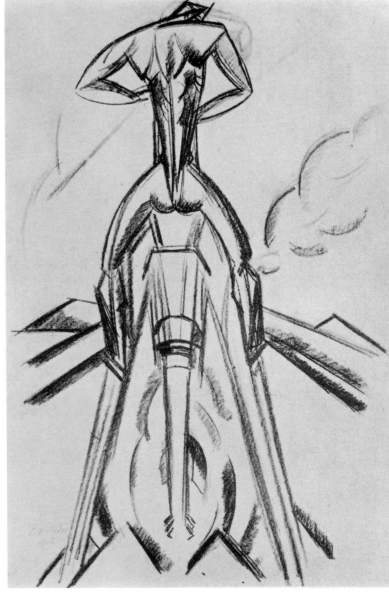

that this driller is riding high above a world which he could easily destroy with his formidable invention. One thing alone was lacking to make the sculpture complete: an exact definition of the drill itself. This drawing thoroughly dodges the issue; but without a fully convincing portrayal of the machine at work, Epstein could not hope to make a purposeful work of art out of his ambitious sketches. The project would stay on the drawing-board, like his extraordinary plan for the copulating totem, and he would be forced to regard it as a marvellous idea that had to be abandoned because of its infeasibility. He must have thought, at one stage, that his driller would never get further than Lewis's *Arghol*, an ink sketch of a figure which bears a remarkable resemblance to Epstein's mechanical operator. Lewis's man strains forward in a tense pose similar to the driller, and his legs are formed into the same kind of metallic curve. The arms swoop down from massively-built shoulders, as if engaged in physical exertions of a Herculean order, but they do nothing: deprived of an instrument, the action turns in on itself and *Arghol* ends up looking sadly impotent, a worker who can only flex his muscles and wait for a suitably impressive task to perform.

Epstein's driller, likewise, was in danger of castration. How could his mechanized phallus and source of strength be rendered into three-dimensional form

△ Jacob Epstein
Study for Rock Drill (back), *c.* 1913

△△ Jacob Epstein
Study for Rock Drill (back), 1913

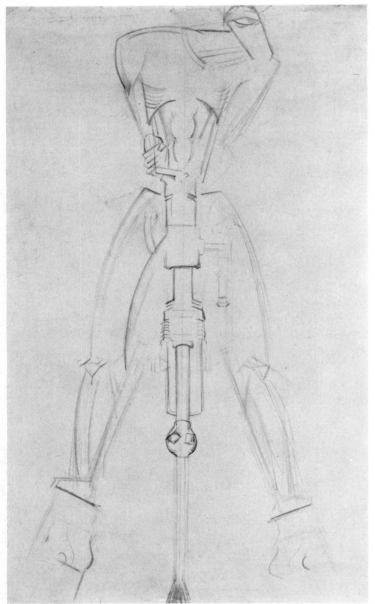

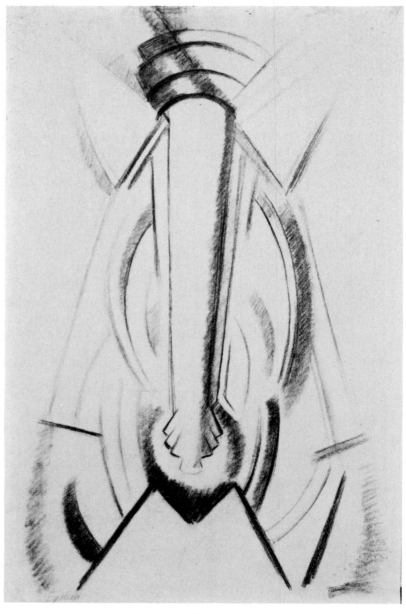

△ Jacob Epstein
Study for Rock Drill (front), *c.* 1913

△△ Jacob Epstein
Study for Rock Drill (drill's head), *c.* 1913

without paling beside a *real* drill, which would always possess far more credibility than anything a sculptor's imagination might produce? It was all very well to draw, as Epstein did, an even more detailed and specific pencil study of the sculpture which showed the driller operating an almost scientifically delineated rendering of a machine. And it was equally possible to execute a powerfully organized composition based on the theme of the drill's teeth striking rock. There, on a sheet of paper, the lines could be disposed in a series of directional curves to show the shattering impact of metal on stone, and a schematized representation of a drill in motion convey just as much force as its genuine equivalent. If this shape was to be transferred to plaster, stone or even bronze, however, it would lose out in comparison with true machinery. The Vorticist painter could use mechanical imagery without any fear of failing to match up to reality: the medium itself immediately removed their visions from any odious comparisons with the world they were reflecting. The Vorticist sculptor, on the other hand, ran a terrible risk if he attempted to beat machinery at its own game, and Epstein knew it only too well. Gaudier had avoided the pitfall by concentrating on animal themes; his *Bird Swallowing Fish* portrayed a

quasi-mechanical operation that would never conceivably be paralleled else-where. But a rock drill could easily be seen in photographs at that time, showing it in powerful action at the Rand Mines or proudly on display in drill manu-facturers' shop windows as a proud substantiation of their claim that 'the condi-tions prevailing on the Rand gold mines (in recent years) were such that they practically revolutionised existing types of drills'.[22] Such an archetypal exemplar of modern mechanical ingenuity might easily put Epstein's personal version to shame.

There was only one course of action open, and he was not afraid to take it. With astonishing audacity, he accepted the full implications of his idea and decided on 'the purchase of an actual drill, second-hand, and upon this I made and mounted a machine-like robot, visored, menacing, and carrying within itself its progeny, protectively ensconced'. Epstein had gone one stage further than any of his Vorticist colleagues in his 'ardour for machinery'. Not only did he finally model a plaster figure of his driller that changed a human being into a mechanized artefact; he also pursued the analogy to its logical conclusion by placing it on a real machine, with the name of the American manufacturers stamped clearly on its side. And he even toyed with the notion of making it move, as a true drill should, for he recalled that 'I had thought of attaching pneumatic power to my rock drill, and setting it in motion, thus completing every potentiality of form and movement in one single work'.[23] Futurist sculp-ture had, of course, already exploited the possibilities of literal dynamism: one head displayed in a Turin exhibition actually rolled its eyes from side to side. Epstein was probably aware of the precedent and it may have affected his decision not to incorporate motion into his piece. Vorticism, after all, was totally opposed to blurred outlines, and he was sufficiently in agreement with the movement to concur with its anti-Futurist aesthetic. Nevertheless, he had adumbrated the whole of Kinetic art by planning to add the extra dimension of motorized movement; and he also complemented Duchamp's 1913 *Bicycle Wheel* by daring to put a ready-made drill on exhibition as a sculpture in its own right, albeit combined with a man-made driller. To do so was to risk incurring the disapproval of his own avant-garde friends as well as the English sculptural establishment: Pound spoke for all the other rebels when he declared

Left to right

Photograph of Driller working with a Rock Drill Tripod, 1910–20

Photograph of a Rock Drill at work in 45·5 cm. Stope, Rand Mines, S. Africa, 1910–20

Photograph of a Rock Drill at work with a spray, Rand Mines, S. Africa, 1910–20

Photograph of the Showrooms at Holman Bros. Rock Drill Works, Camborne, Cornwall, 1910–20

in an 'Affirmations' essay on Epstein's work that 'our respect is not for the subject-matter, but for the creative power of the artist; for that which he is capable of adding to his subject from himself; or, in fact, his capability to dispense with external subjects altogether, to create from himself or from elements'.[24] Did not the glorification of an actual machine come uncomfortably near to the philosophy of mimesis that the Vorticists were at pains to reject? Pound may well have asked such a question when he first saw *Rock Drill*, for Epstein remembered that 'Gaudier Brzeska was very enthusiastic about it when he visited my studio in 1913 with Ezra Pound to view it. Pound started expatiating on the work. Gaudier turned on him and snapped, "shut up, you understand nothing!"'[25]

Gaudier's rebuke may well have been a significant pointer to his own opinion of *Rock Drill*. For although he never committed his specific reaction to print, he did tell Pound late in 1914 that radical sculptors were probably wasting their time vying with real machines in their work. 'The field for combinations of abstract forms is nearly unexplored in occidental painting', he explained to Pound, 'whereas machinery itself has used up so many of the fine combinations of three-dimensional inorganic forms that there is very little use in experimenting with them in sculpture.' The overwhelming impact of *Rock Drill* and its ready-made must have helped engender this belief in Gaudier's mind, and he may in his turn have persuaded Pound that Epstein's monumental assemblage did not after all constitute a sacrilegious creative act. Some such change of heart, at any rate, seems to have motivated the poet to declare in 1916 that 'the forms of automobiles and engines, where they follow the lines of force, where they are truly expressive of various modes of efficiency, can be and often are very beautiful in themselves and in their combinations, though the fact of this beauty is in itself offensive to the school of sentimental aesthetics'.[26]

Even the most cursory glance at the surviving photograph of this courageous masterpiece is, moreover, enough to allay any fears that Epstein had not impressed his own personality on the work. Pictured in the deserted gloom of the sculptor's Lamb's Conduit Street garage, this daunting monument has an air of melancholy that was entirely absent in his preliminary drawings. The drill itself, held firmly upright by three sturdy supporting legs, is subservient to the character of the man-made imaginative product built around it; and this figure, his head peering forward to the right, possesses little of the former surging optimism. Rather is he wary, even fearful, of the effect his machine will have on the world, a man quite different from the driller in the studies who wielded his instrument without a thought for the consequences. Epstein has changed him from a personification of mechanical prowess into a figure haunted by responsibilities: to symbolize his new doubts, the simplified back view of an embryo child is lodged inside the hollow cage of his torso, its biomorphic curves contrasting dramatically with the man's angular physique. For the driller is a potential parent as well as the apogee of an industrialized civilization, and the future welfare of his offspring may well be moulded by the environment his machine will help to bring about.

A careful study which can presumably be linked with this child has survived, and its defenceless pose serves to drive home the inevitability of the father's concern.[27] The huddled figure burrows into its abstracted shelter as if in recoil from the frightening force of the drill; and although Epstein makes the baby relatively calm in the plaster version, it is still positioned dangerously near to the head of the machine. There is, surely, an allegorical significance to be found in the final sculpture's juxtaposition of the foetus and the driller's right hand: even as he turns the handle to operate the mechanism, the man's action is being silently witnessed by the small shape installed in his bowels. Is the driller turning his head away to avoid contemplating the full meaning of this

Jacob Epstein
Birth Drawing, 1913

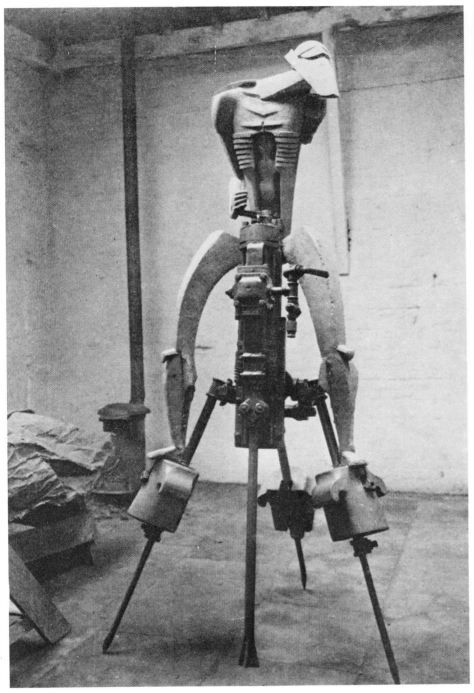

◁△ Jacob Epstein
Two views of *Rock Drill* (original state), 1913–15

symbolic confrontation between his manual gesture and the embryonic form? This hypothesis is reinforced by the brutal amputation of the left arm, severed just below the shoulder to look like an outward manifestation of the man's inward misgivings about his function in life. And the fact that Epstein had previously executed his own self-portrait wearing a similar driller's cap suggests the presence of another meaning, this time concerned with the idea of the sculptor himself as a potentially destructive agent.

That heavy layers of the Symbolism which had been so marked in the early Strand statues should be embedded within such an ostensibly unliterary work only underlines the complexity of Epstein's intentions. The inclusion of a real drill in his sculpture should in theory have utterly precluded the expression of sentiment, and left everything clear for an appreciation of its strong formal

Jacob Epstein
*Portrait of the Artist in a Storm Cap, c.*1912

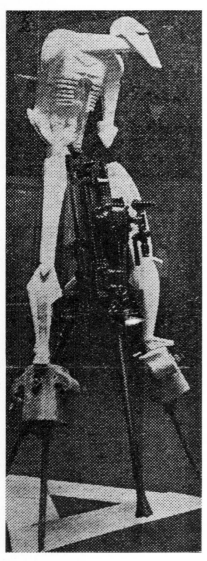

Jacob Epstein
Rock Drill (original state), 1913–15, on show at
the London Group Exhibition, 1915

values. There is enough, after all, to be admired in the bold disposition of the figure's masses, all straight lines and cutting edges in the top half and then widening into the great rounded swoop of the legs lower down. This sudden transition is engineered with the blithe assurance of a virtuoso, as Epstein leads the torso down from its immensely broad shoulders into the progressively tapering narrowness of the waist, only to reverse this diminuendo rhythm in the expansive flourish of the thighs which suddenly burst out from behind the machine and describe an immense arc as they plunge towards the tripod. There, the principle of contrast is carried even further, for these rigid supports contradict the curve of the driller's calves and deny their enclosed movement by jutting sharply downwards to the ground below. Indeed, the main trunk of the drill itself can be seen as more of a natural extension of the torso than can the legs: Epstein has manipulated his elements so carefully that machine and body are married in one integrated whole. The only area which betrays any uncertainty is the arrangement of the arms, where the truncated left shoulder interrupts the full play of the upper section. He obviously wanted to portray hesitation here, in order to mirror the driller's own anxiety, but he could not decide which arm should be sacrificed. A photograph from the *Daily Graphic*, taken in March 1915 when the sculpture was exhibited for the first time at the second London Group show, proves that he extended the original scheme by constructing a left arm as well, which stretches out indecisively towards the drill only to be stopped short through the lack of a hand.[28] A battle had been fought between Epstein's feeling for mechanistic form and his desire to enrich the work with literary meaning, and it was never properly resolved.

He did, however, manage to settle the problem of transforming his figure so that it would take on some of the attributes of its mechanical mount. Treating the idea of analogy as seriously as the Vorticist artists, he turned the driller's body into an unearthly amalgam of human anatomy and machine components. While the head has become an armoured mask, fit for protecting anyone from flying fragments and dust thrown up by the drill's vicious action, its neck is cut into the smooth, metallic planes of a steel girder. Lower down, the arms are changed into levers and pistons, just as Hulme would have wished, and the ribs formalized into two rigid rows of carburettor fins. The driller's thighs are likewise simplified into planes which suggest pre-stressed concrete beams, capable of playing an integral part in the structure of a modern factory, while the knee-caps are scarcely distinguishable from the shafts and bolts which constitute the body of the drill itself. The subtlety of Epstein's mechanical and industrial metaphors lies, all the same, in their ability to escape precise classification. Just as the driller's torso alternates all the time between sections of schematic geometry and areas where a more organic order is given its rein, so it is impossible to decide at any given point whether this ghostly apparition is a human being, a streamlined automaton or a primitive fetish. If it is unnecessary to make these distinctions in *The Mud Bath*, which resembles Epstein's analogical configurations in so many ways that Bomberg may well have been inspired by its example, the same rule applies when appraising the metamorphosis undergone by *Rock Drill*'s etiolated rider. Mounting his cruel charge like a twentieth-century equivalent of the four vengeful Horsemen of the Apocalypse, this hallucinatory cross between an exemplar of virility and an agent of death can easily be imagined demanding obeisance at the heart of a temple devoted to the cult of the machine. Primitivism and technology here meet in a union as unlikely as it is unforgettable.

Rock Drill managed, therefore, to be primarily a product of the imagination, despite its startling acceptance of a ready-made objet-trouvé. The *Daily Graphic* photograph proves, for instance, that Epstein finally decided to remove his drill from the real world by placing it on a triangular plinth, stepped at the front to

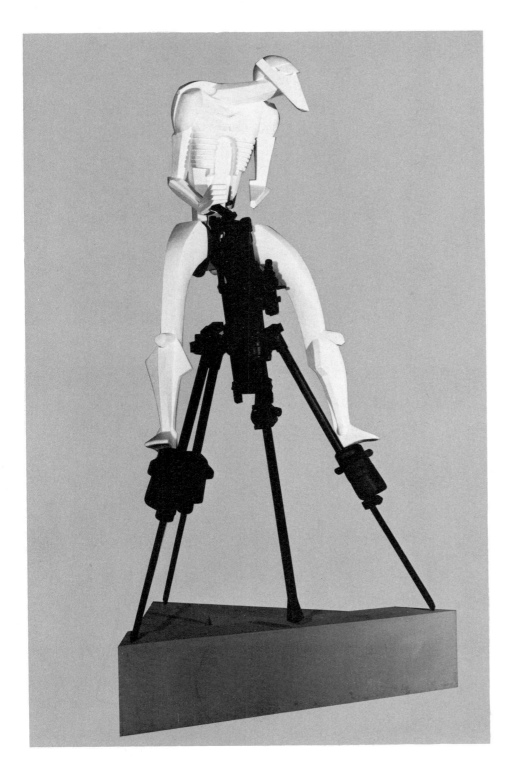

Reconstruction of *Rock Drill* (original state),
1913–15. Made in 1974 by Ken Cook and
Ann Christopher (1st view)

tilt the work back a little. This decision immediately reasserts its identity as a
'sculpture' in the orthodox sense of the word, and anyone who knew how a real
rock drill was operated would also have realised that Epstein had taken another
enormous imaginative liberty in his driller's pose. Nobody could possibly
straddle such a shuddering tool in this way without at the very least rupturing
himself; and although Epstein may have wanted to suggest that this driller could
be castrated by his savage weapon, the principal significance of the straddling
pose lies in the chance it gave Epstein to disclaim any kind of literal prosaism in
the image as a whole.

But this enormous, imposing assemblage still came as a slap in the face of the reviewers, upsetting all their preconceptions, and the *Observer*'s critic recoiled from the sculpture, recording his disgust with 'a ghastly plaster creature that suggests a monstrous insect rather than a human being – a sort of skeleton treated in cubist fashion . . . The whole effect is unutterably loathsome. Even leaving aside the nasty suggestiveness of the whole thing, there remains the irreconcilable contradiction between the crude realism of real machinery (of American make) combined with an abstractly treated figure; and the lack of cohesion between the black iron drill and the white plaster monstrosity perched upon it'.[29] There was no attempt to understand, sympathize with or interpret Epstein's intrepid exhibit: it was merely vilified as a public scandal, an aberration that did not merit serious examination. And the older guard of artists was just as abusive, for Augustus John described in a mystified letter how the driller was 'turning the handle for all he's worth and under his ribs is the vague shape of a rudimentary child or is it something indigestible he's been eating? Altogether the most hideous thing I've seen'.[30]

Epstein, for his part, was embittered by the response accorded his much-deliberated work, and he complained that 'the scribblers have been emboldened by the war, and wish to take an unfair advantage of creative artists by declaring that now we are at war artists have no business to be anything but normal; that is, mediocre. Queer argument that. In abnormal times to be normal'.[31] His comments appear to imply that the harshness of *Rock Drill* was in part caused by an uncanny presage of war, which Epstein shared with many other Vorticists and may help to account for the marked change in feeling between the first sketches and the finished sculpture. Most of the drawings were executed with an amalgam of human potency and inhuman dynamism uppermost in his mind; whereas by the time Bomberg viewed the original version of the assemblage itself in December 1913, he was able to see 'perched near the top of the tripod which held the Drill a tense figure operating the Drill as if it were a Machine Gun, a Prophetic Symbol, I thought later of the impending war'.[32] For Epstein's faith in machines had at some stage been irrevocably impaired, and he gave vent to his mounting disillusion in the haunted attitude of his driller.

These tragic overtones now appear overt, but when the sculpture first went on display everyone was too startled to detect any ambivalence of feeling in its construction. Even the critic of the *Manchester Guardian*, who distinguished himself from his colleagues by writing about it with genuine perception, announced that Epstein had 'found in a rock-drill machine the ideal of all that is expressive in mobile, penetrating, shattering force'. Positively gasping with admiration and astonishment, the reviewer went on to declare that 'he has accepted it all, the actual rock drill is here in this art gallery. Mr Epstein has accepted the rock drill, and says frankly that if he could have invented anything better he would have done it. But he could not. One can see how it fascinated him; the three long strong legs, the compact assembly of cylinder, screws and valve, with its control handles decoratively at one side, and especially the long, straight cutting drill like a proboscis – it all seems the naked expression of a definite force. Mounted upon it Mr Epstein has set a figure of the spirit of the drill – an idea of what a man might be who existed only for rock drilling. Everything is sharp, flanging lines, and the legs describe a curve as strong as a Gothic arch. It is a real piece of invention, a synthetic shape which has a swift, significant interest, even beauty, all its own'. The *Guardian* writer had accepted the challenge that this sculpture offered to his preconceptions about art, and he became a willing convert, asserting that 'I think it is the first convincing proof that what is called Post-Impressionist sculpture has a future'.

But such praise could not go unqualified, and he finished his review by com-

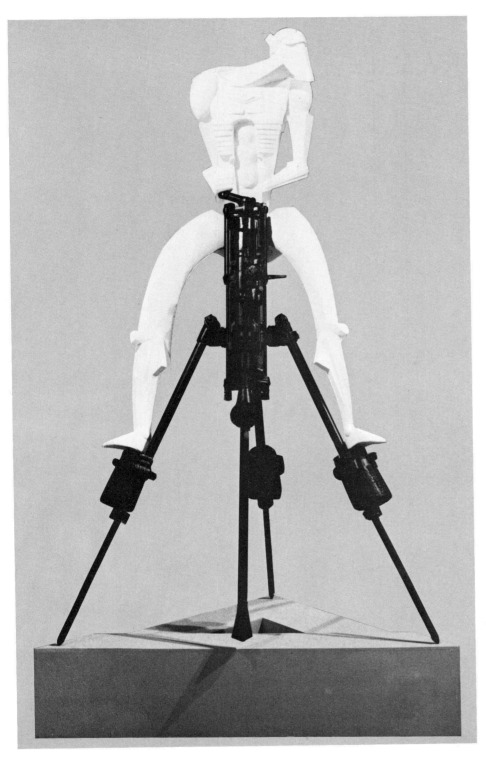

Reconstruction of *Rock Drill* (2nd view)

plaining that 'what is wrong with it is the rock drill itself. Even if the figure is to be cast in iron, the incongruity between an engine with every detail insistent and a synthetic man is too difficult for the mind to grasp. After all, man is a machine more wonderful than a rock drill, and if Mr Epstein can improve on man for his particular purpose it is false modesty to boggle at a rock drill'.[33] The critic was not simply censuring Epstein's unprecedented temerity in making a machine part of a work of art. He was prepared to accept that the gamble had been justified, but he could not reconcile himself to the resounding clash of conventions within the piece. And he was, theoretically, correct: Epstein was

trying to have it both ways, demanding the acceptance of machinery as legitimate sculpture, while at the same time expecting his audience to believe in his
own invented distortions of the human figure.

In principle, this schizophrenic notion should never for one moment have
succeeded; the two halves of the work required completely contradictory
aesthetic responses. Yet in practice, the sheer vigour of Epstein's imagination
welded the disparities together and even managed to command the loyalty of
Lewis, who was not by this time automatically bound to Epstein through any
ties of friendship. After noting that 'the combination of the white figure and
the rock-drill is rather unfortunate and ghost-like', the editor of *Blast No. 2*
wrote in his own periodical that 'its lack of logic has an effectiveness of its own.
I feel that a logical co-ordination was not intended. It should be taken rather
as a monumental, bustling, and very personal whim'. Always at this period an
acute critic of other artists, Lewis realized that Epstein had deliberately flouted
traditional concepts of unity in order to exploit the power of an irrational
ensemble. The subversive intelligence of the work appealed to him, just as its
frankly mechanistic bias confirmed that sculpture was eminently capable of
interpreting Vorticist precepts with outstanding originality; and so he declared
that 'Epstein's "Rock drill" is one of the best things he has done. The nerve-
like figure perched on the machinery, with its straining to one purpose, is a
vivid illustration of the greatest function of life'.[34] What was this function which
Lewis valued so highly: procreation, the aggressive act of destruction, or the
singleminded intensity that alone can create a viable artistic language? All three
concepts were doubtless in his mind when he looked at Epstein's prodigious
achievement, and Pound afterwards echoed Lewis's approbation by using its
name as the title of a group of *Cantos*.

Rock Drill marks the triumph of Vorticist sculpture, but the version beneath
which Lewis remembered 'Epstein and David Bomberg kissed, to seal a truce
. . . in the salons of the Goupil',[35] went the way of so many other vital products
of the movement. 'I lost my interest in machinery', Epstein explained curtly,
'and discarded the drill. I cast in metal only the upper part of the figure.'[36]
Although he never gave his reasons for taking such an extreme step, it is possible
that the rapidly escalating bloodshed in Europe again influenced his decision.
In 1913 and early 1914, when work on the original assemblage was carried out,
war was still widely regarded as a stirring, patriotic crusade. Even then, Epstein
had been sufficiently affected by war's horror to invest his driller with a pervasive anxiety; but by the summer of 1916, when he exhibited his now truncated half-length as *Torso in Metal from the "Rock Drill"* at the fourth London
Group show, the nation's response to the conflagration had turned from eagerness to despair. Too many men had been slaughtered, including Epstein's
friend Gaudier, and aggression was no longer an impulse to be celebrated. It was
inconceivable that the destructive potential of a drill could be admired on any
level: this machine was as much of a lethal weapon as the guns at the Front
which were obliterating English youth in thousands. Years later, Epstein considered *Rock Drill* to be 'a thing prophetic of much of the great war and as
such within the experience of nearly all',[37] which is tantamount to admitting
that the holocaust had caused him to reconsider the true meaning of his iron
instrument. 'I remember Epstein saying that he abandoned the drill because
he hadn't made it himself, it was just a machine',[38] recalled his widow; and this
decision, although ostensibly rising from formal objections to the status of a
ready-made, must have been bound up with his new hatred of the machine's
ability to tear the whole Western world apart. The impersonal finish of a real
drill forbade him to make his altered feelings plain, and so it had to be sacrificed.

Nothing remains in the dismembered bronze cast that now survives of the

◁ Jacob **Epstein**
Torso in Metal from the "Rock Drill", 1913–16
(1st view)

Jacob Epstein
Torso in Metal from the "Rock Drill", 1913–16
(2nd view)

soaring exhilaration expressed in the original studies.[39] Deprived of his gigantic mount, the driller juts his long helmeted beak forward with an air of downtrodden resignation. The foetus has assumed a far greater importance now that the drill has disappeared: it lies there, fully exposed, inside the cavity of the man's stomach, and nothing can hide its vulnerability. Only the driller's left arm seems capable of protecting the unborn child, but it just hangs in the air, inert and useless. Lacking a hand with which to wield the controls of the machine, it simply waits for an impending attack, a limb without a function. And the rest of the robot's anatomy is similarly reduced to a defensive role, for all its impressive array of armature. He is imprisoned in his geometrical format, limited rather than enhanced by his mechanistic attributes. The powerful sinews carved into his right shoulder should belong to a superman, confident of crushing the strongest opponent; and yet their muscular potential is savagely cut short lower down, where Epstein has lopped the arm off before it even had a chance to grow into an elbow. This brusque amputation of the limb that had previously worked the drill has a deleterious effect on the figure. Viewed from the side, his whole body sags and crumples: the upper chest caves in without the iron corsetry of the ribs to stiffen it into shape, while the distended neck bows low in meek acceptance of its fate. And weakness is made horribly explicit in the articulation of the back, which has been mauled by a deep fissure running all the way down the spine. It could have been inflicted during the same fight that

Jacob Epstein
Torso in Metal from the "Rock Drill", 1913–16
(3rd view)

caused the loss of the arm, for this driller looks more like a war victim than a triumphant harbinger of the machine age. He is battered and incomplete, a mere shell shaken by inhuman atrocities, and all he can do is peer apprehensively forward into a future that contains no hope.

'Here is the armed, sinister figure of today and tomorrow', Epstein wrote later, and he made his own feelings clear when he explained that *Rock Drill* possesses 'no humanity, only the terrible Frankenstein's monster we have made ourselves into'.[40] By 1916, he no longer shared the Vorticists' involvement with a mechanical culture, and he made his ultimate version of the sculpture into an indictment of a world that was rapidly becoming tyrannized by the machine, both in the city and at the trenches. The torso's sense of despair is unique in European sculpture of the time; and its nearest stylistic counterparts seem by comparison remarkably innocent manifestations of a belief in industrialized society. When Archipenko metamorphosed the thrusting movements of his *Boxers* into a cluster of non-representational forms, he was simply taking the schematic language that Epstein had employed in the driller's body one stage further into abstraction. Archipenko modelled his work in 1914, at the same time that Epstein was completing his first version of *Rock Drill*, and both sculptors drew on a mechanical vocabulary to express their idea of energy in the most immediate terms. But *Boxers* eschews the static finality of *Rock Drill* in favour of a semi-Futurist glorification of flux. Epstein might easily have been

Left to right

Alexander Archipenko
The Dance, reproduced on the cover of *The Sketch*, 1913

Alexander Archipenko
Boxers, 1914

Raymond Duchamp-Villon
Large Horse, 1914

aware of Archipenko's experiments, from his visits to Paris and photographs like the *Sketch*'s October 1913 cover illustration of *The Dance*, which truncates limbs with the freedom so evident in *Rock Drill*.[41] He would have abhorred the kinetic abandon of *Boxers*, however, preferring to uphold Vorticism's belief in the clearly defined, single image.

The sturdy independence of Epstein's standpoint is conclusively proved if his sculpture is compared with another, closely related continental exploration of the machine theme: Duchamp-Villon's *Large Horse*. It was executed around the same time, in 1914, and grew out of studies initiated the year before, when Duchamp-Villon wrote that 'the power of the machine imposes itself, and we can scarcely conceive living beings any more without it. We are strangely moved by the rapid brushing by of men and things, and accustom ourselves without knowing it to perceive the forces of the former through the forces they dominate'.[42] Epstein would probably have agreed with these sentiments when he originally began to think about *Rock Drill*, and the two men may well have met and discussed the sculpture's development when Duchamp-Villon came to London in the summer of 1914.[43] But as the work developed, Epstein realized with increasing pessimism that 'men' could no longer 'dominate' their mechanized environment. Duchamp-Villon saw nothing sinister in his wholehearted equation of horse and engine, and delighted in the welter of pistons, levers and spirals with which he tried to capture his animal's essential bodily movements. *Large Horse* is a jubilant glorification of twentieth-century speed, and uncoils itself with a leaping certainty that highlights the wavering diffidence of Epstein's figure. While the driller cowers and withdraws into his damaged armour, this archetype of horsepower springs forward with the imperturbable confidence of a motorized dynamo. Duchamp-Villon willingly embraces ambiguous confusion, and seizes on the act of galloping, whereas Epstein emphasizes the precise lines of his paralysed automaton, and stakes all on a knife-edge equipoise.

In the successive stages of one sculpture, he at once defined the English rebels' central tenets and eroded them by introducing an element of tragic doubt. For *Rock Drill* is a pivotal work, summarizing many fundamental premises of Vorticism even as it ushers in the disenchantment that would lead to the movement's downfall. Here, at the very climax of the group's corporate success, its death-knell was sounded; and anyone who viewed Epstein's shattered torso when it was exhibited in the summer of 1916 might have guessed that the revolution was nearing its end. The drill, along with all the iconoclastic hopes it symbolized, had been thrown away for ever.

Chapter 17: Nevinson at War, the New York Vorticist Exhibition and Coburn's Vortographs

Although the spirals of the Great English Vortex were helplessly swallowed up in the larger whirlpool of an international struggle, the Futurists reacted to the war with aplomb and threw themselves into militant activity. To them, the onset of combat came as a welcome confirmation of all that they had prophesied, and they mounted a patriotic crusade to campaign for Italy's intervention. 'There is one man in Europe who must be in the seventh heaven: that is Marinetti', declared Lewis in *Blast No. 2*. 'From every direction come to him sounds and rumours of conflict. He must be torn in mind, as to which point of the compass to rush to and drink up the booming and banging, lap up the blood! He must be a radiant figure now!'[1]

Lewis's satire was scarcely exaggerated: in July 1915, soon after their country committed itself to the fray, Marinetti and his cohorts enlisted and became members of the volunteer cyclists. But over in England, their eagerness had already been anticipated by Nevinson, the faithful disciple, who decided to involve himself in the fight from the instant that hostilities first commenced in the autumn of 1914. 'I was under contract to give a one-man show at the Dorée [sic] Gallery', he recalled, 'but a feeling of futility overwhelmed me and at my request the dealer released me.' Artistic ambitions no longer mattered in comparison with the 'long expected outrage on the Belgians'; and although ill-health prevented him from becoming a soldier, he joined the Red Cross as a compromise solution and went across to Dunkirk with his unit. There, acting not only as an ambulance driver but also as stretcher-bearer and interpreter, he was brought face to face with the agonies of dying men. 'When a month had passed I felt I had been born in the nightmare', he wrote later. 'I had seen sights so revolting that man seldom conceives them in his mind and there was no shrinking even among the more sensitive of us. We could only help, and ignore shrieks, pus, gangrene and the disembowelled.' By the advent of 1915, however, his constitution had become so debilitated that he 'crocked up and was sent home' to London.[2] Yet physical weakness did not deter him from turning his harrowing experiences into pictorial form, and neither did it alter his resolve to support the great cause of Futurism. On the contrary, he was for the moment convinced that the Italian movement would find its ultimate justification in battle paintings.

'This war will be a violent incentive to Futurism, for we believe there is no beauty except in strife, and no masterpiece without aggressiveness', he told the *Daily Express* in February 1915. 'I have tried to express the emotion produced by the apparent ugliness and dullness of modern warfare. Our Futurist technique is the only possible medium to express the crudeness, violence, and brutality of the emotions seen and felt on the present battlefields of Europe . . . Modern art needs not beauty, or restraint, but vitality.'[3] Nor was this empty verbiage, for alongside his interview the *Daily Express* reproduced the first fruit of Nevinson's determination to portray the reality of 'modern warfare' as he had witnessed it. The painting, which was exhibited a month later at the second London Group show, was called *Returning to the Trenches*; and the existence of a considerable number of preparatory studies for the composition indicates how much attention Nevinson lavished on this, perhaps his very first, war-picture.[4]

One of them, a swiftly executed charcoal sketch, shows how he arrived at a compromise between the urge to record his impressions and the urge to subject those memories to a rigorous formal discipline. On the right, where a few sparse lines indicate a skeletal pattern of soldiers' uniforms, baggage and rifles, he seems concerned only to establish the directional movement of the composition. But then, as his hand moves across the paper, simplification turns to elaboration as the paraphernalia of army life claims more of his attention. Faces

Christopher Nevinson
Study for Returning to the Trenches, 1914–15

are specified, limbs are described more fully and the phalanx of marching figures takes on a greater solidity as Nevinson shades his protagonists' forms into a unified mass. A fundamental uncertainty of aim becomes apparent, for the drawing cannot decide how far to abandon a legible theme in the interests of a dynamic diagram. At one point, it lingers over the cubic volume of a soldier's pack in the middle; and then, over on the far left, it starts to impose abstracted contours onto the disappearing column of bodies.

These inconsistencies are resolved with impressive finality in the painting, which manages to retain the full descriptive identity of its subject while marshalling all the incidental elements into a cohesive organization. The air of reportage, of a scene glimpsed vividly and never forgotten, has been crisply presented. And yet narration is made subservient to the demands of an overall structure, which binds the Futurist-inspired 'lines of force' radiating from the soldiers' feet to the diagonal forest of rifles and the sky's slanting rays. This muscular network invests the picture with a sense of urgency and speed, as if the marchers are caught up in a manic race that hurtles them towards their own destruction. Abstraction is used only in so far as it helps Nevinson to reflect the conditions he had experienced: war for these men is, literally, as harsh as the geometric straitjacket inside which they have been placed. The insistent repetition of the poses is not simply a second-hand exercise in Futurist simultaneity; it also forcibly expresses the monotony and grinding routine of an army that confined itself to the trenches and waited for something to happen. Individuality is entirely subsumed in the mechanics of an everyday ritual, and personal hardship takes second place to the impersonal agony of a whole brigade.

If the painting looks like a plain man's guide to Futurist techniques, it is still fully commensurate with the aims of an artist whose instincts always drove him towards the popular. More than ever before, Nevinson now wanted his work to be widely and clearly intelligible, and he had already grown impatient with an avant-garde that alienated the majority. 'My Futurist training . . . had convinced me that a man who lives by the public should make his appeal to that public and meet that public,' he recalled later, 'and that all hole-and-corner cliques, and scratch-a-back societies are disastrous to the artist and his output.'[5] Hence the plain-spoken quality of *Returning to the Trenches*, where radical devices are deployed to ram home the intolerable hardship of conditions at the Front.

Christopher Nevinson
Returning to the Trenches, 1914–15

Active service had catapulted Nevinson into a sudden artistic and emotional maturity, and he found his aesthetic precepts given startling confirmation by the reality of combat. 'I think it can be said that modern artists have been at war since 1912', he told *The New York Times* in a fascinating interview that correlated his pre-war aggression with the new international conflict. 'Everything in art was a turmoil – everything was bursting – the whole talk among artists was of war. They were turning their attention to boxing and fighting of various sorts. They were in love with the glory of violence. They were dynamic, Bolshevistic, chaotic. The intellectuals knew that the war was coming before business men and financiers . . . Everything was being destroyed; canons of art were everywhere sacrificed. And when war eventually came, it found the modern artist equipped with a technique perfectly well able to express war. Some say that artists have lagged behind the war. I should say not! They were miles ahead of it. They were all ready for the great machine that is modern war.'[6] Indeed, Nevinson later remembered that one of his lost pre-war pictures, 'painted mostly with sand to make a contrast with the shining, metallic guns', was actually called *War*.[7]

Like his Futurist counterparts, Nevinson was fully prepared to create images of combat; yet unlike the Italians, he never thought of glorifying in destruction. Callow patriotism and histrionics were firmly rejected in favour of a sombre gravity, poised – like the Vorticists – half-way between Italian dynamism and French monumentality. Over in Paris, Jacques Villon had already achieved a comparable balance when he painted his *Marching Soldiers* in 1913. Diagonal 'lines of force' are employed to denote the advancing motion of the men, just as Nevinson had done in *Returning to the Trenches*. But for Villon, the subject is just a pretext for a refined geometrical exercise, where the figures are lost in a series of cool colour patterns, and the thrust of the march is counteracted by the emphatic diagonal on the right leaning in the opposite direction. His picture strikes an elegant compromise between Cubism and Futurism, but it entirely fails to convey anything about the meaning of an army. Only first-hand experience of slaughter could teach an artist to discount Marinetti's belief in the healthiness of war; and Nevinson, who had been invalided home after tasting the terrors of senseless death, was ideally qualified to present an alternative pessimism. Without abjuring his former allegiances altogether, he still found it necessary to stand against the Futurists' love of destruction: by July 1915 Lewis was able to report that 'Marinetti's one and only (but very fervent and literal) disciple in this country, had seemingly not thought out, or carried to their logical conclusion, all his master's precepts. For I hear that, de retour du Front, this disciple's first action has been to write to the compact Milanese volcano that he no longer shares, that he REPUDIATES, all his (Marinetti's) utterances on the subject of War, to which he formerly subscribed. Marinetti's solitary English disciple has discovered that War is not Magnifique, or that Marinetti's Guerre is not la Guerre. Tant Mieux'.[8]

△ Jacques Villon
Marching Soldiers, 1913

▷ Christopher Nevinson
On the Way to the Trenches, c. 1914–15

Lewis fortified his glee over Nevinson's change of heart by reproducing an outstanding woodcut version of *Returning to the Trenches* in *Blast No. 2*, as if to suggest that the great dissenter had actually joined the ranks of the Vorticists.[9] The picture's clean monochrome construction certainly blended well with the other designs in the magazine, and the woodcut medium gave it a splintered rhythm that put Nevinson momentarily in tune with the rebel movement. Sharp triangles replace the foreground lines delineated in the painting, and the body of the column is now split through with vicious lines that stress the tension vof the situation. Lewis's decision to include the work of a sworn enemy in *Blast No. 2* may come as a surprise, but he helped to account for his tactics by praising *Returning from the Trenches* elsewhere in the periodical. 'As to Mr Nevinson's work, an artist can only receive fair treatment at the hands of one completely in sympathy with him', he wrote in his review of the second London

Group show, scrupulously refusing to make any adverse remarks about the style of Nevinson's contributions. 'So it would not be fair for me to take Mr Nevinson's paintings for criticism, side by side with Wadsworth's, for instance. Nevertheless, I can say that his "Marching Soldiers" have a hurried and harassed melancholy and chilliness that is well seen.'[10] Lewis obviously responded to the mechanistic gloom of the picture, for his own views on the best way to translate war into pictorial terms were closely related to Nevinson's. 'The quality of uniqueness is absent from the present rambling and universal campaign', he declared in another *Blast No. 2* essay, discounting the heroic approach of nineteenth-century war paintings. 'There are so many actions every day, necessarily of brilliant daring, that they become impersonal. Like the multitudes of drab and colourless uniforms – these in their turn covered with still more characterless mud – there is no room, in praising the soldiers, for anything but an abstract hymn.'[11]

Wyndham Lewis
Cover of 'Antwerp', 1915

Returning to the Trenches was just such a work, even if its 'abstract' qualities derived more from Futurism than Vorticism. When Lewis himself drew a military cover for Ford's 'Antwerp', published in January 1915, he avoided Nevinson's simultaneity and concentrated on a characteristically solid definition of one solitary soldier. And he went much further than Nevinson by juxtaposing this fierce automaton with a freewheeling complex of angular forms, one of which scythes across the centre of the page like a shattered gun-barrel. The deliberately harsh, anti-romantic tenor of the drawing is close to Nevinson, however: Lewis's fighter is just as enmeshed in his environment as Nevinson's marchers are in the irresistible drive of their column.[12] Both artists were utterly opposed to the propagandist lies put about through the posters that suddenly proliferated all over England. Indeed, *Returning to the Trenches* could almost be seen as a brutally effective refutation of the poster which sought to win recruits by portraying a similar line of soldiers leaving for France in an orderly, well-scrubbed progression. As Nevinson himself remembered, 'brass bands, union jacks, and even "Kitchener Wants YOU" had no power to move me'.[13] There was a fearful gap separating the civilians' idea of war from the one experienced by the suffering combatants; and by 1915, Nevinson was fully equipped to provide the English public with a more accurate assessment of the fighting. He had been at the Front, and it was his duty as an invalid to present the true facts without attempting to satisfy the chauvinistic demands of those writers who cried out for glamorous war pictures in the national press. 'One is already asking on the Continent who will be the first to immortalise on canvas or in marble the tremendous realities of 1914–15', enthused the *Daily News* on 2 February. 'Defeat inspired the historical painters in the 'seventies. Victory will be the new theme. . . . The campaign of last year and this! What masterpieces must be born!'[14] Nevinson depicted what he had witnessed in the teeth of such rabble-rousing journalism, and it must have required a considerable amount of courage to carry out such a hard-headed programme.

Anon
World War I Recruitment Poster, c. 1915

The Vorticists were soon too embroiled in the war to match Nevinson's productivity, and only Pound was now left behind in London to keep the spirit of pictorial rebellion genuinely alive. After the last of his enlisted friends had departed for the Front in 1916, he found himself entrusted with the task of sustaining the movement in their absence; and no-one could have tackled the task with more flair or enthusiasm. Pound always had pedagogic leanings, and immediately war was declared he attempted to satisfy them by organizing the Vorticists into an official teaching body. On 2 August 1914, *The Egoist* published his 'Preliminary Announcement of the College of Arts', which was obviously meant to be the basis of a full-scale prospectus; and sure enough, by the beginning of November he was able to send a proof of that prospectus to Harriet Monroe, having written another article on the project in the 1 November issue of *The Egoist*. Printed in the form of a leaflet at the Complete Press and distributed in London towards the end of the month, Pound's text was mainly directed at American students who were being prevented from studying in Europe by the advent of hostilities. His encyclopaedic mind was manifestly at work behind the idea of 'a University graduate school' which aimed 'at an intellectual status no lower than that attained by the courts of the Italian Renaissance'. This was the high-flown concept informing the College of Arts, and Pound widened out its appeal to embrace students of all nationalities 'who would otherwise be fugging about in continental pensions, meeting one single teacher who probably wishes them in the inferno'. He claimed that 'no course of study is complete without one or more years in London', and extolled the 'unsurpassed' collections at the British Museum and National Gallery.

But more important still, his College offered 'contact with artists of established position, creative minds, men for the most part who have already suffered in the cause of their art'. The list of faculty members included a nucleus of Vorticists: Gaudier, Lewis, Wadsworth and Pound himself, none of whom would have balked at disseminating the movement's precepts among his pupils. 'Had I been teaching Vorticism at the time I was practising it, in the shadow of the First World War, one of my main doctrines would have run as follows', Lewis wrote later, doubtless recalling the programme he had formulated as the College's professor-designate. 'I would have insisted upon the creation of a language absolutely distinct from what was handed us by nature – such as stones and trees, and men and women, or all the other visual entities of our everyday world. I should have said that the musician does not require these things, and why should we? I should have recommended the construction of an alphabet of as abstract as possible a kind . . . In my class I should have had upon a table objects numbered, or marked by letters, and have excluded those resembling, say, a bottle, or a hand, or an animal, or a flower. Had I been able to start a workshop, like the Omega workshops, I should have had classes developing the above themes, and encouraged the shaping, in clay or in wood, of objects conforming to those theories. In other words, a world of not-stones, not-trees, not-dogs, not-men, not-bottles, not-houses, etc. I should not have insisted upon this world of negation, but I should have used that as a means of teaching repudiation of nature.'[15] Such methods would have revolutionized the whole moribund fabric of English art school teaching, but the College was not to be an exclusively Vorticist institution. 'While the Vorticists are well-represented, the College does not bind itself to a school', Pound explained in 1914;[16] and his prospectus showed how, 'recognising the interaction of the arts, the inter-stimulus, and inter-enlightenment, we have gathered the arts together . . . one art is the constant illuminator of another, a constant refreshment'.[17] And so Pound's American friend Alvin Langdon Coburn was to teach photography, Wilenski and John Cournos were to help deal with the literary side of the course and Arnold Dolmetsch was to propound music, spurred on no doubt by Pound's own suggestion that 'a new Vorticist music would come from a new computation of the mathematics of harmony'.[18]

These enormously wide-ranging proposals never came to anything, of course. Pound's darting intelligence was adept at committing schemes to paper, but he was hopelessly incapable of putting them into practice. The organizational problems must have proved insuperable from the outset, and the very war that had originally inspired the project consumed the energies of its putative teaching staff. It was an ambitious plan, which intended to carry out the cross-fertilization every university aims at in theory but invariably fails to achieve. The arts were not just to be studied: historians would be taught to paint, literary critics to write poetry, and it is a tragedy that these ideas never saw fruition inside the country that needed them most.

Pound, however, was undaunted by the death of his brainchild. His multifarious connections with *The New Age*, *Poetry*, *The Egoist* and many other little magazines ensured that he was able to continue publishing Vorticist propaganda, above all in his own extended series of 'Affirmations' essays. And the news of Gaudier's death in the summer of 1915 affected him so deeply that he began at once to consider commemorating his friend in the permanent form of a book. 'We have lost the best of the young sculptors, and the most promising', he wrote to Felix Schelling in June. 'The arts will incur no worse loss from the war than this is. One is rather obsessed with it.'[19] He set to work immediately, turning his obsession into an elegiac *Memoir* which incorporated all Gaudier's published writings, a rough 'partial catalogue of the sculpture' and a lavish series of reproductions. 'In undertaking this book I am doing what little I can to carry out [Gaudier's] desire for accessibility to students', he explained, 'and I am, moreover, writing it very much as I should have written it if he had lived, save that I have not him leaning over my shoulder to correct me and to find incisive, good-humoured fault with my words.' He also reprinted some of his own most sustained writings on Vorticism, in order to place Gaudier's work in its appropriate context and set down a personal evaluation of the movement as a whole. 'I should in any case have written some sort of book upon vorticism', he added, 'and in that book he would have filled certain chapters.' The *Memoir* was published both in London and New York in 1916, and its partisan tone must have been obvious to all who read it. As well as commemorating Gaudier's talents in a comprehensive manner, Pound was anxious to justify and trace the growth of the movement he had originally christened in the autumn of 1913. And he accounted for his desire to document a rebellion with which he had himself been totally involved by declaring that 'I do not believe that a man's critical activities interrupt his creative activities in the least. As to writing criticism, it is not a question of effort. It is merely a question of whether or no a man writes down what he thinks'.[20]

Pound needed to stand back and analyse the working principles that had inspired him and his artist friends, and their absence in the battlefields of France made the task even more urgent. Besides, one of his own central beliefs was that articulateness and creativity were not mutually exclusive. 'A certain measure of intellect, education, enlightenment', he insisted in the *Memoir*, 'does not absolutely unfit a man for artistic composition.' Hence his determination to use the Gaudier book as a literary credo of Vorticism, and his willingness to assert dogmatic theories throughout the text. 'An artistic principle, even a "formula" is not a circumscription', he declared, anxious to define the precise value of Vorticist tenets. 'These "dogmas" are not limits, not signs saying "thus far and no further", but points of departure, and lines along which the thought or the work may advance. No one can or does "create to a formula", by which phrase people mean "building out a work of art in accordance with a theory without waiting for the creative impulse". No work of value is done that way. On the other hand, a man's antecedent reflection, cogitation, etc., is bound to affect his later expression.' Although Pound would have been the last person to advocate an art that worshipped maxims at the expense of instinct, he despised England for having 'always loved the man incapable of thought', and pointed out that 'the praise of Shakespeare' which the British 'most love is some absolutely inaccurate rubbish about "wood notes wild"'. This fatuous prejudice, he maintained, lay behind 'the fury which greets any "new form of art", new forms of art which are valid being always a product of thought, a double emphasis on

Edmond Dulac
*Caricature of Ezra Pound, c.*1917

some fundamental principle of strength or of a beauty cast aside, or rather buried under the slow accretions of stupidity, carelessness, lack of intensity.'[21]

The *Memoir*, therefore, was written in defiance of such Anglo-Saxon shibboleths, as if to prove that analytical intelligence and creative originality could run hand in hand. But there is nothing dry or pedantic about Pound's final summary of Vorticism's importance at the end of the book. On the contrary, he attempts to pin down its achievement in a personal, almost a private way, asking himself 'what have they done for me these vorticist artists?' And he answered the question in a wonderfully heartfelt passage, explaining how 'they have awakened my sense of form . . . made me more conscious of the appearance of the sky where it juts down between houses, of the bright pattern of sunlight which the bath water throws up on the ceiling, of the great "V's" of light that dart through the chinks over the curtain rings, all these are new chords, new keys of design'.[22] This is a poet's way of saying that Vorticism did indeed manage to formulate an indigenous pictorial language: abrupt, clean-cut, angular and full of abstract vitality.

But the publication of a book, however timely or eloquent, could not ensure that the artists embroiled at the Front found a patron who would support and encourage them by purchasing their work. It was only a happy confluence of chance and coincidence that enabled Pound to contact the one man enthusiastic and rich enough to buy Vorticist works on a large scale: John Quinn, a successful American lawyer and voracious collector of modern art. Pound first met him in America, during an all-day party in August 1910; but this brief acquaintanceship was not renewed until the poet mounted an excoriating attack in *The New Age* on all the wealthy collectors whose backward-looking tastes had caused Epstein to slide into bankruptcy. 'Is it or is it not ludicrous that "The Sun-God" (and two other pieces which I have not seen) should be pawned, the whole lot, for some £60?' he wrote in a January 1915 issue, castigating society for failing to nourish its own finest artists. 'One looks out upon American collectors buying autograph MSS. of William Morris, faked Rembrandts and faked Van-dykes. One looks out on a plutocracy and upon the remains of an aristocracy who ought to know by this time that keeping up the arts means keeping up living artists; that no age can be a great age which does not find its own genius.'[23] Over in New York, Quinn was stung by the accusations contained in the article, and felt that Pound must have been indirectly referring to him. He had, for his part, admired the poet's work for a long time, and was sufficiently wounded to send him a combative letter on 25 February protesting about the *New Age* polemic. 'If there is a "liver" collector of vital contemporary art in this country, for a man of moderate means, I should like to meet him' he asserted confidently, pointing out how he had sold his old manuscripts to finance the acquisition of some Puvis de Chavannes.[24] And any suggestion that he had neglected Epstein was effectively scotched when he reminded Pound of the six works by that very same sculptor already in his collection.

Quinn, in fact, was one of the most enlightened patrons of his time, and Pound was lucky to have instigated a new friendship with such a remarkable man. For this eminently respectable lawyer was fully aware of the need to support the avant-garde, having helped to organize the great Armory Show in 1913 and purchased there almost six thousand dollars' worth of painting and sculpture, the largest single number of works acquired at the exhibition by anyone. His letter to Pound proudly enumerated the impressive roll-call of masterpieces by Cézanne, Van Gogh, Gauguin, Derain, Picasso, Matisse and Duchamp which he had bought over the years. But he was not self-satisfied: Pound's passionate diatribe, full of praise for Gaudier's achievement, prompted him to enquire how he could obtain some of the Frenchman's sculpture. And

Pound, detecting in this request a potential source of assistance for himself and his Vorticist allies, quickly replied with a promise to supply photographs of Gaudier's work. Moreover, he went on to outline the ideal function of a true patron, deploring a situation where one man could pay thirty thousand dollars for two pictures and emphasizing that 'NO artist needs more than 2,000 dollars per year, and any artist can do two pictures at least in a year. 30,000 dollars would feed a whole little art world for five years'. Realizing that Quinn was susceptible to his views, Pound lavished all his rhetorical powers on a description of the collector as a vital adjunct of contemporary art. 'My whole drive is that if a patron buys from an artist who needs money (needs money to buy tools, time and food), the patron then makes himself equal to the artist: he is building art into the world; he creates', Pound urged. 'A great age of painting, a renaissance in the arts, comes when there are a few patrons who back their own flair and who buy from unrecognized men. In every artist's life there is, if he be poor, and they mostly are, a period when £10 is a fortune and when £100 means a year's leisure to work or to travel . . . If you can hammer this into a few more collectors you will bring on another cinquecento.'25

Predictably enough, Quinn was seduced by the prospect of playing an active role in the lives of the artists he cherished, and he rapidly came to lean on Pound's advice. The poet congratulated him 'on having shed your collection of mss. and having "got as far as Derain" ', but was not content to leave it there. 'Mind you', he added, 'I think Lewis has much more power in his elbow, but I wouldn't advise a man to buy "a Lewis" simply because it was Lewis.'26 Quinn's curiosity was aroused. He became interested in Lewis as well as Gaudier, had his appetite whetted by a letter from Pound on 18 March predicting Lewis's imminent fame, and sent Lewis himself £30 on 17 December when Pound told him in a terse cable that 'Lewis enlisted needs money debts'.27 His response had been equally spontaneous during the previous summer when Pound informed him of Gaudier's death. 'Poor brave fellow. There is only the memory now of a brave gifted man. What I can do I will do', he wrote, asking Pound to purchase every available Gaudier for his collection, ordering twenty copies of both issues of *Blast* and – most important of all – promising to underwrite the expense of a Vorticist exhibition in New York.28 'It's a man's letter and I thank you for it', Pound replied with obvious emotion, promising his generous friend some Gaudiers even if it entailed spending part of the advance Quinn had sent 'on firearms as persuaders'.29 Although Sophie Brzeska did her best to thwart the export of any sculptures to America, Quinn eventually managed to secure a number of works, and plans for the projected Vorticist show moved slowly ahead.

Pound remorselessly sang Lewis's praises, telling Quinn in an outright panegyric about 'the vitality, the fullness of the man! Nobody knows it. My God, the stuff lies in a pile of dirt on the man's floor. Nobody has seen it. Nobody has *any* conception of the volume and energy and the variety'. The letter, written in March 1916, announced Pound's determination 'to do a Lewis book to match the Brzeska. Or perhaps a "Vorticists" (being nine-tenths Lewis, and reprinting my paper on Wadsworth, with a few notes on the others)'. He was ecstatic about Lewis's new drawings – 'they are all over the room, and the thing is stupendous' – and defined their quality in unabashedly sexual terms as 'every kind of geyser from jism bursting up white as ivory, to hate or a storm at sea. Spermatozoon, enough to repopulate the island with active and vigorous animals. Wit, satire, tragedy'.30 His enthusiasm paid dividends: Quinn was sufficiently impressed to commit himself to the organization of a Vorticism 'group' exhibition, probably at the Montross Gallery in the late spring of 1916, displaying work by Dismorr, Etchells, Gaudier, Lewis, Roberts, Saunders and Wadsworth.

Pound acted with his usual alacrity, telling Quinn on 9 March that Knewstub of the Chenil Gallery would send the pictures in two separate instalments, since Lewis did not want to entrust his entire contribution to a single ship 'in these torpedoing times'.[31] Then, a week later, he came up with yet another proposal, whereby half of the exhibition would be carried as luggage by T. S. Eliot, who was planning to depart for America on 1 April to sit for his Ph.D. examinations at Harvard. In order to reassure Quinn as to the aesthetic value of the consignment, Pound quipped that 'Eliot's trunk alone . . . would hold enough good art to justify the price of admission'.[32] He hoped Quinn would despatch a clerk to guide Eliot and his precious cargo safely through the New York customs, and felt happy with the idea until Eliot's boat was cancelled and the arrangement fell through.

Quinn, meanwhile, whose main acquisitive designs centred on Gaudier alone, heard that Sophie had forbidden the sculptor's work to be included in the proposed collective shipment, and his interest waned. Suddenly, without any warning, he told Pound to forget about the whole scheme. The poet was outraged: 'Ma che Christo. about the Vorticist show!!!' he exclaimed on 18 March. 'I simply CANT stop it now. The boys have sent in the stuff, and if it don't go I can never look anybody in the face again.'[33] After further indecision on the part of both men, Quinn reluctantly agreed to receive the work; but by the end of June, when the shipment finally arrived in New York, the Montross Gallery had changed its mind about the exhibition and Quinn found himself landed with the heavy cost of packing, insurance and freight.

The unwanted Vorticist works were sent to Quinn's own apartment, where they were examined by two of his American artist friends, Arthur B. Davies and Walt Kuhn. The latter seemed unimpressed and considered them 'too literary',[34] a stricture which embittered Quinn. He told Pound on 1 July that 'you and I were both sentimental about Brzeska'.[35] With unfailing diplomacy, Pound attempted to revive the lawyer's flagging spirits by insisting that 'none of the artists would be disappointed at poor public sales' and stressing that 'they would not be unhappy merely to know that their work had been inspected by Quinn'.[36] The discreet flattery succeeded in encouraging Quinn to spend a total of £438 on pictures by Etchells, Lewis, Roberts and Wadsworth during August, and Pound thanked him for 'absorbing' the work in such a handsome way.[37] A further £46 was spent in September on additional work by Dismorr, Etchells and Saunders, and Pound wrote once more, wondering whether Quinn 'had not absorbed as much Vorticism as was good for him'.[38] He had, however, underestimated Quinn's capacity to sustain an enthusiasm for the English avant-garde. Throughout the summer of 1916, the lawyer was responding with great magnanimity to pleas from Epstein's wife, who begged him to send cables to the Director of Recruiting at the War Office and the clerk of the Exemption Tribunal persuading them to defer the sculptor's enlistment. Epstein, desperately poor, needed time to finish several large works, and so Quinn sent the cables immediately with a letter declaring that 'Mr Epstein is a really great sculptor. His inability to finish the works that he has in hand would be not only a great loss to art and in particular to English art but would be a loss to the world, a loss comparable to which the mere destruction of property or buildings would be nothing. His work as a sculptor is extraordinary'.[39] Quinn reinforced his generous sentiments by purchasing *Cursed Be The Day Wherein I Was Born*, *Figure in Flenite*, and *Marble Mother and Child*, a splendid display of appreciation for Epstein's most radical work.

It was this unstinting sense of concern for the livelihood of artists he admired that also persuaded Quinn to continue his ill-fated efforts to stage a Vorticist exhibition. And eventually, towards the end of 1916, he managed to arrange it at the Penguin Club, 8 East 15th Street, an artists' society founded by Kuhn and a number of his friends after they had fallen out with the Kit Kat Club. With the help of Davies, Quinn converted the drab premises into a lounge and exhibition area, and the Great English Vortex was finally unveiled in New York on 10 January 1917.[40] Quinn printed a thousand copies of a special catalogue entitled *Exhibition of the Vorticists at the Penguin*, issued a couple of thousand handouts and covered all expenses to the tune of two hundred dollars. And his efforts seemed at first to be rewarded, for Walt Kuhn told his wife on the opening day that it 'looks like it's going to be a success – Fine looking "show" '.[41] Kuhn had clearly changed his mind about Vorticism and was hopeful; and so was Horace Brodzky, who as clerk of the works wrote an optimistic review for *Colour* in March 1917, stating that the 'seventy-five paintings and drawings' by Dismorr, Etchells, Lewis, Roberts, Saunders and Wadsworth 'make a brave show, and will do much here to pull painting out of the morass into which it seems to have been lately hopelessly entangled'. The ratio of exhibits was heavily weighed in Lewis's favour, setting his forty-three drawings and three paintings (*Kermesse, Workshop* and *Plan of War*) against nine by Etchells, eight by Wadsworth and four each by Dismorr, Roberts and Saunders. They were represented by several major paintings, including Etchells' *Pigeon and Juggler*, Roberts' *Jeu* and *Overbacks* and Wadsworth's *Combat, Rotterdam, Drydock, Blackpool* and *Isle of Dogs*.

But would-be collectors were hardly encouraged by the fact that fifty-two of the exhibits were loaned and not for sale; that the sparse, four-page, completely unillustrated catalogue contained no introductory statement of intent to explain what exactly Vorticism stood for; and that none of the artists involved was present either at the exhibition or in New York to answer queries and establish first-hand contact with the American vanguard. Arthur B. Davies had originally been enthusiastic enough about the show to promise Quinn that he would bear half its cost, an offer which Quinn refused because he felt that the obligation was his alone. But even Davies could not compensate for the half-hearted character of an event which was more like a retrospective survey than a topical report on work-in-progress. No less than sixteen of Lewis's exhibits dated from 1912 and others were even earlier, including a portfolio of eleven bargee and fishermen sketches which were listed but not numbered in the catalogue, as if in acknowledgement of their extremely marginal relevance. How American visitors were expected to square these pre-Vorticist works with the rest of the show had obviously not been considered by Pound or Quinn, who ought ideally to have arranged the event back in 1915 as a travelling sequel to the Dore Galleries' London exhibition. Only the most recent Vorticist works had been displayed there, and Lewis would certainly not have agreed then to include paintings as old as *Kermesse*. The timing of the New York venture, as well as its location, presentation, selection and brief three-week duration, was all wrong.

Brodzky's brave words, therefore, bore no relation to the lamentable response encountered by the Vorticist exhibition: American artists and critics alike remained singularly unimpressed, hardly anything was sold, and as late as May 1917 the *Art World* was still sarcastically declaring that 'Vorticism is the result when Cubism and Futurism rush into a vacuum from opposite sides, meeting in the centre'.[42] By 1917 abstraction was no longer a shocking intruder in New York, and the Vorticist show, unfortunately weakened by Gaudier's absence, was altogether too modestly staged to have the effect that Pound must originally have hoped for. Brodzky may have asserted that 'the invasion of New York by the Vorticists was a splendid adventure', but his own cheerless etching of a solitary visitor gazing at the overwhelming geometry of Lewis's lost *Kermesse* gives a far more accurate account of the whole dispiriting event. When the

EXHIBITION OF THE
VORTICISTS
AT THE
PENGUIN
8 East 15th Street
New York City

Beginning January 10th
1917
Open weekdays, 1 to 6 P. M

Cover of the New York Vorticist Exhibition catalogue, 1917

Horace Brodzky
Viewing Kermesse, 1917

show finished, all the unwanted exhibits were duly transported back to Quinn's apartment; and there they were ignominiously stored until the following November, when Quinn once more sent them off to be auctioned at the Penguin Club and bought eighteen final items for just over nine hundred and fifty dollars. His gesture did something to ameliorate America's hostility, which was distressingly similar to the reception accorded *Blast No. 1* by the 9 August 1914 issue of *The New York Times*: 'What is Vorticism? Well, like Futurism, and Imagisme, and Cubism, essentially it is nonsense. But it is more important than these other fantastic, artistic, and literary movements because it is their sure conclusion. It is important not because it is the latest, but because it is the last phase of the ridiculous rebellion which has given the world the "Portrait of a Nude Descending the Stairs" and the writings of Gertrude Stein. It is the reductio ad absurdum of mad modernity.'

Despite the signal absence of public acclaim in America, the Vorticists themselves were encouraged by Quinn's patronage. 'Let me say how much I appreciate your action in buying my drawings, and all the kindness and interest you have shown in my work and my friends', Lewis told him on 24 January in an uncharacteristically warm and grateful letter. 'I see what it means for a man to be angel enough to find himself invariably on the side of the angels. Your support is at once a privilege and of incalculable use to the few artists with whom I am associated here: let me speak for them.'[43] Quinn responded to this heartfelt message by purchasing both *Kermesse* and *Plan of War*, and when Pound informed him that Lewis had executed some unnamed 'obscenities', he promptly asked for a choice selection to supplement his discreet private hoard of artistic pornography. 'I don't believe in obscenity for obscenity's sake in art', he explained guardedly to Pound. 'But I have got some peaches by Pascin, and if Lewis's are as good as Pascin's I should like to have them.'[44] There can be no doubt that the other English rebels also appreciated the abortive New York exhibition, if only in terms of financial gain. Saunders must have been delighted to hear from Pound that 'with the exception of Ed Wad he [Quinn] has about cleared up the whole show . . . It runs to 375 pounds, which ought to contradict the premature reports of the death of "le mouvement."'[45] Even Etchells, who admitted that he 'didn't have anything to do with the American affair', thankfully recalled that 'Pound roped in a fair amount of money from it and gave me about eighty pounds, which I hurriedly put into Harrods' bank'.[46] And Roberts recorded, many years afterwards, how the loss of his paybook at the Front 'was a piece of bad luck since it contained £50 in notes sent to me by Ezra Pound who had sold two of my paintings to . . . John Quinn'.[47]

However much Pound may secretly have acknowledged that the Penguin Club exhibition was a virtual fiasco, therefore, he remained undeterred in his efforts to prolong Vorticism's life-span. Ever eager to foster new art forms, he renewed his acquaintance with the outstanding American photographer Alvin Langdon Coburn, who had first taken the poet's portrait in October 1913. The (See frontispiece to Volume One) sittings took place at Pound's Church Walk lodgings, and since he was recovering from a bout of jaundice at the time Coburn agreed to photograph him in his dressing-gown. The result, which Pound told James Joyce was 'seductive and sinister . . . like a cinque, or quattrocento painting', pleased him so much that he used it as the frontispiece to Lustra in 1916. And his old landlady, Mrs Langtry, not only told him it was 'the only photograph that has ever done you justice', but also added, 'as she was sidling out of the door, with increasing embarrassment, "Ah, ah. I. I hope you wont be offended, sir, but it is rather like the good man of Nazareth, isn't it sir?" '[48]

Between 1914 and 1916, Coburn followed up this resounding success by (See frontispiece to Volume One) photographing Lewis and Wadsworth posing in front of Vorticist canvases in their studios, and catching Epstein in sombre mood against a background of tall chimneys. His increasing contact with the rebels made him think hard about the implications of their activities, and confirmed his already growing belief that abstractionist precepts could be applied to his work with the camera. After all, his exhibition of Camera Pictures at the Goupil Gallery in October 1913 had contained, alongside more conventional portraits of established figures like Shaw, Chesterton, Rodin, Sargent and Yeats, a series of adventurous photographs of New York.[49] And he prophesied his future willingness to experiment by claiming in the catalogue preface that his picture of The Thousand Windows was 'almost as fantastic in its perspective as a Cubist fantasy; but why should not the camera artist break away from the worn-out conventions, that even in its comparatively short existence have begun to cramp and restrict his medium, and claim the freedom of expression which any art must have to be alive?'[50] It is not impossible to imagine the English rebel artists visiting Coburn's exhibition and being excited by his images of this archetypal modern city: Lewis, for one, executed his gouache of New York a few months later, and since he had at that time never visited America he would have had to rely for all his urban images on the kind of visual evidence which Coburn's Camera Pictures show so plentifully supplied. London, at that stage in its architectural development, was still rooted in the nineteenth century, and it could well be that photographs like Coburn's helped significantly to shape the Vorticists' vision of the modern world.

▷Alvin Langdon Coburn
The House of a Thousand Windows, New York, 1912

▽ Photograph of Malcolm Arbuthnot, 1905–06

▽ Alvin Langdon Coburn
▽ *Flip Flap*, 1908

Photographic innovation had been in the air in London for some years: Malcolm Arbuthnot, a *Blast* signatory and friend of Coburn's, conducted his daring experiments back in 1908, and in the very same year Coburn's photograph of *Flip Flap*, which closes in on the kind of mechanical structure admired by his Vorticist sitters, adumbrated his future development with great clarity. Arbuthnot never really followed up his promising radical beginnings, except in terms of Post-Impressionist paintings which have since been lost; but Coburn pressed ahead, and in 1911 wrote an impassioned article on 'The Relation of Time to Art' that anticipates everything Vorticism would later uphold. 'Photography born of this age of steel seems to have naturally adapted itself to the necessarily unusual requirements of an art that must live in skyscrapers',[51] he declared from his American viewpoint, expressing sentiments which bear very directly on the concerns of Lewis's 'Vorticist Sketch-Book'. Several photographs of New York taken the following year implement Coburn's convictions to the letter, particularly a celebrated aerial view of *The Octopus* which demonstrates his desire to seek out the underlying abstract framework of a familiar scene and may perhaps have inspired Wadsworth's interest in aerial photography. According to Coburn's autobiography, *The Octopus* was taken 'from the top of

▷ Alvin Langdon Coburn
The Octopus, 1912

▽ Alvin Langdon Coburn
The Lord of the Dynamos, c. 1910–11

▽ Wyndham Lewis
▽ *Composition IX*, 1914–15

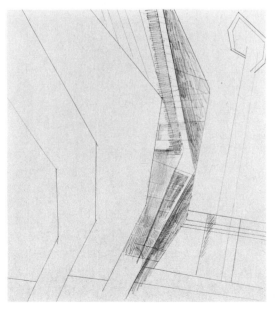

the Metropolitan Tower, looking down on Madison Square where the paths formed a pattern reminiscent of that marine creature. At the time this picture was considered quite mad, and even today it is sometimes greeted with the question "What is it?" The answer is that it is a composition or exercise in filling a rectangular space with curves and masses'. Coburn's explanation echoes the subtitle of Arbuthnot's 1908 *The Doorstep: A Study in Lines and Masses*, which had also defied all the literary, sentimental and picturesque standards of the period and concentrated on minimal form alone.

Two years before *The Octopus*, Coburn had produced a powerful photograph called *The Lord of the Dynamos* which shows a fascination with the potential of mechanical imagery that coincided even more closely with the Vorticists' central pictorial concerns. The title came from a 1911 collection of H. G. Wells short stories, published as *The Door in the Wall*, for which Coburn provided photographic illustrations, and it is extraordinary how Wells' vivid description of the sound of dynamos in action at a Camberwell railway shed expresses the same kind of fascination with machine power that the Vorticists would after-wards share: 'It was a steady stream of din, from which the ear picked out first one thread and then another; there was the intermittent snorting, panting, and seething of the steam-engines, the suck and thud of their pistons, the dull beat on the air as the spokes of the great driving wheels came round, a note the leather straps made as they ran tighter and looser, and a fretful tumult from the dynamos; and, over all, sometimes inaudible, as the ear tired of it, and then creeping back upon the senses again, was this trombone note of the big machine. The floor never felt steady and quiet beneath one's feet, but quivered and jarred. It was a confusing, unsteady place, and enough to send anyone's thoughts jerking into odd zigzags.' The passage could almost have been written by one of the English rebels as he gazed at the source of his own involvement with the machine age: the 'suck and thud of their pistons', no less than the 'thoughts jerking into odd zigzags', would soon be transferred wholesale into the visual language of Vorticism. Coburn's *Lord of the Dynamos* is comparatively restrained, but it was awesome and provocative enough in its subject-matter alone to arouse comment from photographic writers.

'As to A. L. Coburn's mighty machinery, one can but agree that with the proper treatment the things most opposed to simple nature may have a special significance very valuable in invoking a mood', wrote a puzzled but appreciative critic in *Photograms of the Year*. 'The immense wheels in "The Lord of the Dynamos" exert an influence over one that is terrific rather than aesthetic; just as do the pictures of German siege howitzers, for which one has no gentle emotions.'[52] These comments were written towards the end of 1914, when both *Blast* and the war had alerted writers to the idea that machines could be admired for their own sake, albeit outside the boundaries of orthodox 'aesthetics'. But in 1910, when Coburn photographed *The Lord of the Dynamos* and an even more stirring view of *Station Roofs, Pittsburgh*, the imagery he so precociously exploited had scarcely been broached by artists at all. More than any other early Coburn photograph, *Station Roofs* helps to explain why he would later admire Vorticism and add his own postscript to the movement. The way these swooping roofs have been turned into a series of abstract structures, charged with a diagonal dynamism which in itself signifies twentieth-century energy, directly adumbrates both the subject-matter and the style of Wadsworth's woodcuts in particular. Indeed, *Station Roofs* surely represents one of those moments when photography anticipates art, and not vice versa.

The connections with *Blast No. 1*'s manifestos are readily apparent, and if photography had then been regarded as a medium equal to art Coburn might

Alvin Langdon Coburn
Station Roofs, Pittsburgh, 1910

conceivably have added his signature to that journal and exhibited at the 1915 Vorticist show, rather than remaining with the Royal Photographic Society. He himself believed that the camera could be not only equal but superior to painting and sculpture, claiming in 1911 that 'photography is the most modern of the arts . . . in fact, it is more suited to the art requirements of this age of scientific achievement than any other'.[53] But he waited until 1916, when he published a militant credo entitled 'The Future of Pictorial Photography', before bringing the full rebellious extent of his ambitions out in the open. 'It is the revolutionary of today . . . who is the "classic" of tomorrow; there is no escaping the ruthless forward march of time', he announced. 'Yes, if we are alive to the spirit of our time it is these moderns who interest us. They are striving, reaching out towards the future, analysing the mossy structure of the past, and building afresh, in colour and sound and grammatical construction, the scintillating vision of their minds; and being interested particularly in photography, it has occurred to me, why should not the camera also throw off the shackles of conventional representation and attempt something fresh and untried? Why should not its subtle rapidity be utilised to study movement? Why not repeated successive exposures of an object in motion on the same plate? Why should not perspective be studied from angles hitherto neglected or unobserved? Why, I ask you earnestly, need we go on making commonplace little exposures of subjects that may be sorted into groups of landscapes, portraits, and figure studies? Think of the joy of doing something which it would be impossible to classify, or to tell which was the top and which the bottom!'[54]

Futurism had managed to exploit 'successive exposures of an object in motion on the same plate' five years earlier, when Anton Guilio Bragaglia wrote his manifesto on *Photodynamism*.[55] Bragaglia's own photographs were pioneering and very literal studies of human figures hitting, rocking, typing, bowing or 'making a turn'; but Coburn himself seemed more affected by the American photographs, 'of various objects photographed because of their shape and colour value, and with no thought of their sentimental associations', shown at the Royal Photographic Society in 1915. 'The idea was to be as abstract as it is possible to be with the camera', Coburn explained, pointing out that 'Max Weber, the Cubist painter-poet, was responsible for the idea of these designs, and Weber is one of the most sincere artists that it has ever been my good fortune to meet.'

Coburn, however, was an individualist with firm ideas of his own, and suggested in the 1916 essay 'that an exhibition be organised of "Abstract Photography"; that in the entry form it be distinctly stated that no work will be admitted in which the interest of the subject matter is greater than the appreciation of the extraordinary. A sense of design is, of course, all important, and an opportunity for the expression of suppressed or unsuspected originality should prove very beneficial'. One sentence in particular indicated the possible character of Coburn's contributions to this ideal show – 'the use of prisms for the splitting of images into segments has been very slightly experimented with' – and during the next few months he atoned for this neglect.[56]

Following on from the prophetic 1914 *Punch* cartoon of *The Cubist Photographer*, which showed a smart young man-about-town posing happily for a crank portraitist through a large prism, Coburn 'devised the Vortoscope late in 1916'. The instrument, which Coburn afterwards gave to the Royal Photographic Society and cannot now be traced, was according to him 'composed of three mirrors fastened together in the form of a triangle, and resembling to a certain extent the Kaleidoscope . . . The mirrors acted as a prism splitting the image formed by the lens into fragments'.[57] And Helmut Gernsheim, who knew Coburn well, explained that 'the subject was photographed by him through

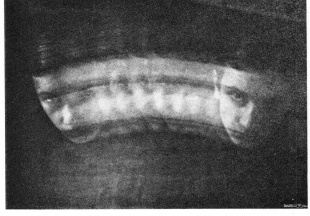

Anton Bragaglia
Young Man Swinging, 1912

George Morrow
The Cubist Photographer, 1914

the middle of [the mirrors] . . . Whilst the mirrors of the kaleidoscope are always enclosed in a cardboard or metal tube, Coburn just used the mirrors in front of the sitter'.[58] To help round out this reconstruction of the instrument, the Curator of the Royal Photographic Society's Museum imagined that the mirrors were hinged, and 'supported in some way between the lens and the sitter'.[59]

It was, apparently, made with the help of broken pieces from Pound's old shaving-mirror, and the first compositions which Coburn attempted to build up through his fragmented invention took the poet as their subject-matter. The mirrors caught Pound's commanding profile and repeated its silhouette, encouraging Coburn to take a whole series of inventive photographs exploiting a dual image of the head alone. One of the most mysterious, which Coburn probably executed at the end of 1916, isolates a two-sided amalgam of Pound's bearded profile against a featureless expanse of white window. The effect is strangely totemic: this Janus-headed mask seems to be impaled on a pole that connects up with the two bars of window to form an almost sculptural whole, suspended in space. It is a hybrid mixture of Cubist double images, African witchcraft and Vorticist geometry, a bizarre brew doubtless concocted with the active help of the sitter himself. And Pound would have been especially im-

Alvin Langdon Coburn
Vortograph of Ezra Pound, c. 1916

Alvin Langdon Coburn
Vortograph of Ezra Pound, c. 1917

Alvin Langdon Coburn
Vortograph of Ezra Pound ('Centre of the Vortex'), 1916

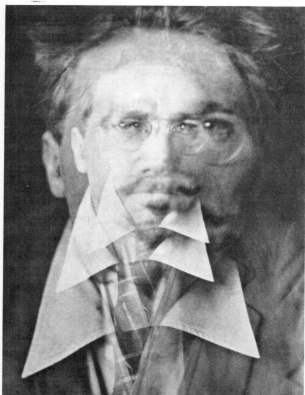

pressed by another multiple portrait nicknamed 'the Centre of the Vortex', a title which acknowledged the extraordinary gyrating motion of the poet's head as it radiates outwards from a calm but whirling centre.

Always quick to find a name for the experimental activities of his friends, Pound lost no time in proclaiming not only that the prismatic device was a Vortoscope but that its products were Vortographs, in recognition of their connections with the rebel movement. And he urged Coburn to continue with his extraordinary researches, posing for him in front of the same window for an extended suite of further photographs, all of which played around with the juxtaposition of head, window-frame and sky. Perhaps the most poetic of these compositions contains several separate readings of Pound's face, doubled, inverted and placed sideways on the paper. They float freely amongst a harsh complex of bars that are as rigid as the structure of a Vorticist picture: the design is in many ways reminiscent of Wadsworth's woodcut *The Open Window*. But Coburn succeeds in making clouds, features and frames cohere by imbuing everything with a soft, deliquescent texture, creating a meditative atmosphere disconcertingly at odds with the aggression of Vorticism.

The only way to approximate more nearly to the rebel aesthetic was to jettison figurative references entirely. Not that Pound necessarily objected to a certain amount of representation: he retained a flexible standpoint on the whole question, just as he had with the Vorticists earlier on, declaring that 'a natural object or objects may perhaps be retained realistically by the vortographer if he chooses, and the vortograph containing such an object or objects will not be injured if the object or objects contribute interest to the pattern, that is to say, if they form an integral and formal part of the whole'.[60] Nevertheless, Coburn wanted to prove that his camera could be as extreme as a painting or a sculpture, for he had declared in 1916 that 'I do not think we have even begun to realise the possibilities of the camera. The beauty of design displayed by the microscope seems to me a wonderful field to explore from the purely pictorial point of view'. With the fervency of a revolutionary, he was determined to make photography as adventurous as the other arts, and 'with her infinite possibilities, do things stranger and more fascinating than the most fantastic dreams .. I want to see [photography] alive to the spirit of progress; and if it is not possible to be "modern" with the newest of all the arts, we had better bury our black boxes'.[61]

In order to delay that funeral, Coburn moved on from the Pound portraits to a large and versatile series of completely abstract designs. Carefully arranging a group of nondescript objects, 'usually bits of wood and crystals', on a glass table-top, he set about turning their multifarious refractions into dazzling configurations of light and shade. Some of them reproduced a relatively solid mass, in which the facets of crystal could easily be discerned. But even these compositions defy all efforts to identify Coburn's subjects, juggling as they do with one image and its reflection, setting the whole complex of glinting shapes to float in an ingeniously undefined spatial area. 'I made many more, all differing from each other and each possessing its own individual character and pattern', Coburn remembered, pointing out how 'photography depends upon pattern for its attractiveness as well as upon quality of tone and luminosity, and in the Vortograph the design can be adjusted at will.'[62] He took full advantage of the infinite permutations Vortography offered, and produced a range of compositions so divorced from any hint of external reality that they have been claimed by photographic historians as the 'first intentionally abstract photographs'.[63]

Paradoxically enough, the more Coburn's images approached the non-representational ideal of Vorticism, the less they succeeded in echoing the movement's actual pictorial vocabulary. They became almost formless, con-

Alvin Langdon Coburn
Vortograph, 1917

Alvin Langdon Coburn
Vortograph, 1917

Alvin Langdon Coburn
Vortograph, c. 1917

Alvin Langdon Coburn
Vortograph, 1917

Alvin Langdon Coburn
Vortograph, c. 1917

Alvin Langdon Coburn
The Eagle (Vortograph), 1917

Alvin Langdon Coburn
Vortograph, 1917

centrating on the bewildering play of light and dissolving everything in their field of vision into gossamer. The explosive quality of a Vorticist picture was achieved, but only at the expense of tangibility: where Lewis had always insisted on solid definition, Coburn's instrument dispersed it in a shower of blurred particles. It was no use Pound affirming that 'in Vortography [Coburn] accepts the fundamental principles of vorticism, and those of vorticist painting in so far as they are applicable to the work of the camera'.[64] The melting confusion of the Vortographs recalled the multiplicity of Futurism rather than Vorticism's belief in the viability of single, static objects.

Occasionally, it is true, Coburn managed to pare the design down to a few well-chosen formal components, slowing the feverish action of his mirrors until they focused with comparative clarity on a succession of thrusting diagonals. Such energetic designs go some way towards justifying Pound's exaggerated claim, in a 1917 letter to Quinn, that Vortography 'will serve to upset the muckers who are already crowing about the death of vorticism'.[65] For they did indeed represent a genuine extension of the rebel programme, demonstrating that the principles first outlined in *Blast No. 1* could be translated with real meaning into a totally different medium. But Coburn found it hard to resist indulging in an instinctive obsession with kaleidoscopic patterns, and some of the most powerful and assured Vortographs turned out to be far removed from the 'cold, hard and plastic' ideal promulgated by their Vorticist counterparts in oil, watercolour or pen. They recalled the flurry of machines in motion, not the stationary essence of a mechanized world advocated in Lewis's theoretical writings; and their soft, feathery luminosity was altogether too melting to achieve the strident energy of the best Vorticist pictures.

Despite the anomalies of Vortography, however, Pound was excited by the new development, and he proudly informed Quinn on 24 January 1917 that 'it, the vortoscope, will manage any arrangement of purely abstract forms. The present machine happens to be rectilinear, but I can make one that will do any sort of curve, quite easily'.[66] The letter was written in the heat of Coburn's greatest activity, for the photographer recalled that 'it was in January 1917 that I created these first purely abstract photographs'. So prolific did he become that a quantity of work was quickly amassed, and he found himself 'invited to hold a one-man show at the Camera Club in London the following month'. Pound immediately offered to write a catalogue introduction for the exhibition, realizing that here was another valuable chance to spread the Vorticist gospel; and Coburn agreed to the proposal, 'on condition that I could hang whatever I liked'.[67] The show opened at the Camera Club in February, and at the private view Coburn remembered that 'Pound elaborated on the theme of his preface, and Bernard Shaw contributed in his usual brilliant manner to make the evening memorable. Photographers inevitably did not know what to make of it all, and I was highly delighted at their confusion; but towards the end of the show they even began to like Vortographs with their strangely fascinating designs'.[68] The exhibition consisted of eighteen Vortographs selected from the total of over forty now extant, and thirteen paintings, including portraits of Stravinsky and Schoenberg, which Pound described in the catalogue as 'roughly speaking, post-impressionist'.[69] The poet ignored the paintings completely, anxious as he was to announce in bold capitals that Vortography meant 'THE CAMERA IS FREED FROM REALITY'.[70] Coburn's show provided him with a perfect opportunity to inveigh against the mimetic tradition which the camera persisted in upholding, and he declared that 'art photography has been stuck for twenty years. During that time practically no new effects have been achieved. Art photography is stale and suburban. It has never had any part in aesthetics. Vortography may have, however, very much the same place in the coming aesthetic that the anatomical studies of the Renaissance had in the aesthetics of the academic school'.[71]

The analogy was slightly deprecating in tone, and led to a public disagreement between the photographer and his critic. For Pound insisted on writing that 'vortography stands below the other vorticist arts in that it is an art of the eye, not of the eye and hand together'. It did not matter that he went on to say that 'it stands infinitely above photography in that the vortographer combines his forms *at will*';[72] the damage was done and Coburn, his pride wounded, rebutted these strictures in a 'postscript' to Pound's introduction. Declaring that his 'opinions most decidedly part company' with his advocate's over the question of whether 'photography is inferior to painting', he boldly affirmed that 'any sort of photograph is superior to any sort of painting aiming at the same result. If these vortographs did not possess distinctive qualities unapproached by any other art method I would not have considered it worth my while to make them. Design they have in common with other mediums, but where else but in photography will you find such luminosity and such a sense of subtle gradations?' So stung was he by the patronizing slant of Pound's words that he went out of his way to scorn other media. 'I took up painting as one takes up any other primitive pursuit, because in these days of progress it is amusing to revert to the cumbersome methods of bygone days, that one may return to modernity with a further appreciation of its vast possibilities.' He stressed that his own paintings were not 'the most important part of the present show', arguing with the tongue-in-cheek logic of the innovator that 'people have been painting now for several years, it is no longer a novelty, but this will go down to posterity as the first exhibition of Vortography'.[73] And so indeed it did; but these squabbles, combined with Coburn's own lack of sustained interest in the possibilities of abstract photography, also ensured that it was the last. Although two vortographs were published for the first time by *The Sketch* in March 1917,[74] the two men did not pursue Vortography any further. Apart from some remarkably Vorticist studies of *Liverpool Cathedral Under Construction* which Coburn took in 1919, it remained a blind alley, only momentarily revived by Pound in 1923 when, with the help of Dudley Murphy, he attached the Vortoscope to a movie-camera over in Paris and considered the possibilities of making an abstract film. The idea was eventually abandoned when the poet realized how much better results both Léger and Man Ray had achieved in comparable experiments.

The brief life-span of Vortography symbolized, in its own eccentric way, the imminent death of the Vorticist movement itself. However hard Pound tried to sustain public interest in the rebels' achievement, he could not succeed single-handed. England was embroiled even more deeply in the escalating carnage of a world war, and in no mood to listen to the ravings of a lunatic who kept shouting about a group that had, to all intents and purposes, ceased to function. How could Pound possibly sound convincing without being able to display new Vorticist work to back up his assertions? Books, articles and photographic adventures could not in themselves bolster up a movement in the eyes of the world, and the miserable anti-climax of the New York exhibition served only to confirm that the rebels no longer possessed the power even to arouse strong feelings. It was simply not enough for the artists at the Front to interest their fellow-soldiers in the movement: Helen Saunders described how she had 'to send two copies' of *Blast* 'to Roberts who is in the fighting and also attempting Vorticist propaganda'.[75] Words alone did not suffice, and the rebels' position was weakened still more grievously by the tragic death of Hulme in September 1917. For although he had ceased to play an active part in championing the avant-garde cause, the philosopher was still regarded by many of the artists as

Alvin Langdon Coburn
Liverpool Cathedral Under Construction, 1919

Photograph of T. E. Hulme, *c.*1916

a towering figurehead. Only two months before, for instance, he had sent Edward Marsh a prolonged and passionate plea to grant Epstein exemption from active service. Hulme was determined that the sculptor whose work he valued above all others should not be sacrificed like Gaudier, and he told Marsh that 'I'd willingly give a year's pay and undergo an extra day's shelling in order to be able to beat those beastly people. Of course Chesterton is quite right on the general principle that the artist has no more claim to immunity than anyone else. We're all equal in that sense, I suppose. But that isn't the point. Is the State making economic use of its material? and ought it not to preserve the only man capable of making some particular kind of instrument – not because instrument-makers were, as men, more valuable than anyone else'.[76]

The urgency of Hulme's letter proves how involved he still was in the fate of his artist friends. Nor had he entirely given up his pre-war critical activities: even when he was serving with the Royal Marine Artillery in Flanders, the bulky manuscript of his monograph on Epstein accompanied him everywhere.[77] His death at Nieuport came, therefore, as a substantial shock to all the rebels: 'we were told it was a direct hit from a very big shell, which literally blew him to bits', Aldington wrote, '– a horrid fate for anyone, but particularly ironical for a philosopher who had doubted the reality of phenomena. Phenomenal or noumenal, the shell got him; and he walked and talked no more among us'.[78] But it was Epstein who was most deeply affected by the news of his mentor's death. 'He had, I believe, the best brains in England and his nature was of the most generous',[79] the sculptor wrote to Quinn on 1 October only hours after hearing of the tragedy. And he later recounted how 'the news of his death, when it reached London, caused widespread pain and sorrow; he had been so much and so strongly alive. It was difficult, for a long time, to believe that he was physically dead. We all felt a personal loss'.[80] Can it be doubted that this new tragedy, coming as it did only two years after the death of Gaudier, helped to destroy the pre-war context of aesthetic innovation even more effectively? Hulme's presence had acted as a cynosure for all the most lively and articulate forces at work in London, and his death left a gap that could never be adequately refilled. He was not even allowed to leave a lasting written monument behind: the book on Epstein, which probably constituted his most sustained and comprehensive analysis of the English aesthetic revolution, perished with him.

A creeping sense of demoralization spread over the artists left behind in London. Deprived of the most vociferous and independent members of the group, Atkinson, Dismorr, Etchells and Saunders failed to sustain the iconoclastic spirit which had once galvanized them into action. It did not matter that abstraction was gradually becoming accepted among other young English artists – men like Phelan Gibb, whose exhibition at the Alpine Club Gallery in the spring of 1917 contained paintings as non-representational as the titles he gave them.[81] Vorticism itself became easy game for hostile critics, and Clive Bell took the opportunity to utter a cry of Bloomsbury triumph over its corpse. Writing in the *Burlington Magazine* in 1917, he castigated British painting once again for being 'hopelessly provincial', the very malady that Vorticism managed with such verve to cure three years before. Only in the last column of his article did he admit that Epstein, Grant and Lewis had 'all seen the sun rise and warmed themselves in its rays'; but this generalized form of praise was quickly followed by the cutting qualification that 'it is to be particularly regretted, therefore, that Mr Lewis should have lent his powers to the canalizing (for the old metaphor was the better) of the new spirit in a little backwater, called English Vorticism, which already gives signs of becoming as insipid as any other puddle of provincialism'.[82] To characterize the movement as a 'backwater', when it had devoted all its energies to avoiding this precise pitfall, was a gross and slanderous insult; and if Lewis had been able to read Bell's allegations, he would have issued a fiery broadside at once. But he was engaged in fierce fighting at the Front – Pound told Quinn in August 1917 that Lewis's 'last note said he had his respirator on for two hours without break, parapet of one of his battery's guns knocked off, and general hotness'[83] – and no-one else was capable of refuting Bell's charges. The nearest Pound came to attacking the Bloomsbury faction was in the privacy of a letter to Lewis, where he reported on having 'had the ineffable pleasure of watching Fry's sylph-like and lardlike length bobbing around in the muddy water off the pier', during a 'dam'd week by the seawaves'.[84] Small wonder that the poet worried about Lewis's safety and told him to invalid himself out of the battle by getting 'a decent and convenient wound in some comparatively tactful part of your anatomy. Say the left buttock'.[85] Deprived of Lewis's driving vitality, the stagnation at home was becoming unbearable.

Even Saunders, who did not join Dismorr in France for voluntary war-work and therefore enjoyed the sheltered vantage of civilian life, languished without his inspiration to spur her on. 'I have done no work for such a long time', she complained to Dismorr in 1916. 'I suppose Art only really comes naturally out of an excess of energy too great for ordinary life. Certainly, I have not got that. Perhaps no woman has. But I should very much like the chance of doing some quite representative painting, as literal as Van Gogh. It would give one a chance I feel of "finding my level" in Art, and perhaps inventing something.'[86] Her disenchanted proposal was to prove prophetic. Before the Armistice was declared, the Vorticists at the Front had come to similar conclusions about the direction their art should take. The inevitable was about to happen.

Chapter 18: The Canadian Commissions, Group X and the Death of Vorticism

In January 1918, Lewis sent an excited letter to Pound from the battle-line in France with welcome news about Roberts. 'Bobby writes me that he has practically got the Canadian job!' he exclaimed. 'That is Watkins (Records Office) has written him asking if he is willing to do the painting on spec: if not found suitable, no £250 but expenses paid.' The jubilation in Lewis's note was understandable, too. Suddenly, after years of heavy fighting in conditions that precluded the execution of anything except rapid sketches – Roberts recalled that 'it was extremely difficult to find the opportunity or the materials to make a drawing of any kind'[1] – the rebels found themselves courted by the heaven-sent patronage of the Canadian War Memorials Fund.

This scheme, which had been instigated in the autumn of 1917 by Sir Max Aitken to provide a visual record of the Canadian war effort, commissioned a wide cross-section of English artists to provide their personal impressions of the struggle on canvases of monumental proportions. It was a wonderful chance for the rebels to extricate themselves from the fighting, and they seized on it with alacrity. The only problem, as Lewis's letter to Pound made clear, was that the Fund's organizers did not relish the prospect of receiving a series of abstract designs for their money. ' "Their advisor" cannot guarantee [Roberts] not doing a "Cubist picture" or something of that rot', Lewis explained scornfully. 'He naturally accepts, with amertume, [*sic*] on any terms.'[2]

None of the rebels was, of course, in a position to turn down or dictate the terms of such an offer; but this ominous proviso in their contracts did pose a grave threat to the integrity of their stylistic development. Before the war, no official body had commissioned work from them, and so the question of compromise never arose. They had been free to create whatever they wished, even if the results remained unsold and despised. Now, however, they were to be judged by a committee consisting not only of Sir Max Aitken, Officer in Charge of War Records, and newspaper magnates like Lord Rothermere and Sir Bertram Lima of the *Daily Mirror*, but also P. G. Konody, who was the fund's 'artistic adviser'. Konody had already shown himself to be largely antipathetic to the Vorticists in the pre-war period, and although he was prepared to accept a certain degree of individualism, he would never for a moment have countenanced abstraction. 'There was bound to be diversity rather than uniformity', he explained in his official capacity, 'but diversity under control, with a definite aim in view'. And this aim, naturally enough, demanded that 'a balance was to be maintained between the historical and the aesthetic aspects of the project'.[3]

In other words, the 'historical' purpose of the scheme meant that each artist would have to work within a representational idiom drastically at odds with the precepts of Vorticism, making the whole commission unpleasantly double-edged. A large group of rebels, embracing Bomberg, Etchells, Lewis, Nevinson, Roberts and Wadsworth, was to be given the opportunity to leave exhausting military duties behind and work on a scale worthy of their talents – but only on condition that they forgot about, or severely modified, their extremist views and complied with the hostile attitude towards avant-garde war pictures summarized so concisely in a 1918 *Punch* cartoon. Nevinson, needless to say, was in the easiest position. As the war progressed, so his paintings became steadily duller and more conventional. Since July 1917, he had spent several months at the Front as an official War Artist for the British Government executing, as he himself recorded, 'rapid short-hand sketches made often under trying conditions in the front line, behind the lines, above the lines in observation balloons, over the lines in aeroplanes and beyond them even to the country at present held by the enemy'.[4] Such a documentary approach might have produced some compelling essays in reportage. But all the moral urgency had by this time disappeared from his work, and with it went the last vestiges of his commitment to radical principles.

"WAR PICTURES."

The Mother. "OF COURSE I DON'T UNDERSTAND THEM, DEAR; BUT THEY GIVE ME A DREADFUL FEELING. I CAN'T BEAR TO LOOK AT THEM. IS IT REALLY LIKE THAT AT THE FRONT?"
The Warrior (who has seen terrible things in battle). "THANK HEAVEN, NO, MOTHER."

Frank Reynolds
War Pictures, 1918

Nevinson was no longer interested in producing morally involved diatribes on the degradation and misery of warfare. He was growing more and more detached, less and less angry, and freely admitted his change of heart in the catalogue preface of his second one-man show, held at the Leicester Galleries in March 1918 two years after his immensely successful London debut. 'This exhibition differs entirely from my last in which I dealt largely with the horrors of War as a motive', he declared. 'I have now attempted to synthesize all the human activity and to record the prodigious organization of our Army.'[5] Instead of condemning the war, and producing savagely anti-heroic dramatizations of human suffering, Nevinson now appeared strangely content with a chauvinistic survey of the army's achievements. It seemed as if the relative comfort and privilege of a war artist's life had softened his emotional responses, encouraging him to ignore his own bitter experiences at the Front in favour of a more picturesque and comfortable view of the conflict. A painting like *Roads of France: Field Artillery and Infantry*, the third in a frieze of four pictures based

Christopher Nevinson
The Roads of France III, 1917–18

on the same theme, is one of the ablest of his later works; and yet it is hard to believe that it was executed by the same man who painted *Returning to the Trenches* three years before.[6] Then, the physical strain and the apprehension of an endless agony was conveyed in a fiercely schematic union of Cubism, Futurism and Vorticism. But now, in this 1918 version, those same marching soldiers have become mere puppets, moving without any evident effort through a gracefully composed landscape of harmless barbed wire, romantic ruins and elegantly arranged bare trees. It is a boudoir vision of war, irreproachably tasteful but almost disgracefully irrelevant.

How Nevinson could possibly have deteriorated into such an anaesthetized complacency is virtually beyond comprehension. But the picture-buying authorities applauded this new emotional and stylistic bankruptcy with even more fervour than before. Konody, for one, lost no time in contacting the artist, and Nevinson joyfully remembered that 'the first thing he did was to come along to my Exhibition and buy four pictures of the "Roads of France" '.[7] Here was one former rebel who had seen the error of his past and come round to a conformist way of working; and Konody, who had already written a fulsome book about Nevinson's war paintings, knew at once that he was the perfect candidate for a Canadian commission. He was transferred to the Canadian army and given every possible form of aid and sympathy; but, as the artist himself later recorded, 'I was set a subject by Konody which was not really suitable for me. He wanted me to illustrate or reconstruct an aerial battle of the great Canadian airman W. A. Bishop . . . But I had not actually witnessed the fight; and although I had seen a good deal of aerial warfare and had myself been attacked by hostile 'planes, I found the task a terribly difficult one. What with flying, ill-health and overwork, I broke down under the strain.'[8] The key remark here is Nevinson's complaint that he 'had not actually witnessed' the subject Konody had given him, for he was an artist who thrived almost exclusively on the visual memory of personal experiences. Hence the particularly dead quality of his later war paintings, where he was operating outside the battle as a subsidized observer of other men's suffering.

And hence, too, the quite extraordinary blandness of his huge Canadian picture, *War in the Air*, which ended up bearing no trace of the problems it had caused during execution. It is difficult, for one thing, to comprehend that a battle is being fought at all. The aeroplanes buzz harmlessly through the sky, frolicking in the clouds and apparently possessing not the slightest connection with each other. The whole scene is portrayed with a photographic literalism worthy of the *Illustrated London News*, and it deteriorates into a lifeless bore lacking any kind of pictorial vitality. There is none of the attack of his first war paintings, no hint of the experimental verve that had aroused the admiration of Lewis. Three years before, Nevinson would never have been satisfied with the tediously amorphous bank of cotton-wool clouds which succeed in depriving the composition of its impact; and yet he was deluded enough to assert later that 'I was the first man to paint in the air, and in all modesty I still think my aeroplane pictures are the finest work I have done. The whole newness of vision, and the excitement of it, infected my work and gave it an enthusiasm which can be felt'.[9] Enthusiasm is precisely what this picture fails to convey, and newness of vision is nowhere to be found.

The critics, needless to say, were delighted with Nevinson's retreat into academicism, and they greeted his one-man show with paeans of reactionary praise. 'Mr Nevinson's contemporary work should be studied by those who laughed at Futurism in its infancy without attempting to understand its underlying ideas, and who have since imagined that it has passed into the limbo of absurdity', declared *The Globe*. 'Mr Nevinson's pictures of war alone disprove

Christopher Nevinson
War in the Air, 1918

this point of view.'[10] The writer could not have been more misinformed. This new Leicester Galleries exhibition was proof positive that Nevinson had completely abjured his Futurist convictions and opted instead for an eclectic approach. He even rejoiced in his volte-face in the catalogue preface, openly confessing that 'since my last exhibition I have experimented with various styles of painting: I wished to create a distinct method in harmony with each new picture. I do not believe the same technique can be used to express a quiet static moonlight night, the dynamic force of a bomber and the restless rhythm of mechanical transport'. Nevinson was obviously tired of the style he had once spent so much energy and imagination evolving: avant-garde concepts were now equated in his mind with facile tricks, foisted on the public by artists who wished to conceal the fundamental poverty of their inspiration. 'Many painters today try to find some particular style of mannerism', his preface continued bitterly, 'and when found they never vary it, hoping always to hall-mark their canvases and deceive their public (the Intellectuals especially) into the idea they have individuality. The truth is that the personality of a painter – if he has any personality, of course – enables him to withstand the test of any technical method.'[11] Unfortunately, Nevinson's own personality had been most strongly defined when he worked inside the very mannerisms he was now at pains to reject. And from the precise moment he discarded them as superficial toys, his own painting descended into a trough of debased realism.

Futurism, and everything it stood for, was now dismissed as a dangerous fad, a game that had encouraged him to glorify the destructive power of the machine. Having been taught by Marinetti to believe in the machine age, he now recoiled from that belief: the war had destroyed too much, given him too many terrifying experiences. His straightforward intelligence could not dissociate the formal discoveries of Futurism from its worship of mechanized aggression. 'It is a black thought for me to look back and see that I was associated with Italian Futurism, which ended in Fascism much as Christianity was quenched by the Spanish Inquisition or charity by angelic Bishops', he wrote later. 'Mussolini seized on it and worked his thug will. What a fate for an intellectual idea!'[12] If Nevinson wanted to escape from the proto-Fascism of his former master, his logical mind insisted too that he turn against the stylistic innovations which Marinetti had helped him to evolve. And so in January 1919, the *Newcastle-on-Tyne Illustrated Chronicle* finally printed his categorical announcement that 'I have now given up Futurism', a preliminary dismissal which was soon followed by an abhorrence of progressive European movements in all their manifestations.[13]

A few months later, he was justifying his return to tradition by linking it up with a widespread revulsion which he considered many of his fellow painters were also experiencing. 'The effect of the war has been to create among artists an extraordinary longing to get static again', he told the *New York Times* in a lengthy interview published in May 1919. 'Having been dynamic since 1912, they are now utterly tired of chaos. Having lived among scrap heaps, having seen miles of destruction day by day, month after month, year after year, they are longing for a complete change. We artists are sick of destruction in art. We want construction.' No more succinct summary of the spiritual exhaustion that war had brought about could possibly have been formulated. Nevinson spoke for the Vorticists as well as himself when he claimed that the horror of real violence had made the aesthetic violence of the pre-war period turn sour. How could any of them face the thought of creating a fundamentally harsh and aggressive pictorial world, or of continuing to indulge in iconoclastic skirmishes, with the aftermath of wholesale slaughter still fresh in the memory? Even on the Continent, as Nevinson pointed out in the same interview, artists were retracing their steps, casting around for affirmation and peace. 'So widespread is this tendency becoming that there is actually a classical reaction among the modern French', he declared. 'They are going back to Ingres.'[14] If a Cubist pioneer like Picasso, or a Futurist virtuoso like his friend Severini, were both busy changing direction, so too was Nevinson; and by the time he was interviewed for *The Studio* in December 1919 he could attach a moral fervour to his premature decline into naturalism. 'The immediate need of the art of today', he cried defiantly, 'is a Cézanne, a reactionary, to lead art back to the academic traditions of the Old Masters, and save contemporary art from abstraction.'[15] Such rotund phrase-making smacked all too strongly of a man who yearned for fame at Burlington House. The young rebel who befriended Marinetti, admired Kandinsky and issued a Futurist Manifesto had altered course for good. He had come full circle, from the Slade to the Canadian War Memorial Fund. The wild oats had been sown long ago, and it was time now to repudiate all this immature abstractionist nonsense.

The climate of world opinion was becoming so hardened against extremism that even Bomberg found his stubborn sense of independence pitched against forces over which he had no control. His spell with the Royal Engineers and the 18th King's Royal Rifles had forced him to undergo a harrowing nightmare: most of his spare time at the Front was devoted to the composition of doom-ridden poetry, he was driven at one stage to administer a self-inflicted wound 'because he had found life too hard to bear'[16] and by 1917 his beloved brother had fallen victim to the slaughter. When he applied to the Canadian War Records Office for transfer to a Canadian regiment, therefore, his natural resilience had already been badly shaken; and to make matters worse, the reply from the Office specified conditions similar to those outlined by Lewis in his letter about Roberts. Bomberg would have to paint a picture at his own risk, declared the communiqué, for the all-powerful Konody was 'not acquainted with your realistic work, and cubist work would be inadmissible for the purpose'.[17] The stipulation was as clear as it could be. But Bomberg, even though he was depressed and desperate for money, remained characteristically undismayed. He had never regarded himself as a mere 'cubist', anyway; and so, blithely ignoring the warning, he selected a subject that would enable him to pursue the preoccupations of his pre-war paintings. The theme he finally settled on, that of a Canadian tunnelling company at work under Hill 60 near St Eloi, offered exactly the same combination of formal elements as all his previous major canvases. As in *Ezekiel*, *Ju-Jitsu*, *In the Hold* and *The Mud Bath*, Bomberg concentrated his attention on a group of figures engaged in frenetic, gesticulating activity within confined surroundings. And if his preliminary oil and watercolour study makes the protagonists appear more nearly human than they had been in *The Mud Bath*, they are nevertheless reduced to a similar amalgam of man and machine.[18]

See next page

The sensitively observed movements of the sappers are translated into a poised diagram in which circles, squares and arcs predominate. But Bomberg's geometry is never starved or over-intellectual; on the contrary, the contrast between the heavy black beams, which serve the same compositional purpose as *The Mud Bath*'s central column, and the tensely straining figures is full of the old vitality. Bomberg makes no distinction between the men and the implements they are undoubtedly wielding: both are welded into the same linear network, and a crisp rhythmic counterpoint is built up as the shapes bend down, coil, twist or stretch into superbly balanced attitudes. Bomberg charts each millimetre of his small design with the exactitude of a man who knows how all the individual details slot together to form a perfectly attuned union of limbs and instruments, sappers and machines. This minor masterpiece represents the essence that Bomberg distilled from a series of on-the-spot sketches, which Alice Mayes testified 'were made direct from Canadian soldiers with authenticity as to uniforms and cap badges',[19] executed under arduous conditions between the spring and autumn of 1918.

If the large canvas completed along the lines of the preliminary oil and watercolour study still survived, it might well stand now as the most radical painting to have come out of the Great War anywhere in the world. But a grave setback occurred when, as Alice Mayes recalled, 'David took it to Burlington House in a taxi' to be inspected by Konody. At the same time she went off to work, 'but some strange instinct caused me to ask my boss if I might leave early. I got home about 2 o'clock to find David huddled in his chair by the fire – in tears.' His reception at the Royal Academy had been worse than either of them ever imagined. 'Konody had almost dissolved into tears himself when he saw what David had produced ... To quote his words, "You submit to me the most wonderful drawings ... and you bring me this futurist abortion. What am I to say to my Committee?" And a great deal more to that effect, while he wrung his hands in annoyance, and stamped round and round the offending painting which had been laid out on the floor for his inspection.'

The situation seemed hopeless, but Bomberg's wife rose courageously to the occasion. 'This aroused all the latent fire in me, and I went straight off to

David Bomberg
*Study for 'Sappers at Work': A Canadian
Tunnelling Company, c. 1918*

Burlington House', she remembered. 'Then I went to work in my best method. I said that I understood he had disapproved of the painting David had submitted, which was a pity, as David had put much thought and endeavour into the work, but would he give David another chance, would he let him work on the painting still further to bring it up to his requirements? I must say that Konody heard me with courtesy and it was finally agreed that David should start on a fresh canvas . . . providing that I should take charge and make sure that no "cubist abortions" should creep into the work.'[20] The compromise solution was duly relayed to Bomberg, who was thereby confronted with an unbearable dilemma: financial need, and a natural desire for some degree of official acclaim, decreed that he castrate his own individuality by embracing the naturalism he had so loftily snubbed in his 1914 Manifesto and bowing to the requirements of the Canadian Fund.

It must have been a bitterly humiliating and painful choice to make. He longed to demonstrate his continuing belief in radicalism on a monumental scale, but found instead that Konody was forcing him to introduce illustrative content that would negate the austere economy of the vision outlined in his studies. In despair, he wrestled manfully with the problem, painting a full-size

David Bomberg
*Study for 'Sappers At Work' : A Canadian
Tunnelling Company, c.* 1918–19

intermediate version that replaced the horizontal format with an upright alternative and sliced off the right portion of the original design.[21] The decision to
sacrifice that particular section was doubtless taken because of Bomberg's
unwillingness to translate the complex configuration depicted there into a more
banal language. But its loss seriously detracted from the stability of the composition, turning the new painting into a crowded jumble of disjointed episodes.
The abstracted forms of beams and mechanical instruments have been partially
retained, above all in the upper half where a giant wheel fills a major part of the
picture-surface. Elsewhere, however, Konody's demands have taken their toll,
and a whole clutter of superfluous description – human anatomy, facial expressions and the tiresome paraphernalia of army uniforms – defiles the purity of
Bomberg's preliminary conception. He tried to arrive at a worthwhile compromise, realizing that if realistic ornament had to be superimposed on the taut
scaffolding of his watercolour sketch, then he ought to compensate by handling
his paint with a certain degree of fluidity and freedom. Such devices helped turn
the picture into a flat, tapestry-like pattern, so that the academicism of two-
dimensional spatial recession was avoided at least.

It is not known whether this hybrid version was discarded by the artist or by
the committee; perhaps Bomberg himself was dissatisfied with the incoherence
of the design. He decided, at any rate, in a worried and over-worked ink drawing,

David Bomberg
Study for 'Sappers At Work': A Canadian Tunnelling Company, c. 1918–19

▷David Bomberg
'Sappers at Work': A Canadian Tunnelling Company, 1918–19

drastically to enlarge the foreground and right side. If figurative dross had to be incorporated in his picture, Bomberg must have argued, he could try and set it off against the sculptural simplicity of the greatly extended beams, but the faltering execution of this sketch shows how little Bomberg believed in his emergency measures. As the list of alternative solutions grew longer, so the last vestiges of real conviction gradually seeped out of the design. It may well be that his rejection by Konody added the finishing touches to a crisis of confidence which Bomberg's war years had initiated. How could he believe in the continuing vitality of his pre-war style now that his brother's death and his own traumatic experiences showed where aggressive extremism and the 'steel city' ultimately led to? Alice Mayes recalled that when Bomberg 'deliberately put the gun to his foot and pulled the trigger' at the Front, 'he was beyond caring about the rules of the war game'. And this sorry ink drawing suggests that he was also, by 1918, beyond caring about the pure form ideal he had evolved during the pre-war period.

The final sacrificial offering submitted to the committee, and duly accepted, is a sadly conventional exercise. Hard pressed by the need for patronage at any cost, Bomberg finished up by relinquishing his cherished ideals. He did all he could, certainly, to dwarf the figures themselves in a stark environment of metallic slabs, extending the foreground even further and according still more space to the angular lattice of girders above. The cubic volume of objects now plays a more dominant role in the painting than the men, who seem by contrast to be overwhelmed by the massive strength of their surroundings. But none of Bomberg's ingenious stylistic ploys can disguise the academic clichés to which he has resorted in the construction of his figures. Each separate sapper adopts a cleverly differentiated and energetic pose, and yet nothing of this energy is actually conveyed. The men are paralysed into frozen stillness by the illustrative shorthand Bomberg has concocted to appease his patrons. Every gesture is artificial, merely theatrical; and it comes as no surprise to find the artist recording that this embarrassing essay in diplomacy was completed in 'an incredibly short time'.[22] Easy to execute it may have been, but Alice Mayes was quite justified when she confessed years later that 'I still wonder if I did the right thing in speaking to Konody as I did – if it would not have been wiser to let David lose his chance of winning the three hundred pounds prize money by withdrawing his work'.[23]

Although Bomberg regarded the final painting as a regrettable but necessary imposition, it turned out to mark a watershed in the development of his life's work. 'The committee's rejection of his first version came as an awful shock to David, a shattering personal blow', declared his second wife, 'and he didn't really recover his earlier strength ever again.'[24] For the first time in the whole of his outstandingly consistent career, his nerve had been broken; and when his Dutch friend Robert Van T'Hoff returned to London in 1919 to persuade Bomberg to join Mondrian in the De Stijl movement over in Holland, he shied away. 'He asked me to return with him to Leyden and join the Group in developing the ideas they had come together for in 1917', Bomberg wrote later; but even though his earlier work had elements in common with the Dutch abstractionists, he was no longer willing to accept such an extremist philosophy. 'The examples of the work he showed me that the Group stood for, I was not impressed with', Bomberg explained. 'There was evidence that they were not sensing design as that which emanated from the sense of mass, but depended more for their appeal on juxtapositions of form that found their way to Leyden via the cubists . . . but more elementary and architecturally integrated. This I felt could only lead again to the Blank Page.'[25] His integrity had already caused him untold anguish at the hands of one committee, and he shrank from any

proposal which threatened to put him at the mercy of another form of collective dogma.

Ironically, Bomberg's own clearest explanation for this dramatic decision came uncomfortably close to echoing Nevinson's call for a return to Cézanne. 'I declined the Leyden invitation', he recalled later. 'I had found I could more surely develop on the lines of Cézanne's rediscovery that the world was round and there was an out through the sunlight – this I have followed and matured in ever since.'[26] Cézanne, who had involuntarily contributed so much towards the evolution of Cubism, was now invoked as a means of escaping from the abstraction which the Cubists had in turn helped to bring about. Bomberg's brief, heroic contribution to the progress of the avant-garde was now over. His revolution had run its course, ending in an agony of doubt, uncertainty and conflicting impulses from which he would never again fully emerge.

△ Edward Wadsworth
View of a Town, 1916

No such tortuous self-criticism affected the evolution of Wadsworth's art during the war. He was far too serene to indulge in the kind of neurotic introspection that beleaguered Bomberg at this time. Between 1915 and 1917, when he served as an Intelligence Officer for the Royal Naval Volunteer Reserve in the Eastern Mediterranean, he found time to execute a few woodcuts inspired by his fresh and largely peaceful surroundings. Some of them were actually subtitled after the idyllic island of Mudros on which he was stationed; but any suspicion that Wadsworth immediately began to move away from the harsh vocabulary of his Vorticist period is allayed by one of the earliest of his wartime woodcuts, the 1916 *View of a Town*. For in this small, exactingly organized design the geometrical bias of Wadsworth's pre-war work is forcefully reasserted. Apart from the lighter, more sunny pitch of the three colours employed in the print, there is little to choose between his interpretation of the old North England industrial centres and his new response to local Greek architecture. Both motifs are similarly reduced to a scaffolding of minimal form, and the assertion of order conveyed by the upright verticals in *View of a Town* is swiftly countered by the overlapping diagonals which rush in from the right side of the composition. Harmony and restless agitation are held in a finely calculated balance, and Wadsworth has not allowed his starting-point in external reality to disrupt the abstract priorities which he carried over intact from his Vorticist work.

◁ Edward Wadsworth
Episode (?), 1916

▽ Edward Wadsworth
Invention, 1917

Neither does the remote suggestion of an island harbour view soften the bare arrangement of formal elements in another 1916 woodcut, even though Wadsworth lets them spread in surprisingly lyrical sweeps of colour across the top of the paper. The print may have called *Episode*, because Etchells singled out a wartime woodcut bearing that name in his introduction to Wadsworth's 1919 exhibition, commending it for 'the curiously interesting "scatter" of the shapes'.[27] They are indeed scattered, with a freedom which Wadsworth seldom attained or desired; and their expansiveness implies that he gradually succumbed to the beneficent influence of his Mediterranean environment. He loved the sea, and a feeling of tidal flow runs through this woodcut's upper half, pacifying the bristling aggression of the forms gathered in ranks towards the bottom of the design.

The new mood of relaxation grew during his stay at Mudros, for a 1917 print called *Invention* extends his interest in curvilinear arabesque until it takes command of the entire picture-surface. If fragments of machinery are still evoked here and there, in the intricacy of *Invention*'s interlocking units, they are nevertheless caught up in a larger rhythm of diving, swaying arcs. They loop their way into each other with a carefree ease hitherto unprecedented in Wadsworth's work, conjuring up an underwater world where everything is

Edward Wadsworth
Scene for a Fairy Tale (?), *c.* 1917

Edward Wadsworth
Interior, 1917

subject to the vagaries of submarine motion. And this impression is confirmed even more decisively in a second, closely related print, which might well bear the openly fanciful title of *Scene for a Fairy Tale*.[28] That, at least, is the name of a wartime woodcut which Etchells admired for its 'brush-script delicacy', and Wadsworth has here loosened his handling so completely that the engraver's knife seems almost to have been exchanged for the watercolourist's wash.[29] Every form is now broken and diffuse, entirely unlike the tight, compact marshalling of components evident only a year before in *View of a Town*. Colour is permitted to wander freely, meandering and splashing among the mysterious crevices of Wadsworth's imaginative dream. And the dancing liberation of the design opens out into an idiom closer to Kandinsky's free-wheeling abstractions than Vorticism's more controlled, inflexible structures.

It was, however, only a momentary departure from the basic line of development in Wadsworth's style. A third 1917 woodcut, *Interior*, marks a categorical return to his pre-war concerns, even if it is infected with a little of the esprit which characterizes the whole Mudros period.[30] Now a group of preponderantly cubic volumes floats and tumbles in an undefined spatial area, freed from all the normal constraints imposed upon such objects by the laws of gravity. Wadsworth emphasizes the massiveness of these shapes; and yet he also enjoys cancelling out the illusion of substance by isolating their edges as planes of brilliant white, bringing them out to the forefront of the picture and thereby detaching them from the surfaces of the entities to which they are supposed to adhere. This is the real subject of *Interior*: the paradoxical nature of an art that is based on illusionism. For the contents of the 'room' Wadsworth has constructed here are reduced to such a simplified equation of geometry and tonal contrasts that they become completely ambiguous. If there is recession, even depth, in the penumbral regions of this environment, it is contradicted by the insistent flatness of the colours printed on the page. No guide-line is given to establish the precise position of any shape inside this confusing space; nothing is fixed with a certitude that would enable the spectator to decide whether one form really does take up a place behind or in front of its companions. Wadsworth is content to leave the question open, and show how easily a cunning use of abstraction throws all our usual perceptual responses into doubt. *Interior* exploits the deceptive qualities of non-representational Vorticism in order to disorient and confuse, and its modest size once again belies the ambitious subtlety of Wadsworth's intentions.

Almost alone among his rebel colleagues, Wadsworth was for the moment able in such superb prints to sustain his pre-war investigations into the possibilities of a remarkably abstract language. He was fortunate: the encounter with classical civilization which his naval posting provided seems to have served to confirm his passion for order and lucidity, enabling him to transfer Vorticist geometry without any sense of hiatus to the articulation of the sea and the Greek landscape which surrounded his working life. And at the same time, as Etchells declared in his introduction to Wadsworth's 1919 exhibition, his friends thought that 'in the Ægean group a great technical advance is shown. In these highly complicated prints the artist has achieved a richness and a fluidity in the use of his medium which gives this series a character wholly personal: they stand, indeed, as a quite new development'.[31] If it is not possible to see why Etchells considered these wartime woodcuts innately superior to the earlier prints, or to view them as a stylistically homogeneous group, their quality and radicalism alike are beyond question.

As luck would have it, Wadsworth was encouraged to continue the same investigations after he had been invalided home. Following a rapid recovery, he found himself employed with other artists on the dazzle-camouflage of ships at a number of English ports. Concentrating largely on Bristol and Liverpool,

Photograph of S.S. New York City at Bristol, April 1918, with dazzle camouflage supervised by Wadsworth

Photograph of R.M.S. Aquitania, *c.* 1918, with dazzle camouflage supervised by Wadsworth

Photograph of the Mauretania at the landing stage in Liverpool, October 1918, with dazzle camouflage supervised by Wadsworth

he supervised the camouflage designs on over two thousand ships within the space of one year; and the problems involved in smothering a surface as huge as the eight-hundred-foot long *Aquitania* with abstract patterns were, of course, intimately related to his own creative concerns. Just as he had once executed paintings which exploited mechanical imagery and fierce linear or tonal oppositions, so now he was able to apply the same kind of pictorial orchestration to the outer covering of real machines. And Etchells pointed out this connection when he wrote in 1919 that 'the camouflaged ship was one of the bright spots of the war and it is not too much to say that it would probably never have developed as it did had it not been for the experiments in abstract design made by a few modern artists during the years immediately prior to 1914'.[32] Although the dazzle technique was invented by the traditional marine painter Norman Wilkinson, who seems to have evolved his ideas more from

optical theories about the distortion produced by violent colour contrasts and
heraldic patterns than from any engagement with the avant-garde, the camouflage designs do possess extraordinary subliminal links with the concerns of
Vorticism. In this sense Wadsworth's appointment as a supervisor acknowledged
those links, and suggested ways in which an élitist language developed in artists'
studios could be applied in the most public manner to functional objects in the
outside world.

With characteristic logic, Wadsworth capitalized on this exhilarating work in
the enormous painting he executed for the Canadian commission by choosing
as his subject *Dazzle-Ships in Drydock at Liverpool*. If the committee required
a realistic approach, then Wadsworth was willing to comply with their request
and provide a documentary record of his own official activities; but he also
made sure that the severe architectonics of the camouflage designs were retained
as well. And so, although his representational content was clear enough to meet
with Konody's approval, the brittle network of coloured bands which enmeshes
most of the picture-surface makes the compromise palatable. Wadsworth has
been careful to make the naturalistic elements diminutive in scale: the tiny men
painting the hull in the foreground pass almost unnoticed, and do nothing to
detract from the impact of the hard-edge stripes swathing the vessel above them
like so many brilliantly coloured bandages. This one gigantic ship has been
positioned with such dramatic frontality that its wild, ragtime grid of asym-
metrical diagonals and verticals is cunningly carried over into the forms of the
surrounding harbour. The converging lines of dock ramps on either side add
their own steely precision, shooting back into space until they meet up with the
heraldic surfaces of two more boats, each neatly converging on the central
vessel so as to prevent any further recession from damaging the picture's overall
pattern. Even the plethora of factual detail gathered behind – warehouses,
chimney-stacks and gasometers – is flattened into a one-dimensional backdrop
which cannot weaken the awesome rigidity of Wadsworth's main structure.

All the same, there is a dryness about the painting which betrays the pressures
under which it was executed. It is altogether too literal, too factual, and Wadsworth's crafty efforts to disguise his stylistic retreat do not entirely dispel the
naturalism of his basic conception. To a man who had previously thrived on
ambiguity, multiple spatial readings and allusion, the necessity to adopt a
commonplace approach inevitably came as a restriction. For all its toughness,
the Canadian picture appears limited and dutiful, constrained by the committee's
insistence on a fundamentally mimetic standpoint. Wadsworth was far more at
ease when he turned to the privacy of his woodcuts, and his first one-man show
at the Adelphi Gallery in March 1919 contained a retrospective survey of
thirty-one prints and four drawings executed over the previous six years,
accompanied by what one critic called 'an excellent and highly appreciative
note of introduction' by Etchells.[33] The latter made his enthusiasm quite obvious,
declaring that 'woodcut is a thing to handle and look at closely . . . its intrinsic
qualities of surface and texture can be achieved in no other way. This much
neglected medium is again beginning to receive the attention it deserves: it
is a good thing'.

Vorticist abstractions mingled uneasily with a new series of more representational scenes depicting camouflaged vessels in dry dock; but Lewis, in one of his
first pieces of post-war critical writing, actively encouraged the public to view
the abstract and representational portions of the exhibition as a unified whole.
'We may really consider then two phases of this artist's work quite simply side
by side', he wrote in the spring issue of *Art and Letters*, 'without any knitting
of the brows and mental readjustment as we pass from the less to the more
abstract works.' By this time, Lewis himself was at pains to justify his own

◁ Edward Wadsworth
Dazzle-Ships in Drydock at Liverpool, 1919

Edward Wadsworth
Dazzled Ship in Drydock, 1918

retreat from the proud extremism of the Vorticist period, and this review of Wadsworth's show gave him a chance to account for his inconsistencies. 'The more genuine and therefore sincere artist who has entered into these experiments has never pretended that this type of work (abstraction) had any mysterious quality that rendered it indefinably superior to the art that plainly represents, and even literally transcribes', he wrote, desperately attempting to minimize the importance of his Vorticist discoveries. 'He claimed certain advantages for it: admitted points in which it must defer to its more "representative" colleague! There are things you cannot do in one, things not in the other: there are valuable things on both sides. But it is too considerable and attractive an innovation not to have come to a stop . . . The writer of this note had written before the war: "I would sign no paper promising never to do a purely naturalistic work again." Similarly I would sign no paper foregoing my, in terms of history, newer enthusiasm.'[34]

The passage is a revelation of the unfortunate pragmatism that Lewis and his allies felt obliged to practise after the war had brought their movement to such a premature end. Instead of stressing the viability of rebel innovations, they now felt able to regard abstraction only as an option, an 'attractive' alternative which could be exchanged for 'purely naturalistic work' at any time. The philosophy came depressingly near to Nevinson's eclecticism, and made nonsense of the high-minded idealism that had first produced the Great English Vortex. But Wadsworth, for one, seemed content with this dramatic shift in creative priorities, and alternated between the two conventions with bewildering assurance throughout 1919. When he designed a woodcut alphabet for T. S. Eliot's *Ara Vos Prec*, his second book of poems published in 1919 by John Rodker's Ovid Press, he executed the capital letters in an elegantly orthodox style and then promptly

Edward Wadsworth
Vorticist Alphabet, c. 1919

contradicted himself by embellishing them with a superb series of Vorticist compositions, each one couched in an idiom which had hardly changed since the great days of 1914.[35] Some of them, particularly the backgrounds of D, W and Y, are drawn in a style strongly reminiscent of Lewis's 'Vorticist Sketch-Book', which helps to explain why Pound also used this alphabet in his 1920 Ovid Press edition of *Hugh Selwyn Mauberley*; while other letters portray groups of faceless robots and instruments of war. The disparity between the muscular angularities of these drawings and the arabesques described by the capitals in front of them is almost absurd: the only way to achieve unity would have been to employ a letterpress similar to the giant black script used in *Blast*. Wadsworth, however, wanted to combine the virtues of two conflicting idioms; and towards the end of the year he abandoned Vorticism altogether in order to return, like Bomberg and Nevinson before him, to nature.

Etchells had undergone a similar metamorphosis in his style by the time he painted a Canadian picture. He had, in fact, been incapacitated with a severe attack of tuberculosis since the onset of war, and was thereby removed from the conflict that had weakened the resistance of so many of his colleagues. 'I was in France at the beginning of hostilities', he recalled later, 'and my blond beard, as big as a spade, combined with my spectacles and foreign accent to make the French suspect me for a German spy. They locked me up in Montaubon jail, and it took all my eloquence to persuade the Mayor to release me. I had a poisoned swollen leg, and after crossing back to England in 1914 spent most of the war laid up on my back.'[36] Eventually, in August 1917, he was given an official certificate which granted him 'rejection as permanently and totally disabled for service under the Military'.[37] But Konody encouraged him to start painting the following year by according him a Canadian commission, and he set to work on a vast panoramic canvas depicting *Armistice Day, Munitions Centre*. Etchells had no memories of active service upon which to draw, and so he turned to a civilian theme 'suggested by the crowd on Armistice Day in a street of an important centre for War Munitions in the Midlands'. As the description printed in a contemporary catalogue of the Canadian paintings indicated, 'the design is that of a crowd of workers and munitionettes pouring forth from works and offices at the announcement of an Armistice with no very clear idea of how to celebrate the occasion'.[38] And the painting itself, which Etchells later admitted to be 'not very good', shows that he had 'no clear idea' about the style he should employ, either.[39]

Apart from a couple of incidental houses and a thin stretch of skyline at the top, the whole picture-surface is choked with figures painted in harsh, brilliant colours. There is a genre, almost anecdotal air about the scene, but Etchells shows a painful uncertainty over the precise nature of the activity he depicts. Despite the proliferation of flag-waving and the hint of festivity contained in the gin advertisement on the left, the prevailing atmosphere is one of listlessness, even downright boredom. Etchells seems to be caught between the impulse to depict a scene of conventionalized gaiety, and a more serious urge to reveal the reality of the ordinary man's indifference to international events. His confused composition expresses very little apart from his own lack of definite purpose: it is the work of an invalid, shut off from the actuality of life outside the sick-room and yet determined to interpret events which illness prevented him from witnessing. He should ideally have relied on his own imaginative resources and dispensed with reportage; but his loss of interest in the Vorticist cause made him embrace the mannerisms of artists like Ginner and Gilman, who had always devoted themselves to the dispassionate recording of everyday events.

Such stylistic comparisons could never have been applied to Roberts' work, which was always conspicuous for its sense of pugnacious independence. And yet even he found himself profoundly affected by the demands of a Canadian committee which obviously regarded his pre-war work as irredeemably esoteric. 'He naturally accepts' the commission, Lewis told Pound, '. . . on any terms';[40] but the painting Roberts finished in November 1918, after having been lent to the Canadian government by the Royal Field Artillery the previous April, shows how much those 'terms' helped to dictate the style of his massive canvas. The subject was an exciting one, unlike those allotted to Bomberg, Etchells and Wadsworth: it set out to commemorate the heroic occasion when the Canadians successfully held the line against the first German surprise attack with gas. And Roberts added to the drama by choosing the precise moment at which the French troops, retreating in chaotic panic from the terrible effects of the gas, ran wildly in amongst the Canadian gunners, almost thwarting their attempts to train the battery on the advancing German infantry. In other words, the painting was bound to be openly illustrational, but Roberts had already resigned himself to that prospect by complying with the official invitation from the Canadian War Records Officer in December 1917, who declared that 'I would be glad to know whether, providing you are given the necessary facilities and leave, you are prepared to paint the picture at your own risk, to be submitted for the approval of the committee. The reason for this request is that the Art Adviser informs us that he is not acquainted with your realistic work and Cubist work is inadmissible for the purpose'. The last sentence of this letter is identical with the one Bomberg received, and Roberts was saddled with the additional disadvantage of not having witnessed his theme: it was merely the last remaining item on Konody's list of subjects to be allotted to the artists concerned, and Roberts told

▷Frederick Etchells
Armistice Day, Munitions Centre, 1918–19

William Roberts
Study for The First German Gas Attack at Ypres, 1918

him that 'I was without experience of that kind of cloud gas warfare'.[41]

To prepare himself for the formidable task of expressing such an emotive theme, he brushed in an admirably spare and controlled watercolour sketch of the composition he had evolved. Little is specified here beyond the limpid contrast of light and shade: lit strongly from the left, the struggling figures become ghostly abstractions in pale yellow, pink and orange, their sinuous shapes vividly reflecting the tumult of the actual event. An arresting Vorticist painting could have been created from such a study; the theme, after all, was tailor-made for the particular kind of schematic dissonance that Roberts had already explored in watercolours like *Twostep*. But it was not to be. The committee required 'a complete and reliable artistic record of Canada's achievements', and it would hardly have been satisfied with such a beautifully allusive work. Roberts was quite willing to comply with their wishes, too: the few sketches he had executed while still on active service show a far more empirical approach to reality than his pre-war pictures ever evinced. Even the Canadian watercolour appears traditional when set beside the work he submitted to the 1915 Vorticist Exhibition. Descriptive curves replace angles and each figure is readily identifiable, announcing Roberts' new determination to lean on visible fact rather than an imaginative substitute of his own.

The finished painting, simply called *The First German Gas Attack at Ypres*, at once accentuates the distortions implied in the watercolour and takes the sorry move towards representation much further. The fantastically contorted attitudes of the panic-striken gas victims successfully correspond with the official Canadian record of the scene, which described 'the anguished faces of many of the French soldiers, twisted and distorted by pain, who were gasping for breath and vainly trying to gain relief by vomiting'.[42] But Roberts goes beyond mere fidelity to history in the organization of his composition, tilting it up even further than he had done four years before in *The Toe Dancer* so that the entire plane of the picture-surface is swarming with bodies. A restless horror vacui results, full of twisting bodies which seem to ape the extravagant contrapposto of a Mannerist altarpiece. Roberts plays off his posturing figures

William Roberts
The First German Gas Attack at Ypres, 1918

against each other with the flair of a theatrical director: the soldiers jerk and
sway, flex their torsos with muscular effort or plunge towards the ground to
pick up shells. He cuts them off arbitrarily at the edge of the canvas, and makes
them collide so violently with their neighbours that it is difficult to divorce one
protagonist from another. They tumble down from the top of the painting in
a grotesque avalanche of rasping colour and convoluted gestures, threatening to
smother the very coherence of the scene with a burgeoning excess of melodrama.
So much has been achieved, and yet the picture as a whole fails to impress. The
surging rhythms of the design outlined in the preliminary watercolour have
become lost in an embarrassment of realistic detail, for Roberts has driven
himself into a naturalism as trite as Bomberg's laboured treatment of the *Sappers*
canvas. The painting suffers from a surfeit of illustrative trivia, the kind of
prosaism that Roberts had always been anxious to avoid in his Vorticist work,
and the uncompromising abstractionist stand which he first took up at the end
of 1913 in the lost *Dancers* picture has now been irrevocably abjured.

Once again, it is tempting to speculate about the effect which horrific war experiences had on Roberts' aesthetic beliefs. Some revealing letters to his future wife Sarah afford glimpses of the physical and mental suffering he had either to undergo or witness in his fellow soldiers. The intense agony of the First World War is such a byword, now, that it is all too easy to take its nightmarish effect for granted, and these letters act as a valuable corrective. 'Dull and stupid isn't it, writing to me out here', he told Sarah in a gloomy message on 11 November 1917. 'I wonder, shall we ever see each other again? Don't for goodness sake stop writing; but there, why the devil shouldn't you; you must live your own way. The difficulty is our two ways of living and environment are so different that my judgement, for you, can have very little point. One whose existence is so absolutely monotonous, repetition always, every day lived to order; the only excitement being to dodge and duck for your bloody miserable life; finds it almost impossible to transport his imagination into the intricasies [*sic*] and complexities of town living.' The urban context which had been an integral part of the Vorticists' programme was brutally replaced by a grotesque alternative reality, and it cut Roberts off from the roots of his pre-war radicalism.

No wonder this prolonged trauma alienated him from his formerly optimistic and high-spirited aggression: now he could see only one consequence of such a militant stance, and it was not a pretty spectacle. 'Marching on the road for days on end with but a few hours sleep at night, then travelling in cattle trucks and working like niggers, with practically no food, whilst, as a welcome at the journey's end, there are bursting shells to greet you', he wrote in a demoralized letter on 7 December 1917. 'I believe I possess the average amount of hope and patience, but this existence beats me.' It must have beaten any continuing belief in Vorticism out of his system as well, for the same letter goes on to channel the angry energy which had previously been directed at the English art establishment into a paradoxical denunciation of all warlike impulses. 'I am feeling very bitter against life altogether just at present', he explained. 'But there is one thing I curse above all others in this world, and that's "open warfare". I could strafe it, as "Fritz" never did strafe Ypres, and if you saw that place you would understand the full extent of my hate.'[43] Roberts had not lost his nerve or his passionate convictions, but they were now dedicated to a wholehearted rejection of an international massacre which could destroy a whole city and its inhabitants. Faced with this appalling waste of human life and civilisation, Roberts can hardly be blamed for also turning away from his own earlier commitment to extremist rebellion.

Lewis was still alive and active, however, having survived exposure to fierce combat in France with the Royal Artillery between 1916 and 1917. And when, in December 1917, he tried to secure a Canadian commission for himself, he found to his amazement that 'Konody received me, almost literally, with open arms. When I asked him if he had among his artists an artillery-artist, to paint howitzers, he shouted N O! When I said I knew all about howitzers – how would it be for me to paint one – he screamed O F C O U R S E !!! With his dramatic mit-european accent he gave this suggestion such a rich Austrian welcome as no suggestion ever had before or since'.[44] Lewis was obviously relieved that Konody seemed prepared to take him seriously as an artist, if only on the tacit understanding that Vorticism and its maxims had been consumed in the holocaust of war. The former editor of *Blast* was as eager for the chance to work as any of his compatriots, and he decided to bow to the conditions imposed by the fund – even though, in the spring of 1917, he had provided an almost completely abstract drawing for the cover of his book, *The Ideal Giant*. It was one of Lewis's last and most assured essays in a style he was about to abandon. Like

Wyndham Lewis
Cover of *The Ideal Giant*, 1917

a vengeful agent of universal destruction, the mechanized object he has brushed onto the page with such commanding strokes of Indian ink bends in the middle, as if in preparation for some mighty act of aggression. Fierce prongs jut out of its headpiece, the antennae that give warning of imminent assault, and the taut energy embodied in the lower half is so powerful that it splays out of the bottom in a flurry of sweeping wash. The whole composition is tightly constructed, all the same, and its compact mass would have been a fitting symbol of Lewis's renewed determination to continue the aesthetic attack he had launched in London before the war.

But conditions had changed, and he had altered with them. The soldier who returned from battle no longer wanted to prolong his investigations into the potential of a non-representational language, and *The Ideal Giant* remained an isolated reminder of preoccupations which had now been superseded by other, more conventional priorities. In *Blast No. 2* he had declared that 'there is no reason why very fine representative paintings of the present War should not be done',[45] and he proceeded to implement his own prophecy on the monumental scale prescribed by the Canadians. There is no reason to suppose, nevertheless, that the pressures implicit in the commission's patronage did not irritate Lewis's congenitally restless temperament. In April 1918, Pound reported that his friend was 'nearly dying of the attempt to paint something bad enough *in the right way*',[46] and Lewis himself complained to Herbert Read in December that 'on looking at my Canadian painting today I came to the conclusion that Konody had succeeded in making me paint one of the dullest good pictures on earth. I have just done another painting in an afternoon which is at least 17 times as alive. What a nightmare this wicked war has been!'[47] A nightmare indeed, and one which had confused Lewis's sense of artistic direction as thoroughly as that of his rebel allies. How on earth was he to marry Vorticism to the naturalistic requirements of the Canadian brief? The subject, *A Canadian Gun Pit*, certainly made use of his own personal experience in combat; but did he therefore have to work on the reconstruction of outward appearances with as much pettifogging diligence as Nevinson, Bomberg, Etchells and Roberts? The dilemma

Wyndham Lewis
A Canadian Gun Pit, 1918

remained unsolved in the final canvas: Lewis clearly could not make up his mind while he was painting it, and the weakness shows. As Augustus John told a mutual friend at the time, Lewis was 'painting his gun-pit and striving to reduce his "Vorticism" to the level of Canadian intelligibility – a hopeless task I fear'.[48]

There is a curious deadness about the picture, a quality that has nothing to do with the desolation of the scene he was portraying. The composition does not hang together properly; it looks almost as if Lewis had worked in sections which were ultimately pieced together without any real sense of pictorial cohesion. The soldiers stand around dejectedly, as unsure as Lewis himself as to their precise formal function, and the grotesque masks of the two men staring out of the centre make no sense up against the normative way in which their uniforms have been drawn. All over the painting this hesitation is painfully apparent. The camouflage hanging down over the roof of the improvised shelter gives Lewis the opportunity to indulge in some fragmented Vorticist pattern-making; but it contrasts unhappily with the tentative naturalism of the stones, boxes, and miscellaneous bric-a-brac scattered so feebly across the foreground of the composition. It soon becomes clear that no coherent stylistic convention has been adopted: Lewis's brush hovers indecisively between distortion and documentation, fantasy and fact.

This sudden descent from the summit of abstraction was continued in Lewis's first one-man show at the Goupil Gallery in February 1919. Brusquely entitled *Guns*, it contained a large number of drawings portraying life in the Royal Artillery. Some were elaborate compositions, others individual figures sketched from life or studies of the weapons themselves. The catalogue listed such items as *Pill-Box*, *Walking Wounded* or *Battery Salvo*; and all of them, although decidedly angular, were naturalistic. 'I have attempted here only one thing', Lewis stated with disarming modesty in his catalogue foreword: 'namely, in a direct ready formula to offer an interpretation of what I took part in in France'. A direct, ready formula: words that would suit the way in which Nevinson had used his knowledge of Cubism and Futurism, but a surprise from the man who more than anyone else had once brought a new art movement into being. The sometime revolutionary now wrote in his own preface that 'experimentation has been waived', explaining how 'I have tried to do with the pencil and brush what the storyteller does with his pen'. A far cry indeed from the pre-war artist who had made of his *Portrait of an Englishwoman* an abstract arrangement of line and colour, and had bravely affirmed in *Blast No. 2* that it was ridiculous to question 'whether Mr Wyndham Lewis, Mr Brzeska, Mr Wadsworth, Mr Etchells, Mr Roberts are going to recant and paint and sculpt on the mental level of Mr Lavery or Mr Herkomer, or to put it another way, whether such a terrific interest will be awakened in Mr Lavery, Mr Wilson Steer and Mr Caton Woodville that attempts at a purifying of taste and renovation of formulas will obtain no hearing'.[49] For now he himself seemed to view the whole idea of 'renovation' with disapproval.

What had happened? The simile of the storyteller, so innocently inserted into his catalogue foreword, provides one clue. The completion of his first novel, *Tarr*, in the winter of 1914, followed as it was by the publication of a series of short stories in 1916 and the following year, had considerably altered his aesthetic theories. 'It became evident to me at once', he explained later, '... that words and syntax were not susceptible of transformation into abstract terms, to which process the visual arts lent themselves quite readily ... Writing – literature – dragged me out of the abstractist cul-de-sac'. The irresistible urge to split his creative activities in two, becoming both a painter and a novelist, had a profound effect on his extremist doctrines. 'My great interest in this first novel – essentially so different a type of expression from more or less abstract compositions in pure form and colour – so humanist and remote from implications of the machine, turned me into other paths', he recalled; 'one form of expression must affect the other if they co-exist within the confines of one brain.'[50]

But this justification, convincing though it appears, was not written until many years later; and the preface to the *Guns* exhibition contained nothing half as intelligent or understandable. Far from it: he wrote to Quinn in February 1919 defending his new 'representative treatment' as a means of convincing public, critics and hostile fellow artists that the Vorticists were not just charlatans who hid their lack of orthodox talent in a blaze of gimmicks. '*It will be more difficult henceforth in the set politics of London* for certain gentlemen to assert that myself or my companions are "spoofers" & so on', he asserted triumphantly. 'The show . . . has won over a number of people. Every day fresh things are being sold.'[51] It looks as if Lewis was set on the very objective he had dismissed so haughtily in earlier days: proving his prowess as a traditional draughtsman, showing the world that he had not cultivated abstraction as a hoax alone. 'The public, surprised at finding eyes and noses in this exhibition, will begin by the reflection that the artist has conceded Nature, and abandoned those vexing diagrams by which he puzzled and annoyed', he wrote in the *Guns* catalogue. 'The case is really not quite that. All that has happened is that in these things the artist has set himself a different task. A Tchekhov story, or the truth of a drawing by Rembrandt, is a highly respectable thing, and in the highest degree worth doing.' Respectability, not rebellion, was now the order of the day.

The motives behind his new style, then, were sadly muddled. Part of him – the shrewder, more practical and cynical side – realized that if he was to establish his reputation in post-war England he must rethink his priorities, consider again how best to communicate with his potential audience. When the war broke out he was still filled with the hope that Vorticism could form the basis of an accepted and independent national movement which would grow and flourish. Had he not written in *Blast No. 2* that 'it seems to me that, as far as art is concerned, things will be exactly the same after the War as before it . . . All art that matters is already so far ahead that it is beyond the sphere of these disturbances'?[52] It reads like wishful thinking now, but in 1915 the rebels persisted in regarding the war with a certain amount of guarded hope. Establishments would be destroyed, and it might prove easy to usher in the new way of seeing once the old barriers had finally been ripped down. But Lewis's literary ambitions clashed head-on with his artistic ideas. After the highly experimental prose of 'The Enemy of the Stars' in *Blast No. 1*, which consciously sought a verbal equivalent for his visual images, he began to acknowledge that his pictorial theories were forcing his writing to strive for a degree of stylization impossible to maintain. In fact, as his obsession with fiction snowballed, he found that he had strictly to separate the two activities. 'From 1924 onwards writing became so much a major interest that I have tended to work at my painting and drawing in prolonged bursts,' he noted later, 'rather than fit them into the intervals of the writing or planning of books.'[53] A serious clash took place between the two occupations, and it began increasingly to be resolved in favour of literature. The choice had to be taken, and Lewis arrived at it with a characteristic sense of impatience.

There was, after all, something of the gadfly in his tireless pursuit of multifarious activities. Just as one form of creative exploration failed to satisfy his yearning after versatility, so he never found it possible to settle on one single line of development for very long. On the whole, his work between the 1912 *Timon* designs and the huge geometrical canvas seen in Coburn's 1916 photograph of Lewis represented a consistent development, evolving from Cubo-Futurism to the Vorticists' ideal of an abstraction which retains multiple references to the visible world. But there were inevitable aberrations within that development, and the very nature of the Vorticist synthesis enabled him to reserve fairly extensive options. On the one hand, he could announce in *Blast No. 2* that 'whatever happens, there is a new section that has already justified its existence, which is bound to influence, and mingle with the others, as they do with each other; that is, for want of a better word, the Abstract'. And on the other, he could just as easily swing over to the other side of his surprisingly adjustable fence and declare outright, in the same essay, that 'I think a great deal of effort will automatically flow back into more natural forms from the barriers of the Abstract'. In other words, Lewis was advocating an essentially flexible approach to the problem of evolving a definitive Vorticist language, and he did not for one moment consider that this evolution had come to fruition before he departed for active service. In the summer of 1915, he predicted that the 'ferocious and unfriendly' character of the movement would gradually blossom with the passing of time. 'This rigidity, in the normal process of Nature, will flower like other things', he wrote. 'THIS simple and massive trunk or stem may be watched . . . It is too commonly suggested that rigidity cannot flower without "renouncing" itself.'[54] Could it be maintained, therefore, that Lewis's post-war style represented the 'flowering' of his Vorticist beliefs into a new maturity that did not involve 'renunciation' of any kind? Unfortunately not: he sacrificed far too many rebel precepts to be acquitted on such a score.

Lewis himself later convincingly described the Vorticist period as 'a little narrow segment of time, on the far side of world war i. That first war, you have to regard, as far as I am concerned, as a black solid mass, cutting off all that went before it'.[55] And he was, at heart, correct: the soldier who returned from the Front was profoundly different from the polemicist who had blasted England in the summer of 1914. 'The war was a sleep, deep and animal, in which I was visited by images of an order very new to me', he explained afterwards. 'Upon waking I found an altered world: and I had changed, too, very much. The geometrics which had interested me so exclusively before, I now felt were bleak and empty. They wanted *filling*. They were still as much present to my mind as ever, but submerged in the coloured vegetation, the flesh and blood, that is life.'[56] Sure enough, the metamorphosis so succinctly described here can be seen enacted in the large painting commissioned by the Imperial War Museum in 1918 and completed the following year.[57] Lewis settled once again for a military theme, but this time it was a far more dramatic idea: *A Battery Shelled*. His picture shows the aftermath of destruction. The jagged fragments twisting up into the air are still close in spirit to the splintered violence of his Vorticist designs, and on the ground below their rhythms are subtly echoed in the tortuous configurations of gouged mud. Mechanistic robots pick their way through the labyrinthine patterns formed by the mud and these automatons, too, recall the 'creaking men machines' of his pre-war drawings. Indeed, the central figure of the trio in the middle of the picture could almost stand as the pictorial equivalent of the dehumanized man perched on top of Epstein's *Rock Drill*.

This main section of the painting retains a more impressive balance between representation and abstraction than the *Gun Pit* canvas, and suggests how logical Lewis's shift in artistic direction must have appeared to the artist himself at the time. 'War, and especially those miles of hideous desert known as "the Line" in Flanders and France', he pointed out in retrospect, 'presented me with a subject-matter so consonant with the austerity of that "abstract" vision I had

Wyndham Lewis
A Battery Shelled, 1919

developed, that it was an easy transition.'[58] His explanation makes very good
sense; but the argument crumbles somewhat when the huge figures in dark
green on the left of the picture are considered. They are blatantly inconsistent,
naturalistic intruders placed in a stylized environment, and the conjunction of
two irreconcilable idioms is jarring. These contemplative observers could almost
be standing in front of a completely separate painting, gravely meditating on the
change of style that Lewis has made himself undergo. They make nonsense of
the mechanical imagery employed in the rest of the canvas; and the smaller,
robot soldiers, bathed in a harsh orange that blends bitterly with the chalk-white
sky and the acid mud, appear as a consequence arbitrarily conceived, the product
of a quirky literary whim rather than a compulsive vision of the world.

A Battery Shelled dramatizes the most decisive turning-point in Lewis's life
as an artist, and by extension sounds the Last Post for the Vorticist movement
as a whole. Its chronic, unconcealed schizophrenia highlights the crisis of
confidence which he, as much as his colleagues, was experiencing; and Roberts
later admitted that 'in the two large paintings he did as an Official artist, Lewis
made no attempt to depict the war in a Vorticist or abstract manner'. Roberts, in
fact, had agreed to help Lewis 'in transferring his design on to the canvas', and
recalled how acutely sensitive Lewis was about the realistic elements in the
picture. 'My method of working did not satisfy him', Roberts wrote. ' "You
have photographed it onto the canvas", he objected, adding: "It looks like a
Jacob Kramer!" Just how the slight pencil work I had done on the canvas
could resemble a picture by Kramer and at the same time be photographic
puzzled me. The painting was continued without my assistance.' Lewis was
obviously touchy about his adoption of more traditional stylistic procedures;
but it did not deter him, as Roberts confirmed, from using Wadsworth 'as a
model for the figures on the left of the scene'.[59] Drawing from life was to
become an integral part of his programme in the years ahead, as Lewis insisted

more and more on 'acquiring a maximum amount of skill in work from nature
– still of course subject to the disciplines I had acquired and which controlled
my approach to everything'.[60]

For a while, however, Lewis still clung to the deluded idea of reviving
Vorticism, and even before the war ended the old group began to meet once
more at its favourite haunt. 'After the battle interlude, the Eiffel again became
our assembly point, but it no longer resembled La Nouvelle Athène', Roberts
remembered. 'Military uniforms and shaven chins had replaced the sombreros
and beards. We were now Official War Artists. As a precaution against surprise
night attacks from over-exuberant bohemians in uniform and their warrior
companions, a small hole bored through the street door enabled Joe the waiter
to inspect all late callers before admission.'[61] The cavalier insouciance and exhibitionism of the movement's pre-war evenings had disappeared, and with it
the essential spirit that had informed the Vorticists' activities. But Lewis was,
for the moment, indefatigable and uncowed by the new mood of sobriety: by
the autumn of 1919 he was even preparing to edit a third edition of the rebels'
magazine. 'I am bringing out another volume of *Blast* (about November I
expect)', he told Quinn buoyantly on 3 September. 'This will be, one half, the
matter of my pamphlet: these theories illustrated by fifteen or twenty designs by
Roberts, Etchells, Wadsworth, Turnbull, Dismorr and myself; the other half
consisting of less specific matter: a story by myself, a long, new poem by Eliot,
and some other things.'[62] Despite Lewis's confidence, the project was never
brought to fruition; and part of the reason may be that Pound, who played
such a major role in the compilation of previous *Blast* issues, had decided to
give up his struggle to sustain the Vorticist cause and leave England for good.

The last effort the poet made to perpetuate the memory of the movement was
in the summer of 1918, when he organized a Memorial Exhibition of Gaudier's
work at the Leicester Galleries. In his preface to the catalogue he reaffirmed his
commitment to his friend's achievement by stating that 'his death... at Neuville
St. Vaast is, to my mind, the gravest individual loss which the arts have sustained during the war'.[63] But after paying this generous final tribute to Gaudier's
memory, Pound seemed to grow more cynical about the future of radicalism in
London. Possibly he realized, as he looked at the work his allies were now
executing, that the original spark was being extinguished and his much-
cherished 'primary pigment' slowly 'dispersed' in 'secondary applications'.[64]
Even though he continued to admire Lewis's pictures,[65] doubt is discernible
in his review of the *Guns* one-man show, where he wrote that 'although I give
no jot of my admiration, of my preference for his "abstract" work, I consider
the present work an advance, or at any rate not an artistic retrogression'. Pound's
former unqualified enthusiasm for Lewis was now significantly absent, and the
highest compliment he could pay the exhibition was to describe it as 'a phase,
and by no means the most important phase of the work of one of the chief living
artists; it is dispassionate; it is without rhetoric; it is at the furthest remove from
any vulgarity'. Negative virtues indeed; but Pound did go on to offer a valuable
explanation for the fact that Lewis had 'lost some of the apparent vigour of his
Timon drawings; some of the bonhomie of his sailors; some of the savagery of
his post-Daumier satires'. For the poet stressed that 'the war was no joking
matter, and satire has no place in the treatment of tragic situations; the point of
satire is for smugness and hypocrisy and stupidity, not for grave unavoidable
horror'.[66] Pound realised only too well that it would be impossible to recapture the
context in which his beloved Vorticism had flourished ever again.

His attitude therefore remained enigmatic, diplomatically countering a stated
'preference' for Vorticism with a guarded and indecisive murmur of approval
for the war pictures. He was obviously finding it hard to reconcile himself to

Lewis's new style, and he avoided participating in the projected issue of *Blast* by peripatetic trips to Paris and the South of France. 'Pound has vanished into France and is in a mist of recuperation and romance', Lewis told Quinn rather aggrievedly in September 1919. 'I have not heard from him, so I don't expect he will take part in this, although he may.'[67] The poet returned to London for sporadic visits, but his disenchantment with life in the city grew stronger. When Aldington returned from the war in 1919, he found his old Imagist ally 'still in the same apartment in Kensington, rather overwhelmingly obstructed with one of Dolmetsch's spinets and a quantity of poor Gaudier's statues', and realized at once that 'Ezra had become violently hostile to England . . . he kept tapping his Adam's apple and assuring me that the English stopped short there. I thought at first he meant that he had been menaced by the returning troops as a slacker, but it eventually came out that the English had no brains . . . He told me that he was moving to Paris where he would be among intelligent people'.[68] Eventually, in the autumn of 1920, Pound acted on his discontent: after complaining to Carlos Williams that 'there is no longer any intellectual *life* in England',[69] he moved to France, thereby depriving London of one more vital agent of its brief avant-garde renaissance.

Lewis was left behind with the solitary burden of producing new theoretical writings for the movement he hoped to relaunch; and he finally published them as a separate pamphlet with the outspoken title of *The Caliph's Design. Architects! Where is your Vortex?* in October 1919. It turned out to be one of Lewis's most provocative and prophetic essays on art, although a certain lack of co-ordination tallied with his own description of it as 'a painter's notebook . . . mostly rough notes; not planned, but written down hastily, from time to time, as some problem presented itself'.[70] As might be expected, they reiterated many of *Blast*'s earlier attacks on Futurism, but there is a new note of constructive criticism, a plea for the fruitful integration of the modern artist with the society in which he lives. 'What is the use of taking all the useful Gods and Goddesses away, and leaving the artist with no role in the social machine, except that of an entertainer, or a business man?' he asked passionately, raising the most important issue in the entire broadside. For Lewis was worried about the isolation of the experimental painter, and wanted to see the implications of the recent aesthetic innovations harnessed by the world at large. Forgetting about his own new espousal of representational doctrines, he argued that abstraction should be incorporated in the everyday fabric of big cities, not left to cultivate its own alienation among a select clique of misunderstood pioneers. 'The energy at present pent up (or rather too congested) in the canvas painted in the studio and sold at the dealers, and written of with a monotonous emphasis of horror or facetiousness in the Press, must be released and used in the general life of the community', he stormed. 'And from thence, from the life outside, it will come back and enrich and invigorate the studio. When accepted, modern painting is accepted as a revolutionary oasis in the settled, dreary expanse of twentieth-century commercial art: a place where bright colours, exciting and funny forms, a little knot of extravagant people, are to be found; and that it is amusing sometimes to visit. Listlessness, dilettantism is the mark of studio art. *You must get Painting, Sculpture, and Design out of the studio and into life somehow or other* if you are not going to see this new vitality dessicated in a Pocket of inorganic experimentation.'[71]

The impassioned urgency of Lewis's outburst reflected, of course, the impasse in which he found himself when he returned from the war. If the *Guns* show had brought him popular acclaim, he was still a grossly neglected artist whose talents were simply not being put to good use. His frustration inevitably mounted, and in some sections of the pamphlet erupted into satire: the unifying theme of these notes was focused in the story of a mythical and immensely powerful Caliph, who suddenly summons his trembling architects and tells them angrily that 'I am extremely dissatisfied with the shape of my city, so I have done a design of a new city, or rather of a typical street in a new city. It is a little vorticist effort that I threw off while I was dressing this morning'.[72] The whimsical fairy-tale vein of the allegory does not wholly conceal Lewis's admiration for such dictatorial tactics, a bias that foreshadows his political inclinations in the thirties. For the Caliph story is tantamount to an exercise in wish-fulfilment on Lewis's part, knowing as he did that Vorticism was now regarded as an outdated joke, and that he would never be capable of sustaining such a comprehensive revolt on his own.

The pamphlet can almost be seen as a blueprint of the way in which the rebel movement *should* have developed after the war, disseminating its principles outwards from the studio into every department of creative activity. Indeed, one particularly inspiring passage proceeds to outline the ideal aesthetic behind such a Vorticist crusade, emphasizing as it does that 'machinery should be regarded as a new resource, as though it were a new mineral or oil, to be used and put to different uses than those for which it was originally intended'. Lewis might have rejected the influence of mechanical imagery in his own work, but he was still prepared to sit down and write that 'a machinery for making the parts of a 6 in. Mk. 19 gun should be regarded apart from its function. Absorbed into the aesthetic consciousness it would no longer *make* so much as a pop-gun: its function thenceforward would change, and through its agency emotions would be manufactured, related, it is true, to its primitive efficiency, shinyness [*sic*], swiftness or slowness, elegance or power but with its meaning transformed'. What a tragedy that Lewis did not act on his own theories and produce work in accordance with the concepts outlined here! He could have built on the achievements of Vorticism and fulfilled his pamphlet's astonishing declaration that 'if the world *would only build temples to Machinery* in the abstract then everything would be perfect. The painter and sculptor would have plenty to do, and could, in complete peace and suitably honoured, pursue their trade without further trouble'.[73]

The Caliph's Design, however, remained a fantasy and did nothing to alleviate Lewis's compromised position as an artist. He could easily explain to Quinn that the pamphlet was 'a consideration of how an abstract design of direction and masses can be applied to a street or a city. It is an appeal to the better type of artist to take more interest in and more part in the general life of the world . . . and to attempt to change the form-content of civilized life'.[74] But in reality, he was himself an artist of immeasurable energy and resourcefulness who had already found his hands tied and given up the struggle for radicalism. Even in October 1918, Herbert Read realized – after meeting Lewis for only a few hours – that 'he is very bitter about the war: he feels that four years of the most vital period of his career have been torn from his life'.[75] And this sense of bitterness rapidly turned into a sour deprecation of the importance he had once attached to the rebel movement. 'To a good painter, with some good work to do in this world . . . the only point of the "new movement" that he finds there when he comes on the scene (for there is *always* a new movement) is quite cynically recognized to be a movement that suits *him*', he protested in *The Caliph's Design*. 'To look for anything more than the swing of the pendulum would be an absurdity. That *more* is supplied at the moment of every movement by the individual. And the painter who is at the same time an individual and the possessor of that "more", is not likely to try and find in a movement what he has in himself. It is for the public to take "movements" seriously – not for the artist.'[76] The implications were clear. Vorticism was now regarded as little

Edward Wadsworth
Suggestion for a Building, 1919

more than a starting-point, to be discarded by any artist capable of moving beyond a communal endeavour towards private fulfilment.

The only immediate result of the outpourings in his pamphlet was Wadsworth's *Suggestion for a Building*, a curiously eccentric plaster model of a Vorticist monument which was shown in November 1919 at an exhibition organized by the Arts League of Service at the Twenty-One Gallery.[77] Intended for construction in ferro-concrete, the extraordinary brutality of its façade was obviously designed as a loyal reinforcement of Lewis's vow in the *Caliph's Design* to 'flood those indolent commercial offices, where architects pursue their trade, with abstract design. I am sure the result would be to cram the world with form and intention'.[78] And the reception accorded this formidable invention was, predictably, vociferous. 'The stir and hullabaloo of the month is not . . . among painters, but among architects', commented *The New Age*. 'Following their perturbation over the "Caliph's Design", and their natural defence – i.e., that the pamphlet was merely destructive – Mr Wadsworth has had the temerity to exhibit a plaster model of a Vorticist building.'[79] The *Daily Mirror* was horrified, declaring that 'it is enough to make Wren, who did so much to beautify London, turn in his grave. The builder is supposed to find places for the windows from the "plan"'.[80] But Rutter, writing in the *Sunday Times*, was fascinated by the model, and announced that 'it is entirely original, no building like it has ever been seen before. How far it is practicable I should not like to say . . . from the model it is not clear where the doors and windows are, but an accompanying drawing shows the openings through which the interior of this crystalline structure gets its light'. After lamenting the absence of an interior plan, Rutter decided that 'as a suggestion it is certainly stimulating and exciting, an adaptation to architecture of those principles of abstract design advocated by cubist and vorticist painters. Mr Wadsworth has at least shown architects how to scrap what his friend Wyndham Lewis calls their "silly antique fakes", and his suggestion has a solidity that suggests a house built on a rock that will endure for ages. If only we were still in the Middle Ages it would have made a splendid stronghold for a robber baron on the Rhine, and from the scale of the man before the model the building would be about a hundred feet high – a colossal structure'.[81]

Wadsworth's monolith was never built, and soon became a forgotten remnant of ambitions that the Vorticists themselves would never fulfil. But Lewis's plea for the widespread dissemination of abstractionist principles in everyday life did receive striking expression in the poster designs of the American Edward McKnight Kauffer, who met the rebels after he settled in London in 1914, went on to exhibit with some of them at the 1916 London Group show and finally collaborated with Lewis on an exhibition project in 1920. His most outstanding poster, the celebrated *Early Bird* composition used to launch the *Daily Herald* in 1919, was a strikingly successful adaptation of Vorticist tenets, and showed how easily the movement's vocabulary lent itself to the need for a bold public image.[82] The flurry of birds in flight has been turned, not into a glorification of blurred motion like Balla's painting of *Swifts: Paths of Movement + Dynamic Sequences*, but a hard and crisply defined pattern of angular segments. Kauffer presents a simplified ideogram of the birds' characteristics and then reassembles them at will to form the most streamlined essence of flight he can devise. The result is a glancing, chequerboard complex of tensely sprung fragments, half bird and half aeroplane, which would not have looked at all out of place as an illustration in *Blast*. And Kauffer later explained that he was aiming at a Vorticist amalgam of natural and machine forms, which would have particularly appealed to Gaudier, when he described how 'the design was not

Edward McKnight Kauffer
Early Bird Poster for the Daily Herald, 1918–19

Giacomo Balla
Swifts: Paths of Movement + Dynamic Sequences, 1913

Jacob Epstein
The Tin Hat, 1916

Lawrence Atkinson
Dance Movement, c. 1914–20

invented in a studio. It came after much observation of birds in flight. The problem seemed to me at any rate a translation into design terms of three factors, namely, bird identification, movement, and formalization into pattern and line. Birds in flight and aeroplane formations are singularly alike. The arrowhead thrust is the dominant motif. But wings flapping have a contrary movement – so this too has to be considered'.[83]

The *Early Bird* employs a Vorticist-inspired vocabulary to rise above those aspects of poster design Kauffer hated, and it could easily be seen as the direct answer to Lewis's insistence in his preface to the Vorticist Exhibition catalogue that 'in poster advertisement by far the most important point is a telling design. Were the walls of London carpeted with abstractions rather than the present mass of work that falls between two stools, the design usually weakened to explain some point, the effect architecturally would be much better, and the Public taste could thus be educated in a popular way to appreciate the essentials of design better than the picture-galleries have ever done'. Kauffer did not let Lewis down, either, for he went on to produce a superb series of posters throughout the following decade which can reasonably be seen as the only way the rebel movement's doctrines ever won approval in the eyes of the nation at large.

As for the other allies, they all followed Lewis's example and controverted their earlier ideals in a faint-hearted attempt to return to representational frames of reference. Epstein, who had never been closely involved in the internal politics of the movement anyway, found that his departure from Pett Level in 1916 brought about a change from the abstract severity of the dove and Venus carvings. He later mentioned, somewhat wistfully, that his stay in Sussex had definitely marked 'a period of intense activity and were it not for the war and the impossibility of living in the country and making a living, I would have stayed there forever'.[84] There can be no doubt that this disruption, along with his desperate need to sell work, caused Epstein to relinquish his position as a leader of the sculptural vanguard and move back towards the rugged, dramatic realism which was soon to become the hallmark of his portrait busts. His shifting views are clearly expounded in a letter to Quinn, written in February 1917, where he berated the collector for favouring radicalism to the exclusion of all else. 'I think you are inclined to over rate what you call advanced work', he complained with a significant note of impatience; 'not all advanced work is good, some of it is damn damn bad. I say this because there is a tendency to slight work that has any resemblance to natural objects. My own essays into abstract art have always been natural and not forced. I make no formula, and only when I see something to be done in abstract form that better conveys my meaning than natural forms then I use it. There is a solidity in natural forms though that will always attract a sculptor, and great work can be done on a natural basis.'[85]

No longer committed to the abstractionist cause, and increasingly attracted to the 'solidity' of naturalistic sculpture, Epstein eschewed the extremism of the *Venus* carvings, and returned to nature. Even before he was called up, he executed in *The Tin Hat* a work that already heralded the reactionary bias of his post-war work. Completed in time to be displayed at his Leicester Galleries one-man show in the spring of 1917, this bronze head combines a machine-made object – the helmet – with an invented form, like the original version of the *Rock Drill*. But the latter's bleak geometry could not be further removed from the straightforward modelling of the Tommy's face, with its profusion of pitted, incidental detail and faithful adherence to anatomical propriety. The older he grew, the more Epstein came to regard his Vorticist work as a form of apprenticeship which lacked the humanism of a bronze like *The Tin Hat*. 'I cannot see that sculptors who took up abstraction later and used it made any advance on the 1913–14 period, or produced more novel forms', he wrote many years later, attempting to justify his own return to tradition. 'In our attempts to extend the range of sculpture we are led into extravagance and puerility.'[86] His work continued to arouse calumny in England throughout his career, but he had obviously abandoned experimentation in favour of a heightened, vaguely Expressionist naturalism, alternated only sporadically with monumental carvings which still bore traces of his earlier daring. 'When I returned to a normal manner of working', he wrote defensively, 'and was so bold as again to carve and model a face with its features, the advanced critics spoke of my having "thrown in the sponge". I was lost to the movement.' By this time, Epstein was equating realism with 'boldness', and insisted that 'I feel easy about this. The discipline of simplification of forms, unity of design, and co-ordination of masses is all to the good, and I think this discipline has influenced me in my later works like the "Behold the Man" and the "Adam". But to think of abstraction as an end in itself is undoubtedly letting oneself be led into a cul-de-sac, and can only lead to exhaustion and impotence'.[87] His explanation is remarkably similar to Lewis's account of his return to external appearances, even if the end results were very different. Both men had been assailed by the same doubts and misgivings, and both simultaneously decided to brush aside esoteric investigations in an attempt to communicate with a wider cross-section of the community.

Lawrence Atkinson
Limelight, c. 1914–20

Lawrence Atkinson
Abstract Figure Drawing, c. 1914–18

Only the secretive Atkinson pursued the implications of abstraction, undisturbed by the loss of faith around him; and all through the war years, from 1916 to 1919, he stubbornly exhibited non-representational pictures as a non-member at successive London Group shows. None of these contributions can be identified, although a lost watercolour afterwards known as *Dance Movement* may be the *Abstract Drawing of a Dancer* which Atkinson displayed at the 1916 London Group exhibition. It is fascinating to discover how many assumptions about the non-representational essence of dance rhythm this picture shares with Bomberg's many treatments of the same theme. An identical concentration on arabesque for its own sake and on the linear charting of movement underlies the interpretation in each man's work, proving once again how very unified two distinct individuals who never acknowledged any mutual agreement could be during this period of English art. Of the two, Atkinson adheres more closely to the idea of a sculptural form isolated from its surrounding space, and his dancer can therefore be said to appear more figurative than Bomberg's. The same is even more true of another lost watercolour called *Limelight*, where the elongated, slightly theatrical figure seems to have stepped out from behind a dark structure as artificial as a flat on a stage set. In this connection, it is reminiscent of earlier drawings by Lewis, and so is a surviving ink *Abstract Figure Drawing* which might perhaps be the *Abstract Drawing of Figure in Room* also exhibited by Atkinson in the 1916 London Group show. Despite its obvious interest in relating the linear structure of the figure to the lines of its immediate environment, the drawing still clings to the integrity of a human image; and it was only in a lost watercolour called *Marchers* that Atkinson really dispensed with that recurrent image and organized his untypically military theme into the kind of massed geometrical ranks seen in *Red Duet*. The colours may well have marked the picture out as definably Atkinson's, but in the extant photograph his diagrammatic forms have an impersonal air, as if he was deliberately rescinding his own personality for the sake of the rebel movement.

On this score alone, *Marchers* should belong to a relatively early period: by

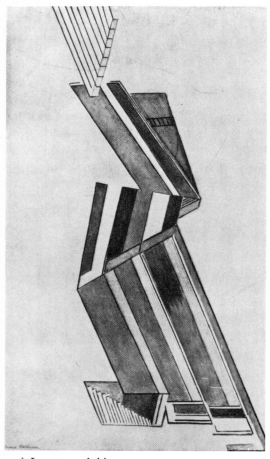

1918, when Atkinson's first securely dated work was reproduced as *The Sky Pilot* on the cover of Edith Sitwell's poetry magazine *Wheels*, he had broken away from Vorticism for ever. But in terms both of its style and its archetypally modern subject-matter, *The Sky Pilot* still belongs within the movement's frames of reference; and it shows that Atkinson, unlike most of the other rebels, had no intention of abrogating his abstract convictions now that the war was over. Following on from the precedent set by Wadsworth's *A Short Flight*, this lean, aggressive structure certainly does communicate 'the feeling of mechanism, throbbing down a channel of night-blue with blackness closing in on either hand', as Horace Shipp maintained in his monograph on Atkinson. 'Such a subject could only be presented in representational art as a study in arrested movement – a method which misses the basic essential of the theme', Shipp continued. 'Treated in semi-abstraction by Atkinson, and expressed by a repetition of his forms in cubic perspective, the picture conveyed a sense of actual flight through the air.' The original design must have been much less inflammatory than the surviving scarlet cover, however, for Shipp declared that he 'would like to ask the talented editress of "Wheels" why this significant blue was changed to

△ Lawrence Atkinson
Marchers, c. 1914–20

▷ Lawrence Atkinson
Vital, c. 1919

▽ Lawrence Atkinson
The Sky Pilot (Cover for *Wheels*), 1918

meaningless red when the design was used as a cover'.[88] Atkinson would only rarely have employed such a strident colour, as another delicate but impressive post-war composition called *Vital* proves.

Vital has a puritanical reserve which reflects Atkinson's new mood of aloofness and self-abnegation, but its angular severity could not have been achieved without his earlier contact with the rebel movement. The image looks like a preliminary study for one of the free-standing carvings which gave him a certain limited fame in the post-war period as a sculptor who worked in extraordinary isolation, cut off from every official group and organized alliance. Horace Shipp's monograph on his work was published in 1922, and it made clear that he had rejected Cubism, Futurism, and Vorticism because 'these schools are primarily interested in surfaces and appearances, whilst Atkinson has always tended to see through these to the deeper things behind them of which they were the result'.[89] The explanation was tenuously expressed and more than a little absurd – Shipp blithely labels Atkinson's final phase as 'Pure Abstraction' and leaves it at that – for the later sculpture does not substantiate this heady claim to reveal 'deeper' truths than the rebels had unearthed half-a-dozen years before. Indeed, when he staged a one-man show of *Abstract Sculpture and Painting* at the Eldar Gallery in May 1921, the catalogue listed two drawings as *Vortex No. 1* and *Vortex No. 2*, as if in recognition of his continuing debt to the movement.[90]

Konody, of all people, contributed a friendly essay to the catalogue called 'In Defence of Abstract Art' – an almost incredible irony in view of everything he had previously done to break the Vorticists' abstract beliefs over the Canadian commissions – and Lewis proceeded to write down his only recorded thoughts on Atkinson a year later. 'As regards purely "abstract" work, or extreme experimental work, none has appeared since the war, unless we except Mr Laurence [*sic*] Atkinson', he declared in a review intended for *The Tyro No. 2*, openly admitting that Atkinson alone sustained the pre-war spirit of radicalism in English art. 'He is a busy practitioner in music, who produces his plastic abstract phantasies in his spare time.' A note of subtly veiled sarcasm ran all the way through Lewis's article, particularly when he recorded that 'a piece of sculpture of his was awarded the gold medal, or something very grand, at the Milan Exhibition'. Lewis did not quite approve of Atkinson's work, even though he admitted that the Eldar Gallery show was 'very interesting', because 'an admirable and delicate sense of design was somewhat let down, in his exhibition, by a lack of ordinary virtuosity and the substance and strength that it gives'. It was in many ways an accurate criticism of Atkinson's often faulty draughtsmanship, but Lewis went on to assert that 'there were several designs for sculpture there, that, executed on a proper scale, would have been, in the public places of a modern city, appropriate monuments, and a welcome contrast to the obscene and idiotic rubbish that is hourly raised to commemorate and to parody some heroism. As regards the Milan cup, or medal, it is natural that a foreign city should honour this vorticist artist of whom England had never heard'.[91] Perhaps Lewis had second thoughts about deflating Atkinson in print: the article was published in a trial copy only, leaving Atkinson to the altogether more devoted comments of Horace Shipp.

But despite his admirable independence, and success in the Milan Exhibition of 1921, Atkinson remained an obscure figure. By the time he died in September 1931, he was known only to a few friends and collectors, and in recent years his name has virtually been forgotten. It comes as a surprise to rediscover his work and to realize that, with all its evident limitations, it marks Atkinson out as one of the very first English artists consistently to explore the possibilities of an abstract language until the end of his life.

▷Frederick Etchells
Armistice – Suburbia, 1918–20

◁ Cuthbert Hamilton
Self-Portrait, 1919–20

▽ Cuthbert Hamilton
Glass Factory, 1919–20

Most of the other lapsed revolutionaries, meanwhile, came together under the title of 'Group X' for an exhibition at Heal's Mansard Gallery in March 1920, but not even the domineering Lewis was willing to be known as their leader. The man who had coerced such a prickly band of artistic egos into the collective endeavour of *Blast* now confessed in the catalogue preface that 'the members of this group have agreed to exhibit together twice annually, firstly for motives of convenience, and with no theory or dogma that would be liable to limit the development of any member. Each member sails his own boat, and may lift his sails to any wind that may seem . . . to promise a prosperous cruise.' It was the most overt admission of defeat that Lewis had so far permitted himself to publish: for in a show possessing no manifesto, little homogeneity of style and artists as diverse as Frank Dobson, Ginner, Jock Turnbull and the Group's initiator McKnight Kauffer, it was no longer practicable to pretend that a common purpose informed the venture. Dismorr, Etchells, Hamilton, Roberts and Wadsworth joined Lewis in the proceedings, but none of them had any illusions about the uncommitted nature of the undertaking. The *Drawing* which Dismorr exhibited did prove that she regarded Vorticist imagery with affection and was loath to abandon it altogether. It was one of her most assured works, an incisive foray into the world of dancing automatons which Lewis had formulated so many years before, and yet it marked the end of her rebel phase.

Jessica Dismorr
Drawing, 1919–20

Frederick Etchells
Gunwalloe, c. 1922

Disillusion with the whole concept of radical art was rampant, and Etchells was so affected by it that he decided to give up painting, study for an A.R.I.B.A. and pursue a completely new career as a professional architect who would in 1930 provide London with one of its first truly modernist buildings, Crawford's advertising agency in Holborn. 'Lewis spent nearly a week trying to persuade me not to throw up painting', he recalled;[92] but the conservative style of the *Armistice – Suburbia* drawing he exhibited at the Mansard show must have proved to Lewis that his friend no longer had any interest in preserving even a vestige of his interest in Vorticism. After executing a few final watercolours like the markedly architectural *Gunwalloe*, which Etchells remembered was 'done about 1922 – when I spent some 2 or 3 weeks at Gunwalloe, with Charlie Ginner . . . & other minor high-brows of the period',[93] he never again returned to the medium which had given him so much temporary notoriety in the pre-war period.

Surprisingly enough, the only contributor to display any genuine love for the movement was Cuthbert Hamilton, who had been the most shadowy of all the rebels at the time. Although he too turned away from painting after relinquishing his war duties as a special constable, and started to make ceramics at the Yeoman Potteries which he himself had founded,[94] the drawings he sent in to the 'Group X' show demonstrated an unfaltering concern for abstractionist principles. One of them, a *Self-Portrait*, excludes so much of outward appearances that its reference to a head can be discerned only with difficulty. Hamilton has reduced his face to a blunt summary of essential form, a structure which snubs the naturalism so favoured by his friends and stands as a gesture of confidence in the fragmentation exploited by the Vorticists. Nor was the drawing an isolated phenomenon. Its companion at the 'Group X' exhibition, *Glass Factory*, persisted in seizing on the subject-matter recommended for the artist in *Blast No. 1* and treating it with the aggressive vitality of a vintage rebel design.[95] The very workings of the factory itself are exposed in the energetic simplification of Hamilton's composition: the building seems to have exploded with mechanized vigour and then reassembled its segmented parts into a new order, which is not afraid to employ ambiguity and spatial deception in the interests of a frenetic impact.

And in another design, which is probably to be identified as the exhibit listed

Cuthbert Hamilton
Decorated Plate, c.1919

▷Cuthbert Hamilton
Reconstruction (?), c. 1919–20

in the Mansard catalogue as *Reconstruction*, this same feeling is translated into an even more immense convulsion of urban activity.[96] If the title is correct, Hamilton's theme must be concerned with post-war rebuilding, but the image he produces could just as easily be conveying the familiar Vorticist idea of positive destruction. The minuscule figure standing beside the house just below the centre of the composition extends his arm in a gesture of seeming despair, as a cataclysmic tremor runs through the jumble of metal and masonry around him and convulses it into violent life. He is the only human element in a work which defines universal upheaval with a whiplash linear precision and objectivity, welding chimneys and crane forms with complete confidence to more abstract configurations like the zigzag leaping up towards the top right corner of the picture. If the colours of the gouache are restricted to muted oranges and dull greys, there is still no real difference between its ordered aggression and the iconoclasm of other Vorticist designs. It has, in fact, sometimes been known as *Devastation*; and its inclusion in the Mansard show, alongside the pottery which was afterwards to claim most of Hamilton's attention, stands as a resilient symbol of Vorticism's ability, even at this late stage, to fire the enthusiasm of its disaffected followers.

Hamilton's contributions were, however, the solitary exception in a group show devoted to a resurrection of naturalism. *The Times* was all too accurate when it pointed out, with a discernible sigh of relief, that 'only one of the artists, Mr C. J. Hamilton, persists in design that looks entirely abstract'.[97] And even this small outpost of Vorticist endurance came under attack from the critics who reviewed the 'Group X' exhibition. *Truth* maintained, with a scathing hostility reminiscent of the pre-war days, that 'Mr Hamilton's black-and-white designs in the catalogue suggest that he might make a good designer of carpets and cretonnes, but fragments of the "innards" of a piano do not make pleasant pictures'.[98] And it was left to Michael Sadleir to make his lonely amends in an article declaring that 'Cuthbert Hamilton, to my mind, justifies the extreme in non-representation. There are suggestions of accepted form in his clear, cool compositions, but they become an acceptable part of the delightful whole and one is content that they should be there, and neither more nor less'.[99]

All the same, nothing could hide the fact that the Mansard exhibition was staged as a miscellaneous bran-tub into which ten widely incommensurable artists could pour their own particular sweetmeats. It was in vain that Lewis spoke in the catalogue preface of their collective belief that 'the experiments undertaken all over Europe during the last ten years should be utilised directly and developed, and not be lightly abandoned or the effort allowed to relax'.[100] For his contributions, and those of his colleagues, flatly contradicted the crusading urgency of this statement; and Frank Rutter was much nearer the truth when he asserted in his *Sunday Times* review of the show that 'the real tendency of the exhibition is towards a new sort of realism, evolved by artists who have passed through a phase of abstract experiment'.[101]

Paradoxically enough, 'Group X's corporate attitude was now much closer to the timidity castigated by Lewis in his catalogue preface, when he sternly admonished the 'many people today who talk glibly of the "victory" of the Cubist, Vorticist or Expressionist movements, and in the next breath of now putting the armour off and becoming anything that pays best, repairing wherever, after the stress of a few years, the softest time is to be secured'.[102] If the subsequent development of the rebels cannot with justice be seen as commercially cynical – all of them stayed true to their personalities, and none ever reaped the rewards of the time-serving artist – it is equally certain that they failed to 'develop' the Vorticist language in the way Lewis pretended to advocate in his preface. They did indeed 'relax', in a variety of wayward and disparate directions,

and never for one moment recaptured their briefly-held positions as leaders of the European avant-garde. Looking back on the fate of the Mansard exhibition, Roberts afterwards gave a far more accurate and clear-eyed assessment of its significance than the one provided by Lewis at the time. 'For want of something better, a large uninspiring "X" was adopted as the group's device', he recalled wrily. 'This time no manifestos were issued; our plain "X" offered no message or new theory of art. But what could possibly be done with an "X"? Art at the cross-roads? . . . Group "X" set out, but got nowhere. "X" marked our beginning and end.'[103]

If Vorticism had finally been abandoned, so too had the movements that originally inspired it. During the war, most continental artists found themselves separated from one another, and many of them were obliged to forsake their work. When, therefore, they found it possible to take up the threads of civilian life once again, they discovered that all feeling of continuity had been irretrievably dispersed. Italy's entry into the war in May 1915 fatally disrupted Futurism, which came to the end of its energies the following year with the death of two vital figureheads, Saint 'Elia and Boccioni. At the same time, Carrà sensed the waning intensity, renounced his membership of the movement and joined de Chirico in the Scuola Metafisica; while Severini abandoned Futurism in favour of an ornamental Cubist idiom. And even though the indefatigable Marinetti continued his literary and political activities with a sprinkling of second-generation Futurist artists, the Fascist dictatorship frowned on the violent individualism that had furnished the earlier group with so much of its strength, and encouraged the weaker decorative tendencies of its surviving members. The whole context of pre-war Europe, which had provided a vital background of extraordinary excitement and revolutionary fervour, had been effectively demolished; and none of the collective groups weaned in that intoxicating ambience could hope to survive its passing. Futurism, moreover, had required of its disciples an emotional recklessness that could only be expected of young men. By its very nature it was destined to have only a short life, and it is somehow very fitting that the war, in so many ways a practical demonstration of Futurist gospels, should have swept it away.

Cubism, likewise, emerged profoundly altered from the holocaust. Although dealers and artists busied themselves more than ever before with one-man shows and mixed exhibitions dedicated to celebrating the resurrection of the Cubist impulse, the movement had in reality all but spent itself. By 1914 its fundamental tenets had been established, and all the most durable discoveries comprehensively explored. The post-war revival added nothing to this achievement, and succeeded only in producing a quantity of work in which hard-won Cubist principles degenerated into second-hand mannerisms. Even Gleizes, who helped to organize the 1920 *Section d'Or* exhibition and originally planned it as a phoenix-like demonstration of Cubism's lasting vitality, confessed a few years later that it had merely revealed how 'the idea [of Cubism] as it developed had burst the tidy envelope of the *word* Cubism'.[104] In a sense, however, Cubism did not need to continue after the war. Its nature had been so thoroughly and brilliantly expounded that its outstanding participants felt free to develop as individual artists who could use its precepts as the basis of their own particular stylistic developments.

Unlike the Vorticists, they did not on the whole deny their origins: Léger, for instance, whose pre-war work had paralleled the English movement in so many ways, carried on painting in an idiom commensurate with his earlier experiments. Not that he was any less affected by his spell of active service than the Vorticists; on the contrary, he afterwards described how his period in the trenches had dramatically altered his conception of art. 'During those four war years I was abruptly thrust into a new reality which was both blinding and new', he remembered. 'When I left Paris my style was thoroughly abstract: period of pictorial liberation . . . I was dazzled by the breadth of a 75-millimetre gun which was standing uncovered in the sunlight: the magic of light on white metal. This was enough to make me forget the abstract art of 1912–13.'[105] His account is immediately reminiscent of Lewis's description of his conversion at the Front; but – and the difference is an important one – Léger's revelation did not result in a complete renunciation of his previous work. He may have explained that 'once I got my teeth into that sort of reality I never let go of objects again';[106] yet 'reality' to him did not mean, as it did to Lewis and most of his allies, going back to nature and starting all over again from scratch.

Although Léger did not have the Canadian commission to contend with, it must be obvious that he was a more formidably singleminded personality than any of his English counterparts. And even if they had possessed the Frenchman's imperturbable vision, the Vorticists were still helplessly crippled by the abrupt intrusion of world events. Their nascent movement was not granted the period of uninterrupted peace which both Cubism and Futurism had been able to enjoy, and Lewis himself was afterwards forced to admit that the Great English Vortex remained more of 'a programme, rather than an accomplished fact'.[107] The war had temporarily forbidden it to develop beyond its noisy beginnings, and only an obsession of unusual consistency could have produced enough stamina to pick up the scattered remnants of such an unformed philosophy after peace returned. None of the Vorticist artists was of that stature, and apart from Atkinson they all variously succumbed to the pervasive spirit of moderation that England urged them to embrace.

Besides, there had all along been a strain of hysterical desperation in the rebels' crusade which suggested that they never really imagined that their efforts would bear fruit. In the early summer of 1914, when most of them finally decided to band together and fight, the declining state of Europe must have been ominously apparent, and caused them to wonder whether they would be heard at all amid the clamour of an international conflict. 'Pre-war Europe was guttering down to its end', Pound wrote later, in an attempt to describe the ambivalent mood of fatalism and euphoria which lay behind the Vorticists' revolt. 'One tried to persuade it to make a "good end". One may even have thought one was in the act of succeeding. In any case the years immediately before the great slaughter were full of exhilaration for those in the middle of the action – I suppose one must call it the intellectual scene – it was rather like a battle between a weasel and a cow with all the fun for the weasel. Whether we supposed we could trans-animate the cow and produce a miraculous super-antelope or springbok, I doubt.'[108] Pound had perhaps laid his finger on one reason why Vorticism faded so quickly: for such feelings of 'doubt', realistic though they may have been, do not help to sustain a movement beyond its first flush of revolt.

After the war the rebels were, at heart, no longer prepared to whip themselves up into that kind of manic frenzy. They could now see exactly how impracticable and idealistic the entire venture had been; and maybe they could also appreciate how the frenetic explosiveness of Vorticism carried within itself a kind of death-wish. When Lewis advocated in *Blast No. 1* the use of 'the most perishable colours in painting', explaining that 'we should hate other ages, and don't want to fetch £40,000, like a horse',[109] he pinpointed the suicidal element which was lodged like a time-bomb inside the fabric of his movement. With hindsight, the Vorticists' iconoclasm can be seen to have blown up in their own faces: the Great War was in that sense only an outward manifestation of the acute weariness which their exhibitionism inevitably brought about.

Most of the insurgents would, moreover, have been more willing to carry on if Vorticism itself did not owe quite so much of its impetus to Lewis alone. Had the movement been communal in the truest sense of the word, its capacity for a more prolonged resilience might have proved larger. But without Lewis's continuing initiative, the other members saw no compelling reason why they should adhere to a group impulse any more. Indeed, their relief at escaping from Lewis's hegemony was probably as great as the sense of loss they may have felt over Vorticism's demise. None of them, it is fair to say, shared his critical dislike of Cubism, Futurism or English culture with anything like the same degree of ferocious passion. And it was the presence of these very targets which had prompted much of the motivation behind both Vorticism and *Blast*. However much Lewis may have hated these Aunt Sallys, the fact remained that he drew a large part of his revolutionary energy from the attempt he made to knock them down flat. And once he had thrown his brick-bats as vigorously as he knew how, his energy evaporated.

Lewis gradually shifted his attention to other sources of annoyance, because his creative resources throve on a combative stance; but his erstwhile colleagues did not need it. And so Vorticism, which was as much the product of a polemical moment in time as it was the embodiment of its artists' inner needs, obviously could not be expected to outlive the peculiar context against which it had been pitted. There was, heaven knows, plenty that deserved blasting in English art during the twenties. But by then, the Vorticists' individual needs had taken precedent over group solidarity, and the context had irrevocably changed. Hence their resigned refusal to team up and attempt the same kind of wholesale conversion all over again. Weary and disillusioned, they opted out of the struggle without a murmur, and left the future of modernism in the far more determined hands of the artists affiliated with De Stijl, Dada and Surrealism. Disgusted with this corporate volte-face, Quinn berated Pound in 1921 for ever recommending the movement, and hit out at 'your monumental folly re that sort of stuff and my monumental assinnity [*sic*] in falling for it and buying it'.[110] And the following year, Clive Bell issued another dismissive verdict on the rebels when he announced from his Bloomsbury standpoint that 'the French know enough of Vorticism to know that it is a provincial and utterly insignificant contrivance which has borrowed what it could from Cubism and Futurism and added nothing to either'.[111]

The memory of the movement soon became submerged, and it had little direct impact on the course of English art. Disclaimed by the men who had first conspired to produce it, Vorticism was already forgotten and despised by the time Pound told Lewis in a 1924 letter from Rapallo that 'I have just, ten years an' a bit after its appearance and in this far distant locus, taken out a copy of the great MAGENTA cover'd opusculus (*Blast*). We were hefty guys in them days; an' of what has come after us, we seem to have survived without a great mass of successors'.[112] The poet's proud recollection of the rebels' militancy and daring was tempered by the realization that their own failure to sustain the group impulse had enabled English artists to ignore Vorticism completely. In 1925, the only reference to the movement made by one of its closest former observers, John Rodker, in a book on modern artistic experiment, was that 'Futurism may now mean almost any unconventional activity in the contemporary arts, whether Vorticist, Cubist, Symbolist, Vers Librist, etc.'[113] For Rodker, as for the world at large, the Great English Vortex had lost its significance; and it became an easy target for layman satirists like W. Hugh Higginbottom, who described in a 1928 book called *Frightfulness in Modern Art* how 'we find ... the staled kickshaws of Picasso and Marinetti served up, *réchauffés*, with a *sauce piquante* prescribed by the latter, at the tardy table of the English Vorticists'.

Bent on securing some easy laughs at the movement's expense, Higginbottom declared that the rebels 'borrowed Marinetti's automobile', tried to 'run it on hot-air alone, and registered surprise when they found themselves in possession of the motor without the "go"'. And having scored his point, Higginbottom then proceeded to dismiss the Vorticists completely. 'Without a single idea of their own, these "Mother Hubbards" of latter-day art lacked even the wit to conceal the bareness of their cupboard . . . But I do not propose to waste words upon those who have wasted so many upon themselves.'[114]

On a more serious level, the movement was once again spurned when England gave birth to another abstractionist group with the formation of Unit One in 1933. Although both Paul Nash and Ben Nicholson had attended the Slade with some of the Vorticists before the war, and Wadsworth himself became a member of Unit One, none of them bothered to acknowledge a debt to Vorticism's pioneering example. In many ways, the ideals outlined by Nash – 'to stand for the expression of a truly contemporary spirit, for that thing which is recognised as peculiarly of *today* in painting, sculpture and architecture' – echoed the aims promulgated twenty years before by the rebels.[115] But Nash pushed aside any Vorticist links which Unit One could be suspected of possessing when he described in a 1933 *Listener* article how 'England, in spite of her habitual aloofness, contributed a small revolt of her own in 1913; the half-remembered "Vorticist" movement, organised by Wyndham Lewis. This, however, was chiefly literary in inspiration, not excluding many of the "Cubist" paintings. The immense intervention of the War left very little of the substance or spirit of Vorticism surviving, although some of its chief exponents made valuable pictorial War records'.[116]

Nash's condescending history of the 'small revolt' showed only too clearly how irrelevant Vorticism had become to the artists who eventually succeeded in persuading England of abstraction's lasting value. And it was only much later that the balance was redressed when two of the principal architects of this second non-representational phase in British art, Henry Moore and Ben Nicholson, actually paid tribute to Vorticism's inspiration. 'Wyndham Lewis meant a lot to me in my early days, because at that time the Bloomsbury Group dominated English art', Moore recalled. 'When I came to London as a raw provincial student, I read things like *Blast* and what I liked was to find somebody in opposition to the Bloomsbury people, who had a stranglehold on everything. Lewis was literally a blast of fresh air to me: offering not so much a belief or particular attitude as an opening-up, a freeing, which was a great help. Gaudier's writings and sculpture meant an enormous amount as well – they, and *Blast*, were a confirmation to me as a young person that everything was possible, that there were men in England full of vitality and life.'[117] Moore was obviously excited by the spirit of the movement rather than by its stylistic contribution, whereas Ben Nicholson pointed out that the pictures themselves had a liberating influence on his work. 'My recollection is simply that Vorticism was of use in freeing me from many conventional (visual) ideas', he wrote, 'but once I'd seen "Cubism" in Paris Vorticism had little to give me.'[118] The French movement was bound, ultimately, to be more valuable to an artist of Nicholson's unaggressive disposition; and yet he particularly remembered that 'Bomberg I suppose was a part of it & early work by [him] I found v. interesting',[119] while his greatest admiration was reserved for Gaudier, whom he thought 'both in achievement & potential head & shoulders above any other artist involved'.[120] Even Atkinson, obscure though he soon became, exerted a palpable effect: Merlyn Evans, who helped to pioneer English abstraction in the 1930s, testified that he was enormously excited at the age of 17 by the reproductions in Horace Shipp's Atkinson monograph, and decided that his work 'ought ideally to carry

Dorothy Shakespear
Hommages – To Vorticism, c. 1937–8

on from where Atkinson's sculpture left off'.[121]

Vorticism's influence on later British painting and sculpture cannot, therefore, be considered wholly negligible. It acted as a catalyst on some members of the succeeding generation, even if they chose at the time to discount its importance altogether. At the very least, it proved that something could be done – with the requisite amount of conviction – to shake England out of its insular torpor and realize what was happening to modern art on an international scale. But it had no pupils or linear descendants. The movement's example lingered on in an indirect manner alone, through Lewis's wavering concern with geometrical forms, Atkinson's ascetic sculpture, Dismorr's resumption of an abstract idiom in the thirties, Wadsworth's association with Unit One, and Roberts' lifelong adherence to one rigidly inflexible formula. All the latter's figures are transformed into tubular giants, basically naturalistic but stiff and schematic enough to account for Lewis's belief that Vorticism did survive in 'works produced since that time which are touched with the authentic fire. I can think of dozens of drawings which would not be the original things they are if it had not been for their "Vorticist" ancestry'.[122] Dorothy Shakespear obviously agreed, for she paid specific tribute to the continuing inspiration of the movement with a celebratory thirties watercolour called *Hommages – To Vorticism*, which groups her initials with those of Eliot, Gaudier, Lewis and Pound and includes a Gaudier carving and a Lewis abstract canvas in an interior based on the small castle at Rapallo she knew so well. Pound, doubtless touched by this heartfelt gesture, told her that the watercolour was 'the best you've done yet'.[123]

Thirty years after *Hommages – To Vorticism*, when the movement was all but forgotten and its place in the history of modern art thoroughly traduced, another unexpected tribute was paid to the rebels by the English fabric designer Bernard Nevill. An admirer of *Blast*, which he had come across accidentally when some friends found mint copies of both issues and gave them to him at his request,[124] Nevill used the magazines' powerful visual attack as the springboard for his new collection of fashion prints. At that time he was designing for Liberty's – famous, ironically enough, for pioneering the popularization of Art Nouveau and William Morris in the late nineteenth century – and *Blast* helped him develop the abstract themes he had already employed in his previous collection, the Art Deco-oriented *Jazz* series. 'The direct wood block techniques of the illustrations in *Blast* made me realise that even simpler and more basic shapes and forms were the answer', he told an interviewer when his Vorticist designs were published in the *Sunday Times* colour magazine in 1967. 'I had already been an admirer of Wyndham Lewis as a portraitist, and of Vorticists and the literary movement of that time, but what excited me most in the manifestos was the advanced style of the graphic and typographical content.'[125]

He executed the designs early in 1966,[126] thereby adding a series of dynamic non-representational compositions to his current *Tango* range and paying specific homage to Wadsworth's *Rotterdam* and Lewis's *Slow Attack*. Some of Nevill's monochrome prints were faithful reflections of the Vorticist originals, but *Blast* gave him no guide to the colours he should use elsewhere. The fierce red, blue, yellow and green primaries slashed across the fabric which appeared on the mini-dress worn by the *Sunday Times* model therefore owed more to the inspiration of Sonia Delaunay (a personal friend of Nevill's)[127] than to *Blast*, even though their strident impact did not contradict Vorticism's own preference for scabrous colour oppositions. Created at the height of the 'swinging London' era, these highly energized designs successfully reinterpret the Vorticist spirit according to the no less frenetic standards of England in the sixties, and can be seen as a belated, indirect realization of the ambitions which briefly fired the applied art experiments conducted at the Rebel Art Centre in 1914. If the cur-

Bernard Nevill
Two dress design fabrics, 1966

tains, fans, screens and tables made in Kate Lechmere's Great Ormond Street *atelier* still survived today, they would probably have more than a little connection with Nevill's updated alternatives.

The *Sunday Times* cautiously thought that Lewis's reactions to the *Tango* fabrics would have been 'the same predictable reactions that he held for anything frivolous', and that Nevill would probably have qualified for inclusion in *Blast*'s list of the damned. But although Lewis had indeed declared in *Blast No. 1* that 'to believe that it is necessary for or conducive to art, to "improve" life, for instance – make architecture, dress, ornament, in "better taste", is absurd',[128] he was only objecting to the prevailing decorative criteria of his day. By the time he wrote his 'Review of Contemporary Art' in *Blast No. 2*, he was prepared to announce that 'if Tube Posters, Magazine Covers, Advertisement and Commercial Art generally, were ABSTRACT, in the sense that our paintings at present are, they would be far less harmful to the EYE, and thence to the minds, of the Public'.[129] Nevill's designs are thus a fortuitous answer to Lewis's idealist dream, and disarm the scruples of purists who – according to the *Sunday Times* – 'feel that it's wrong to use forms designed to be seen as part of a flat rectangular surface on materials that are going to be cut-up, pleated, swathed, draped and curved round thighs, waists, breasts or bottoms'. Besides, as the same newspaper pointed out, 'Vorticist designs do lend themselves rather well to being fragmented in this way', and its final verdict on the *Tango* collection was enthusiastic: 'fabrics, like any other part of fashion, are sensitive recorders of what's happening; they can reflect current art trends, invention and technological achievements. And if these fabric designs are any sort of guideline, there could be a strong

Vorticist revival'.[130]

It is doubtful whether Roberts would agree with such a viewpoint. His later books and polemical pamphlets have been directed above all at angrily disclaiming the significance of the Vorticist period in his work, while at the same time contesting what he saw as Lewis's attempt to present the movement as a one-man affair.[131] He felt, understandably, that his fanatically consistent style is now his own, and owes little to the theories and pictures produced by others so many decades before. He is a member of the Royal Academy, the very institution against which he reacted so impatiently in his youth, and the resemblance his later paintings bear to the rebel movement is a superficial one. Over the last fifty years his work has been representational in origin, and its persistent angularity is only a means of presenting a vision that rejects abstraction of any kind. Roberts is a man defiantly out of step with the avant-garde principles he once helped to introduce as a youthful prodigy.

In 1961, however, a curious idea took shape in his mind. He started to execute a huge, imaginative reconstruction of a typical rebel dinner, and named his setpiece *The Vorticists at the Restaurant de la Tour Eiffel, Spring 1915*.[132] The finished picture turned out to be one of his most lively and endearing works. There is a spirit of festive gaiety and bonhomie rarely seen in his paintings: the Vorticists are all openly convivial, champagne is being consumed in liberal quantities, and only Roberts – sandwiched rather uncomfortably between the dominating bulk of Pound on the left and Lewis in the middle – appears quizzical and slightly detached.[133] Lewis is placed unequivocally at the centre of the proceedings, a sinister figure dressed in black with his characteristic 'sombrero' and a long scarf; but the monochromatic solemnity of his dress is counteracted by the bright puce covers of *Blast No. 1*, which sing out behind Saunders' arms in the doorway, beneath Roberts' interlocking fingers and between Etchells' hands on the table. The merrymakers jerk with ponderous deliberation from side to side, caught up in the heavy ballet that Roberts' paintings always insist on. Hamilton, seated on the left, waves a cigarette in one hand and a champagne glass in the other, but his body is nevertheless cast into an unyielding straitjacket; and although there is plenty of animated movement in the picture, it is frozen into an awkward tableau. Even the slice of cake that Stulik offers to the assembled company is a stark, geometrical affair: a triangle surmounted by a circle. And as if to comment on the metamorphosis his style has undergone since those early days, Roberts includes a glimpse of a Vorticist decoration on the right wall. Presumably a reference to the commissioned abstract panels which Lewis executed at that time, it offers only a parody of the rebel style. The whole conception of this elaborate souvenir comes as an odd and unexpected gesture from the author of a broadside which, only a few years before, had carried the biting words 'BLAST VORTICISM' in fiercely satirical block capitals across its back cover.[134] The painting appears to be affectionate, commemorating an enterprise which Roberts can now, despite his intermittent complaints, look back on with genuine warmth. The Tour Eiffel picture might, indeed, reasonably be seen as a Vorticist Last Supper, with copies of *Blast* being passed round like a sacrament by a group of intense rebels who look as if they would have agreed with Aldington when he declared in 1914 that 'the profound intellectuality, the love of abstract design, of abstract colour, the serious revolt against the Renaissance and all sensuousness – all of which I agree is perfectly and truthfully English – give to this movement something which I can only call religious'.[135] In this sense, Roberts' painting achieves the remarkable feat of blessing *Blast*.

He is right: Vorticism deserves to be cherished. If it is a matter for intense regret that the movement did not live longer, or produce a more substantial

William Roberts
*The Vorticists at the Restaurant de la Tour
Eiffel: Spring 1915*, 1961–2. Left to right, seated:
Hamilton, Pound, Roberts, Lewis, Etchells and
Wadsworth. Standing: Dismorr, Saunders, Joe
the waiter and Stulik

corpus of work, enough can be reconstructed to bear out Herbert Read's judgement that 'while Vorticism lasted, it was a vitalising influence, perhaps the most lively effort ever made to infuse our timid English aestheticism with Latin intellectualism'. Despite his appreciation of the need for such an insurrection, Read nevertheless considered that the rebels destroyed their own cause by attempting to bully with propaganda and aggression when they should have been content with the creation of artefacts alone. 'Like the Italian Futurists, the English Vorticists tried to take the mind by assault', he wrote, 'forgetting that art wins its positions by subtle infiltration.'[136] But in 1914 there was no time for subtlety: the whole of Europe was moving towards war, and the only language that anyone would really listen to was bombastic and explosive. It is all too easy to forget the mood of the period, which positively demanded a manifesto and an attack before a group could even think of securing recognition for itself. There was, too, the all-pervasive presence of Marinetti, a fearless self-publicist who – if he was to be ousted – had to be fought on his own exhibitionist terms. And over-shadowing everything, casting a chilly eye of disapproval over the activities of the entire English vanguard, was the stifling conservatism of the artistic establishment. Victorian London was still a potent memory, the Royal Academy was ruled by a President with unshakeable nineteenth-century values, and the New English Art Club spread its pallid influence over anyone who operated outside the portals of Burlington House. Faced with such stultifying odds, the one course a dissenting movement could be expected to take was extreme, irreverent and subversive.

For the Vorticists were all young men who had run out of patience, and desperately wanted to make a fresh start. They were ambitious and – more vital still – idealistic enough to act with presumption. It is difficult, today, to comprehend just how sacrilegious their views must have seemed at the time; but Lewis characterized the positive spirit behind the revolt most convincingly when he declared that 'it was, after all, a new civilisation that I – and a few other people – was making the blueprints for: these things never being more than that. A rough design for a way of seeing for men who as yet were not there'.[137] This, in essence, was the ideal which Lewis and his friends must have held before them. They were feeling their way, groping towards a form of art that would express the rapidly changing environment created by a new century. It was an urgent business, too: they felt it incumbent upon them to persuade the nation to discard outworn conventions and be taught to see in an utterly new way. 'I, like all the other people in Europe so engaged, felt it to be an important task', Lewis continued. 'It was more than just picture-making: one was manufacturing fresh eyes for people, and fresh souls to go with the eyes. That was the feeling.'[138]

Only now, well over fifty years after *Blast* first appeared, is it possible to understand the full truth of those words. The English needed an art that would make them more aware of the speed with which their lives were being transformed, and Vorticism was determined to provide it. All the rebels realized that, as Pound wrote in 1915, 'new masses of unexplored arts and facts are pouring into the vortex of London. They cannot help bringing about changes as great as the Renaissance changes, even if we set ourselves blindly against it. As it is, there is life in the fusion. The complete man must have more interest in things which are in seed and dynamic than in things which are dead, dying, static'. That was why the Vorticists were, in Pound's words, '"arrogant" enough to dare to intend "to wake the dead" (quite as definitely as did Cyriac of Ancona)'.[139] And this thirst for an uprising should not, in the final analysis, be confused either with soul-destroying aggression or with unqualified admiration for the changes which industrialised society had brought about. Vorticism's iconoclastic urges were level-headed and constructive in their underlying aims: the fact that the real violence of the Great War shattered the rebels' earlier militancy shows just how little they had to do with genuine bloodlust. Their desire to overthrow was inextricably bound up with an affirmative concept of an art which would acknowledge that the industrial revolution had, for better or worse, invaded the very fabric of contemporary life.

Before the Vorticist movement arrived, such an acknowledgement had only been occasional and fragmentary in English art. The *Blast* manifestos were quite right when they claimed that Britain had been too 'busy with this LIFE-EFFORT', this determination to overhaul every practical facet of civilisation, to develop for itself 'the Art that is an organism of this new Order and Will of Man'.[140] Eighteenth-century forerunners like de Loutherbourg and Wright of Derby, who realised that the iron works of Coalbrookdale at night or Arkwright's cotton mill were legitimate subjects for the painter, never got beyond a picturesque approach to their material and certainly did not let it affect in any profound way the substance of their style. Later on, both John Martin and Turner allowed their work to be touched by a generalized, romantic consciousness of an industrial nation, but it could never be seen as the central focus of their ideas. Nor are Ford Madox Brown's *Work* or William Bell Scott's *Iron and Coal*, two paintings justly famous for their decision to portray the key function of the urban worker in modern life, anything more than isolated and relatively literal exceptions which prove the rule that Victorian art remained impervious to, or else fearful about, the presence of dynamic change.

The Vorticists rectified this damaging omission by ensuring that both their attitudes and their art were impregnated with a programmatic yet spontaneous involvement in the mechanized age. And although our view of technological advance is considerably more wary and disillusioned than the *Blast* manifestos would ever have thought possible, their refusal to embrace Futurist optimism stands squarely in their favour today. Vorticism viewed its chosen subject-matter with a gaze directed half-way between a romantic enthusiasm for technology's ability to instigate renewal, and a classical awareness of its capacity for horrific strength. In the end, this balancing act did not quite work: the classicism was not hard enough to sustain the shock of witnessing machinery at war, and the romantic fervour failed to carry over its appetite for regeneration into the post-war period. Nowadays, we find it easy to understand why the Vorticists recoiled from the vision they had created for England, and we can with hindsight fault them for being rather too ready to depersonalize themselves and brutalize their environment. But if the raucous high spirits with which they established this contemporary diagnostic sometimes sound over-strident in our ears, we ought to remember that the twin forces of dehumanization and colossal machine power could only be tackled by artists resilient enough to face this reality on its own harsh terms. The triumph of the Vorticists and their allies is that they succeeded, not only in making themselves as tough as their raw material, but in wringing a keen and totally unsentimental vitality out of the confrontation.

By doing so, the rebels proved themselves capable of playing an integral role in the evolution of their society at large, and they achieved this eminently desirable union in three principal ways. They managed to forge an identifiably national art, as homegrown and pugnacious as Hogarth, from an absorbed critical awareness of their most radical international context; they created a highly abstract vocabulary which nevertheless retained manifold and enriching links with the form-language of the visible world; and they demonstrated in a taut, bracing and often exhilarating manner how it might be possible not to escape from or rhapsodize about industrialization's steady march, but to fully take account of even the most terrifying aspects of twentieth-century life. On all these counts they still deserve to be referred to as a model for any ongoing attempt to implement *Blast*'s belief that 'an Art must be organic with its time',[141] and a full recognition of the energy they devoted to this ambitious task is long overdue.

Notes

The full reference to a book or publication is only given the first time it is mentioned. Page numbers are given for books and *Blast*, not for magazines, catalogues and newspapers.

Chapter Twelve

1. Pound, note at the end of 'Vorticism', *The Fortnightly Review*.
2. Roberts, 'Wyndham Lewis, the Vorticist'.
3. Pound, *Memoir of Gaudier*, pp.15–16.
4. Ibid., pp.108–9.
5. Pound, *The New Age*, 11 February 1915.
6. Lewis, *Blast No. 1*, p.39.
7. Ibid., p.148.
8. Lewis, *Wyndham Lewis the Artist, from 'Blast' to Burlington House* (London, 1939), p.79.
9. Etchells, interview. In the 1927 Quinn Sale catalogue this lost design was described as: 'An arch of the bridge over the Serpentine, with figures'. (No. 294A).
10. Boccioni, 'Fondamento Plastico . . .', *Lacerba*, 15 March 1913, p.52.
11. Lewis, *Wyndham Lewis the Artist*, pp.78–9.
12. Lewis, *Blast No. 1*, p.13.
13. Lewis, *Blast No. 2*, p.44.
14. Lewis, *Blast No. 1*, p.141.
15. Lewis, *Blast No. 2*, p.38.
16. Lewis, *Blast No. 1*, p.140.
17. Lewis, ibid., pp.135, 148.
18. Léger, 'Les Origines de la Peinture et sa Valeur Représentative', *Montjoie!* Paris, 29 May 1913 and 14–29 June 1913. Translated in Edward F. Fry's *Cubism* (London, 1966), p.125.
19. Lewis, *Blast No. 2*, p.45.
20. Pound, *The Egoist*, 15 June 1914.
21. Pound to H. L. Mencken, 17 March 1915, *Letters*, p.101.
22. Lewis, 'Introduction' to the catalogue of his exhibition at the Redfern Gallery, London, May 1949.
23. Lewis to Leonard Amster, *c.*August 1940, *Letters*, p.274.
24. Lewis, *Wyndham Lewis the Artist*, pp.77–8.
25. Rutter, *Sunday Times*, 18 June 1911.
26. Lewis to John, *c.*1914, *Letters*, p.64.
27. *Blast No. 1*, pp.23–4.
28. *Blast No. 2*, p.46.
29. Ibid., p.45.
30. Lewis, *Blast No. 1*, p.71.
31. Lewis, *Blast No. 2*, p.91.
32. It is possible that this gouache is a study for a lost painting executed, like *Design for Red Duet*, in 1915. If so, that painting rather than the extant gouache was shown at the Vorticist Exhibition.
33. Lewis, *Blast No. 1*, p.138.
34. Dorothy Shakespear's opinion was relayed to the author by her son, Omar Pound. She was by no means definite about the picture's starting-point, but it is sufficiently convincing to suggest that she was remembering something either Lewis or Pound originally told her.
35. Saint'Elia, *Messaggio*, 1914, trans.

Reyner Banham, *Theory and Design in The First Machine Age* (London, 1960; third impression 1967), p.129.
36. Lewis, *Blast No. 2*, p.44.
37. Lewis did not visit New York until the late twenties, and may not have approved of this title which Wadsworth, the picture's former owner, probably invented.
38. This description of *Workshop* is taken from the 1927 Quinn Sale Catalogue where it is listed as No. 353, merely 'attributed to Wyndham Lewis' and described as an 'Interior'. But it was listed as *Workshop* in the catalogue of the 1917 New York Vorticist Exhibition (No. 36), where Quinn acquired it.
39. This passage does not appear in the 1918 edition of *Tarr*: Lewis added it to the revised edition published in 1928. (Quoted here from the Jupiter Book edition (London, 1968), p.279.)
40. Lewis, *Blast No. 2*, p.9.
41. Ibid.
42. Lewis, *Blast No. 1*, p.142.
43. *The Crowd* was entitled *Revolution* by its former owner, Dr Barnett Stross.
44. Rutter, *Sunday Times*, 21 March 1915.
45. Lewis, *Blast No. 1*, p.144.
46. Ibid., p.141.
47. Lewis, *Blast No. 2*, p.94.
48. Lewis to Pound, January 1915 (?), *Letters*, p.67.
49. Lewis to James Thrall Soby, 9 April 1947, *Letters*, p.406.
50. Roberts, *Cometism and Vorticism*, pp. unnumbered.
51. Lewis, 'The Vorticists', *Vogue*, September 1956.
52. Aldington, *The Egoist*, 15 July 1914.
53. Pound to Harriet Monroe, 9 November 1914, *Letters*, p.87.
54. This print of *Newcastle* was exhibited at the 1956 *Wyndham Lewis and Vorticism* exhibition at the Tate Gallery (No. 190).
55. Neither of the two impressions of *Mytholmroyd* which the author has been able to trace is dated. But the woodcut is listed as No. 1 in the catalogue of the *Exhibition of Original Woodcuts and Drawings by Edward Wadsworth* held in March 1919 at the Adelphi Gallery, 9 Duke Street, Adelphi, London. And Etchells, in 'A Note' published in the catalogue, states that 'the first group, Nos. 1–8, are cuts produced before the war'. The fact that *Mytholmroyd* was listed at the beginning of this group, therefore, argues an early date of *c.* 1914, and this would also seem feasible on stylistic grounds. Two colour variants are known.
56. Lewis, 'Introduction' to the exhibition catalogue of *Wyndham Lewis and Vorticism*.
57. Lewis, 'Edward Wadsworth: 1889–1949', *The Listener*, 30 June 1949.
58. Ibid.
59. Neither of the two colour variants which the author has seen is titled. But

the Victoria and Albert Museum's copy of it was presented by Wadsworth in 1920, and is confidently captioned *Yorkshire Village*. And Etchells, in his 'Note' for the catalogue of Wadsworth's 1919 one-man show, says of *Yorkshire Village* (No. 5) that 'the pyramid of box forms in no. 5 conveys convincingly the bleakness and solidity of a northern hill village . . . in spite of the economy of the means employed, the effect is peculiar in depth and body'. This comment seems to apply very well to the woodcut reproduced here. The version in steel blue and black (not reproduced here) has an extra segment added two-thirds of the way up the right edge of the woodcut.
60. One impression of this print is entitled 'Bradford' in Wadsworth's own hand. But others are simply inscribed *View of a Town*, which was listed as No. 2 in Wadsworth's 1919 exhibition catalogue. Etchells, in his 'Note', wrote that 'Print no. 2 shows an interesting simplification of planes and the closely knitted composition of roofs and chimney stacks seems to be a very complete abstract of a modern industrial town'. It is on the strength of this description that the print is here named *Bradford: View of a Town* and given to the pre-war period. Several colour variants of this print are known.
61. Several impressions of *The Open Window* are titled, but none dated. It was listed as No. 29 in the 1919 exhibition catalogue, and therefore is not included in the groups which Etchells' 'Note' mentions. At least six different colour variants of this print are known to the author.
62. Only one print of this is known, and it is titled in Wadsworth's own hand. It is not dated, however, and neither was it listed in the 1919 exhibition catalogue.
63. Again, only one impression of this woodcut is known, titled by the artist but not listed. It is not listed in Wadsworth's 1919 exhibition catalogue.
64. Neither of the two extant colour variants of *New Delight* is dated, and it was not included in the 1919 exhibition catalogue.
65. Pound, 'Edward Wadsworth, Vorticist', *The Egoist*, 15 August 1914.
66. Lewis, *Blast No. 2*, p.46.
67. Etchells, 'A Note'. (See footnote 55.)
68. Despite the strong overtones of industrial machinery conveyed by *Untitled: Abstract Woodcut*, it could well have been executed during the war. For Pound reproduced it alongside five other Wadsworth woodcuts from the Mudros (1916–18) period in the *Little Review*, February–March 1919. Mark Glazebrook gives it the title *Brown Drama* in his exhibition catalogue *Edward Wadsworth 1889–1949* (Colnaghi's, July–August 1974, no.118) but his reasons are inconclusive.

69. *Facade* was listed as No. 4 in Wadsworth's 1919 exhibition catalogue and therefore belongs to the pre-war group of woodcuts singled out by Etchells in his catalogue 'Note'.

70. *Street Singers* was listed as No. 8 in the 1919 exhibition catalogue and therefore belongs to the pre-war period according to Etchells' 'Note'.

71. This untitled woodcut is called *Staircase and Scaffolding* in Anthony d'Offay's catalogue of *Abstract Art in England 1913–1915* (No. 38). There is no supporting evidence for this title, but it is again accepted by the catalogue of *The Tate Gallery 1968–70* (p.107). Working on the possibility that it may be based, like *Cape of Good Hope*, on an aerial view of a harbour, this woodcut could be *The Port*, exhibited as No. 6 in Wadsworth's 1919 one-man show. Three colour variants are known.

72. None of the surviving impressions of this print is titled, but the copy in the British Museum is inscribed with the quotation from Conrad's *Typhoon* quoted in the present book. And this text is also quoted underneath the catalogue entry for *Illustration*, listed as No. 31 in Wadsworth's 1919 exhibition catalogue.

73. From the description in the 1927 Quinn Sale catalogue where *Rotterdam* is listed as No. 374. The catalogue also states that the painting of *Rotterdam* was dated 1914 and measured $127 \times 101 \cdot 5$ cm.

74. Gaudier to Wadsworth, 18 November 1914, Pound, *Memoir of Gaudier*, p.81.

75. Lewis, reprinted in *Blast No. 1*, p.136.

76. Gaudier, *The Egoist*, 15 June 1914. *Cape of Good Hope* was listed in the 1914 AAA catalogue as No. 113.

77. This watercolour is not titled, and is linked here with *Cape of Good Hope* on stylistic grounds alone.

78. *Blast No. 1*, p.23. The passage was printed there as a vertical column stretching down the page, without some of the punctuation added here for the purposes of legibility.

79. Etchells, interview.

80. See two letters from Wadsworth to Lewis, 4 February 1914 and *c.* spring 1914, Wyndham Lewis Collection, Cornell University.

81. Pound, *The New Age*, 11 February 1915.

82. Gaudier, *The Egoist*, 15 June 1914.

83. See Chapter Three, footnote 29 and text, where *Long Acre* is discussed.

84. Lewis, *Blast No. 2*, p.77. Rutter's review of *Blackpool* in the *Sunday Times*, 21 March 1915, declared that 'the crudeness of the brilliant colour may be thought to give no inaccurate impression of a town where pleasure takes a very noisy form'.

85. *Gouache 1915* is the title under which Wadsworth himself lent *Composition* to an exhibition of *40 Years of Modern Art, 1907–1947*, held at the I.C.A., London, February–March 1948. But it was called *Composition (gouache)* in *Sélection* (Anvers, Mai 1933), p.34.

86. The 1927 Quinn Sale catalogue states that it was painted 'in strong colours' and measured $183 \times 212 \cdot 5$ cm (No. 381).

87. *Study for a Vorticist Painting* (?) may be connected with *The Port*, No. 157 in the May–June 1914 *Twentieth Century Art* exhibition at the Whitechapel Art Gallery.

88. Lewis, 'Introduction' to the catalogue of the *Wyndham Lewis and Vorticism* exhibition.

89. The title of *Abstract Composition* is taken from the 1956 Tate Gallery exhibition catalogue, where it was listed as No. 191. It is probable, however, that this gouache is the picture included in the 1927 Quinn Sale catalogue with precisely the same dimensions and simply called *Abstraction* (No. 323). To clinch the connection the Quinn catalogue also stated that *Abstraction* was 'signed lower left Edward Wadsworth, and dated 1915'.

90. Gaudier to Wadsworth, 18 November 1914, Pound, *Memoir of Gaudier*, p.81.

91. Lewis, *Blast No. 2*, p.94.

92. Recounted to the author by Mrs Elaine Bailey, *Enclosure*'s former owner.

Chapter Thirteen

1. Etchells, interview.

2. Saunders to Dismorr, undated, but probably late 1917 or early 1918, since the letter also states that Lewis 'is in the Canadian Artists Corps' and preparing to 'paint a picture of a gun-pit for the Canadian Government'. Collection R. H. M. Ody.

3. Introduction to the catalogue of the Whitechapel Art Gallery's exhibition of *Twentieth Century Art. A Review of Modern Movements*, May–June 1914.

4. Roberts, *Abstract & Cubist Paintings & Drawings*, p.8.

5. The authority for ascribing this undated and uncharacteristically figurative drawing to 1914 comes from Roberts himself, who identified it when it was sent for the sale at Sotheby's, 11 December 1968 (No. 284).

6. *The Toe Dancer* is not dated, but Roberts implied that it was executed around 'the autumn of 1914' in *Abstract & Cubist Paintings & Drawings*, p. 8.

7. Ibid.

8. Epstein, *Let There Be Sculpture*, p.137.

9. The double portraits of Stewart Gray are pointed out by Ronald Alley in the November–December 1965 *William Roberts ARA* exhibition catalogue, No. 118.

10. Lewis, *Blast No. 2*, p.77.

11. Roberts, *Abstract & Cubist Paintings & Drawings*, p.8.

12. Ibid.

13. *Observer*, 14 March 1915.

14. Lewis, *Blast No. 2*, p.77.

15. Konody, *Observer*, 1 August 1915.

16. Roberts, *Cometism and Vorticism*, pp. unnumbered.

17. *Street Games* was sent for sale at Sotheby's, 11 December 1968 (No. 291). Roberts authenticated it, ascribed it to the period 1914–15, and later signed it along the bottom. But he did not identify it with *Overbacks* and this connection remains pure supposition on the part of the author.

18. 1927 Quinn Sale catalogue; the picture is listed as No. 369 and its measurements given as $133 \cdot 5 \times 108$ cm.

19. In 1969, when Roberts reproduced the drawing in his *8 Cubist Designs*, he stated that it was a study for *Jeu*.

20. 1927 Quinn Sale catalogue, No. 368, states that it was 'signed lower right, William Roberts' and gives its measurements as $156 \times 112 \cdot 5$ cm.

21. The unorthodox spelling of *Twostep* is here taken from the entry in the Doré Galleries catalogue (no. 3b). Roberts repeats this spelling in the text, but not the plate captions, of his *8 Cubist Designs*.

22. *The Athenaeum*, 19 June 1915.

23. Roberts, *Abstract & Cubist Paintings & Drawings*, p.9.

24. See in particular Roberts' 1974 pamphlet, *In Defence of English Cubists*, where he writes of the term Vorticism: 'I agree with Lewis, that it should only be used in reference to his own work; and that the term Cubist should be employed, to describe the abstract painting of his contemporaries of the 1914 period.'

25. Meninsky's design is now lost, and is reproduced here from the illustration which appeared in the *Evening News*, 23 April 1915. The accompanying caption drily explained that 'the horse's head is at the top, the dragon's neck swings up at the left side, and St. George himself is evidently at the right top corner of the drawing. There is no competition in connection with this'.

26. Roberts, *Abstract & Cubist Paintings & Drawings*, p.5.

27. Before the original pencil study illustrated here appeared at Sotheby's sale on 11 December 1968 (No. 288), *St. George and the Dragon* was known only through the stark black and white version reproduced in the *Evening News*. In *8 Cubist Designs* Roberts simply states that this pencil drawing 'is a study for the line block, that was reproduced in the *Evening News*'. The line block version reproduced here is taken from an illustration in Roberts' *Abstract & Cubist Paintings & Drawings*, because it is in every way more satisfactory than the poor reproduction which originally appeared in the *Evening News*. However, a close comparison of the two versions reveals that they are not the same:

although Roberts has never explained why, the version illustrated in *Abstract & Cubist Paintings & Drawings* looks like a later copy which he executed after the *Evening News* original.

28. *Evening News*, 23 April 1915.
29. Roberts, *Abstract & Cubist Paintings & Drawings*, pp.7–8.
30. In *A Reply to My Biographer, Sir John Rothenstein* (pp.13–14) Roberts explained the changes in the title of his *Machine Gunners* drawing by recounting how, 'early in 1915 Lewis, as editor, asked me to contribute two drawings to Blast No. 2, the War number. He said "keep them simple, it is easier for the Block-maker". I did two "simple" line drawings, one I called "Machine Gunners" the other "Combat". When I gave Lewis these drawings I did not know what his contributions would be. Later when Blast was published my "Machine Gunners" carried the plain title "A drawing", whilst upon the front cover appeared a large intricate line drawing of machine gunners by Lewis'. Roberts also acidly comments that 'In Art, above all, a Leader must be wide awake or he may find himself his disciple's disciple; in Art being a Leader is also an Art'.
31. Sonia Joslen, interview.
32. Rebecca West, interview.
33. *The Athenaeum*, 19 June 1915.
34. Hulme, *The New Age*, 9 July 1914.
35. Sonia Joslen, interview.
36. Brown, *Exhibition, The Memoirs of Oliver Brown* (London, 1968), p.44.
37. Goldring, *South Lodge*, pp.72–3.
38. Binyon, *The Flight of the Dragon* (London, 1914). All three passages are quoted by Pound in *Blast No. 2*, p.86. Pound regarded them only as exceptional 'moments' of insight in 'a book otherwise unpleasantly marred by his [Binyon's] recurrent respect for inferior, very inferior people'.
39. No trace survives of the original design which Bomberg executed for the cover of Rodker's *Poems*, and the precise medium employed is by no means certain.
40. The dedication simply reads 'To Sonia'.
41. Rodker, *Collected Poems 1912–1925* (Paris, 1930), date of composition given as 1915. Rodker also published a 'prose poem' called 'Dancer' in the *Little Review*, October 1918. It too seems to refer to Bomberg's treatment of the theme.
42. Alice Mayes to Lilian Bomberg, 27 September 1965, Lipke, *David Bomberg*, p.115, footnote 37.
43. Alice Mayes, *The Young Bomberg*, p.26.
44. Alice Mayes to Lilian Bomberg, 27 September 1965, Lipke, *David Bomberg*, p.115.
45. Bomberg, unpublished writings, 1957, in the possession of Mrs Lilian Bomberg.
46. Alice Mayes, *The Young Bomberg*, pp.10, 4.

47. Ibid., p.4.
48. Ibid., p.5.
49. Lewis to Pound, 1915, *Letters*, p.68.
50. Nevinson to Lewis, June 1915, Lipke, *David Bomberg*, p.46.
51. Lechmere, interview.
52. Sonia Joslen, interview.
53. Bomberg, *The Bomberg Papers*, p.185.
54. Bomberg, unpublished writings, 23 April 1957, owned by Mrs Lilian Bomberg.
55. Etchells, interview.
56. Sonia Joslen, interview.
57. Lewis, *Blasting and Bombardiering*, p.39.
58. Bomberg, memoir entitled *Reflections on Art and Artists*, Lipke, *David Bomberg*, p.125.

Chapter Fourteen
1. Roberts, *Abstract & Cubist Paintings & Drawings*, p.7.
2. Roberts, *Cometism and Vorticism*, pp. unnumbered.
3. Rutter, *Sunday Times*, 15 March 1914.
4. The British Council, which now owns this gouache, describes it simply as *Composition 1914*. But its measurements accord so well with the dimensions of an Etchells 'watercolour' called *Stilts* (listed in the 1927 Quinn Sale Catalogue, No. 292B) that it seems reasonable to call the British Council picture by this name.
5. Pound, 'Vorticism', *The Fortnightly Review*.
6. Etchells, interview.
7. 1927 Quinn Sale catalogue (No. 501).
8. Its size, 76 × 54·5 cm, is given ibid.
9. By 1927, when it appeared in the Quinn Sale catalogue, it was described as a 'watercolour', so Etchells must have added the watercolour sometime before *Progression* was shown in the 1917 New York Vorticist Exhibition (No. 49).
10. *Group* was reproduced in *Blast No. 1* as Illustration xviii. There is no way of telling what medium it was executed in (it does not appear listed in any of the catalogues of the exhibitions to which Hamilton contributed at this time) apart from examining the *Blast No. 1* reproduction. From there, it seems likely that *Group* was an oil painting rather than a watercolour or gouache.
11. Bell, *The Nation*, 25 October 1913.
12. Bomberg, *Memoir*, Lipke, *David Bomberg*, p.41.
13. Shipp, *The New Art*, pp.62, 72–3.
14. Ibid., p.69.
15. Pound, 'Vorticism'.
16. Shipp, pp.23, 82.
17. Ibid., pp.77, 82.
18. This picture has in recent years been called *Abstract*, but it has been changed here to *Painting* because of its clear figurative content. In the absence of any date on the picture itself, and the almost

complete lack of any other Atkinson paintings with which to compare it, the unsatisfactory umbrella dating 1914–18 cannot be improved upon. There is, however, no good reason why *Painting* should not be at least connected with the paintings Atkinson contributed to the 1915 Vorticist Exhibition. Each of them was simply listed as *Painting*, which suggests that they were relatively abstract in character.
19. Shipp, pp.88–9.
20. Ibid., pp.85–6.
21. As with Atkinson's previous *Painting* (see footnote 18) there is nothing to prevent connecting this picture with the three *Paintings* which Atkinson displayed in the 1915 Vorticist Exhibition. It must be stressed, however, that until more is known about Atkinson's development as an artist such suppositions will remain provisional.
22. Because of its close similarities with Vorticist work by other artists, *Abstract Composition* stands as an example of Atkinson's work which can confidently be placed in the 1914–15 period.
23. Shipp, p.62.
24. It should be emphasized that the titles of all the Atkinson works discussed in this chapter are, apart from *The Lake*, quite arbitrary and not supplied by the artist.
25. Shipp, pp.22–3, 66, 90.
26. Pound to Quinn, 24 January 1917, *Letters*, p.158.
27. Goldring, *South Lodge*, p.68.
28. Ody to the author, 8 September 1971.
29. Lewis to Dismorr, 1915, Lipke, unpublished 'Introduction' written for the *Jessica Dismorr Memorial Exhibition* held at the Mayor Gallery, April–May 1965.
30. Ody to the author, 8 September 1971.
31. Lechmere, interview.
32. Etchells, interview.
33. Dismorr, *Blast No. 2*, p.66.
34. The reproduction of *The Engine* published on p.27 of *Blast No. 2* is the only record which survives of this picture.
35. See *The Tate Gallery Acquisitions 1968–9* (London, 1969), p.4.
36. Dismorr, *Blast No. 2*, p.65.
37. Dismorr, ibid., pp.67–8.
38. Possibly identifiable as the *Edinburgh Castle* which Dismorr showed at the New York Vorticist exhibition. An oil painting version of *Landscape*, measuring 51·5 × 47 cm, used to exist in the collection of R. H. M. Ody, who described it as 'an enlarged version of the "Landscape" drawing in the V. and A.' (Letter to the author, 14 July 1971). But Mr Ody explained in another letter to the author (7 July 1971) that this painting no longer survives.
39. Etchells, interview.
40. Saunders, notes on Harriet Weaver, 24 February 1962, Jane Lidderdale and Mary Nicholson, *Dear Miss Weaver* (London, 1970), pp.119–20.

41. Saunders to Dismorr, 7 November 1915, collection R. H. M. Ody.
42. See the entry under Saunders in Chamot, Farr and Butlin's *The Tate Gallery*, Vol. 2.
43. See, for example, Delaunay's painting *Sun, Moon*, executed in 1912–13.
44. Delaunay, *Notes sur le Developpement de la Peinture de Robert Delaunay*, Pierre Francastel, *Du Cubisme à l'Art Abstrait* (Paris, 1957), p.67.
45. Saunders, *Blast No. 2*, p.73.
46. Lewis, *Blast No. 2*, p.38.
47. This design was donated to the Victoria and Albert Museum by the late Miss Ethel Saunders. The Museum thinks that it could be the gouache and pencil composition entitled *Design for a Book Jacket*, c.1915–20, listed in the *Wyndham Lewis and Vorticism* exhibition catalogue as No. 189. It was lent to the exhibition by Saunders herself, who presumably supplied this title. It is not known for what specific purpose the *Book Jacket* was designed.
48. *Dance* is actually untitled, and has been given this name for reasons of convenience by the author, but it may be identifiable as *Dance* which Saunders contributed to the New York Vorticist exhibition (No. 67).
49. *Vorticist Composition in Green and Yellow* has similarly been titled by the author.
50. Lewis, *Blast No. 1*, p.148.
51. The *Island of Laputa*, illustrated on p.8 of *Blast No. 2*, has since been lost; but the 1927 Quinn Sale catalogue listed the picture as No. 431A, confirmed its medium as 'pen' and gave its measurements as $25 \cdot 5 \times 21 \cdot 5$ cm. It was listed in the Vorticist Exhibition catalogue 'Drawings' section as No. 3a.
52. *Blast No. 1*, p.26.
53. Etchells, interview.

Chapter Fifteen
1. Gaudier, *Blast No. 1*, p.158.
2. Ibid., p.155.
3. Ibid., pp.156, 155.
4. Ibid., p.156.
5. Pound, *Memoir of Gaudier*, p.125.
6. Gaudier, *Blast No. 1*, pp.156, 158.
7. Lewis, *Blast No. 2*, p.78.
8. Lewis, *Blast No. 1*, p.40.
9. Lewis, *Blast No. 2*, p.78.
10. The original *Dog* carving was executed in marble, broken but now repaired, and used to be owned by Sir James Dyer Simpson. The author apologizes for reproducing a bronze cast which radically distorts Gaudier's original intentions: he would no doubt have insisted that a sculpture conceived in marble should never be transposed into bronze. But it proved impossible to obtain an adequate photograph of the marble version.

11. Pound, *Memoir of Gaudier*, p.91.
12. Fry, *The Nation*, 14 March 1914.
13. Pound, *The Egoist*, 16 March 1914.
14. Lewis, *Rude Assignment*, p.128.
15. Celia Clayton to the author, 15 October 1972. Mrs Clayton, the present owner of *Fish*, is Mrs Kibblewhite's granddaughter, and her information therefore comes from that source.
16. There is no definitive way of telling whether this gunmetal *Bird* was indeed the first cast of *Bird Swallowing Fish*. But no other Gaudier sculpture fits this title, and it is a fact that *Bird Swallowing Fish* was listed as *The Sea Bird* when it was exhibited (in a 'bronze' version) at Gaudier's 1918 Memorial Exhibition at the Leicester Galleries (No. 95).
17. Gaudier, *The Egoist*, 15 June 1914.
18. If this picture is viewed horizontally, the gazelles' heads become clearly legible.
19. Pound implied a very late date for *Birds Erect* when he placed it at the end of his 'Partial Catalogue of the Sculpture'.
20. Hulme, *The New Age*, 26 March 1914.
21. Gaudier, *Blast No. 1*, p.155.
22. Brodzky, *Henri Gaudier-Brzeska*, p.111.
23. Gaudier, *The Egoist*, 15 June 1914.
24. Aldington, *Life for Life's Sake*, pp.153–4.
25. Brodzky, *Henri Gaudier-Brzeska*, p.92.
26. Pound, *Memoir of Gaudier*, p.161.
27. Aldington, *Life for Life's Sake*, pp.151–2.
28. Gaudier, *The Egoist*, 15 June 1914.
29. Pound states in his *Memoir of Gaudier* (p.160), that Gaudier executed two 'cut brass' door-knockers.
30. Gaudier, *The Egoist*. Gaudier exhibited both *Door-Knockers* at the 1914 AAA Salon (Nos. 48, 49).
31. Pound, *Memoir of Gaudier*, p.38.
32. Pound, *The New Age*, 4 February 1915.
33. *Carved Toothbrush Handle* appears in Gaudier's List of Works of 9 July 1914, thereby disproving Mervyn Levy's statement in *Gaudier-Brzeska Drawings and Sculpture* (London, 1965), p.30, that it dates from 1915 and 'is the only surviving fragment of the sculptor's war-time carving'.
34. Pound, *Memoir of Gaudier*, p.160. This title for the carving is confirmed by its present owner, Grattan Freyer, whose father was a 'close friend of Hulme' and 'always spoke of this piece as "Toy for Tommy Hulme" ... and described Hulme carrying the piece about with him'. (Letter to the author, 14 August 1972.) Pound also wrote in his *Memoir* (p.167) that 'it interests me that Mr Hulme in his boyhood should have pestered the village blacksmith ... to forge him a piece of metal absolutely square'.
35. See H. S. Ede, *A Life of Gaudier-Brzeska*, p.200. The carving was listed as *Ornament* in the catalogue of the 1914 AAA Salon (No. 46).
36. *Blast No. 1*, p.30.

37. Grattan Freyer to the author, 14 August 1972.
38. Grattan Freyer, 'Blast and Counter-blast', *Irish Times*, 12 August 1972.
39. Lewis, *Blast No. 2*, p.78.
40. Pound, *Memoir of Gaudier*, p.57.
41. Aldington, *Life for Life's Sake*, p.152.
42. Pound, *Memoir of Gaudier*, p.160.
43. Ibid.
44. Lewis to the editor of the *Partisan Review*, c.April 1949, *Letters*, pp.491–2.
45. Lewis, *Blasting and Bombardiering*, p.114.
46. Gaudier to Pound, 24 October 1914, Pound, *Memoir of Gaudier*, p.61.
47. Gaudier, *Blast No. 2*, p.33.
48. Ibid., p.34.
49. Ibid. Pound wrote to Harriet Monroe on 9 November 1914 that Gaudier 'has done a figure, working with his jackknife and an entrenching tool' (*Letters*, p.86).
50. Ford, *The Outlook*, 31 July 1915.
51. Gaudier to Pound, 27 January 1915, Pound, *Memoir of Gaudier*, p.65. Pound summarized the contents of his lost letter in a footnote on the same page.
52. Gaudier to Mrs Shakespear, 11 April 1915, Pound, *Memoir of Gaudier*, p.75.
53. Ibid. Pound remembered Gaudier saying 'those *damn* Greeks' in discussions with Aldington (*Memoir*, p.23).
54. Pound, *Memoir of Gaudier*, pp.89–90.
55. Fry, 'Gaudier-Brzeska', *Burlington Magazine*, August 1916.
56. Pound, *Memoir of Gaudier*, pp.16–17.
57. Gaudier, *Blast No. 2*, p.33.
58. Lewis, *Blast No. 2*, p.78.

Chapter Sixteen
1. Gaudier to Pound, 27 January 1915, Pound, *Memoir of Gaudier*, p.65.
2. Epstein, *Let There Be Sculpture*, p.59.
3. Lechmere, interview.
4. Epstein, *Let There Be Sculpture*, p.216. He finally acquired the *Brummer Head* in 1935.
5. Ibid.
6. Lewis, *Blast No. 2*, p.78.
7. Epstein, *Let There Be Sculpture*, p.64.
8. Epstein's *Blast No. 1 Drawing* could have been any one of a number of drawings listed in the Twenty-One Gallery exhibition catalogue: *Design for Sculpture* (No. 3), *Design for l'Être* (No. 4), *L'Être* (No. 6), *Drawing for Flenite* (No. 7), or *Creation* (No. 8).
9. Hulme, *Speculations*, p.107.
10. A slightly different version of the Allinson caricature reproduced here still exists in a London private collection.
11. Epstein, *Let There Be Sculpture*, p.217.
12. Ibid., pp.217, 216.
13. Epstein, *Let There Be Sculpture*, p.11.
14. The title of this sculpture is usually given in a form which changes the word 'Wherein' to 'Whereon'. But while this latter version makes more

sense grammatically, the original title listed in the second London Group exhibition (No. 92) gives it as 'Wherein'. Epstein may have been using an Old Testament quotation from the Book of Job, for Hulme's photograph of the sculpture, preserved at Hull University Library, is entitled *Cursed Be The Day Wherein I Was Born* (*Job*).
15. *The Star*, 6 March 1915.
16. Epstein, 'Foreword' to *Speculations*.
17. 'Man Woman' is cited in a telegram sent by Epstein's wife to John Quinn on 25 June 1916, in which she describes Epstein's works in progress. (B. L. Reid, *The Man from New York. John Quinn and his Friends*, Oxford 1968, p.259.)
18. Epstein, *Let There Be Sculpture*, p.70.
19. Epstein's contributions to the 'Cubist Room' were listed in the catalogue as *Drawing, Drawing for Sculpture*, and *The Rock Drill* (Nos. 147, 148, 179).
20. Bomberg, draft of unsent letter to Roberts, 1957, unpublished, owned by Mrs Lilian Bomberg. Bomberg's draft went on to remember 'the tripod which held the Drill' as well, thereby implying that the sculpture was then almost complete.
21. Lewis, 'Introduction' to the 'Cubist Room' catalogue.
22. 'Foreword' to the trade catalogue of *The Holman Standard Reciprocating Rock Drills*, Camborne, Cornwall, 1920.
23. Epstein, *Let There Be Sculpture*, p. 70; ibid.
24. Pound, *The New Age*, 21 January 1915.
25. Epstein, *Let There Be Sculpture*, p.70.
26. Pound, *Memoir of Gaudier*, p.17. Gaudier's comments are recorded on the same page.
27. The photograph of this drawing, once owned by T. E. Hulme and now preserved at Hull University Library, is captioned *Birth Drawing*, thereby raising the possibility that it is not directly connected with the genesis of *Rock Drill*.
28. *Daily Graphic*, 5 March 1915, under the headline 'War as the Futurist Sees It'.
29. *Observer*, 14 March 1915.
30. John to Quinn, 3 April 1915, B. L. Reid, *The Man from New York*, p.203.
31. Epstein to Quinn, 28 March 1915, ibid.
32. Bomberg, draft of unsent letter to Roberts, 1957, unpublished, owned by Mrs Lilian Bomberg.
33. *Manchester Guardian*, 15 March 1915.
34. Lewis, *Blast No. 2*, p.78.
35. Lewis, *Blasting and Bombardiering*, p.39.
36. Epstein, *Let There Be Sculpture*, p.56.
37. Epstein and Arnold Haskell, *The Sculptor Speaks* (London, 1931), p.45.
38. Lady Epstein, interview with the author.
39. The original bronze cast of *Torso in Metal from the "Rock Drill"* was probably the version purchased by the National Gallery of Canada in 1956. The present reproductions are taken from the cast in the Tate Gallery.
40. Epstein, *Let There Be Sculpture*, p.70.

41. *The Sketch*, 29 October 1913. Underneath, a sarcastic caption asks: 'Shall we see this in our streets if the present statues are veiled, according to Mr Birrell's prophecy?'
42. Duchamp-Villon to Walter Pach, 16 January 1913, Pach, *Queer Thing, Painting* (New York, 1938), p.145. The translation used here is taken from another version given in the catalogue of the Duchamp Brothers' Exhibition, Guggenheim Museum and Museum of Fine Arts, Houston, 1957.
43. In his unpublished 1957 writings, Bomberg records that Duchamp-Villon visited Bomberg's July 1914 one-man show at the Chenil Gallery. (Memoirs owned by Mrs Lilian Bomberg.)

Chapter Seventeen
1. Lewis, *Blast No. 2*, p.25.
2. Nevinson, *Paint and Prejudice*, pp.71, 74, 78.
3. Nevinson, interview with *Daily Express*, 25 February 1915.
4. See the *Vorticism and its Allies* catalogue, Arts Council 1974, Nos. 165–70, for a complete survey of these studies.
5. Nevinson, *Paint and Prejudice*, pp.91–2.
6. Nevinson, interview with the *New York Times*, 25 May 1919.
7. Nevinson, *Paint and Prejudice*, p.64.
8. Lewis, *Blast No. 2*, p.25.
9. *Blast No. 2*, p.89, titled *On the Way to the Trenches*.
10. Lewis, *Blast No. 2*, p.77. Although Lewis refers to the painting by the inaccurate title of *Marching Soldiers*, he is obviously discussing *Returning to the Trenches*: Nevinson's only other contributions to the second London Group show were *My Arrival at Dunkirk* (No. 27), *Taube Pursued by Commander Samson* (No. 28), and *Ypres After the Second Bombardment* (No. 87).
11. Lewis, *Blast No. 2*, p.25.
12. The soldier is probably inspired by Ford's description of 'this Belgian man in his ugly tunic'.
13. Nevinson, *Paint and Prejudice*, p.70.
14. *Daily News*, 2 February 1915.
15. Lewis, 'The Vorticists', *Vogue*.
16. Pound to Harriet Monroe, 10 November 1914, *Letters*, p.89.
17. College of Arts prospectus, Pound's *Letters*, pp.88–9.
18. Pound, 'Vorticism', *The Fortnightly Review*.
19. Pound to Felix Schelling, June 1915, *Letters*, p.106.
20. Pound, *Memoir of Gaudier*, p.6; ibid.; p.144.
21. Ibid., p.151; pp.144–5; p.145.
22. Ibid., pp.155–6.
23. Pound, *The New Age*, 21 January 1915.
24. Quinn to Pound, 25 February 1915, B. L. Reid, *The Man from New York*, p.198.

25. Pound to Quinn, 8 March 1915, ibid., pp.199–200.
26. Ibid.
27. Pound to Quinn, 17 December 1915, ibid., p.204.
28. Quinn to Pound, 27 July 1915, ibid.
29. Pound to Quinn, 11 August 1915, ibid. The last four words are taken from B. L. Reid's paraphrase of the letter, not Pound's actual words.
30. Pound to Quinn, 10 March 1916, *Letters*, pp.121–2. The passage about 'spermatozoon' is not included in the *Letters*, and is quoted here from B. L. Reid, p.252.
31. Pound to Quinn, 9 March 1916, B. L. Reid, p.253.
32. Pound to Quinn, 16 March 1916, ibid. This passage is taken from Reid's paraphrase.
33. Pound to Quinn, 18 March 1916, ibid.
34. Walt Kuhn's opinion was quoted by Quinn in a letter to Pound, 1 July 1916, ibid.
35. Ibid., p.254.
36. Pound to Quinn, 19 July 1916, ibid. Reid's paraphrase of the letter is quoted here.
37. Pound to Quinn, 25 August 1916, ibid.
38. Pound to Quinn, 9 September 1916, ibid. The passage is taken from Reid's paraphrase of Pound's letter. 'I have succeeded in selling a lot of pictures in New York, by Lewis, Wadsworth, Etchells and Roberts', Pound told Joyce early in September. 'So they are no longer on my mind either. I shall devote the next six months entirely to my own interests.' But it was not to be. (Pound to Joyce, 1 and 2 September 1916, *Pound/Joyce*, p.82.)
39. Quinn to Margaret Dunlop Epstein, 27 June 1916, B. L. Reid, p.259.
40. The opening date of the exhibition is printed on the title-page of the catalogue.
41. Only one library owning this catalogue has been traced by the author: the Archives of American Art in Washington, among the papers of Walt Kuhn. They also contain a copy of the exhibition's invitation card, on which Kuhn wrote the note to his wife quoted here in the text. Elsewhere in his papers, another copy of the catalogue states in his hand that a thousand copies were printed. B. L. Reid states (p.292) that Quinn 'composed and proofread the catalog', but the Kuhn papers make clear that Quinn's involvement did not extend very far. Garnett McCoy, Deputy Director-Archivist of the Archives of American Art, wrote to the author on 9 January 1974: 'That [the catalogue] is all there is, which makes the Quinn connection seem a little thin'.
42. Don Marquis, 'The First Intelligible Answer', *Art World*, May 1917.
43. Lewis to Quinn, 24 January 1917, *Letters*, p.86.

44. Quinn to Pound, 29 April 1917, B. L. Reid, p.293.
45. Pound to Saunders, c.November 1917, Cornell University Library.
46. Etchells, interview.
47. Roberts, *Memories of the War to End War*, p.26.
48. Pound to Joyce, c.June 1915, *Pound/Joyce*, p.35.
49. Coburn's other portrait photographs in the exhibition included H. G. Wells, Brangwyn, William Nicholson, Galsworthy, Arnold Bennett, Roger Fry and Matisse.
50. Coburn, introduction to the exhibition catalogue of *Camera Pictures by Alvin Langdon Coburn*, Goupil Gallery, October 1913.
51. Coburn, 'The Relation of Time to Art', *Camera Work*, No. 36, 1911.
52. F. C. Tilney, 'Observations on Some Pictures of the Year', *Photograms of the Year, 1914*.
53. Coburn, 'The Relation of Time to Art'.
54. Coburn, 'The Future of Pictorial Photography', *Photograms of the Year, 1916*.
55. An English translation of Bragaglia's manifesto by Caroline Tisdall is published, along with five of his photographs, in *Creative Camera*, May 1973, pp.162–5.
56. The last few passages are all taken from Coburn's 'The Future of Pictorial Photography'.
57. Coburn, *Alvin Langdon Coburn, Photographer. An Autobiography* (London, 1966), p.102.
58. Gernsheim to the author, 28 July 1972.
59. Arthur Gill to the author, 27 August 1972.
60. Pound, introduction to the catalogue of Coburn's *Vortographs and Paintings* exhibition at the Camera Club, February 1917. A revised edition of this essay, called 'Vortographs', was published in Pound's *Pavannes and Divisions* (London, 1918), p.231.
61. Coburn, 'The Future of Pictorial Photography'.
62. Coburn, *Autobiography*, p.102; ibid.
63. Nathan Lyons (ed.) *Photographers on Photography* (Rochester, New York, 1966), p.180. Gernsheim, *Creative Photography. Aesthetic Trends 1839–1960* (London, 1962), p.163, makes a similar claim.
64. Pound, introduction to Coburn's 1917 exhibition catalogue.
65. Pound to Quinn, 24 January 1917, *Letters*, p.158.
66. Ibid.
67. Coburn, *Autobiography*, p.104.
68. Ibid.
69. Coburn executed most of these paintings in 1916, for in 'The Future of Pictorial Photography' he revealed that 'all the summer I have been painting, and so I can come back to photography with a more or less fresh viewpoint, and it makes me want to shout, "Wake up!" to many of my photographic colleagues'.
70. Pound, introduction to Coburn's 1917 exhibition catalogue.
71. Ibid.
72. Ibid.
73. Coburn, 'Postscript' to the 1917 Camera Club exhibition catalogue.
74. *The Sketch*, 14 March 1917. Another Vortograph was reproduced as Plate XLIV in *Photograms of the Year, 1917–18*.
75. Saunders to Dismorr, undated, but probably c.1917, collection R. H. M. Ody.
76. Hulme to Marsh, July 1917, Christopher Hassall, *Edward Marsh*, p.382.
77. A large collection of photographs of Epstein's work now constitutes the only surviving record of Hulme's lost monograph. Hull University Library, which owns the photographs, kindly supplied the author with a list of them, and the selection at least reveals which Epstein sculptures Hulme considered to be important. As such, it is well worth recording here. There are thirty-five photographs in all, several showing different views of the same sculpture, and they represent: *Head of Romilly John, Small Carving in Flenite, Large Carving in Flenite, Cursed be The Day Wherein I was Born (Job), Mother and Child (marble), Pigeons (marble), Head of Iris Tree, Large Female Figure, Garden Carving, The Sun God, Wilde Memorial, Rock Drill, Venus, Head of T. E. Hulme, 'Rock Drilling' drawing, 'Birth' drawing, 'Birth' drawing*. Apart from this list there are, according to Hull University Library, 'no notes by Hulme, except for another list of the contents, in his handwriting, on the fly-leaf'. (Letter to the author, 16 September 1971.)
78. Aldington, *Life for Life's Sake*, pp.152–3.
79. Epstein to Quinn, 1 October 1917, B. L. Reid, p.302.
80. Epstein, *Let There Be Sculpture*, p.76.
81. *Twenty-three by Sixty-two Inches* is a typical Gibb picture illustrated in the catalogue of *Exhibition of the Latest Pictures and Pottery Decorations by Phelan Gibb*, the Alpine Club Gallery, London, 19 February–19 March 1917. Altogether 90 'Pictures' are listed, all titled simply by their measurements.
82. Bell, 'Contemporary Art in England', *Burlington Magazine*, July 1917.
83. Pound to Quinn, 21 August 1917, B. L. Reid, p.293.
84. Pound to Lewis, July 1916, *Letters*, p.136.
85. Pound to Lewis, 25 August 1917, ibid., p.175.
86. Saunders to Dismorr, c.1916, collection R. H. M. Ody. Saunders worked at a London Censor's Office during the war.

Chapter Eighteen

1. Roberts, *Memories of the War to End War*, p.23. He also recalled that Captain Guy Baker wrote to him from London suggesting that he apply for a Canadian commission. He did so by submitting a drawing he had furtively made on a newspaper.
2. Lewis to Pound, 16 January 1918, *Letters*, p.97.
3. R. F. Wodehouse, *A Check List of the War Collections of World War I, 1914–18 and World War II, 1939–45* (National Gallery of Canada, n.d.), p.4.
4. Nevinson, preface to the catalogue of his *Exhibition of Pictures of War*, Leicester Galleries, London, March 1918.
5. Ibid.
6. *Roads of France* was shown in Nevinson's 1918 exhibition as No. c.
7. Nevinson, *Paint and Prejudice*, p.111.
8. Ibid.
9. Ibid., p.96.
10. *The Globe*, 1 March 1918.
11. Nevinson, preface to his 1918 exhibition catalogue.
12. Nevinson, *Paint and Prejudice*, p.66.
13. Nevinson, interview with the *Newcastle-on-Tyne Illustrated Chronicle*, 22 January 1919.
14. Nevinson, interview with the *New York Times*, 25 May 1919.
15. Nevinson, quoted by Malcolm C. Salaman in 'The Art of C. R. W. Nevinson', *The Studio*, December 1919.
16. Alice Mayes, *The Young Bomberg*, p.22.
17. Communiqué addressed to Bomberg by the Canadian War Records Office, dated 29 December 1917, collection Mrs Lilian Bomberg.
18. Another, very similar study, in a less advanced stage than the one reproduced here but with no significant variations, is reproduced in Lipke's *David Bomberg*, plate 11.
19. Alice Mayes, *The Young Bomberg*, p.25.
20. Ibid., pp.27–9.
21. There is a possibility that this painting is in fact the original version rejected by Konody, but it cannot be proved either way.
22. Joanna Drew, 1967 Bomberg exhibition catalogue, p.27.
23. Alice Mayes, *The Young Bomberg*, p.29.
24. Lilian Bomberg, interview.
25. Bomberg to Siegfried Gideon, 27 July 1953, Lipke, *David Bomberg*, p.49.
26. Ibid.
27. Etchells, 'A Note'. *Episode* was listed as No. 14 in the 1919 exhibition catalogue.
28. Although only one untitled and undated copy of this woodcut has so far been traced, Wadsworth did call it *Mudros* when it was reproduced in *The Tyro, No. 2* (London, 1922) plate XVI. Stylistically, it would seem to belong to the war-time period; and the fact that Wadsworth placed it beside a photograph of *Invention* in his album also suggests a c. 1917 dating.

29. Etchells, 'A Note'.
30. The British Museum's copy of this print is signed and dated 'Mudros 1917'. But in the Victoria and Albert Museum's copy it is signed and dated 'Lemnos 1917' middle right and then at bottom left inscribed 'Interior'. *Interior* was listed as No. 13 in Wadsworth's 1919 exhibition catalogue. Wadsworth exhibited another work called *Interior*, presumably a painting, in the 'Pictures' section of the 1915 Vorticist Exhibition as No. 5(c).
31. Etchells, 'A Note'.
32. Ibid.
33. *World*, 22 March 1919.
34. Lewis, 'Mr. Edward Wadsworth's Exhibition of Woodcuts', *Art and Letters*, Spring 1919.
35. A precise date of execution for this alphabet is not known, but Wadsworth exhibited it in the Exhibition of Practical Arts arranged by the Arts League of Service at the Twenty-One Gallery in November 1919 (where the *Evening Standard*, 23 November 1919, noted that Wadsworth's 'Initial letters, in woodcut . . . have considerable merit'). The illustration of the letters reproduced here is taken from a sheet inscribed 'Wadsworth. Proof' in a London private collection. The same sheet also contains two leaping horse designs which were used in Wadsworth's *The Black Country* (Ovid Press, London, 1920). Thirteen of the letters were later used as letter-heads at the start of John Rodker's *Collected Poems 1912–1925* (The Hours Press, Paris, 1930).
36. Etchells, interview.
37. The certificate, dated 18 August 1917, was shown to the author by Etchells in June 1970.
38. Catalogue, *Canadian War Memorials Paintings Exhibition – 1920 – New Series. The Last Phase* (Canada, 1920), p.9.
39. Etchells, interview.
40. Lewis to Pound, 16 January 1918, *Letters*, p.97.
41. Roberts, *Memories of the War to End War*, p.32. The letter to Roberts from Captain Harold Watkins of the Canadian War Records Office, dated 28 December 1917, is published in full on p.24 of the same memoir.
42. Passage taken from *Canada in Flanders*, Vol. I.
43. Roberts' two letters quoted here appear on p.42 and p.45 of his *Memories of the War to End War*.
44. Lewis, *Blasting and Bombardiering*, pp.188–9.
45. Lewis, *Blast No. 2*, p.26.
46. Pound to Quinn, 3 April 1918, *Letters*, p.193.
47. Lewis to Read, 17 December 1918, *Letters*, p.102.
48. Michael Holroyd, 'Damning and Blasting', *The Listener*, 6 July 1972.
49. Lewis, *Blast No. 2*, p.24.
50. Lewis, *Rude Assignment*, p.129.
51. Lewis to Quinn, 7 February 1919, *Letters*, p.104.
52. Lewis, *Blast No. 2*, p.13.
53. Lewis, *Rude Assignment*, p.130.
54. Lewis, *Blast No. 2*, p.46; ibid., p.79.
55. Lewis to James Thrall Soby, 9 April 1947, *Letters*, p.406.
56. Lewis, *Rude Assignment*, p.129.
57. Roberts, who helped Lewis with the picture, states in 'Wyndham Lewis, the Vorticist' that *A Battery Shelled* 'was painted during the winter of 1918 in his new studio at Notting Hill'.
58. Lewis, *Rude Assignment*, p.128.
59. Roberts, 'Wyndham Lewis, the Vorticist'.
60. Lewis, *Rude Assignment*, p.129.
61. Roberts, 'Wyndham Lewis, the Vorticist'.
62. Lewis to Quinn, 3 September 1919, *Letters*, p.111.
63. Pound, 'Prefatory Note' to the Leicester Galleries exhibition catalogue.
64. Pound, *Blast No. 1*, pp.153–4.
65. Pound told Quinn in a 25 October 1919 letter that 'Lewis's portrait of me was on the way to being excellent when I last saw it'. (*Letters*, p.214.)
66. Pound, 'The War Paintings of Wyndham Lewis', *The Nation*, 8 February 1919.
67. Lewis to Quinn, 3 September 1919, *Letters*, p.111.
68. Aldington, *Life for Life's Sake*, p.198.
69. Pound to William Carlos Williams, 11 September 1920, *Letters*, p.223.
70. Lewis, *Rude Assignment*, p.154.
71. Lewis, *The Caliph's Design. Architects! Where is Your Vortex?* (London, 1919), pp.29, 7.
72. Ibid., p.11.
73. Ibid., p.29.
74. Lewis to Quinn, 3 September 1919, *Letters*, p.110.
75. Read to 'a friend', 28 October 1918, *The Contrary Experience. Autobiographies* (London, 1963), p.141.
76. Lewis, *The Caliph's Design*, p.47.
77. Illustration taken from *Daily Sketch*, 6 November 1919.
78. Lewis, *The Caliph's Design*, p.18.
79. *The New Age*, 11 December 1919.
80. *Daily Mirror*, 18 November 1919.
81. Rutter, *Sunday Times*, 23 November 1919.
82. Kauffer's *Daily Herald* poster, *The Early Bird*, was designed in 1918 and issued the following year. But it was preceded by a closely related design published in *Colour* in January 1917, and by a woodcut called *Flight* which Kauffer probably executed around 1915–16. It is the actual poster which is illustrated here.
83. Kauffer, printed sheet now in the Cooper-Hewitt Museum, New York, quoted by Mark Haworth-Booth in 'E. McKnight Kauffer', *The Penrose Annual 1971* (London, 1971), p.88.
84. Epstein, *Let There Be Sculpture*, p.64.
85. Epstein to Quinn, 11 February 1917, B. L. Reid, p.299.
86. Epstein, *Let There Be Sculpture*, p.70.
87. Ibid., p.71.
88. Shipp, *The New Art*, p.86.
89. Ibid., pp.91–2.
90. Atkinson's *Vortex* drawings were listed as Nos. 41 and 71 respectively in the Eldar Gallery catalogue. They remain unidentified.
91. Lewis, 'Dobson. Atkinson', printed only in a trial copy of *The Tyro, No. 2* (London, 1922), in a London private collection.
92. Etchells, interview.
93. Etchells, letter to the author, 21 March 1971. *Gunwalloe* was reproduced in *The Tyro, No. 2* (London, 1922), pl. XII.
94. Hamilton showed some of his Yeoman Pottery bowls in the Exhibition of Practical Arts arranged by the Arts League of Service at the Twenty-One Gallery, November 1919. They were singled out for praise in an *Evening Standard* review on 23 November 1919.
95. Both *Self-Portrait* and *Glass Factory* are lost, and are reproduced here from the Mansard Gallery catalogue, pp.24–5.
96. The design reproduced here can be identified with *Reconstruction* because of its close stylistic resemblance to *Glass Factory*, another of Hamilton's Mansard Gallery exhibits.
97. *The Times*, 1 April 1920.
98. *Truth*, 7 April 1920.
99. Sadleir, *Educational Times*, May 1920.
100. Lewis, preface to the Mansard Gallery catalogue.
101. Rutter, *Sunday Times*, 28 March 1920.
102. Lewis, preface to the Mansard Gallery catalogue.
103. Roberts, *Abstract & Cubist Paintings & Drawings*, pp.11–12.
104. Gleizes, 'L'Epopée', *Le Rouge et le Noir*, June–July 1929, trans. taken from John Golding, *Cubism*, 1968 ed., p.182.
105. Léger, trans. Douglas Cooper, *Fernand Léger et le Nouvelle Espace* (London and Paris, 1940), vii, pp.74–5.
106. Ibid.
107. Lewis, *Wyndham Lewis the Artist*, p.76.
108. Pound, 'Gaudier: A Postscript', *Esquire* (New York), August 1934.
109. Lewis, *Blast No. 1*, p.134.
110. Quinn to Pound, 1 May 1921, B. L. Reid, p.491.
111. Bell, *Since Cézanne* (London, 1922), 1929 ed., p.9.
112. Pound to Lewis, 3 December 1924, *Letters*, p.261.
113. Rodker, *The Future of Futurism* (London, 1925), pp.7–8.
114. W. Hugh Higginbottom, *Frightfulness in Modern Art* (London, 1928), pp.77, 79.
115. Nash to *The Times*, 2 June 1933, *Unit 1. The Modern Movement in English Architecture, Painting and Sculpture* (London, 1935).

116. Nash, 'Unit One', *The Listener*, 5 July 1933.
117. Moore, conversation with the author, 23 October 1972.
118. Nicholson to the author, 12 August 1972.
119. Ibid.
120. Nicholson to the author, 26 August 1972.
121. Merlyn Evans, interview with the author, autumn 1973. Evans, in fact, thought that Atkinson had influenced him far more than had Lewis, who is usually supposed to have inspired Evans' work quite considerably.
122. Lewis, 'The Vorticists', *Vogue*, September 1956.
123. Quoted in Shakespear, *Etruscan Gate* (Exeter, 1971).
124. Nevill, interview with the author.
125. Nevill, interview with Meriel McCooey in 'Blast', *Sunday Times* colour magazine, 8 January 1967.
126. The date of execution for these prints was supplied to the author by Nevill, who explained that the *Tango* range already contained designs carried out before he came across *Blast*.
127. Nevill told the author that Sonia Delaunay's portfolio *Ses peintures, ses objets, ses tissus simultanés, ses modes* (Paris, Librarie des Arts Decoratifs), which she gave Nevill around that time, was one specific inspiration for the colours employed in *Tango*.
128. Lewis, *Blast No. 1*, p.33.
129. Lewis, 'A Review of Contemporary Art', *Blast No. 2*, p.47.
130. Meriel McCooey, 'Blast', *Sunday Times* colour magazine, 8 January 1967.
131. Roberts' bitterness stems originally from the way in which the *Wyndham Lewis and Vorticism* exhibition was organized at the Tate Gallery, July–August 1956. In reality, the show was a straightforward retrospective survey of Lewis's work; but its small section called 'Other Vorticists' was, as Roberts bitingly pointed out in a series of broadsides, pamphlets and books listed here in the bibliography, a derisory misrepresentation of the other rebels' roles at that period. Roberts himself was permitted seven pictures, one dating from his student days and the rest from 1918 or even later. Only three of Wadsworth's exhibits – two woodcuts and a gouache – could possibly have been described as Vorticist. Bomberg was allowed one work, a relatively traditional drawing executed while he was at the Slade. And Epstein was omitted altogether. The other rebels fared equally badly, while Frank Dobson and Jacob Kramer, neither of whom could possibly be thought of as Vorticist, were unaccountably included. Small wonder that Roberts was incensed, and his indignation knew no bounds when he read Lewis's demonstrably inflated claim in the catalogue 'Introduction' (p.3) that 'Vorticism, in fact, was what I, personally, did, and said, at a certain period'. The details of Roberts' various counterattacks are too lengthy to be spelled out here, but many of them are historically justified. Perhaps he came closest to an accurate rebuttal of Lewis's assertion when he wrote in *The Resurrection of Vorticism and the Apotheosis of Wyndham Lewis at the Tate* (London, 1956, pages unnumbered) that: 'To be correct, Lewis's statement should run thus . . . "Vorticism" in fact was a word used to symbolise the painting and sculpture of the artists named below who agreed to be known as the "Vorticist Group" at a certain period . . . Gaudier-Brzeska, Wadsworth, Etchells, Dismorr, Saunders, Roberts, Lewis.' For the record, Sir John Rothenstein told the author that it was his idea to have a Vorticism section in the 1956 exhibition, and that Lewis was from the outset very unhappy with the plan.
132. It ought to be noted here that in 1974 Roberts issued a special monochrome reproduction of this painting, on card measuring $16 \cdot 5 \times 18 \cdot 5$ cm, with a revised title printed on the back: *The English Cubists at the Hotel de la Tour Eiffel 1915*. The presence of Lewis, Pound, Wadsworth and above all *Blast* in a picture with this title therefore becomes something of a mystery.
133. The figures represented are, from left to right, seated: Hamilton, Pound, Roberts, Lewis, Etchells and Wadsworth. Standing: Dismorr, Saunders, the waiter Joe and Stulik, the restaurant's proprietor.
134. Roberts, back cover of *The Resurrection of Vorticism and the Apotheosis of Wyndham Lewis at the Tate*.
135. Aldington, review of *Blast No. 1* in *The Egoist*, 15 July 1914.
136. Read, *Contemporary British Art* (London, 1951), p.16.
137. Lewis, *Rude Assignment*, p.125.
138. Ibid.
139. Pound, 'Affirmations. VI. Analysis of this Decade', *The New Age*, 11 February 1915.
140. *Blast No. 1*, p.39.
141. Ibid., p.34.

Bibliography

For the sake of clarity, this bibliography is divided into two sections. The first is a collection of background and general reading for Vorticism and the period as a whole. The second concentrates on the most important participating individuals, likewise restricted in its reference to the Vorticist period, and is presented under the names of the people themselves.

Since the major source-material for contemporary continental developments has already been comprehensively listed in authoritative studies of Cubism, Futurism, etc., it is not included here. Only the catalogues for relevant continental exhibitions held in London are cited.

SECTION 1

ABBOTT, CLAUDE COLLEER, and ANTHONY BERTRAM, ed. *Poet and Painter: Being the Correspondence between Gordon Bottomley and Paul Nash, 1910–1946.* Oxford, 1955.

ALDINGTON, RICHARD. 'M. Marinetti's Lectures'. *The New Freewoman,* 1 December 1913.

—. 'Books, Drawings, and Papers'. *The Egoist,* 1 January 1914.

—. 'Anti-Helenism'. *The Egoist,* 15 January 1914.

—. 'Presentation to Mr. W. S. Blunt'. *The Egoist,* 2 February 1914.

—. 'Blast'. *The Egoist,* 1 July 1914.

—. 'Blast'. *The Egoist,* 15 July 1914.

—. 'Free Verse in England'. *The Egoist,* 15 September 1914.

—. 'The Poetry of Ezra Pound'. *The Egoist,* 1 May 1915.

—. 'Periodical Not Received'. *The Egoist,* 2 August 1915.

—. *Images, 1910–1915.* London, 1915.

—. *Images of War.* London, 1919.

—. *Life for Life's Sake. A Book of Reminiscences.* London, 1968.

The London Salon of the Allied Artists' Association, Ltd. July 1908. First Year. Royal Albert Hall. Exhibition catalogue.

The London Salon of the Allied Artists' Association, Ltd. July 1909. Second Year. Royal Albert Hall. Exhibition catalogue.

The London Salon of the Allied Artists' Association, Ltd. July 1910. Albert Hall. Third Year. Exhibition catalogue.

The London Salon of the Allied Artists' Association, Ltd. July 1911. Fourth Year. Albert Hall. Exhibition catalogue.

The London Salon of the Allied Artists' Association, Ltd. July 1912. Fifth Year. Albert Hall. Exhibition catalogue.

The London Salon of the Allied Artists' Association, Ltd. July 1913. Sixth Year. Albert Hall. Exhibition catalogue.

The London Salon of the Allied Artists' Association, Ltd. July 1914. Seventh Year. Holland Park Hall. Exhibition catalogue.

The London Salon of the Allied Artists' Association, Ltd. March 1916. Eighth Year. Grafton Galleries. Exhibition catalogue.

ALLINSON, ADRIAN. *Painter's Pilgrimage.* Unpublished autobiographical manuscript in the possession of Miss M. Mitchell-Smith, London.

AYRTON, MICHAEL. 'The Stone Guest'. *New Statesman,* 21 July 1956.

BAGNOLD, ENID. *Enid Bagnold's Autobiography (from 1889).* London, 1969.

BARON, WENDY. *Sickert.* London, 1973.

BARR, ALFRED H., JR., ed. *Cubism and Abstract Art.* New York: Museum of Modern Art, 1936.

BELL, CLIVE. 'The London Salon at the Albert Hall'. *The Athenaeum,* 27 July 1912.

—. 'The English Group'. Introduction to the catalogue of the *Second Post-Impressionist Exhibition. British, French and Russian Artists.* Grafton Galleries: London, October 1912–January 1913.

—. 'Rutter's Post-Impressionist and Futurist Exhibition'. *The Nation,* 25 October 1913.

—. *Art.* London, 1914.

—. 'Contemporary Art in England'. *Burlington Magazine,* July 1917.

—. *Pot-Boilers.* London, 1918.

—. 'Wilcoxism'. *The Athenaeum,* 5 March 1920.

—. *Since Cézanne.* London, 1922.

—. 'How England Met Modern Art'. *Art News,* October 1950.

—. *Old Friends. Personal Recollections.* London, 1956.

BELL, QUENTIN. *Roger Fry. An Inaugural Lecture.* Leeds, 1964.

—. 'Bloomsbury and the Arts in the Early Twentieth Century'. *Leeds Arts Calendar,* No. 55, 1964.

—. *Bloomsbury.* London, 1968.

—. *Virginia Woolf. A Biography. Volume One. Virginia Stephen, 1882–1912.* London, 1972.

—. *Virginia Woolf. A Biography. Volume Two. Mrs Woolf, 1912–1941.* London, 1972.

BELL, QUENTIN and STEPHEN CHAPLIN. 'The Ideal Home Rumpus'. *Apollo,* October 1964.

—. Letter about Walter Michel's 'Tyros and Portraits' article. *Apollo,* January 1966. (Cf. Section 2, under LEWIS.)

BELL, QUENTIN and PHILIP TROUTMAN. Introductions to the exhibition catalogue of *Vision and Design: The Life, Work and Influence of Roger Fry, 1866–1934.* London: Arts Council, 1966.

BENNETT, ARNOLD. *Books and Persons.* London, 1917.

—. *The Journals.* Selected and edited by Frank Swinnerton. New ed., incorporating Journal Volume 6 and Florentine Journal, first published London, 1971.

BERTRAM, ANTHONY. *A Century of British Painting, 1851–1951.* London, 1951.

—. *Paul Nash. The Portrait of an Artist.* London, 1955.

BILLCLIFFE, ROGER and PAOLO ROSSI. Introduction to the exhibition catalogue of *Cubism in England, 1910–1920,* Glasgow University Print Room, April–May 1970.

BINYON, LAURENCE. *The Flight of the Dragon.* London, 1914.

BOWNESS, ALAN. Introduction and notes to the exhibition catalogue of *Decade 1910–1920. Painting in England.* London: Arts Council, 1965.

BOWNESS, ALAN and DENNIS FARR. Note to the catalogue of the *London Group 1914–64 Jubilee Exhibition.* Tate Gallery, July–August 1964.

BROWN, DAVID. 'Introduction' to the catalogue of *We Are Making a New World. Artists in the 1914–18 War,* an exhibition held at the Scottish National Gallery of Modern Art, Edinburgh, October–November 1974.

BROWN, FRED. 'Wander Years'. *Artwork,* Autumn 1930.

BROWN, OLIVER. *Exhibition. The Memoirs of Oliver Brown.* London, 1968.

BROWSE, LILLIAN. *Sickert.* London, 1960.

Preliminary Prospectus (Cabaret Theatre Club). London, April 1912.

Cabaret Theatre Club. The Cave of the Golden Calf. An illustrated pamphlet. London, May 1912.

The Café Royalists. Catalogue of exhibition held at Parkin Gallery, London, September–October 1972.

The First Exhibition of the Camden Town Group. Catalogue of exhibition held at the Carfax Gallery, London, June 1911.

The Second Exhibition of the Camden Town Group. Catalogue of exhibition held at the Carfax Gallery, London, December 1911.

The Third Exhibition of the Camden Town Group. Catalogue of exhibition held at the Carfax Gallery, London, December 1912.

Exhibition by the Camden Town Group and Others. Catalogue of exhibition held at Brighton Public Art Galleries, December 1913–January 1914.

Canadian War Memorials Exhibition. Catalogue of exhibition held at the Royal Academy, London, January–February 1919.

CARRINGTON, NOEL, ed. *Mark Gertler. Selected Letters.* London, 1965.

CHAMOT, MARY, DENNIS FARR and MARTIN BUTLIN. *The Tate Gallery: The Modern British Paintings, Drawings and Sculpture*. Volume I, A–L, London, 1964.

—. Volume II, M–Z, London, 1965.

CHARLTON, GEORGE. 'The Slade'. *The Studio*, October 1946.

CLUTTON-BROCK, ALAN. Introduction to the catalogue of the *Duncan Grant* exhibition held at the Tate Gallery, London, May–June 1959.

COFFMAN, STANLEY K., JR. *Imagism. A Chapter for the History of Modern Poetry*. Oklahoma: University of Oklahoma Press, 1951.

CONSTABLE, W. G. *Duncan Grant*. London, 1927.

CONWAY, MARTIN. *A Concise Catalogue of Paintings, Drawings and Sculpture of the First World War, 1914–1918*. London, 1963.

COOPER, DOUGLAS. *The Courtauld Collection: A Catalogue and Introduction*. London, 1954.

—. *The Cubist Epoch*. London, 1971.

CORK, RICHARD. Essay and notes for the catalogue of *Vorticism and its Allies*, an exhibition held at the Hayward Gallery, London, March–June 1974.

COURNOS, JOHN. 'The Death of Vorticism'. *Little Review*, June 1919.

—. *Autobiography*. New York, 1935.

Exhibition of Works by Members of the Cumberland Market Group. Catalogue of exhibition held at the Goupil Gallery, London, 1915.

CURLE, RICHARD. *Caravansary and Conversation*. London, 1937.

DAVIES, W. H. *Later Days*. London, 1925.

DEGHY, GUY and KEITH WATERHOUSE. *Café Royal. Ninety Years of Bohemia*. London, 1955.

DENVIR, BERNARD. Introduction to catalogue of *Jacob Kramer* exhibition, Parkin Gallery, London, March–April 1973.

d'OFFAY, ANTHONY. *Abstract Art in England 1913–1915*. Catalogue of the exhibition held at the d'Offay Couper Gallery, London, November–December 1969.

—. Introduction to the catalogue of the *Alfred Wolmark Exhibition* held at the Fine Art Society, London, October–November 1970.

DUNCAN, RONALD. 'BLAST and About and About'. *The Townsman*, January 1938.

DUNLOP, IAN. *The Shock of the New*. London, 1972.

EASTON, MALCOLM. *Art in Britain, 1890–1940*. Catalogue of an exhibition held at the University of Hull in 1967.

—. 'Augustus John: Drawings and Etchings'. Introduction to catalogue of exhibition held at Colnaghi's, London, September–October 1974.

EASTON, MALCOLM, and MICHAEL HOLROYD. *The Art of Augustus John*. London, 1974.

EDDY, ARTHUR JEROME. *Cubists and Post-Impressionism*. Chicago, 1914.

ELSEN, ALBERT E. *Origins of Modern Sculpture: Pioneers and Premises*. London, 1974.

EMMONS, ROBERT. *The Life and Opinions of Walter Richard Sickert*. London, 1941.

FISHMAN, SOLOMON. *The Interpretation of Art*. California, 1963.

FLETCHER, JOHN GOULD. *My Life is My Song*. London, 1937.

FLINT, F. S. 'Imagisme'. *Poetry* (Chicago), March 1913.

—. 'The History of Imagism'. *The Egoist*, 1 May 1915.

—. *Cadences*. London, Poetry Bookshop, 1915.

FORD, FORD MADOX. 'The Poet's Eye'. *The New Freewoman*, 1 September 1913.

—. 'On a Notice of "Blast"'. *The Outlook*, 31 July 1915.

—. *Thus to Revisit. Some Reminiscences*. London, 1921.

—. 'A Haughty and Proud Generation'. *The Yale Review*, July 1922.

—. *The Marsden Case*. London, 1923.

—. *Return to Yesterday. Reminiscences, 1894–1914*. London, 1931.

—. *Mightier than the Sword. Memories and Criticisms*. London, 1938.

FORGE, ANDREW. *The Slade, 1871–1960*. London, n.d.

FOTHERGILL, JOHN. *The Slade. A Collection of Drawings and Some Pictures Done by Past and Present Students of the London Slade School of Art, 1893–1907*. London, 1907.

—. 'Essay on Drawing'. *Encyclopaedia Britannica*, Volume VIII, London, 1911.

—. *James Dickson Innes*. Ed. Lillian Browse. London, 1946.

Catalogue of An Exhibition of Pictures by Members of the Friday Club. Alpine Club Gallery, London, February 1912.

Catalogue of An Exhibition of Pictures by Members of the Friday Club. Alpine Club Gallery, London, January–February 1913.

Catalogue of An Exhibition of Pictures by Members of the Friday Club. Alpine Club Gallery, London, February–March 1914.

Catalogue of An Exhibition of Pictures by Members of the Friday Club. Alpine Club Gallery, London, 1915.

Catalogue of An Exhibition of Pictures by Members of the Friday Club. Alpine Club Gallery, London, March–April 1916.

FRY, ROGER. 'The Grafton Gallery, I'. *The Nation*, 19 November 1910.

—. 'The Post-Impressionists'. *The Nation*, 3 December 1910.

—. 'A Postscript on Post-Impressionism'. *The Nation*, 24 December 1910.

—. 'Post-Impressionism'. *The Fortnightly Review*, 1 May 1911.

—. 'The Allied Artists at the Albert Hall'. *The Nation*, 20 July 1912.

—. Introduction to the catalogue of the *Second Post-Impressionist Exhibition. British, French and Russian Artists*, Grafton Galleries, London, October 1912–January 1913.

—. 'The Allied Artists' Association'. *The Nation*, 2 August 1913.

—. 'Two Views of the London Group'. *The Nation*, 14 March 1914.

—. Notes to the exhibition catalogue of *Works Representative of the New Movement in Art*. Contemporary Art Society, Mansard Gallery, London, October 1917.

—. *Vision and Design*. London, 1920.

—. *Duncan Grant*. London, 1923.

Exhibition of Works by the Italian Futurist Painters. Catalogue of the exhibition held at the Sackville Gallery, London, March 1912.

Exhibition of Works by the Italian Futurist Painters and Sculptors. Catalogue of the exhibition held at the Doré Galleries, London, April 1914.

GARNETT, DAVID. *The Golden Echo. The First Part of an Autobiography*. London, 1954.

—. *The Flowers of the Forest*. London, 1955.

—. Introduction to and selection of *Carrington: Letters and Extracts from her Diaries*. London, 1970.

GATHORNE-HARDY, ROBERT, ed. *The Early Memoirs of Lady Ottoline Morrell*. London, 1963.

—. *Ottoline at Garsington*. London, 1974.

Modern German Art. Catalogue of exhibition held at the Twenty-One Gallery, London, February–March 1914.

Exhibition of the Latest Pictures and Pottery Decorations by Phelan Gibb. Catalogue of exhibition held at the Alpine Club Gallery, London, February–March 1917.

GILL, ERIC. *Autobiography*. London, 1940.

GILL, WINIFRED. Typescript of a taped interview with Winifred Gill, and her letters to Duncan Grant. Care of Carol Hogben, Circulation Dept., Victoria and Albert Museum, London.

GINNER, CHARLES. 'Neo-Realism'. *The New Age*, January 1914.

—. 'Modern Painting and Teaching'. *Art and Letters*, July 1917.

—. 'The Camden Town Group'. *Studio*, November 1945.

GOLDRING, DOUGLAS. *Odd Man Out. The Autobiography of a 'Propaganda' Novelist*. London, 1935.

—. *South Lodge. Reminiscences of Violet Hunt, Ford Madox Ford and the English Review Circle*. London, 1943.

—. *The Last Pre-Raphaelite. A Record of the Life and Writings of Ford Madox Ford*. London, 1948.

—. *Life Interests*. Preface by Alec Waugh. London, 1948.

The Grafton Group: Vanessa Bell, Roger Fry, Duncan Grant, Second Exhibition. Catalogue of exhibition held at the Alpine Club Gallery, London, January 1914.

GRANT, JOY. *Harold Monro and the Poetry Bookshop*. London, 1967.

Group X. Catalogue of an exhibition held at the Mansard Gallery, London, March 1920.

HAMILTON, GEORGE HEARD. *Painting and Sculpture in Europe, 1880–1940*. London, 1967.

HAMNETT, NINA. *Laughing Torso*. London, 1932.

HARRISON, CHARLES. 'The Origins of Modernism in England'. *Studio International*, September 1974.

HASSALL, CHRISTOPHER. *Edward Marsh. Patron of the Arts. A Biography*. London, 1959.

HASTINGS, BEATRICE. *The Old 'New Age', Orage—and Others*. London, 1936.

HAWORTH-BOOTH, MARK. 'E. McKnight Kauffer'. *The Penrose Annual 1971*, London, 1971.

—. In preparation: a biographical study of Edward McKnight Kauffer.

H. D. (HILDA DOOLITTLE). *Collected Poems*. New York, 1925.

HERON, PATRICK. *The Changing Forms of Art*. London, 1955.

—. Introduction to the catalogue of the *Exhibition of the Work of B.S. Turner*, Leeds City Art Gallery, October–November 1964.

HIGGINBOTTOM, W. HUGH. *Frightfulness in Modern Art*. London, 1928.

HIND, C. LEWIS. *The Post-Impressionists*. London, 1911.

HOLMAN-HUNT, DIANA. *Latin Among Lions: Alvaro Guevara*. London, 1974.

HOLMES, CHARLES. *Notes on the Post-Impressionist Painters*. London, 1910.

HOLROYD, MICHAEL. *Lytton Strachey. A Critical Biography. Volume II. The Years of Achievement (1910–1932)*. London, 1968.

—. *Augustus John. Volume I. The Years of Innocence*. London, 1974.

—. *Augustus John. Volume II. The Years of Experience*. London, 1975.

HONE, JOSEPH. *The Life of Henry Tonks*. London, 1939.

HUBBARD, HESKETH. *A Hundred Years of British Painting, 1851–1951*. London, 1951.

HUGHES, GLENN. *Imagism and the Imagists. A Study in Modern Poetry*. California: Stanford University Press, 1931.

HUNT, VIOLET. *The Flurried Years*. London, 1926.

HUTCHISON, SIDNEY C. *The History of the Royal Academy, 1768–1968*. London, 1968.

HYNES, SAM. *The Edwardian Turn of Mind*. London, 1968.

Des Imagistes. London, 1914.

Some Imagist Poets. London, 1915.

JAMES, PHILIP. Foreword to exhibition catalogue of *The Camden Town Group*. London: Arts Council, 1953.

JEPSON, EDGAR. *Memories of an Edwardian and Neo-Georgian*. London, 1937.

JERROLD, DOUGLAS. *Georgian Adventure*. London, 1937.

JOHN, AUGUSTUS. *Chiaroscuro. Fragments of an Autobiography: First Series*. London, 1937.

—. *Finishing Touches*. Edited and introduced by Daniel George London, 1964.

JOHNSTONE, J. K. *The Bloomsbury Group*. London, 1954.

JONES, ALUN R. 'Notes Toward a History of Imagism'. *South Atlantic Quarterly*, LX, 1961.

—. 'Imagism: A Unity of Gesture'. *American Poetry*, Stratford-on-Avon Studies, No. 7, Arnold, 1965.

JONES, PETER, ed. Introduction to *Imagist Poetry*. London, 1972.

KANDINSKY, WASSILY. *The Art of Spiritual Harmony*. First English translation by M. T. H. Sadleir. London, 1914.

KAUFFER, EDWARD MCKNIGHT. Notes to the *Posters of McKnight Kauffer*. New York: Museum of Modern Art, 1937.

E. McKnight Kauffer. Memorial exhibition catalogue. Victoria and Albert Museum, October–November 1955.

KEENAN, PETER. 'Memories of Vorticism'. *The New Hope*, October 1934.

KONODY, P. G. *Art and War: Canadian War Memorials*. London, n.d.

LAIDLAY, W. J. *The Origin and First Two Years of the New English Art Club*. London, 1907.

LAUGHTON, BRUCE. Introduction to the exhibition catalogue of *The Slade, 1871–1971*, Royal Academy, London, November–December 1971.

LAVER, JAMES. *Portraits in Oil and Vinegar*. London, 1925.

LEA, F. A. *The Life of John Middleton Murry*. London, 1959.

LECHMERE, KATE. 'Recollections of Vorticism'. Interview with Della Denman. *Apollo*, January 1971.

LEWIS, WYNDHAM, ed. *Blast No. 1. June 20th, 1914. Review of the Great English Vortex*. With contributions by Epstein, Etchells, Ford, Gaudier, Gore, Hamilton, Lewis, Pound, Roberts, Wadsworth and Rebecca West. London, 1914.

—. *Blast. War Number. No. 2. July, 1915. Review of the Great English Vortex*. With contributions by Dismorr, Etchells, Ford, Gaudier, Kramer, Lewis, Nevinson, Roberts, Saunders, Dorothy Shakespear and Wadsworth. London, 1915.

LEWIS, WYNDHAM and LOUIS F. FERGUSSON. *Harold Gilman: An Appreciation*. London, 1919.

LIDDERDALE, JANE and MARY NICHOLSON. *Dear Miss Weaver. Harriet Shaw Weaver, 1876–1961*. London, 1970.

LILLY, MARJORIE. *Sickert. The Painter and His Circle*. London, 1971.

LIPKE, WILLIAM C. 'Vorticism and the Modern Movement'. *The Arts Review*, 21 August–4 September 1965.

—. *A History and Analysis of Vorticism*. Unpublished doctoral thesis for the University of Wisconsin, 1966.

—. 'Futurism and the development of Vorticism'. *Studio International*, April 1967.

—. 'The New Constructive Geometric Art in London, 1910–1915'. One chapter of *The Avant-Garde*, ed. Thomas B. Hess and John Ashbery, *Art News Annual*, XXXIV, New York, 1968.

—. 'The Omega Workshops and Vorticism'. *Apollo*, March 1970.

The London Group. Catalogue of *The First Exhibition of Works by Members of The London Group*, held at the Goupil Gallery, London, March 1914.

The London Group. Catalogue of *The Second Exhibition of Works by Members of The London Group*, held at the Goupil Gallery, London, March 1915.

The London Group. Catalogue of *The Third Exhibition of Works by Members of The London Group*, held at the Goupil Gallery, London, November–December 1915.

The London Group. Catalogue of *The Fourth Exhibition of Works by Members of The London Group*, held at the Goupil Gallery, London, June 1916.

LUDOVICI, ANTHONY. *An Artist's Life in London and Paris, 1870–1925.* London, 1926.

LUDWIG, RICHARD M., ed. *The Letters of Ford Madox Ford.* Princeton, 1965.

MACCARTHY, DESMOND. 'The Post-Impressionists'. Unsigned introduction to the exhibition catalogue of *Manet and the Post-Impressionists,* Grafton Galleries, London, November 1910–January 1911.

—. 'The Art-Quake of 1910. Desmond MacCarthy on the Post-Impressionist Exhibition'. *The Listener,* 1 February 1945.

MACCOLL, D. S. *Confessions of a Keeper and other papers.* London, 1931.

MACSHANE, FRANK. *The Life and Work of Ford Madox Ford.* London, 1965.

MARRIOTT, CHARLES. *Modern Art.* London, 1917.

—. *Modern Movements in Painting.* London, 1920.

MARTIN, WALLACE. *The New Age Under Orage.* Manchester, 1967.

MCLUHAN, MARSHALL. *Counterblast.* Toronto: privately printed, 1954.

MIDDLETON, CHRISTOPHER. 'Documents on Imagism from the Papers of F. S. Flint'. *The Review,* April 1965.

MIZENER, ARTHUR. *The Saddest Story. A Biography of Ford Madox Ford.* London, 1972.

Modernism in England 1910–20. The Vorticists and their Circle. Exhibition catalogue. The Tate Gallery, London, April–June 1973.

MONROE, HARRIET. *A Poet's Life: Seventy Years in a Changing World.* New York, 1938.

MOORE, GEORGE. *Conversations in Ebury Street.* London, 1924.

MOORE, HENRY. *Henry Moore on Sculpture.* Edited Philip James. London, 1966.

MORPHET, RICHARD. *British Painting 1910–1945.* London, 1967.

—. 'The Significance of Charleston'. *Apollo,* November 1967.

—. 'The Art of Vanessa Bell'. Introduction to exhibition catalogue of *Vanessa Bell Paintings and Drawings,* Anthony d'Offay, London, November–December 1973.

MORTIMER, RAYMOND. *Duncan Grant.* London, 1948.

MURRY, JOHN MIDDLETON. *Between Two Worlds: An Autobiography.* London, 1935.

NASH, PAUL. *Outline. An Autobiography and Other Writings.* With a preface by Herbert Read. London, 1949.

Catalogue of the Forty-Third Exhibition of Modern Pictures, by the New English Art Club at the Galleries of the Royal Society of British Artists. Summer, 1910.

Catalogue of the Forty-Fourth Exhibition of Modern Pictures, by the New English Art Club at the Galleries of the Royal Society of British Artists. Winter, 1910.

Catalogue of the Forty-Fifth Exhibition of Modern Pictures, by the New English Art Club at the Galleries of the Royal Society of British Artists. Summer, 1911.

Catalogue of the Forty-Sixth Exhibition of Modern Pictures, by the New English Art Club at the Galleries of the Royal Society of British Artists. Winter, 1911.

Catalogue of the Forty-Seventh Exhibition of Modern Pictures, by the New English Art Club at the Galleries of the Royal Society of British Artists. Summer, 1912.

Catalogue of the Forty-Eighth Exhibition of Modern Pictures, by the New English Art Club at the Galleries of the Royal Society of British Artists. Winter, 1912.

Catalogue of the Forty-Ninth Exhibition of Modern Pictures, by the New English Art Club at the Galleries of the Royal Society of British Artists. Summer, 1913.

Catalogue of the Fiftieth Exhibition of Modern Pictures, by the New English Art Club at the Galleries of the Royal Society of British Artists. Winter, 1913.

Catalogue of the Fifty-First Exhibition of Modern Pictures, by the New English Art Club at the Galleries of the Royal Society of British Artists. Summer, 1914.

Catalogue of the Fifty-Second Exhibition of Modern Pictures, by the New English Art Club at the Galleries of the Royal Society of British Artists. Winter, 1914.

Catalogue of the Fifty-Third Exhibition of Modern Pictures, by the New English Art Club at the Galleries of the Royal Society of British Artists. Spring, 1915.

Catalogue of the Fifty-Fourth Exhibition of Modern Pictures, by the New English Art Club at the Galleries of the Royal Society of British Artists. Winter, 1915.

Catalogue of the Fifty-Fifth Exhibition of Modern Pictures, by the New English Art Club at the Galleries of the Royal Society of British Artists. Summer, 1916.

Catalogue of the Fifty-Sixth Exhibition of Modern Pictures, by the New English Art Club at the Galleries of the Royal Society of British Artists. Winter, 1916.

NICOLSON, BENEDICT. 'Post-Impressionism and Roger Fry'. *Burlington Magazine,* January 1951.

The Omega Workshops Ltd. Official catalogue of *The Ideal Home Exhibition Organised by the Daily Mail.* London, 1913.

Omega Workshops, Ltd., Artist Decorators. Prospectus, London, n.d.

The Omega Workshops. Catalogue of an *Exhibition of Furniture, Textiles and Pottery Made at the Omega Workshops, 1913–1918.* London, Arts Council, May 1946.

ORAGE, A. R. *Readers and Writers, 1917–1921.* London, 1922.

OVERY, PAUL. Essay on *Vorticism* in *Concepts of Modern Art.* London, 1974.

—. 'Puce Monster'. *The New Review,* June 1974.

PALMER, J. WOOD. Introduction to the exhibition catalogue of *Harold Gilman 1876–1919.* London: Arts Council, 1954.

—. Introduction and notes to the exhibition catalogue of *Spencer Frederick Gore 1878–1914.* Paintings and drawings. London: Arts Council, 1955.

—. Introduction and notes to the exhibition catalogue of *Robert Bevan 1865–1925.* Paintings and drawings. London: Arts Council, 1956.

—. Introduction and notes to the exhibition catalogue of *Drawings of the Camden Town Group: An Exhibition to mark the 50th Anniversary of the Founding of the Group in 1911.* London: Arts Council, 1961.

PARKIN, MICHAEL. Introduction to catalogue of *The Appalling Loss,* exhibition of 1914–18 War Artists held at Parkin Gallery, London, June–July 1973.

PEVSNER, NIKOLAUS. 'Omega'. *Architectural Review,* August 1941.

PICKVANCE, RONALD. Introduction and notes to the catalogue of *Vanessa Bell 1879–1961.* Memorial exhibition of paintings. London: Arts Council, 1964.

—. Introduction and notes to the exhibition catalogue of *Sickert 1860–1942.* Paintings and drawings. London: Arts Council, 1964.

Poetry and Drama. September 1913. Special issue devoted to Futurism.

John Quinn 1870–1925. Collection of Paintings, Water Colors, Drawings & Sculpture. Foreword by Forbes Watson. New York, 1926.

Paintings and Sculptures. The Renowned Collection of Modern and Ultra-Modern Art, Formed by the Late John Quinn. Including Many Examples Purchased By Him Directly From the Artists. Sale catalogue. New York, 1927.

READ, HERBERT. *Contemporary British Art*. London, 1951.
—. *The Philosophy of Modern Art*. London, 1952.
—. *The Contrary Experience. Autobiographies*. London, 1963.
READ, HERBERT and many others. *Jacob Kramer. A Memorial Volume*. Leeds, 1969.
Prospectus. The Rebel Art Centre. London, 1914.
Prospectus: The Art School. (Rebel Art Centre). London, 1914.
REEVES, JAMES, ed. *Georgian Poetry*. London, 1962.
REID, B. L. *The Man from New York. John Quinn and His Friends*. Oxford, 1968.
RITCHIE, ANDREW CARNDUFF. *Masters of British Painting, 1890–1950*. New York, 1956.
RODKER, JOHN. 'The New Movement in Art'. *Dial Monthly*, May 1914.
—. *Poems*. London: privately printed, 1914.
—. *The Future of Futurism*. London, 1926.
—. *Collected Poems 1912–1925*. Paris, 1930.
ROSS, ROBERT H. *The Georgian Revolt. Rise and Fall of a Poetic Ideal, 1910–1922*. London, 1967.
ROTHENSTEIN, JOHN. *British Artists and the War*. London, 1931.
—. *Augustus John*. London, 1944.
—. *Modern English Painters. Volume One. Sickert to Grant*. London, 1952.
—. *Modern English Painters. Volume Two. Innes to Moore*. London, 1956.
—. *British Art Since 1900. An Anthology*. London, 1962.
—. 'Introduction' to the catalogue of the *Alvaro Guevara* exhibition, held at Colnaghi's, London, December 1974 – January 1975.
ROTHENSTEIN, WILLIAM. *Men and Memories. Recollections of William Rothenstein 1900–1922*. London, 1932.
RUMNEY, RALPH. 'Kill John Bull with Art! What went wrong?' *Studio International*, December 1969.
RUTTER, FRANK. *Revolution in Art*. London, 1910.
—. Foreword to the catalogue of the *Post-Impressionist and Futurist Exhibition*, Doré Galleries, London, October 1913.
—. 'Extremes of Modern Painting: 1870–1920'. *Edinburgh Review*, April 1921.
—. *Some Contemporary Artists*. London, 1922.
—. *Evolution in Modern Art: A Study of Modern Painting, 1870–1925*. London, 1926.
—. *Since I Was Twenty-Five*. London, 1927.
—. *Art in My Time*. London, 1933.
—. *Modern Masterpieces. An Outline of Modern Art*. London, 1940.

SADLEIR, MICHAEL. *Michael Ernest Sadleir. A Memoir by His Son*. London, 1949.
SEGONZAC, A. DUNOYER DE. Introduction to catalogue of *Vanessa Bell* exhibition, held at the Adams Gallery, London, October 1961.
SELVER, PAUL. *Orage and the New Age Circle*. London, 1959.
SEVERINI, GINO. Preface to the catalogue of *The Futurist Painter Severini Exhibits His Latest Works*. Marlborough Gallery, London, April 1913.
—. 'Get Inside the Picture'. *Daily Express*, 11 April 1913.
SHEWRING, WALTER, ed. *Letters of Eric Gill*. London, 1947.
SHONE, RICHARD. Introduction to the exhibition catalogue of *Portraits by Duncan Grant*, held at the Arts Council Gallery, Cambridge, November 1969.
—. *Bloomsbury Portraits*. London, 1976.
SICKERT, WALTER. 'The Allied Artists' Association'. *Art News*, 14 July 1910.
—. 'The Post-Impressionists'. *The Fortnightly Review*, January 1911.
—. 'The Old Ladies of Etching-Needle Street'. *The English Review*, January 1912.

—. 'The Futurist "Devil-among-the-Tailors" '. *The English Review*, April 1912.
—. 'Mesopotamia—Cézanne'. *The New Age*, 5 March 1914.
—. Letter to the *Pall Mall Gazette*, 11 March 1914.
—. 'On Swiftness'. *The New Age*, 26 March 1914.
—. 'Democracy in Ease at Holland Park'. *The New Age*, 25 June 1914.
—. 'O Matre Pulchra'. *Burlington Magazine*, April 1916.
SITWELL, OSBERT, ed. *A Free House! Or, The Artist as Craftsman* (*Being the Writings of Walter Richard Sickert*). London, 1947.
—. *Great Morning. Being the Third Volume of Left Hand, Right Hand! An Autobiography*. London, 1948.
SKIPWITH, PEYTON. Foreword to the exhibition catalogue of *The Art of War 1914–1918. Wyndham Lewis, Paul Nash, C. R. W. Nevinson, William Roberts*. The Morley Gallery, London, May–June 1971.
SOBY, JAMES THRALL. *Contemporary Painters*. New York, 1948.
SOREL, GEORGES. *Reflections on Violence*. Trans. with a bibliography by Hulme. London, 1916.
SPEAIGHT, ROBERT. *William Rothenstein. The Portrait of an Artist in his Time*. London, 1962.
—. *The Life of Eric Gill*. London, 1966.
SPENCER, HERBERT. *Pioneers of Modern Typography*. London, 1970.
SQUIRE, J. C. *The Honeysuckle and the Bee*. London, 1937.
STIRNER, MAX. *The Ego and his Own*. Ed. John Carroll. London, 1971.
SUTTON, DENYS. Introduction to the catalogue of the *Duncan Grant* exhibition held at Wildenstein's, London, November 1964.
—. 'A Silver Age in British Art'. Introduction and notes to the catalogue of *British Art 1890–1928*, an exhibition held at the Columbus Gallery of Fine Arts, Columbus, Ohio, February–March 1971.
—. Introduction and ed. *Letters of Roger Fry*. Two volumes. London, 1972.
SWINNERTON, FRANK. *The Georgian Literary Scene*. London, 1935.

TARRATT, MARGARET. ' "Puce Monster". The two issues of *Blast*, their effects as Vorticist propaganda and how the rebellious image faded'. *Studio International*, April 1967.
The Tate Gallery Report 1964–65. London, 1966.
The Tate Gallery Report 1966–67. London, 1967.
The Tate Gallery Acquisitions 1968–9. London, 1969.
The Tate Gallery 1968–70. London, 1970.
The Tate Gallery 1970–72. London, 1972.
The Tate Gallery 1972–74. London, 1975.
TAYLOR, BASIL. 'Blasted and Blessed'. *The Listener*, 15 February 1970.
THORNTON, ALFRED. *Fifty Years of the New English Art Club, 1886–1935*. London, 1935.
THORP, JOSEPH. *Eric Gill*. London, 1929.
TONKS, HENRY. 'Wander Years'. *Artwork*, Winter 1929.
Twentieth Century Art. A Review of Modern Movements. Catalogue of exhibition at Whitechapel Art Gallery, May–June 1914.

VENGEROVA, ZINAIDA. 'English Futurists'. *The Archer*, 1915.
The First Exhibition of the Vorticist Group, opening 10th June 1915, at the Doré Gallery, London. Catalogue, with a 'Note' by Lewis.
Exhibition of the Vorticists at the Penguin. Catalogue of the exhibition held at the Penguin Club, 8 East 15th Street, New York City, 10–31 January 1917.

WEES, WILLIAM C. 'England's *Avant-Garde*: The Futurist-Vorticist Phase'. *The Western Humanities Review*, Spring 1967.
—. *Vorticism and the English Avant-Garde*. Toronto and Manchester, 1972.

WEISSTEIN, ULRICH. 'Vorticism: Expressionism English Style'. *Yearbook of Comparative and General Literature*, 1964.

WELLINGTON, HUBERT. Introduction to exhibition catalogue of *Charles Ginner 1878–1952*. London: Arts Council, 1953.

WHITE, GABRIEL. Introduction to the exhibition catalogue of *Notes and Sketches by Sickert from the Walker Art Gallery*, Liverpool. London: Arts Council, 1949.

—. Introduction to the exhibition catalogue of *Sickert Paintings and Drawings*. London: Arts Council (held at the Tate Gallery), May–June 1960.

WHITTET, G. S. Introduction to the catalogue of *Horace Brodzky (1885–1969)*, an exhibition held at the Fieldborne Galleries, London, September 1973.

WILENSKI, R. H. *The Modern Movement in Art*. London, 1926.

—. *The Meaning of Modern Sculpture*. London, 1928.

WODEHOUSE, R. F. *A Check List of the War Collections of World War I, 1914–1918 and World War II, 1939–1945*. National Gallery of Canada, Ottawa, n.d.

WOODALL, MARY. Introduction to the exhibition catalogue of *The Early Years of the New English Art Club, 1886–1918*. Birmingham City Museum and Art Gallery, 1952.

WOODESON, JOHN. Introduction and notes for the exhibition catalogue of *Spencer Gore, 1878–1914*. Colchester, Oxford and Sheffield, March–June 1970.

—. Introductory essay and notes for the exhibition catalogue of *Mark Gertler 1891–1939*. Colchester, London, Oxford and Sheffield, March–June 1971.

—. *Mark Gertler. Biography of a Painter 1891–1939*. London, 1972.

WOOLF, LEONARD. *Beginning Again. An Autobiography of the Years 1911–1918*. London, 1964.

WOOLF, VIRGINIA. *Roger Fry. A Biography*. London, 1940.

WORRINGER, WILHELM. *Abstraction and Empathy*. Translated by Michael Bullock. London, 1953.

WRIGHT, WILLARD HUNTINGTON. *Modern Painting: Its Tendency and Meaning*. London, 1928.

YEATS, W. B. *Memoirs. Autobiography—First Draft. Journal*. Transcribed and edited by Denis Donoghue. London, 1972.

SECTION 2

MALCOLM ARBUTHNOT.

ARBUTHNOT, MALCOLM. 'Where to Go'. *The Amateur Photographer and Photographic News*, 25 January 1901.

—. 'The Gum-Bichromate Process. A Few Hints on Producing Multiple-Coated Prints'. *The Amateur Photographer and Photographic News*, 26 May 1904.

—. 'The Gum-Bichromate Process, practically described by M. Arbuthnot' (Part 1). *The Amateur Photographer and Photographic News*, 6 March 1906.

—. 'The Gum-Bichromate Process' (Part 2). *The Amateur Photographer and Photographic News*, 13 March 1906.

—. 'My Exhibition Prints, and How I Make Them'. *The Photographic News*, 13 December 1907.

—. 'A Simple Method of Preparing Paper for Oil Printing'. *The Photographic News*, 20 March 1908.

—. 'The Evolution of an Exhibition Picture'. *The Amateur Photographer*, 16 June 1908.

—. 'A Plea for Simplification and Study in Pictorial Work'. *The Amateur Photographer*, 12 January 1909.

—. 'The Gum-Platinum Process'. *The Amateur Photographer*, 2 March 1909.

—. 'A New Gelatine Pigment Process for Pictorial Workers'. *The Amateur Photographer*, 13 December 1910.

—. *Exhibition of Camera Portraits by Malcolm Arbuthnot*. Catalogue of one-man show held at the Goupil Gallery, London, June–July 1912.

—. *Random Recollections*. Unpublished writings in the possession of Miss A. E. Wisdom, Jersey. Written *c*.1956.

ARMSTRONG, MICHAEL. 'Malcolm Arbuthnot'. *Magnet Magazine*, 19 December 1973.

EDITOR OF PHOTOGRAMS OF THE YEAR. 'Photograms of the Year 1908. A Fragmentary Retrospect'. *Photograms of the Year*, 1908.

—. Note on Malcolm Arbuthnot's *Lulworth Cove*. *Photograms of the Year*, 1911.

—. 'The Year's Work. A Retrospect and some Comments'. *Photograms of the Year*, 1912.

—. 'The Year's Work. Some comments on photographic pictorialism and pictures by the editor'. *Photograms of the Year*, 1913.

GUEST, ANTONY. 'Malcolm Arbuthnot's "Impressions" at the A. P. Little Gallery, 52, Long Acre, W.C.'. *The Amateur Photographer*, 9 March 1909.

JOHNSON, J. DUDLEY. 'Phases in the Development of Pictorial Photography in Britain and America'. *The Photographic Journal*, December 1923.

"PORTRAIT LENS" (pseud.). 'Some Professional Picture Makers and Their Work by "Portrait Lens". Malcolm Arbuthnot'. *The Amateur Photographer*, 12 June 1916.

TILNEY, F. C. 'Observations on Some Pictures of the Year'. *Photograms of the Year*, 1914.

LAWRENCE ATKINSON.

ATKINSON, LAWRENCE. *Aura*. London, 1915.

HENRY, LEIGH. 'A Link with the Pyramids'. Essay on Atkinson in the catalogue of *Laurence [sic] Atkinson. Abstract Sculpture & Painting. On Exhibition at the Eldar Gallery, 40, Gt. Marlborough Street, London, W1*, May 1921.

KONODY, P. G. 'In Defence of Abstract Art'. Essay on Atkinson in the catalogue of his one-man show at the Eldar Gallery, May 1921.

LEWIS, WYNDHAM. 'Dobson. Atkinson'. Review of Atkinson's Eldar Gallery show printed only in a trial copy of *The Tyro No. 2*, London, 1922, in a private collection.

SHIPP, HORACE. 'The Sculpture of Laurence [sic] Atkinson. A Brochure of Preferences' (Booklet). London, *c*.1922.

—. *The New Art. A Study of the Principles of Non-Representational Art and their Application in the Work of Lawrence Atkinson*. London, 1922.

DAVID BOMBERG.

ALLEY, RONALD. 'David Bomberg's "In the Hold"', 1913–14'. *Burlington Magazine*, Vol. CX, 1968.

BOMBERG, DAVID. Foreword to the exhibition catalogue of *Works by David Bomberg*, held at the Chenil Gallery, London, July 1914.

—. *Russian Ballet*. Text and six colour lithographs. London, The Bomb Shop, Hendersons, 66 Charing Cross Road, 1919.

—. 'The Bomberg Papers'. Ed. David Wright and Patrick Swift. *X, A Quarterly Review*, June 1960.

—. Unpublished writings about his early career, 1957. Owned by Mrs. Lilian Bomberg.

David Bomberg 1890–1957. Drawings and Watercolours. Catalogue of exhibition held at Marlborough Fine Art, London, March 1967.

David Bomberg. Drawings, Watercolours and Prints 1912–1925. Catalogue of exhibition held at the d'Offay Couper Gallery, London, June–July 1971.

CORK, RICHARD. Introduction to the exhibition catalogue of *Paintings and Drawings by David Bomberg (1890–1957) and Lilian Holt*. Reading Museum and Art Gallery, June–July 1971.

FORGE, ANDREW. Introduction to the catalogue of *David Bomberg*

1890–1957: An Exhibition of Paintings and Drawings. London: Arts Council, 1958.

FORGE, ANDREW, WILLIAM LIPKE and DAVID SYLVESTER. Essays in the exhibition catalogue of *David Bomberg 1890–1957 Paintings and Drawings.* Catalogue by Joanna Drew. Tate Gallery, London, March–April 1967.

HULME, T. E. 'Modern Art. IV. – Mr. David Bomberg's Show'. *The New Age,* 9 July 1914.

LIPKE, WILLIAM. *David Bomberg. A Critical Study of his Life and Work.* With an appendix devoted to a selection of Bomberg's unpublished manuscripts. London, 1967.

MAYES, ALICE. *The Young Bomberg, 1914–1925.* Unpublished memoir, 1972, in Tate Gallery Archives.

SYLVESTER, DAVID. 'The Discovering of a Structure'. Introductory essay to the exhibition catalogue of *David Bomberg: 1890–1957.* Marlborough Fine Art, London, March 1964.

—. 'Selected Criticism'. A compiled and annotated essay in the exhibition catalogue of *Bomberg. Paintings, Drawings, Watercolours and Lithographs.* With a 'Biographical Note' by Joanna Drew. Fischer Fine Art, London, March–April 1973.

ALVIN LANGDON COBURN.

'American Photographs in London'. *Photo-Era,* January 1901.

'Artists of the Lens; the International Exhibition of Pictorial Photography in Buffalo'. *Harper's Weekly,* 26 November 1910.

CAFFIN, CHARLES H. Critical essay on Coburn with six reproductions of his work. *Camera Work,* April 1904.

Camera Work, July 1906. Five reproductions of Coburn's work and a reprint of Shaw's preface to the catalogue of Coburn's London and Liverpool exhibitions, 1906.

Camera Work, January 1908. Twelve reproductions of Coburn's work.

'The Work of Alvin Langdon Coburn'. *Photography,* 13 February 1906.

'Alvin Langdon Coburn'. *Contemporary Photography,* Summer 1961. A selection of photographs and a reprint of Shaw's 1906 catalogue preface.

COBURN, ALVIN LANGDON. 'Ozotype: a Few Notes on a New Process'. *Photo-Era,* August 1900.

—. 'My Best Picture'. *Photographic News,* 1 February 1907.

—. 'The Relation of Time to Art'. *Camera Work,* No. 36, 1911.

—. 'Men of Mark'. *Forum,* Vol. 50, 1913.

—. *Men of Mark.* With an introduction by Coburn. London, 1913.

—. 'Alvin Langdon Coburn, Artist-Photographer, by Himself'. *Pall Mall Magazine,* Vol. 51, 1913.

—. 'Photogravure'. *Platinum Print,* October 1913.

—. Notes to the exhibition catalogue of *Camera Pictures by Alvin Langdon Coburn,* held at the Goupil Gallery, London, October 1913.

—. 'Modern Photography'. *Colour,* November 1914.

—. 'British Pictorial Photography'. *Platinum Print,* February 1915.

—. Preface to the catalogue of an Old Masters of Photography exhibition organised by Coburn at the Albright Art Gallery, Buffalo, January–February 1915.

—. 'The Old Masters of Photography'. *Century Magazine,* October 1915.

—. 'The Future of Pictorial Photography'. *Photograms of the Year,* 1916.

—. Postscript to the exhibition catalogue of *Vortographs and Paintings by Alvin Langdon Coburn,* held at the Camera Club, London, February 1917.

—. *More Men of Mark.* London, 1922.

—. 'Photography and the Quest of Beauty'. *The Photographic Journal,* Vol. 64, 1924.

—. 'Retrospect'. *The Photographic Journal,* Vol. 98, 1958.

—. 'Photographic Adventures'. *The Photographic Journal,* Vol. 102, 1962.

—. *Alvin Langdon Coburn, Photographer. An Autobiography.* Edited Helmut and Alison Gernsheim. London, 1966.

COBURN, ALVIN LANGDON and H. G. WELLS. *The Door in the Wall.* London, 1911.

CUMMINGS, T. H. 'Some Photographs by Alvin Langdon Coburn'. *Photo-Era,* Vol. 10, 1903.

DOTY, ROBERT M. *Photo-Secession: Photography as a Fine Art.* Foreword by Beaumont Newhall. Rochester, New York, 1960.

EDGERTON, GILES. 'Photography as One of the Fine Arts; the Camera Pictures of Alvin Langdon Coburn as a Vindication of this Statement'. *The Craftsman,* Vol. 12, 1907.

FIREBAUGH, JOSEPH J. 'Coburn: Henry James's Photographer'. *American Quarterly,* Vol. 7, 1955.

'The Function of the Camera'. *Liverpool Courier,* 16 May 1906. Review of Coburn's 1906 exhibition.

GERNSHEIM, HELMUT. *Creative Photography. Aesthetic Trends 1839–1960.* London, 1962.

GRUBER, L. FRITZ. 'Ueber einen Fotografen, Alvin Langdon Coburn'. *Foto Magazin,* April 1962.

GUEST, ANTONY. 'Alvin Langdon Coburn's Vortographs'. *Photo-Era,* 1917.

HALL, NORMAN. 'Alvin Langdon Coburn'. *Photography,* October 1961.

HOPPE, E. O. 'Alvin Langdon Coburn'. *Photographische Rundschau,* 1906.

JOHNSTON, J. DUDLEY. 'Phases in the Development of Pictorial Photography in Britain and America'. *The Photographic Journal,* December 1923.

LYONS, NATHAN, ed. *Photographers on Photography. A Critical Anthology.* Rochester, New York, 1966.

NEWHALL, NANCY. *A Portfolio of Sixteen Photographs by Alvin Langdon Coburn.* Rochester, New York, 1962.

POUND, EZRA. Unsigned essay in the exhibition catalogue of *Vortographs and Paintings by Alvin Langdon Coburn,* the Camera Club, London, February 1917. (Revised version entitled 'Vortographs', republished in Pound's *Pavannes and Divisions,* London, 1917).

RICE, H. L. 'The Work of Alvin Langdon Coburn'. *The Photographer,* Vol. 1, 1904.

SCHARF, AARON. *Art and Photography.* London, 1968.

SHAW, GEORGE BERNARD. Preface to the catalogue of Coburn's exhibition at the Royal Photographic Society, London, February–March 1906.

JESSICA DISMORR.

DISMORR, JESSICA. 'Poems and Notes'. *Blast No. 2, July 1915. Review of the Great English Vortex.* London, 1915. Comprising 'Monologue', 'London Notes', 'June Night', 'Promenade', 'Payment' and 'Matilda'.

—. 'Poems', comprising 'Spring', 'The Enemy', 'Promenade', 'Islands', 'Twilight', and 'Landscape'. *Little Review,* August 1919.

—. 'Critical Suggestions'. *Little Review,* September 1919.

—. 'Some Russian Artists'. *The Tyro No. 2,* London, 1922.

Jessica Dismorr 1885–1939. Paintings and Drawings. Catalogue of the exhibition held at the Mayor Gallery, London, April–May 1965.

LIPKE, WILLIAM and R. H. M. ODY. Introduction to Jessica Dismorr's work and a chronology of her life. Compiled for the catalogue of the Mayor Gallery's 1965 Dismorr exhibition. Introduction unpublished; owned by R. H. M. Ody.

STEVENSON, QUENTIN. Foreword to the exhibition catalogue of *Jessica Dismorr and Her Circle.* With a chronology of her life and watercolours by Catherina Giles and Gertrude Leese. The Archer Gallery, London, February 1972.

—. Introduction to the exhibition catalogue of *Jessica Dismorr 1885–1939*, held at the Mercury Gallery, London, April–May 1974.

—. In preparation: *A Biographical Study of Jessica Dismorr and her Circle.*

JACOB EPSTEIN.

BLACK, ROBERT. *The Art of Jacob Epstein.* Cleveland, 1942.

BUCKLE, RICHARD. Introduction to the *Catalogue of the Epstein Memorial Exhibition.* Edinburgh Festival Society, 1961.

—. Introduction to *Epstein Drawings.* With notes by Lady Kathleen Epstein. London, 1962.

—. *Jacob Epstein, Sculptor.* London, 1963.

CORK, RICHARD. 'The Rock Drill Period'. Introduction to the catalogue of the *Jacob Epstein. The Rock Drill Period* exhibition, held at Anthony d'Offay, London, October–November 1973.

COURNOS, JOHN. 'The Sculpture of Epstein'. *The Fortnightly Review*, June 1917.

DIEREN, BERNARD VAN. *Jacob Epstein.* London, 1920.

EPSTEIN, JACOB. *Let There Be Sculpture.* London, 1940.

Drawings and Sculpture by Jacob Epstein. Catalogue of one-man exhibition held at the Twenty-One Gallery, 21 York Buildings, Adelphi, London, December 1913–January 1914.

Catalogue of an Exhibition of the Sculpture of Jacob Epstein. Leicester Galleries, London, February–March 1917.

Catalogue of Egyptian, Greek and Roman Antiquities and Primitive Works of Art of Africa, Asia, North and South America, Oceania and Australasia from the Epstein Collection. Sale at Christie's, London, 15 December 1961.

Catalogue of an Exhibition of Sculpture and Drawings from 1900 to 1932 by Sir Jacob Epstein (1880–1959). Leicester Galleries, London, June–July 1971.

EPSTEIN, JACOB and ARNOLD HASKELL. *The Sculptor Speaks. A Series of Conversations on Art.* London, 1931.

FAGG, WILLIAM. Introduction to the exhibition catalogue of *The Epstein Collection of Tribal and Exotic Sculpture.* London: Arts Council, 1960.

HULME, T. E. 'Mr. Epstein and the Critics'. *The New Age*, 25 December 1913.

JAMES, PHILIP. Introduction to the catalogue of *Epstein. An Exhibition held at the Tate Gallery.* London: Arts Council, September–November 1952.

—. 'Foreword' to the catalogue of *Epstein. An Exhibition held at the Tate Gallery: Book of illustrations including a number of works not exhibited.* London: Arts Council, September–November 1952.

POUND, EZRA. 'Affirmations. III. Jacob Epstein'. *The New Age*, 21 January 1915.

POWELL, L. B. *Jacob Epstein.* London, 1932.

ROTHENSTEIN, JOHN. Introduction to the exhibition catalogue of *Epstein.* London: Arts Council, 1961.

The Works of Sir Jacob Epstein From the Collection of Mr. Edward P. Schinman. With an 'Introduction' by Kathleen Epstein. Catalogue of an exhibition held at the Farleigh Dickinson University, Rutherford, New Jersey, 1967.

WELLINGTON, HUBERT. *Jacob Epstein.* London, 1925.

FREDERICK ETCHELLS.

BETJEMAN, JOHN. Obituary on Frederick Etchells. *Architectural Review*, October 1973.

Obituary notice. *The Times*, 18 August 1973.

ETCHELLS, FREDERICK. A Note to the catalogue of the *Exhibition of Original Woodcuts and Drawings by Edward Wadsworth*, held at the Adelphi Gallery, London, March 1919.

HENRI GAUDIER-BRZESKA.

BRODZKY, HORACE. *Henri Gaudier-Brzeska 1891–1915.* London, 1933.

—. *Gaudier-Brzeska Drawings.* London, 1946.

COLE, ROGER. Introduction and notes to the exhibition catalogue of *Henri Gaudier-Brzeska (1891–1915) Sculptures. With a selection of drawings from Kettle's Yard, Cambridge.* Edinburgh, Leeds and Cardiff, August–November 1972.

COURNOS, JOHN. 'Henri Gaudier-Brzeska'. *The Egoist*, 2 August 1915.

—. 'Henri Gaudier-Brzeska's Art'. *The Egoist*, 1 September 1915.

EDE, H. S. *A Life of Gaudier-Brzeska.* London, 1930.

—. *Savage Messiah.* London, 1931.

—. 'Un Grand Artiste Méconnu: Henri Gaudier-Brzeska'. *Le Jardin des Arts*, Paris, November 1955.

FRY, ROGER. 'Gaudier-Brzeska'. *Burlington Magazine*, August 1916.

GAUDIER-BRZESKA, HENRI. 'Mr. Gaudier-Brzeska on "The New Sculpture"'. *The Egoist*, 16 March 1914.

—. 'The Allied Artists' Association Ltd., Holland Park Hall'. *The Egoist*, 15 June 1914.

—. 'VORTEX. GAUDIER BRZESKA'. *Blast No. 1. June 20th, 1914. Review of the Great English Vortex.* London, 1914.

—. 'VORTEX GAUDIER-BRZESKA (Written from the Trenches)'. *Blast No. 2. July, 1915. Review of the Great English Vortex.* London, 1915.

Henri Gaudier-Brzeska: An Exhibition of Drawings and Statues reproduced in 'Henri Gaudier-Brzeska' by H. S. Ede. Catalogue of an exhibition held at The Old Court House of St. Marylebone, April–May 1931.

Roy de Maistre and Henri Gaudier-Brzeska. Catalogue of an exhibition held at Temple Newsam, Leeds, June–August 1943.

Sculptures, Paintings and Drawings by Gaudier-Brzeska. Catalogue of an exhibition held at the Cardiff Gallery, Cardiff, July–August 1953.

Gaudier-Brzeska. Catalogue of an exhibition held at the Folio Society, London, April–May 1964.

Gaudier-Brzeska. Catalogue of an exhibition held at Marlborough Fine Art, London, February 1965.

GILL, WINIFRED. *A Faggot of Verse: Poems by Five Women.* London, 1930.

LEVY, MERVYN. *Gaudier-Brzeska Drawings and Sculpture.* London, 1965.

MENIER, M. 'La Salle Gaudier-Brzeska au Musée National d'Art Moderne'. *La Revue du Louvre*, No. 3, 1965.

MURDOCK, W. G. BLAIKIE. 'Henri Gaudier-Brzeska'. *Bruno's Weekly*, 29 July 1916.

PALMER, J. WOOD. Introduction to *Henri Gaudier-Brzeska, 1891–1915.* Catalogue of an exhibition of sculpture, pastels and drawings. London: Arts Council, 1956.

—. 'Henri Gaudier-Brzeska (1891–1915)'. *Studio*, CLIII, 1957.

POUND, EZRA. 'Affirmations. V. Gaudier-Brzeska'. *The New Age*, 4 February 1915.

—. *Gaudier-Brzeska. A Memoir by Ezra Pound. Including the Published Writings of the Sculptor, and a Selection from his Letters.* London, 1916.

—. *Gaudier-Brzeska.* (ibid.) Milan, 1957.

—. *Gaudier-Brzeska.* (ibid.) Yorkshire, 1960. With more recent writings by Pound and a different selection of illustrations.

—. Prefatory Note to the catalogue of *A Memorial Exhibition of the Work of Henri Gaudier-Brzeska.* Leicester Galleries, London, May–June 1918.

—. 'Gaudier: A Postscript'. *Esquire*, New York, August 1934.

ROBINSON, DUNCAN and ELISABETH. *Kettle's Yard. University of Cambridge.* Illustrated Handlist of the Paintings, Sculptures and Drawings. Introduction by H. S. Ede. Cambridge, 1970.

Twenty Drawings from the Note-books of Henri Gaudier-Brzeska. London, 1919.

VARIN, RENE and JACQUELINE AUZAS-PRUVOST. Exhibition catalogue of *Henri Gaudier-Brzeska, Sculptor Orléannais, 1891–1915.* Musée des Beaux-Arts, Orléans, March–April 1956.

WEISNER, ULRICH. Essay on Gaudier's drawings in the exhibition catalogue of *Henri Gaudier-Brzeska 1891–1915.* With a note by H. S. Ede and extracts from Gaudier's letters and writings. Kunsthalle der Stadt, Bielefeld, 1969.

T. E. HULME.

HULME, T. E. 'The New Philosophy'. *The New Age,* 1 July 1909.
—. 'Notes on the Bologna Congress'. *The New Age,* 27 April 1911.
—. 'Notes on Bergson. I'. *The New Age,* 19 October 1911.
—. 'Notes on Bergson. II'. *The New Age,* 26 October 1911.
—. 'Notes on Bergson. III'. *The New Age,* 23 November 1911.
—. 'Notes on Bergson. IV'. *The New Age,* 30 November 1911.
—. 'The Complete Poetical Works of T. E. Hulme'. *The New Age,* 23 January 1912.
—. 'Notes on Bergson. V'. *The New Age,* 22 February 1912.
—. Authorised translation of *Introduction to Metaphysics* by Henri Bergson. London, 1913.
—. 'Mr. Epstein and the Critics'. *The New Age,* 25 December 1913.
—. 'Modern Art. I.—The Grafton Group (at the Alpine Club)'. *The New Age,* 15 January 1914.
—. 'Modern Art. II.—A Preface Note and Neo-Realism'. *The New Age,* 12 February 1914.
—. 'Modern Art. III.—The London Group'. *The New Age,* 26 March 1914.
—. 'Contemporary Drawings'. *The New Age,* 2 April 1914.
—. 'Contemporary Drawings'. *The New Age,* 16 April 1914.
—. 'Contemporary Drawings'. *The New Age,* 30 April 1914.
—. 'Modern Art. IV.—Mr. David Bomberg's Show'. *The New Age,* 9 July 1914.
—. *Diary from the Trenches.* 30 December 1914–19 April 1915. Published in *Further Speculations.*
—. 'The Translator's Preface to Sorel's "Reflections on Violence"'. *The New Age,* 28 October 1915.
—. *Speculations. Essays on Humanism and the Philosophy of Art.* Edited Herbert Read. With a Frontispiece and Foreword by Jacob Epstein. Including 'Modern Art and its Philosophy'. London, 1924.
—. *Further Speculations.* Edited Sam Hynes. Minneapolis, University of Minnesota Press, 1955.
JONES, ALUN R. *The Life and Opinions of T. E. Hulme.* London, 1960.
POUND, EZRA. Prefatory Note to the *Complete Poetical Works of T. E. Hulme.* Published as an appendix to Pound's *Ripostes,* London, 1912. (Originally published in *The New Age,* 23 January 1912.)
—. 'This Hulme Business'. *Townsman,* January 1939.
ROBERTS, MICHAEL. *T. E. Hulme.* Includes the text of Hulme's 'Lecture on Modern Poetry'. London, 1938.

WYNDHAM LEWIS.

AYRTON, MICHAEL. 'Tarr and Flying Feathers'. *Shenandoah,* Autumn 1955.
—. 'Homage to Wyndham Lewis'. *Spectrum,* Spring–Summer 1957.
BRIDSON, D. G. *The Filibuster. A Study of the Political Ideas of Wyndham Lewis.* London, 1972.
CASSIDY, VICTOR M. In preparation: a biography of Wyndham Lewis.
CHAPMAN, ROBERT T. *Wyndham Lewis: Fictions and Satires.* London, 1973.
COOKSON, WILLIAM, ed. 'Wyndham Lewis Special Issue'. Including 'Tarr' by Rebecca West, 'Wyndham Lewis the Painter' by Walter Michel, 'The War Paintings of Wyndham Lewis' by Ezra Pound, 'Wyndham Lewis and the Modern Crisis of Painting' by Edmund Gray, 'Pound and Lewis: The Crucial Years' by W. K. Rose and 'Some Notes on Vorticism and Futurism' by Annamaria Sala. *Agenda,* Autumn-Winter, 1969–70.
DARRACOTT, JOSEPH. 'Wyndham Lewis'. *The Connoisseur,* March 1963.
ELIOT, T. S. 'Tarr'. *The Egoist,* September 1918.
—. 'The Importance of Wyndham Lewis'. *Sunday Times,* 10 March 1957.
—. 'Wyndham Lewis.' *The Hudson Review,* Summer 1957.
GRIGSON, GEOFFREY. *A Master of Our Time. A Study of Wyndham Lewis.* London, 1951.
HANDLEY-READ, CHARLES. *The Art of Wyndham Lewis.* With a critical evaluation by Eric Newton. London, 1951.
HOLROYD, MICHAEL. 'Damning and Blasting—Michael Holroyd writes about the volcanic friendship between Wyndham Lewis and Augustus John'. *The Listener,* 6 July 1972.
KENEDY, R. C. 'Wyndham Lewis or, the Stand against Aphrodite's Sunset-Struck Star'. *Art International,* November 1971.
KENNER, HUGH. *Wyndham Lewis.* London, 1954.
KIRK, RUSSELL. 'Wyndham Lewis' First Principles'. *Yale Review,* XLIV, 1955.
LECHMERE, KATE. *Wyndham Lewis from 1912.* Memoir, 1971, owned by Kate Lechmere, London.
LEWIS, WYNDHAM. 'The Pole'. *The English Review,* May 1909.
—. 'Some Innkeepers and Bestre'. *The English Review,* June 1909.
—. 'Les Saltimbanques'. *The English Review,* August 1909.
—. 'A Spanish Household'. *The Tramp: an Open Air Magazine,* June–July 1910.
—. 'A Breton Innkeeper'. *The Tramp: an Open Air Magazine,* August 1910.
—. 'Le Père François (A Full-Length Portrait of a Tramp)'. *The Tramp: an Open Air Magazine,* September 1910.
—. 'Grignolles (Britanny)'. *The Tramp: an Open Air Magazine,* December 1910.
—. 'Unlucky for Pringle'. *The Tramp: an Open Air Magazine,* February 1911.
—. *Timon of Athens.* Portfolio, with designs on front and back covers, containing sixteen sheets of Lewis designs (six coloured, ten monochrome). Cube Press, London, late 1913.
—. 'The Cubist Room'. Preface to the exhibition catalogue of the *Exhibition by the Camden Town Group and Others,* Brighton Public Art Galleries, December 1913–January 1914. Reprinted under the same title in *The Egoist,* 1 January 1914.
—. 'Epstein and His Critics, or Nietzsche and His Friends'. *The New Age,* 8 January 1914.
—. 'Mr. Arthur Rose's Offer'. *The New Age,* 12 February 1914.
—. 'Note' to catalogue of *Modern German Art,* exhibition held at Twenty-One Gallery, Adelphi, London, February–March 1914.
—. 'Modern Art'. *The New Age,* 2 April 1914.
—. 'Rebel Art in Modern Life'. Lewis interviewed by 'M.M.B.' *Daily News and Leader,* 7 April 1914.
—. 'Preface' to the catalogue of *Exhibition, Leeds,* dated 16 May 1914. (Proof copy owned by Omar Pound).
—. 'A Man of the Week: Marinetti'. *The New Weekly,* 30 May 1914.
—. 'Automobilism'. *The New Weekly,* 20 June 1914.
—. 'Long Live the Vortex!' 'Manifesto', 'Enemy of the Stars', 'Vortices and Notes', 'Frederick Spencer Gore'. *Blast No. 1. June 20th 1914. Review of the Great English Vortex.* London, 1914.
—. 'Futurism and the Flesh. A Futurist's Reply to Mr. G. K. Chesterton'. *T.P.'s Weekly,* 11 July 1914.
—. 'Kill John Bull with Art'. *The Outlook,* 18 July 1914.

—. 'Note'. Catalogue of *The First Exhibition of the Vorticist Group, opening 10th June, 1915 at the Doré Galleries, London.*

—. 'Editorial', 'War Notes', 'Artists and the War', 'The Exploitation of Blood', 'The Six Hundred, Verestchagin and Uccello', 'Marinetti's Occupation', 'A Review of Contemporary Art', 'The Art of the Great Race', 'Five Art Notes', 'Vortex "Be Thyself"', 'The Crowd-Master'. *Blast No. 2. July 1915. Review of the Great English Vortex.* London, 1915.

—. 'The French Poodle'. *The Egoist*, 1 March 1916.

—. 'Imaginary Letters, I'. *The Little Review*, May 1917.

—. 'Imaginary Letters, II'. *The Little Review*, June 1917.

—. 'Imaginary Letters, III'. *The Little Review*, July 1917.

—. 'Inferior Religions'. *The Little Review*, September 1917.

—. 'Cantleman's Spring-Mate'. *The Little Review*, October 1917.

—. 'A Soldier of Humour, I'. *The Little Review*, December 1917.

—. 'A Soldier of Humour, II'. *The Little Review*, January 1918.

—. 'Imaginary Letters, VIII'. *The Little Review*, March 1918.

—. 'Imaginary Letters, IX'. *The Little Review*, April 1918.

—. 'The Ideal Giant'. *The Little Review*, May 1918.

—. *Tarr.* London, 1918.

—. 'The War Baby'. *Art and Letters*, Winter 1918.

—. *Fifteen Drawings.* Ovid Press, London, 1919.

—. Foreword to the exhibition catalogue of *Guns by Wyndham Lewis*, Goupil Gallery, London, February 1919.

—. 'The Men Who Will Paint Hell. Modern War as a Theme for the Artist'. *Daily Express*, 10 February 1919.

—. 'Mr. Wadsworth's Exhibition of Woodcuts'. *Art and Letters*, Spring 1919.

—. 'What Art Now?' *The English Review*, April 1919.

—. 'I. Nature and the Monster of Design'. *The Athenaeum*, 21 November 1919.

—. 'Prevalent Design. II. Painting of the Soul'. *The Athenaeum*, 12 December 1919.

—. 'Prevalent Design. III. The Man behind the Eyes'. *The Athenaeum*, 26 December 1919.

—. *The Caliph's Design. Architects! Where Is Your Vortex?* London, 1919.

—. 'Prevalent Design. IV. The Bulldog Eye's Depredations'. *The Athenaeum*, 16 January 1920.

—. 'Mr. Clive Bell and "Wilcoxism"'. *The Athenaeum*, 12 March 1920.

—. 'Mr. Clive Bell and "Wilcoxism"'. *The Athenaeum*, 26 March 1920.

—. 'Foreword'. Exhibition catalogue of *Group X*, Mansard Gallery, London, March 1920.

—. 'Group X'. *Evening News*, 20 March 1920.

—. *Time and Western Man.* London, 1927.

—. *Tarr.* Revised edition. London, 1928.

—. *Blasting and Bombardiering.* London, 1937.

—. *Wyndham Lewis the Artist, from 'Blast' to Burlington House.* London, 1939.

—. 'Early London Environment'. *T. S. Eliot. A Symposium.* Edited Richard March and Tambimuttu. London, 1948.

—. Introduction to catalogue of *Exhibition of Paintings, Drawings, and Watercolours by Wyndham Lewis.* Redfern Gallery, London, May 1949.

—. 'Ezra: The Portrait of a Personality'. *Quarterly Review of Literature*, December 1949.

—. *Rude Assignment: A Narrative of My Career Up-to-Date.* London, 1950.

—. 'The Rock Drill'. (Review of Pound's *Letters*). *New Statesman*, 7 April 1951.

—. 'Augustus John Looks Back'. *The Listener*, 20 March 1952.

—. Introduction to the exhibition catalogue of *Wyndham Lewis and Vorticism*, Tate Gallery, London, July–August 1956.

—. 'The Vorticists'. *Vogue*, September 1956.

LEWIS, WYNDHAM, FREDERICK ETCHELLS, CUTHBERT HAMILTON and EDWARD WADSWORTH. 'Round Robin'. Autumn 1913. Reprinted in W. K. Rose's *The Letters of Wyndham Lewis*, London, 1963, pp. 47–50.

LEWIS, WYNDHAM AND OTHERS. 'The Futurist Manifesto'. Letter to the *Observer*, 14 June 1914.

MAYNE, RICHARD. 'Wyndham Lewis'. *Encounter*, February 1972.

MCALMON, ROBERT. *Being Geniuses Together, 1920–30.* Revised and with supplementary chapters by Kay Boyle. London, 1970.

MCLUHAN, MARSHALL. 'Wyndham Lewis: His Theory and Art of Communication'. *Shenandoah*, IV, 1953.

MICHEL, WALTER. 'Vorticism and the Early Wyndham Lewis'. *Apollo*, January 1963.

—. 'Tyros and Portraits. The Early 'Twenties and Wyndham Lewis'. *Apollo*, August 1965.

—. Letter replying to letter from Quentin Bell and Stephen Chaplin. *Apollo*, January 1966.

—. *Wyndham Lewis. Paintings and Drawings.* With an introductory essay, 'The Visual World of Wyndham Lewis', by Hugh Kenner. London, 1971.

MICHEL, WALTER and C. J. FOX, ed. *Wyndham Lewis on Art. Collected Writings 1913–1956.* London, 1969.

PORTEUS, HUGH GORDON. *Wyndham Lewis: A Discursive Exposition.* London, 1932.

POUND, EZRA. 'Wyndham Lewis'. *The Egoist*, 15 June 1914.

—. 'On Wyndham Lewis'. *Shenandoah*, Summer–Autumn 1953.

PRITCHARD, WILLIAM H. *Wyndham Lewis.* New York, 1968.

ROBERTS, WILLIAM. 'Wyndham Lewis, the Vorticist'. *The Listener*, 21 March 1957.

ROSE, W. K. *Wyndham Lewis at Cornell. A Review of the Lewis Papers presented to the University by William G. Mennen.* Cornell University Library, Ithaca, New York, 1961.

ROSE, W. K. ed. *The Letters of Wyndham Lewis.* London, 1963.

ROSENTHAL, T. G. 'Introduction to Wyndham Lewis and Michael Ayrton Exhibitions at the National Book League 1971'. Exhibition catalogue of *Word and Image I & II. Wyndham Lewis 1882–1957. Michael Ayrton b. 1921*, London: National Book League, 1971.

ROTHENSTEIN, JOHN. *Wyndham Lewis, 1882–1957.* Chapter in *Modern English Painters. Volume One. Sickert to Grant.* London, 1952.

STEIN, GERTRUDE. *The Autobiography of Alice B. Toklas.* London, 1933.

TOMLIN, E. W. F. *Wyndham Lewis.* London, 1955.

—. *Wyndham Lewis. An Anthology of His Prose.* Edited with an introduction by E. W. F. Tomlin. London, 1969.

WAGNER, GEOFFREY. 'Wyndham Lewis and the Vorticist Aesthetic'. *Journal of Aesthetics and Art Criticism*, September 1954.

—. *Wyndham Lewis. A Portrait of the Artist as the Enemy.* London, 1957.

C. R. W. NEVINSON.

APOLLINAIRE, GUILLAUME. 'Echos et on-Dit des Lettres et des Arts'. *L'Europe Nouvelle*, 20 July 1918. Reprinted in *Apollinaire, Chroniques d'Art (1902–1918).* Edited L. C. Breunig, Paris, 1960.

CRAWFORD-FLITCH, J. E. *C. R. W. Nevinson. The Great War. Fourth Year.* London, 1918.

DODGSON, CAMPBELL and C. E. MONTAGUE. Introductions to *British Artists at the Front. I. C. R. W. Nevinson.* London, 1918.

KONODY, P. G. *Modern War: Paintings by C. R. W. Nevinson.* London, 1917.

LEVY, MERVYN. 'C. R. W. Nevinson: Undertones of Peace'. *The Studio*, Vol. CLXII, 1961.

MARINETTI, F. T. and NEVINSON, C. R. W. 'Vital English Art. A Futurist Manifesto'. *The Observer*, 7 June 1914.

NEVINSON, C. R. W. 'Post-Impressionism and Cubism'. *Pall Mall Gazette*, 7 March 1914.

—. 'Futurism'. *The New Weekly*, 20 June 1914.

—. 'The Vorticists and the Futurists'. *The Observer*, 12 July 1914.

—. Interview with the *Daily Express*. 25 February 1915.

—. 'Art and War'. *Daily Graphic*, 11 March 1915.

—. Preface to the catalogue of *Exhibition of Pictures of War*. Leicester Galleries. London, March 1918.

—. Interview with the *Newcastle-on-Tyne Illustrated Chronicle*. 22 January 1919.

—. Interview with the *New York Times*. 25 May 1919.

—. 'Modern Art'. *The World*, 4 October 1919.

—. *Paint and Prejudice*. London, 1937.

—. 'Studio Reminiscences'. *The Studio*, Vol. CXXIV, 1942.

Catalogue of an Exhibition of Paintings and Drawings of War by C. R. W. Nevinson. Leicester Galleries, London, September–October 1916.

Nevinson's Collection of Press Cuttings. Vol. I: 1910–1914. Vol. II: 1914–1918. Tate Gallery Library.

NEVINSON, HENRY W. 'Marinetti'. *Newark Evening News*, 17 January 1914.

—. 'The New Art Gospel'. *Glasgow Herald*, 13 June 1914.

—. 'A New Venture in Art'. *The Times*, 9 July 1914.

—. 'The Impulse to Futurism'. *The Atlantic Monthly*, November 1914.

—. 'New Pictures; Principles of the X Group'. *The Times*, 1 April 1920.

—. *The Fire of Life*. (Abbreviation of autobiography published in three vols. as *Changes and Chances*, 1923–28.) London, 1935.

—. *Visions and Memories*. Collected and arranged by Evelyn Sharp. With an introduction by Gilbert Murray. London, 1944.

NEVINSON, MARGARET WYNNE. 'Futurism and Woman'. *The Vote*, 31 December 1910.

ROTHENSTEIN, JOHN. *C. R. W. Nevinson, 1889–1946*. Chapter in *Modern English Painters. Volume Two. Innes to Moore*. London, 1956.

SALAMAN, MALCOLM C. 'The Art of C. R. W. Nevinson'. *The Studio*, December 1919.

SITWELL, OSBERT. *C. R. W. Nevinson*. London, 1925.

—. Introduction to the catalogue of the *Memorial Exhibition of Pictures by C. R. W. Nevinson, 1889–1946*. Leicester Galleries, London, May–June 1947.

EZRA POUND.

ALDINGTON, RICHARD. 'The Poetry of Ezra Pound'. *The Egoist*, 1 May 1915.

COOKSON, WILLIAM (ed.) *Selected Prose 1909–1965 by Ezra Pound*. London, 1973.

DELL, FLOYD. 'Friday Literary Review'. *Chicago Evening Post*, 6 January 1911.

DEUTSCH, BABETTE. 'Ezra Pound, Vorticist'. *Reedy's Mirror*, 21 December 1917.

ELIOT, T. S. *Ezra Pound: His Metric and Poetry*. New York, 1917.

—. 'Ezra Pound'. *Poetry* (Chicago), September 1946.

—. Introduction and ed. *Literary Essays of Ezra Pound*. London, 1954.

FRASER, G. S. *Ezra Pound*. London, 1960.

GALLUP, DONALD. *A Bibliography of Ezra Pound*. London, 1963.

HALL, DONALD. 'Ezra Pound: an Interview'. *Paris Review*, Summer–Autumn 1962.

HESSE, EVA, ed. *New Approaches to Ezra Pound. A co-ordinated investigation of Pound's poetry and ideas*. London, 1969.

HUTCHINS, PATRICIA. 'E.P. as a Journalist'. *Twentieth Century*, January 1960.

—. *Ezra Pound's Kensington: An Exploration, 1885–1913*. London, 1965.

KENNER, HUGH. *The Poetry of Ezra Pound*. Norfolk, Conn., 1951.

—. *The Pound Era*. London, 1972.

LANDINI, RICHARD G. 'Vorticism and *The Cantos* of Ezra Pound'. *Western Humanities Review*, XVI, 1960.

LEWIS, WYNDHAM. 'Ezra: The Portrait of a Personality'. *Quarterly Review of Literature*, December 1949.

—. 'The Rock Drill'. (Review of Pound's *Letters*). *New Statesman*, 7 April 1951.

LIPKE, WILLIAM C. and BERNARD ROZRAN. 'Ezra Pound and Vorticism: A Polite Blast'. *Wisconsin Studies in Contemporary Literature*, Summer 1966.

LUDWIG, RICHARD M. 'Ezra Pound's London Years'. *Aspects of American Poetry*, Ohio State University, 1962.

MULLINS, EUSTACE. *This Difficult Individual, Ezra Pound*. New York, 1962.

NORMAN, CHARLES. *Ezra Pound. A Biography*. London, 1969.

PACK, ROBERT. 'The Georgians, Imagism and Ezra Pound: A Study in Revolution'. *Arizona Quarterly*, XII, 1956.

PAIGE, D. D. ed. *The Letters of Ezra Pound, 1907–1941*. London, 1951.

PATMORE, BRIGIT. 'Ezra Pound in England'. *Texas Quarterly*, Autumn 1964.

POUND, EZRA. *Canzoni*. London, 1911.

—. 'Prologomena'. *Poetry Review*, February 1912.

—. *Ripostes*. London, 1912.

—. 'To Whistler, American'. *Poetry*, October 1912.

—. 'Status Rerum'. *Poetry*, January 1913.

—. 'A Few Don'ts By an Imagiste'. *Poetry*, March 1913.

—. 'The Serious Artist'. *The New Freewoman*, 15 October 1913.

—. 'Rabindranath Tagore'. *The New Freewoman*, 1 November 1913.

—. 'The Divine Mystery'. *The New Freewoman*, 15 November 1913.

—. 'The New Sculpture'. *The Egoist*, 16 February 1914.

—. 'Exhibition at the Goupil Gallery'. *The Egoist*, 16 March 1914.

—. Letter to the *Daily News and Leader*, 8 April 1914.

—. 'Wyndham Lewis'. *The Egoist*, 15 June 1914.

—. 'Edward Wadsworth, Vorticist'. *The Egoist*, 15 August 1914.

—. 'Vorticism'. *The Fortnightly Review*, 1 September 1914.

—. 'Preliminary Announcement of the College of Arts'. *The Egoist*, 2 November 1914.

—. 'A Blast from London'. *Dial*, 1 January 1915.

—. 'Affirmations. I. Arnold Dolmetsch'. *The New Age*, 7 January 1915.

—. 'Affirmations. II. Vorticism'. *The New Age*, 14 January 1915.

—. 'Affirmations. III. Jacob Epstein'. *The New Age*, 21 January 1915.

—. 'Affirmations. IV. As for Imagisme'. *The New Age*, 28 January 1915.

—. 'Affirmations. V. Gaudier-Brzeska'. *The New Age*, 4 February 1915.

—. 'Affirmations. VI. Analysis of this Decade'. *The New Age*, 11 February 1915.

—. 'Affirmations. VII. The Non-existence of Ireland'. *The New Age*, 25 February 1915.

—. 'Status Rerum—The Second'. *Poetry*, April 1916.

—. *Pavannes and Divisions*. London, 1918.

—. 'The Death of Vorticism'. *The Little Review*, February–March 1919.

—. *Personae*. London, 1926.

—. 'Small Magazines'. *English Journal*, May 1930.

—. *Profile: An Anthology Collected in MCMXXXI*. Milan, 1932.

—. 'Past History'. *English Journal*, May 1933.

—. 'This Hulme Business'. *Townsman*, January 1939.

—. 'Verse is a Sword: Unpublished Letters of Ezra Pound'. *X, A Quarterly Review*, October 1960.

READ, FORREST, ed. *The Letters of Ezra Pound to James Joyce; with Pound's Essays on Joyce*. London, 1968.

RECK, MICHAEL. *Ezra Pound: A Close-Up*. London, 1968.

ROZRAN, BERNARD W. 'A Vorticist Poetry with visual implications: the "forgotten" experiment of Ezra Pound'. *Studio International*, April 1967.

RUSSELL, PETER, ed. *Ezra Pound: A Collection of Essays*. London, 1950.

SCHNEIDAU, HERBERT N. 'Vorticism and the Career of Ezra Pound'. *Modern Philology*, February 1968.

STOCK, NOEL. *The Life of Ezra Pound*. London, 1969.

WEES, WILLIAM C. 'Ezra Pound as a Vorticist'. *Wisconsin Studies in Contemporary Literature*, Winter–Spring 1965.

—. 'Pound's Vorticism: Some New Evidence and Further Comments'. *Wisconsin Studies in Contemporary Literature*, Summer 1966.

WILLIAM ROBERTS.

ALLEY, RONALD. 'Introduction' and notes to the catalogue of *William Roberts ARA. Retrospective Exhibition*. Tate Gallery, London, November–December 1965.

CORK, RICHARD. 'A Blast from the Past'. *Evening Standard*, 28 March 1974.

ROBERTS, WILLIAM. 'Portrait of the Artist'. *Art News and Review*, 5 November 1949.

—. *The Resurrection of Vorticism and the Apotheosis of Wyndham Lewis at the Tate*. Pamphlet. London, 1956.

—. *Cometism and Vorticism. A Tate Gallery Catalogue Revised*. Pamphlet. London, 1956.

—. *A Press View at the Tate Gallery*. Pamphlet. London, 1956.

—. 'Wyndham Lewis, the Vorticist'. *The Listener*, 21 March 1957.

—. *A Reply to My Biographer Sir John Rothenstein*. Pamphlet. London, 1957.

—. *Abstract & Cubist Paintings & Drawings*. London, n.d. (1957).

—. *Vorticism and the Politics of Belles-Lettres-ism*. London, 1958.

—. *The Vortex Pamphlets 1956–1958*. London, 1958.

—. *Paintings 1917–1958*. London, 1960.

—. *8 Cubist Designs*. London, 1969.

—. *Fame or Defame. A Reply to Barrie Sturt-Penrose*. London, 1971.

—. *Memories of the War to End War 1914–18*. London, n.d. (1974).

—. *In Defence of English Cubists*. Pamphlet. London, 1974.

—. 'Postscript' (to the *English Cubists* pamphlet). Leaflet. London, 1974.

—. Revised title, *The English Cubists at the Hotel de la Tour Eiffel*, on a privately printed monochrome reproduction of Roberts' painting. London, 1974.

—. *Paintings and Drawings by William Roberts R.A.* London, 1976.

William Roberts R.A. Drawings and Watercolours 1915–1968. Catalogue of an exhibition held at the d'Offay Couper Gallery, London, September–October 1969.

William Roberts R.A. A Retrospective Exhibition. Catalogue of the exhibition at the Hamet Gallery, London, February–March 1971.

ROTHENSTEIN, JOHN. *William Roberts, b. 1895*. Chapter in *Modern English Painters. Volume Two. Innes to Moore*. London, 1956.

HELEN SAUNDERS.

SAUNDERS, HELEN. 'A Vision of Mud'. Poem published in *Blast No. 2. July, 1915. Review of the Great English Vortex*. London, 1915.

—. Notes on Harriet Weaver. 24 February 1962. Quoted in *Dear Miss Weaver*, by Jane Lidderdale and Mary Nicholson, London, 1970.

—. Letter to Walter Michel. 1962. Quoted by Michel in his *Wyndham Lewis. Paintings and Drawings*, London, 1971.

—. Unpublished poems and notes. Owned by Mrs. Helen Peppin.

DOROTHY SHAKESPEAR.

Obituary notice. *The Times*, 13 December 1973.

Dorothy Shakespear Pound. Etruscan Gate. Includes a notebook written by Dorothy Shakespear in 1909–11 and 26 pages of her drawings. The Rougemont Press, Exeter, 1971.

WINDELER, B. C. *Elimus: A Story by B. C. Windeler, with Twelve Designs by D. Shakespear*. Paris, 1923.

In preparation: A Portfolio of Fifteen Watercolours by Dorothy Shakespear.

EDWARD WADSWORTH.

ATTERBURY, PAUL. 'Dazzle Painting in the First World War'. *The Antique Collector*, April 1975.

BENNETT, ARNOLD. Introduction to *The Black Country. A Book of Twenty Drawings by Edward Wadsworth*. London, 1920.

CORK, RICHARD. Introduction to the catalogue of *Edward Wadsworth Early Woodcuts*, an exhibition presented jointly by Christopher Drake and Alexander Postan at Christopher Drake Limited, London, March–April 1973.

DREY, O. RAYMOND. *Edward Wadsworth*. Modern Woodcutters Series. London, 1921.

EARP, T. W. Introduction to the catalogue of *Edward Wadsworth 1889–1949. A Memorial Exhibition*, held at the Tate Gallery, London, February–March 1951.

ETCHELLS, FREDERICK. A Note to the catalogue of the *Exhibition of Original Woodcuts and Drawings by Edward Wadsworth*, held at The Adelphi Gallery, London, March 1919.

GEORGE, WALDÉMAR, MICHAEL SEVIER AND OSSIP ZADKINE. Tributes in 'Edward Wadsworth'. *Sélection (Chronique de la Vie Artistique) Cahier 13*, Anvers, 1933.

GLAZEBROOK, MARK. Introduction and notes to the catalogue of *Edward Wadsworth 1889–1949. Paintings, Drawings and Prints*, an exhibition held at Colnaghi's, London, July–August 1974.

HARLING, ROBERT (ed.) *Image 5: English Wood Engraving, 1900–1950*. London, 1950.

LEWIS, WYNDHAM. 'Mr. Wadsworth's Exhibition of Woodcuts'. *Art and Letters*, Spring 1919.

—. 'Edward Wadsworth: 1889–1949'. *The Listener*, 30 June 1949.

NEWTON, ERIC. Conversation with Edward Wadsworth. *The Listener*, 20 March 1935.

POUND, EZRA. 'Edward Wadsworth, Vorticist'. *The Egoist*, 15 August 1914.

—. Reproductions of six Wadsworth woodcuts from the Mudros period accompanying Pound's 'The Death of Vorticism', *Little Review*, February–March 1919.

ROTHENSTEIN, JOHN. *Edward Wadsworth, 1889–1949*. Chapter in *Modern English Painters. Volume Two. Innes to Moore*. London, 1956.

WADSWORTH, EDWARD. Letter to *The Nation*, 9 February 1913.

—. 'Inner Necessity'. Introduction to specially translated extracts by Wadsworth from Kandinsky's *The Art of Spiritual Harmony*. *Blast No. 1. June 20th 1914. Review of the Great English Vortex*. London, 1914.

—. 'The Aesthetic Aspect of Civil Engineering'. Sixth lecture in series delivered at the Institute of Civil Engineers and published by them in book form in 1945.

Index to both volumes